ISB

Hundbook

June 1997

British Bus Publishing

The Scottish Bus Handbook

The Scottish Bus Handbook is part of the Bus Handbook series that details the fleets of stage carriage and express coach operators. Where space allows other significant operators in the areas covered are also included. These handbooks are published by *British Bus Publishing* and cover Scotland, Wales and England north of London. The current list is shown at the end of the book. Together with similar books for greater London published by Capital Transport, they provide comprehensive coverage of all the principal operators' fleets in the British Isles.

The operators included in this edition cover those who provide stage and express services in Scotland. Also included are a number of those operators who provide significant coaching activities.

Quality photographs for inclusion in these, and other areas covered by the series are welcome, for which a fee is payable. The publishers unfortunately cannot accept responsibility for any loss and request you show your name on each picture or slide. Details of changes to fleet information are also welcome.

More information on the Bus Handbook series is available from:

British Bus Publishing,
The Vyne,
16 St Margaret's Drive
Wellington
Telford,
Shropshire TF1 3PH

Series Editor: Bill Potter

Principal Editors for *The Scottish Bus Handbook:* David Donati

Acknowledgements:
We are grateful to Ernest Barnett, Keith Grimes, Mark Jameson, Iain MacGregor
Colin Lloyd, Royal Mail, Stuart Martin the PSV Circle and the operating
companies for their assistance in the compilation of this book.

The front cover photo is by Tony Wilson
The rear cover photographs are by ...

Contents correct to May 1997

ISBN 1 897990 20 0
Published by *British Bus Publishing Ltd*
The Vyne, 16 St Margarets Drive, Wellington,
Telford, Shropshire, TF1 3PH
© British Bus Publishing Ltd, May 1997

CONTENTS

AA BUSES / DODDS COACHES

Dodds of Troon Ltd, 4 East Road, Heathfield, Ayr, South Ayrshire, KA8 9BA

p	OKM317	AEC Regent III 9612E	Saunders	H30/26R	1949	Ex Law, Prestwick, 1957
p	GSD779	Guy Arab IV	Roe	H37/28RD	1955	
p	SJW515	Guy Warrior	Burlingham Seagull	C41F	1956	Ex Guy demonstrator, 1957
	GMB654T	Leyland National 10351B/1R (Gardner)		B40F	1978	Ex Glasgow Airport, 1993
	ASJ206T	Leyland Fleetline FE30AGR	Alexander AL	H45/33F	1979	
	ASJ207T	Leyland Fleetline FE30AGR	Alexander AL	H45/33F	1979	
	BAO867T	AEC Reliance 6U3ZR	Plaxton Supreme IV Express	C53F	1979	Ex Marshall, Troon, 1992
	YSJ14T	Leyland National 11351A/1R		B52F	1979	
	FSD687V	Leyland National 2 NL116L11/1R		B52F	1980	
	JSD595W	Leyland National 2 NL116L11/1R		B52F	1980	
	LSD732W	Leyland National 2 NL116AL11/1R		B52F	1981	
	LSJ871W	Leyland National 2 NL116AL11/1R		B52F	1981	
	LSJ872W	Leyland National 2 NL116AL11/1R		B52F	1981	
	NSJ550X	Leyland National 2 NL116AL11/1R		B52F	1981	
	USJ491Y	Leyland National 2 NL116TL11/1R		B52F	1983	
	A306YSJ	Leyland National 2 NL116TL11/1R		B52F	1984	
	WSV540	Volvo B10M-61	Van Hool Alizée	C53F	1984	Ex Park's, Hamilton, 1986
	C112GSJ	Leyland National 2 NL116HLXCT/1R		B52F	1985	
	MIL4693	Scania K92CRB	Jonckheere TransCity	B47D	1986	Ex Smith, Alcester, 1992
w	C352SVV	Scania K92CRB	Jonckheere TransCity	B47D	1986	Ex Smith, Alcester, 1992
	TJI5393	Volvo B10M-61	Plaxton Paramount 3200 II	C53F	1986	Ex Shearings, 1993
	TJI5394	Volvo B10M-61	Plaxton Paramount 3200 II	C53F	1986	Ex Shearings, 1993
	E76RCS	Scania N112CRB	East Lancashire	B51F	1987	
	E77RCS	Scania N112CRB	East Lancashire	B51F	1987	
	NIW2230	Volvo B10M-61	Plaxton Paramount 3500 III	C53F	1987	Ex Beaton, Blantyre, 1994
	TJI5391	Volvo B10M-61	Van Hool Alizée	C46FT	1988	Ex Excelsior, 1989
	TJI5392	Volvo B10M-61	Van Hool Alizée	C53F	1988	Ex Excelsior, 1989
	UJI5789	Volvo B10M-61	Van Hool Alizée	C53F	1988	Ex Excelsior, 1989
	E499TSJ	Mercedes-Benz 609D	Devon Conversion	C23F	1988	
	TJI5399	Scania K112CRB	Van Hool Alizée	C49FT	1988	
	F85XCS	Leyland Lynx LX112L10ZR1R	Leyland Lynx	B51F	1989	
	F262WSD	Leyland Lynx LX112LXCTZR1S	Leyland Lynx	B51F	1989	
	G362FOP	Iveco Daily 49.10	Carlyle Dailybus 2	B25F	1989	Ex Sherratt, Cold Meece, 1993
	TJI5390	Scania K93CRB	Plaxton Paramount 3200 III	C53F	1990	Ex Shearings, 1994
	H455WGG	Scania N113CRB	Alexander PS	B51F	1990	
	H466WGG	Scania N113CRB	Alexander PS	B51F	1990	

Opposite: **Typical of the AA operation on the Ayrshire coast is Leyland National LSJ872W photographed at Irvine Cross and Dennis Dart M389KVR. The Dart has become the most popular of the modern buses, AA operating four with Northern Counties Paladin bodies.** *Billy Nicol/Phillip Stephenson*

Dodds of Troon has announced that the AA Buses operation will be passing to Western Buses at the end of June 1997. Shown left while heading for Ayr is H455WGG one of a pair of Scania N113s with Alexander PS bodywork.

For much of the 1980s AA's purchasing policy required two new buses each year and these were usually supplied by the Leyland plant at Lillyhall. After a long association with the National there are just two Lynx in the fleet. Seen passing through Irvine is F262WSD. *Malc McDonald*

J460YDT	Mercedes-Benz 811D	Reeve Burgess Beaver	B27F	1991	Ex Plaxton demonstrator, 1992
UJI5786	Toyota Coaster HDB30R	Caetano Optimo II	C21F	1992	Ex Excelsior, Bournemouth, 1995
UJI5787	Toyota Coaster HDB30R	Caetano Optimo II	C21F	1992	Ex Excelsior, Bournemouth, 1995
J277OSJ	Mercedes-Benz 709D	Reeve Burgess Beaver	B25F	1992	
M100AAB	Scania L113CRL	Alexander Strider	B51F	1994	
M949EGE	Dennis Dart 9.8SDL3054	Plaxton Pointer	B40F	1994	
M950EGE	Dennis Dart 9.8SDL3054	Plaxton Pointer	B40F	1994	
M386KVR	Mercedes-Benz 709D	Plaxton Beaver	B27F	1995	Ex TGWU, Chelmsford, 1995
M387KVR	Dennis Dart 9.8SDL3054	Northern Counties	B40F	1995	
M388KVR	Dennis Dart 9.8SDL3054	Northern Counties	B40F	1995	
M389KVR	Dennis Dart 9.8SDL3054	Northern Counties	B40F	1995	
M395KVR	Mercedes-Benz 709D	Alexander Sprint	B27F	1995	
M396KVR	Mercedes-Benz 709D	Alexander Sprint	B27F	1995	
M397KVR	Mercedes-Benz 709D	Alexander Sprint	B27F	1995	
M630RCP	DAF SB220LT550	Northern Counties Paladin	B49F	1995	
N585WND	Mercedes-Benz 709D	Alexander Sprint	B27F	1995	
N586WND	Mercedes-Benz 709D	Alexander Sprint	B27F	1995	
N7DOT	Scania K113CRB	Van Hool Alizée	C49FT	1996	
N610WND	Dennis Dart 9.8SDL3054	Plaxton Pointer	B40F	1996	
N611WND	Dennis Dart 9.8SDL3054	Northen Counties Paladin	B40F	1995	
N612WND	Dennis Dart 9.8SDL3054	Plaxton Pointer	B40F	1996	
N590GBW	Dennis Javelin 12SDA2146	Caetano Algarve II	C51FT	1996	
N591GBW	Dennis Javelin 12SDA2146	Caetano Algarve II	C51FT	1996	
N592GBW	Dennis Javelin 12SDA2146	Caetano Algarve II	C53F	1996	
N594GBW	Dennis Javelin 12SDA2146	Caetano Algarve II	C53F	1996	
P741HND	Dennis Dart SLF	Plaxton Pointer	B39F	1996	
P606WND	Dennis Dart SLF	Plaxton Pointer	B41F	1996	

Previous Registrations:

MIL4693	C351SVV	TJI5394	C520DND
NIW2230	E552UHS	TJI5399	E755TCS
TJI5390	G883VNA	UJI5786	A20XEL, J351YHO
TJI5391	E312OPR	UJI5787	A19XEL, J372YHO
TJI5392	E314OPR	UJI5789	E318OPR
TJI5393	C519DND	WSV540	A650UGD

Livery: Green and cream; white and lilac (North British Tours) NIW2230, N592/4GBW; white and red (Clyde Coaster) N611WND, M630RCP, MIL4693

ALLANDER TRAVEL

Allander Coaches Ltd, Unit 19, Cloberfield Industrial Estate,
Milngavie, Glasgow, G62 7LN

758WNN	Volvo B58-56	Plaxton P'mount 3200(1991)	C53F	1979	Ex Marbill, Beith, 1991
LHS748V	Ailsa B55-10	Alexander AV	H44/35F	1979	Ex KCB Network, 1995
CBZ4622	Volvo B10M-61	Duple Goldliner	C50F	1982	Ex Marbill, Beith, 1997
OJI5506	Volvo B10M-61	Duple Goldliner	C50F	1982	Ex Marbill, Beith, 1997
GIW111	Volvo B10M-61	Duple 320	C57F	1988	Ex McCall's Cs, Gartocharn, 1996
K332MOS	Renault Trafic	Holdsworth	M8	1993	Ex MoD 1996
3786AT	Volvo B10M-62	Van Hool Alizée	C53F	1994	Ex Park's, Hamilton, 1995
4143AT	Volvo B10M-62	Van Hool Alizée	C53F	1994	Ex Park's, Hamilton, 1995
XAT11X	Volvo B10M-62	Van Hool Alizée	C53F	1994	Ex Park's, Hamilton, 1996
7726AT	Volvo B10M-62	Van Hool Alizée	C48FT	1995	Ex Dave Parry, Cheslyn Hay, 1996
7921AT	Volvo B9M	Van Hool Alizée	C38F	1995	
2367AT	Volvo B9M	Van Hool Alizée	C40FT	1995	
M818ECS	Volvo B10M-62	Van Hool Alizée	C53F	1996	
9446AT	Volvo B10M-62	Jonckheere Deauville	C53F	1996	
N812NHS	Volvo B10M-62	Jonckheere Deauville	C53F	1996	Ex Park's, Hamilton, 1997
N813NHS	Volvo B10M-62	Jonckheere Deauville	C53F	1996	Ex Park's, Hamilton, 1997
P502XGA	Volvo B10M-62	Van Hool Alizée	C48F	1997	
P503XGA	Volvo B10M-62	Van Hool Alizée	C48F	1997	

Previous Registrations:

2367AT	M75FGG	CBZ4622	OHE268X, UTC872, YFJ67X
3786AT	KSK984, L717ADS	GIW111	E538WEC
4143AT	KSK983, L718ADS	K682SHS	K714TSD, 2367AT
758WNN	GRF447V	M818ECS	M74VGG, 7921AT
7726AT	M133SKY	OJI5506	OHE264X
7921AT	P622TGE	XAT11X	LSK844, L635AYS
9446AT	N243OUS		

Livery: Orange and black; yellow and blue (Scottish Citylink) XAT11X, 9446AT

The latest arrival with Allander Travel, P503XGA, is one of a pair of Volvo B10Ms with Van Hool Alizée bodywork. With the exception of the minibus, all the fleet are now Volvo-based with Belgian-built bodies now dominating.
Billy Nicol

ARGYLL BUS GROUP

Ashton Coach Hire Ltd; Coastline Express Services Ltd; Greenock Motor Services Ltd;
School Bus Scotland Ltd, Easdale Ind. Est, 8 Ardgowan Street,
Port Glasgow, Argyle & Bute, PA14 5DG

Reg	Chassis	Body	Seat	Year	History
TJI1692	Leyland Leopard PSU3E/4R	Duple Dominant II Express	C49F	1980	Ex Taylor, Widnes, 1996
TOS866X	Volvo B10M-61	Duple Dominant IV	C49F	1982	Ex Clyde Coast, Ardrossan, 1997
C929SLT	Renault-Dodge G10	Wadham Stringer Vanguard	B30F	1985	Ex Lune Valley Transport, Lancaster, 1996
C279MDS	Renault-Dodge Commando G08	Wadham Stringer Vanguard	B39F	1986	Ex MoD, 1996
C308SPL	Mercedes-Benz L608D	Reeve Burgess	B20F	1986	Ex London & Country, 1996
C310SPL	Mercedes-Benz L608D	Reeve Burgess	B20F	1986	Ex London & Country, 1996
C312SPL	Mercedes-Benz L608D	Reeve Burgess	B20F	1986	Ex London & Country, 1996
D82CFA	Ford Transit VE6	Dormobile	B16F	1986	Ex Midland Red North, 1996
D86CFA	Ford Transit VE6	Dormobile	B16F	1987	Ex Midland Red North, 1996
D103CFA	Ford Transit VE6	Dormobile	B16F	1987	Ex Midland Red North, 1996
D613MDB	MCW MetroRider MF151/3	MCW	B23F	1987	Ex Stagecoach Manchester, 1997
D621MDB	MCW MetroRider MF151/3	MCW	B23F	1987	Ex Stagecoach Manchester, 1997
D626MDB	MCW MetroRider MF151/3	MCW	B23F	1987	Ex Stagecoach Manchester, 1997
D665NNE	MCW MetroRider MF151/3	MCW	B23F	1987	Ex Stagecoach Manchester, 1997
E319LHG	Peugeot-Talbot Pullman	Talbot	B20F	1988	Ex A1A, Birkenhead, 1995
E565MAC	Peugeot-Talbot Pullman	Talbot	B20F	1988	Ex Topping, Sancreed, 1995
E422MAC	Peugeot-Talbot Pullman	Talbot	B20F	1988	Ex Slocoach, Johnstone, 1996
E52KJU	Peugeot-Talbot Express	Dormobile	M14	1988	Ex Cochrane, Armadale, 1997
G32OHS	Mercedes-Benz 811D	Alexander AM	B33F	1989	Ex Westside, Gourock, 1996
G902MNS	Mercedes-Benz 811D	Reeve Burgess	B33F	1989	Ex Stevensons, 1995

	Peugeot-Talbot Pullman	Talbot	B22F	1989-90	Ex Kentish Bus, 1996
G701RNE	G133AHP	G870SKE	G872SKE		G878SKE

H675AGD	Mercedes-Benz 609D	Rapier	C24F	1991	Ex Boyd, Paisley, 1996
H183CNS	Mercedes-Benz 609D	Made-to-Measure	B26F	1991	Ex Westside, Gourock, 1996
H185CNS	Mercedes-Benz 609D	Made-to-Measure	B26F	1991	Ex Westside, Gourock, 1996
J916HGD	Peugeot-Talbot Pullman	Talbot	B25F	1991	Ex Stonehouse Coaches, 1996
K731AOG	Peugeot-Talbot Pullman	TBP	B18F	1993	Ex Lofty's, Bridge Trafford, 1995
K732AOG	Peugeot-Talbot Pullman	TBP	B18F	1993	Ex Lofty's, Bridge Trafford, 1995
L263VSU	Mercedes-Benz 709D	Dormobile Routemaker	B29F	1994	Ex Redline, Penwortham, 1995
L970VGE	Mercedes-Benz 709D	WS Wessex II	B29F	1994	Ex Lofty's, Bridge Trafford, 1996
M878DDS	Mercedes-Benz 709D	WS Wessex II	B29F	1994	Ex Lofty's, Bridge Trafford, 1996
M880DDS	Mercedes-Benz 709D	WS Wessex II	B29F	1994	Ex Lofty's, Bridge Trafford, 1996
M883DDS	Mercedes-Benz 811D	WS Wessex II	B33F	1994	
M583SSX	Iveco TurboDaily 59-12	Keillor	B29F	1994	Ex Rennies, Dunfermline, 1995
M95EGE	Mercedes-Benz 709D	WS Wessex II	B33F	1995	

	Mercedes-Benz 709D	TBP	B27F	1995	
M791EUS	M792EUS	M793EUS	M794EUS		M423GUS

	Mercedes-Benz 811D	WS Wessex II	B33F	1995	
M799EUS	M277FNS	M278FNS	M422GUS		N991KUS
M276FNS					

N26KYS	Mercedes-Benz 811D	Plaxton Beaver	B31F	1995	Ex Daybird Roadline, Killamarsh, 1996
N27KYS	Mercedes-Benz 811D	Plaxton Beaver	B31F	1995	Ex Daybird Roadline, Killamarsh, 1996
N750LUS	Mercedes-Benz OH1416	Wright	B47F	1995	
N941MGG	Mercedes-Benz 709D	Marshall C19	B29F	1995	Ex Lofty's, Bridge Trafford, 1996
N942MGG	Mercedes-Benz 709D	Marshall C19	B29F	1995	Ex Lofty's, Bridge Trafford, 1996
N935ETU	Iveco TurboDaily 59-12	Mellor	B25F	1995	Ex Lofty's, Bridge Trafford, 1996
N936ETU	Iveco TurboDaily 59-12	Mellor	B25F	1995	Ex Lofty's, Bridge Trafford, 1996
N752LUS	Mercedes-Benz 709D	UVG CitiStar	B29F	1996	
N753LUS	Mercedes-Benz 709D	UVG CitiStar	B29F	1996	
N253PGD	Mercedes-Benz 811D	UVG CitiStar	B33F	1996	

Argyll Bus Group have purchased many minibuses of varying types for their operation south of the Clyde. Shown here are M883DDS, a Mercedes-Benz 811 with WS Wessex II bodywork while below is D621MDB, one of four second-hand MetroRiders which previously operated with Stagecoach Manchester. *Phillip Stephenson/Andrew Jarosz*

Pictured in Irvine is Coastline Express's Mercedes-Benz 811 N809PDS, one of six that carry the longer C16 version of the Marshall-built minibus body. *Murdoch Currie*

	Mercedes-Benz 709D	Marshall C19	B29F	1996	
N754LUS	N256PGD	N258PGD	N802PDS		N804PDS
N228MUS	N257PGD	N801PDS	N803PDS		N805PDS
N254PGD					

	Mercedes-Benz 811D	Marshall C16	B33F	1996	
N806PDS	N808PDS	N809PDS	N81PUS		N82PUS
N807PDS					

P490TGA	Mercedes-Benz 711D	UVG CitiStar	B29F	1996
P491TGA	Mercedes-Benz 711D	UVG CitiStar	B29F	1996
P492TGA	Mercedes-Benz 711D	UVG CitiStar	B29F	1996
P526UGA	Mercedes-Benz 711D	Marshall C19	B29F	1996
P527UGA	Mercedes-Benz 711D	Marshall C19	B29F	1996
P528UGA	Mercedes-Benz 709D	Plaxton Beaver	B29F	1997
P529UGA	Mercedes-Benz 709D	Plaxton Beaver	B29F	1997
P930YSB	Mercedes-Benz 709D	Plaxton Beaver	B29F	1997
P931YSB	Mercedes-Benz 709D	Plaxton Beaver	B29F	1997
P932YSB	Mercedes-Benz 811D	Mellor	B33F	1997
P936YSB	Mercedes-Benz 811D	Mellor	B33F	1997
P937YSB	Mercedes-Benz 811D	Mellor	B33F	1997

Livery: White, green and gold

Names vehicles: M883DDS *Coastline Cruiser*; M791EUS, *Coastline Cutter*; M423GUS *Coastline Coaster*; M95EGE, *Coastline Classic*; M793EUS, *Coastline Connect*.

Previous Registrations:

C279MDS	?		TOS886X	FHS753X, 1528RU	TJI1692	EYH808V

AVONDALE

C Irving & T McIntyre, 11 Houston Street, Greenock, Renfrewshire, PA16 8DA

100	E518JHG	Mercedes-Benz 609D	Reeve Burgess Beaver	C25F	1988	Ex A Woods, Standish, 1994
101	E511YSU	Mercedes-Benz 709D	Alexander AM	B25F	1988	Ex KCB Network, 1995
104	H991YUS	Mercedes-Benz 709D	Reeve Burgess Beaver	B25F	1990	Ex KCB Network, 1995
105	H913XGA	Mercedes-Benz 709D	Dormobile Routemaker	B29F	1990	Ex Walker, Paisley, 1992
106	H914XGA	Mercedes-Benz 709D	Dormobile Routemaker	B29F	1990	Ex Walker, Paisley, 1992
109	L922UGA	Mercedes-Benz 709D	Dormobile Routemaker	B29F	1993	
110	L139XDS	Mercedes-Benz 709D	WS Wessex II	B29F	1994	
111	L140XDS	Mercedes-Benz 709D	WS Wessex II	B29F	1994	
112	N249PGD	Mercedes-Benz 709D	UVG CitiStar	B29F	1996	
113	N250PGD	Mercedes-Benz 709D	UVG CitiStar	B29F	1996	
114	N799PDS	Mercedes-Benz 709D	Marshall C19	B29F	1996	
115	N798PDS	Mercedes-Benz 709D	Marshall C19	B29F	1996	
116	D536RCK	Mercedes-Benz L608D	Reeve Burgess	B20F	1986	Ex Ribble, 1996
117	D537RCK	Mercedes-Benz L608D	Reeve Burgess	B20F	1986	Ex Ribble, 1996
1	D510RCK	Mercedes-Benz L608D	Reeve Burgess	DP19F	1986	Ex Ribble, 1996
121	D521RCK	Mercedes-Benz L608D	Reeve Burgess	DP19F	1986	Ex Ribble, 1996
122	D515RCK	Mercedes-Benz L608D	Reeve Burgess	DP19F	1986	Ex Ribble, 1996

Livery: Red and white

Avondale operate a fleet that comprises entirely of Mercedes-Benz minibuses, though a variety of body styles can be found. Shown here is 110, L139XDS which is one of two with WS Wessex bodywork that date from 1994. The latest arrivals have featured Marshall bodywork.
Phillip Stephenson

BLUEBIRD BUSES

Bluebird Buses Ltd, Guild Street, Aberdeen, AB9 2DR

Depots : Hillview Road, East Tullos, Aberdeen; Montgarrie Road, Alford; Golf Road, Ballater; Castleton Place, Braemar; March Road, Buckie; Pinefield, Elgin; North Road, Forres; Hanover Street, Fraserburgh; Schoolhill, Fyvie; Burnett Road, Inverness; Union Road, Macduff; Longside Road, Mintlaw; Ruthvenfield Road, Perth; St Peter Street, Peterhead; Spittalfield; Spurryhillock Ind Est, Stonehaven and Scotsburn Road, Tain. **Outstations** : Bellabeg, Strathdon; Stirling Road, Crieff; Ellon; Castle Street, Fochabers and Inverurie.

002-007

		Leyland Olympian ONLXB/1R	Alexander RL		H45/32F	1981	

002	SSA2X	004	SSA4X	005	SSA5X	006	SSA6X	007	SSA7X
003	SSA3X								

008	K508ESS	Leyland Olympian ON2R50G13Z4	Alexander RL	DPH43/27F	1992	
009	K509ESS	Leyland Olympian ON2R50G13Z4	Alexander RL	DPH43/27F	1992	
010	K510ESS	Leyland Olympian ON2R50G13Z4	Alexander RL	DPH43/27F	1992	
011	K511ESS	Leyland Olympian ON2R50G13Z4	Alexander RL	DPH43/27F	1992	
012	TSO12X	Leyland Olympian ONLXB/1R	Eastern Coach Works	H45/32F	1982	Ex Stagecoach, 1994
013	TSO13X	Leyland Olympian ONLXB/1R	Eastern Coach Works	H45/32F	1982	Ex Stagecoach, 1994
014	TSO14X	Leyland Olympian ONLXB/1R	Eastern Coach Works	H45/32F	1982	Ex Stagecoach, 1994
015	K515ESS	Leyland Olympian ON2R50G13Z4	Alexander RL	DPH43/27F	1992	
016	TSO16X	Leyland Olympian ONLXB/1R	Eastern Coach Works	H45/32F	1982	Ex Stagecoach, 1994
017	TSO17X	Leyland Olympian ONLXB/1R	Eastern Coach Works	H45/32F	1982	Ex Stagecoach, 1994
018	K518ESS	Leyland Olympian ON2R50G13Z4	Alexander RL	DPH43/27F	1992	
019	OMS910W	Leyland Olympian B45-6LXB	Eastern Coach Works	H45/32F	1981	Ex Stagecoach, 1994

020-025

		Leyland Olympian ONLXB/1R	Eastern Coach Works		H45/32F	1982	Ex Stagecoach, 1994

020	TSO20X	022	9492SC	023	TSO23X	024	TSO24X	025	TSO15X
021	TSO21X								

026	L26JSA	Volvo Olympian YN2RV18Z4	Northern Counties Palatine I	DPH43/25F	1993	
027	L27JSA	Volvo Olympian YN2RV18Z4	Northern Counties Palatine I	DPH43/25F	1993	
028	L28JSA	Volvo Olympian YN2RV18Z4	Northern Counties Palatine I	DPH43/25F	1993	
029	TSO29X	Leyland Olympian ONLXB/1R	Eastern Coach Works	H45/32F	1982	Ex Stagecoach, 1994
030	TSO30X	Leyland Olympian ONLXB/1R	Eastern Coach Works	H45/32F	1982	Ex Stagecoach, 1994
031	TSO31X	Leyland Olympian ONLXB/1R	Eastern Coach Works	H45/32F	1982	Ex Stagecoach, 1994
032	TSO32X	Leyland Olympian ONLXB/1R	Eastern Coach Works	H45/32F	1982	Ex Stagecoach, 1994

Bluebird Buses encompass the operations of Inverness Traction and Stagecoach Buses from their base in Aberdeen. Seen heading for Tain is Northern Counties-bodied Olympian 028, L28JSA.
Andrew Jarosz

033-060 — Leyland Olympian ONLXB/1R* · Alexander RL · H45/32F* · 1983-85 · *044 is DPH41/29F · *049 has a 5LXCT engine

033	YSO33Y	039	YSO39Y	045	A45FRS	051	B351LSO	056	B356LSO
034	YSO34Y	040	YSO40Y	046	A46FRS	052	B352LSO	057	B357LSO
035	YSO35Y	041	YSO41Y	047	A47FRS	053	B353LSO	058	B358LSO
036	YSO36Y	042	YSO42Y	048	B348LSO	054	B354LSO	059	B359LSO
037	YSO37Y	043	YSO43Y	049	B349LSO	055	B355LSO	060	B360LSO
038	YSO38Y	044	A44FRS	050	B350LSO				

061-066 — Leyland Olympian ONLXB/1RV · Alexander RL · DPH43/27F · 1986

061	C461SSO	063	C463SSO	064	MHS4P	065	MHS5P	066	C466SSO
062	C462SSO							

067-071 — Leyland Olympian ONLXB/1RV · Alexander RL · H47/30F · 1986

067	C467SSO	068	C468SSO	069	C469SSO	070	C470SSO	071	GSO1V

072	UWV605S	Bristol VRT/SL3/6LXB	Eastern Coach Works	CO43/31F	1977	Ex East Midland, 1992
074	UWV611S	Bristol VRT/SL3/6LXB	Eastern Coach Works	CO43/31F	1978	Ex Stagecoach South, 1996
075	UWV613S	Bristol VRT/SL3/6LXB	Eastern Coach Works	CO43/31F	1978	Ex Stagecoach South, 1996
076u	MAU146P	Bristol VRT/SL3/6LX	Eastern Coach Works	H39/31F	1976	Ex Stagecoach, 1992
077	VTV171S	Bristol VRT/SL3/6LXB	Eastern Coach Works	H43/31F	1978	Ex Stagecoach South, 1996
078	EAP996V	Bristol VRT/SL3/6LXB	Eastern Coach Works	H43/31F	1980	Ex Stagecoach South, 1996
079u	EAP983V	Bristol VRT/SL3/6LXB	Eastern Coach Works	H43/31F	1980	Ex Stagecoach South, 1996

085-089 — Leyland Olympian ONLXB/1RV · Alexander RL · DPH43/27F · 1987

085	D385XRS	086	D386XRS	087	D387XRS	088	D388XRS	089	D389XRS

090-099 — Leyland Olympian ON2R56G13Z4 Alexander RL · DPH47/27F · 1991-92

090	J120XHH	092	J122XHH	097	J197YSS	098	J198YSS	099	J199YSS
091	J121XHH	096	J196YSS						

100	L100JLB	Volvo Olympian YN2RV18Z4	Northern Counties Palatine I	DPH43/25F	1993	
101	L101JSA	Volvo Olympian YN2RV18Z4	Northern Counties Palatine I	DPH43/25F	1993	
102	L102JSA	Volvo Olympian YN2RV18Z4	Northern Counties Palatine I	DPH43/25F	1993	
103	FDV810V	Bristol VRT/SL3/6LXB	Eastern Coach Works	H43/31F	1980	Ex Stagecoach, 1994
104	JAK209W	Bristol VRT/SL3/6LXB	Eastern Coach Works	H43/31F	1980	Ex Western Scottish (A1), 1995
105	FDV816V	Bristol VRT/SL3/6LXB	Eastern Coach Works	H43/31F	1980	Ex Stagecoach, 1994
106	UWV608S	Bristol VRT/SL3/6LXB	Eastern Coach Works	CO43/31F	1977	Ex Stagecoach, 1991
107	FDV819V	Bristol VRT/SL3/6LXB	Eastern Coach Works	H43/31F	1980	Ex Stagecoach, 1994
108	UWV609S	Bristol VRT/SL3/6LXB	Eastern Coach Works	CO43/31F	1977	Ex Stagecoach, 1991
109	FDV840V	Bristol VRT/SL3/6LXB	Eastern Coach Works	H43/31F	1980	Ex Stagecoach, 1994
110	JAK210W	Bristol VRT/SL3/6LXB	Eastern Coach Works	H43/31F	1980	Ex Stagecoach, 1994
111	KWA213W	Bristol VRT/SL3/6LXB	Eastern Coach Works	H43/31F	1981	Ex Western Scottish (A1), 1995
112	JAK212W	Bristol VRT/SL3/6LXB	Eastern Coach Works	H43/31F	1980	Ex Stagecoach, 1994

The Inverness Town and Culloden Tour is operated by Bluebird Buses with Guide Friday marketing as shown in this picture of 108, UWV609S. This batch of former Southdown convertible-top buses have been spread to many of the group's operations.
Phillip Stephenson

13

113	HWG207W	Bristol VRT/SL3/6LXB	Eastern Coach Works	H43/31F	1980	Ex Western Scottish (A1), 1995		
114	KWA219W	Bristol VRT/SL3/6LXC	Eastern Coach Works	H43/31F	1981	Ex Western Scottish (A1), 1995		
115	FAO429V	Bristol VRT/SL3/6LXB	Eastern Coach Works	H43/31F	1980	Ex Western Scottish (A1), 1995		
116	EWE205V	Bristol VRT/SL3/6LXB	Eastern Coach Works	H43/31F	1980	Ex Western Scottish (A1), 1995		
117	KKY222W	Bristol VRT/SL3/6LXB	Eastern Coach Works	H43/31F	1981	Ex Western Scottish (A1), 1995		
120	SAO410R	Bristol VRT/SL3/501	Eastern Coach Works	H43/31F	1977	Ex Cumberland, 1991		
122	SAO412R	Bristol VRT/SL3/501	Eastern Coach Works	H43/31F	1977	Ex Cumberland, 1991		
123	EWE202V	Bristol VRT/SL3/6LXB	Eastern Coach Works	H43/31F	1980	Ex Western Scottish (A1), 1995		
124	KWA215W	Bristol VRT/SL3/6LXC	Eastern Coach Works	H43/31F	1981	Ex Western Scottish (A1), 1995		
125	KWA216W	Bristol VRT/SL3/6LXC	Eastern Coach Works	H43/31F	1981	Ex Western Scottish (A1), 1995		
126	KRM430W	Bristol VRT/SL3/6LXB	Eastern Coach Works	H43/31F	1980	Ex Western Scottish (A1), 1995		
128	RJT155R	Bristol VRT/SL3/6LXB	Eastern Coach Works	H43/31F	1977	Ex Stagecoach, 1992		
131	RRS46R	Leyland Leopard PSU3E/4R	Duple Dominant I	C49F	1977			
132	RRS47R	Leyland Leopard PSU3E/4R	Duple Dominant I	C49F	1977			
133	RRS48R	Leyland Leopard PSU3E/4R	Duple Dominant I	C49F	1977			
134	PRA109R	Leyland Leopard PSU3C/4R	Alexander AT	C49F	1976	Ex East Midland, 1995		
135	RRS50R	Leyland Leopard PSU3E/4R	Duple Dominant I	C49F	1977			
136u	PRA110R	Leyland Leopard PSU3C/4R	Alexander AT	C49F	1976	Ex East Midland, 1995		
137	PRA112R	Leyland Leopard PSU3E/4R	Alexander AT	C49F	1976	Ex East Midland, 1995		
138	RRS53R	Leyland Leopard PSU3E/4R	Duple Dominant I	C49F	1977			

139-144
Leyland Leopard PSU3E/4R — Alexander AT — DP49F — 1979

139	CRS60T	141	CRS62T	142	CRS63T	143	CRS68T	144	CRS69T
140	CRS61T							

145	CRS70T	Leyland Leopard PSU3E/4R	Duple Dominant I	C49F	1979			
146	CRS71T	Leyland Leopard PSU3E/4R	Duple Dominant I	C49F	1979			
147	CRS73T	Leyland Leopard PSU3E/4R	Duple Dominant I	C49F	1979			
148	CRS74T	Leyland Leopard PSU3E/4R	Duple Dominant I	C49F	1979			
149u	OSJ635R	Leyland Leopard PSU3C/3R	Alexander AY	B53F	1977	Ex East Midland, 1995		
150u	OSJ643R	Leyland Leopard PSU3C/3R	Alexander AY	B53F	1977	Ex East Midland, 1995		
151u	OSJ644R	Leyland Leopard PSU3C/3R	Alexander AY	B53F	1977	Ex East Midland, 1995		

152-158
Leyland Leopard PSU3E/4R — Alexander AYS — DP49F* — 1980 — Ex Stagecoach, 1994
*155/7 are B53F

152	GSO89V	154	GSO91V	156	GSO93V	157	GSO94V	158	GSO95V
153	GSO90V	155	GSO92V					

160	KRS531V	Leyland Leopard PSU3E/4R	Duple Dominant II Express	C49F	1980			
161	KRS532V	Leyland Leopard PSU3E/4R	Duple Dominant II Express	C49F	1980			
162u	OSJ634R	Leyland Leopard PSU3C/3R	Alexander AY	B53F	1977	Ex East Midland, 1995		
163	JSA101V	Leyland Leopard PSU3F/4R	Alexander AT	DP49F	1980			
164	JSA102V	Leyland Leopard PSU3F/4R	Alexander AT	DP49F	1980			
165	JSA103V	Leyland Leopard PSU3F/4R	Alexander AT	DP49F	1980			
166	JSA104V	Leyland Leopard PSU3F/4R	Alexander AT	DP49F	1980			
167	HSR136W	Leyland Leopard PSU3G/4R	Duple Dominant II Express	C49F	1981	Ex Stagecoach, 1994		
169	NUF276	Leyland Leopard PSU3G/4R	Duple Dominant II Express	C49F	1981	Ex Stagecoach, 1994		
170	VLT272	Leyland Leopard PSU3G/4R	Duple Dominant II Express	C49F	1981	Ex Stagecoach, 1994		
171	866NHT	Leyland Leopard PSU3G/4R	Duple Dominant II Express	C49F	1981	Ex Stagecoach, 1994		
172	KRS682V	Leyland Leopard PSU3E/4R	Duple Dominant II Express	C53F	1980	Ex Western Scottish (A1), 1995		
188	DWF188V	Bristol VRT/SL3/6LXB	Eastern Coach Works	H43/31F	1979	Ex Stagecoach, 1994		
190	DWF190V	Bristol VRT/SL3/6LXB	Eastern Coach Works	H43/31F	1979	Ex Stagecoach, 1994		
191	DWF191V	Bristol VRT/SL3/6LXB	Eastern Coach Works	H43/31F	1979	Ex Stagecoach, 1994		
193	DWF193V	Bristol VRT/SL3/6LXB	Eastern Coach Works	H43/31F	1979	Ex Stagecoach, 1994		
213	HNE252V	Leyland Leopard PSU5C/4R	Duple Dominant II Express	C53F	1980	Ex Stagecoach, 1994		
214	HNE254V	Leyland Leopard PSU5C/4R	Duple Dominant II Express	C53F	1980	Ex Stagecoach, 1994		
215	JND260V	Leyland Leopard PSU5C/4R	Duple Dominant II Express	C53F	1980	Ex Stagecoach, 1994		
216	XRM772Y	Leyland Leopard PSU5C/4R	Duple Dominant III	C57F	1983	Ex Hardie's Coaches, Aberchirder, 1994		
217	D523KSE	Bedford YNV Venturer	Duple 320	C57F	1986	Ex Hardie's Coaches, Aberchirder, 1994		
221	WFS135W	Leyland Leopard PSU3F/4R	Alexander AYS	B53F	1980	Ex Stagecoach, 1994		
223	WFS137W	Leyland Leopard PSU3F/4R	Alexander AYS	B53F	1980	Ex Stagecoach, 1994		

Opposite: **Bluebird have become one of the most respected operations within Britain in recent years being awarded the prestigious title of Bus Company of the Year in 1996. The company is also only the second coach operation to be awarded the Royal Warrant for its services to the Crown. Copies of the Royal Warrant have been applied to a selection of the vehicles, principally those based at Ballater. Looking splendid with their Royal Arms are Alexander-bodied Olympian express 061 and Plaxton Interurban 582, N582XSA.** *Billy Nicol/Bill Potter*

Five Optare StarRiders previously with Stagecoach East London are now in the Bluebird Buses fleet. Photographed in Aberdeen, 294, E714LYU is one a pair currently allocated to Ballater. *Paul Wigan*

230	D435RYS	Mercedes-Benz 609D	Scott	C24F	1987	Ex Airpark, Linwood, 1990
231	D436RYS	Mercedes-Benz 609D	Scott	C24F	1987	Ex Airpark, Linwood, 1990
233	E364YGB	Mercedes-Benz 609D	Scott	C24F	1988	Ex Airpark, Linwood, 1990
234	E842KAS	Mercedes-Benz 609D	Reeve Burgess	C23F	1988	Ex Glenlivet & District, 1990
235	E947BHS	Mercedes-Benz 609D	Scott	C24F	1988	Ex Whitelaw, Stonehouse, 1990
236	F77HAU	Mercedes-Benz 609D	Scott	C24F	1988	Ex Skills, Sheffield, 1990
237	F164XCS	Mercedes-Benz 609D	Scott	C24F	1989	Ex Clyde Coast, Ardrossan, 1990
238	F862FWB	Mercedes-Benz 609D	Whittaker	C24F	1989	Ex Metcalfe, Ferryhill, 1990
241w	C901HWF	Mercedes-Benz L608D	Reeve Burgess	DP19F	1985	Ex Fife Scottish, 1994

256-292		Mercedes-Benz 709D	Alexander AM	B25F*	1990	Ex Stagecoach, 1991-92

*279-292 are B23F

256	G256TSL	262	G262TSL	275	G275TSL	283	G283TSL	288	G288TSL
257	G257TSL	270	G270TSL	276	G276TSL	284	G284TSL	289	G289TSL
258	G258TSL	271	G271TSL	277	G277TSL	285	G285TSL	290	G290TSL
259	G259TSL	272	G272TSL	278	G278TSL	286	G286TSL	291	G291TSL
260	G260TSL	273	G273TSL	279	G279TSL	287	G287TSL	292	G292TSL
261	G261TSL	274	G274TSL	282	G282TSL				

293	E713LYU	Mercedes-Benz 811D	Optare StarRider	B28F	1988	Ex Stagecoach East London, 1995
294	E714LYU	Mercedes-Benz 811D	Optare StarRider	B28F	1988	Ex Stagecoach East London, 1995
295	F169FWY	Mercedes-Benz 811D	Optare StarRider	B26F	1989	Ex Stagecoach East London, 1995
296	F177FWY	Mercedes-Benz 811D	Optare StarRider	B26F	1989	Ex Stagecoach East London, 1995
297	F180FWY	Mercedes-Benz 811D	Optare StarRider	B26F	1989	Ex Stagecoach East London, 1995
298	G86KUB	Mercedes-Benz 811D	Optare StarRider	B26F	1989	Ex Stagecoach East London, 1995
299	L550JFS	Mercedes-Benz 814D	Dormobile Routemaker	B33F	1993	Ex John G Gordon, Dornoch, 1996
301	L301JSA	Mercedes-Benz 709D	Alexander Sprint	DP25F	1993	
302	L302JSA	Mercedes-Benz 709D	Alexander Sprint	DP25F	1993	
303	L303JSA	Mercedes-Benz 709D	Alexander Sprint	DP25F	1993	

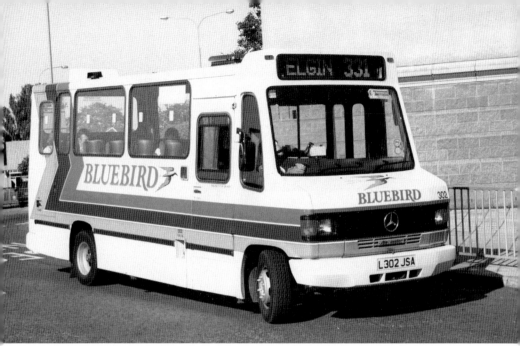

The standard Stagecoach minibus is the Mercedes-Benz 709D with Alexander Sprint bodywork. For 1997, the minibus delivery will consist of the new Mercedes-Benz Vario model and will have Plaxton's Beaver 2 bodywork. Photographed at Elgin is 302, L302JSA, one of fourteen minibuses based in the city. *Phillip Stephenson*

304-314

Mercedes-Benz 709D · Alexander AM · DP25F · 1990 · Ex Stagecoach, 1991-94

304	G193PAO	307	G196PAO	309	G198PAO	311	G200PAO	313	G202PAO
305	G194PAO	308	G197PAO	310	G199PAO	312	G201PAO	314	G203PAO
306	G195PAO								

315-321

Mercedes-Benz 709D · Alexander Sprint · DP25F · 1993-94

315	L315JSA	317	M317RSO	319	M319RSO	320	M320RSO	321	M321RSO
316	L316JSA	318	M318RSO						

336-352

Mercedes-Benz 709D · Alexander Sprint · B25F · 1996

336	N636VSS	340	N640VSS	344	P344ASO	347	P347ASO	350	P350ASO
337	N637VSS	341	P341ASO	345	P345ASO	348	P348ASO	351	P351ASO
338	N638VSS	342	P342ASO	346	P346ASO	349	P349ASO	352	P352ASO
339	N639VSS	343	P343ASO						

421	A116ESA	Leyland Tiger TRBTL11/2R	Alexander P	B52F	1983
422	A117ESA	Leyland Tiger TRBTL11/2R	Alexander P	B52F	1983
423	A118ESA	Leyland Tiger TRBTL11/2R	Alexander P	B52F	1983

424-430

Leyland Tiger TRBLXB/2RH · Alexander P · B52F · 1984

424	A121GSA	426	A123GSA	428	A125GSA	429	A126GSA	430	A127GSA
425	A122GSA	427	A124GSA						

431	PES190Y	Leyland Tiger TRCTL11/3R	Duple Laser	C55F	1983	Ex Busways, 1995
433	A940XGG	Leyland Tiger TRCTL11/3R	Duple Laser	C51F	1984	Ex Busways, 1995
434	A941XGG	Leyland Tiger TRCTL11/3R	Duple Laser	C51F	1984	Ex Stagecoach Transit, 1995
435	A942XGG	Leyland Tiger TRCTL11/3R	Duple Laser	C51F	1984	Ex Busways, 1995

442-446

Leyland Tiger TRCTL11/2RP · Alexander TC · C51F* · 1985 · *443 is C49F; 446 is C47F

442	TSV718	443	TSV719	444	TSV720	445	TSV721	446	TSV722

Transferred from East Midland during 1991 was this Leyland Tiger with Alexander TE-type bodywork pictured in Aberdeen. Numbered 459, A40XHE has been re-registered since its arrival and now carries the mark RIB4309. *Tony Wilson*

447	126ASV	Leyland Tiger TRBTL11/2R	Alexander TE	C51F	1983	Ex Kelvin Scottish, 1986
448	127ASV	Leyland Tiger TRBTL11/2R	Alexander TE	C51F	1983	Ex Kelvin Scottish, 1986
449	128ASV	Leyland Tiger TRBTL11/2R	Alexander TE	C51F	1983	Ex Kelvin Scottish, 1986

450-454

		Leyland Tiger TRCTL11/3RH	Alexander TC	C57F	1987	

450	D744BRS	451	LSK547	452	LSK548	453	147YFM	454	BSK756

455	HSK760	Leyland Tiger TRCLXC/2RH	Duple 320	C53F	1986	Ex Central Scottish, 1989
456	C111JCS	Leyland Tiger TRCLXC/2RH	Duple 320	C53F	1986	Ex Central Scottish, 1989
457	B291YSL	Leyland Tiger TRCTL11/2RP	Alexander TC	C47F	1985	Ex Fife Scottish, 1997
458	WAO643Y	Leyland Tiger TRCTL11/2R	Alexander TE	C47F	1983	Ex Ribble, 1994
459	RIB4309	Leyland Tiger TRCTL11/2R	Alexander TE	C49F	1983	Ex East Midland, 1991

460-465

		Leyland Tiger TRCTL11/3R	Duple Laser	C53F	1984	Ex National Welsh, 1992

460	AAX600A	462	AKG232A	463	AAX589A	464	AAX601A	465	AKG162A
461	AAX631A								

466	NIB4138	Leyland Tiger TRCTL11/3RH	Duple Laser	C51F	1984	Ex Stagecoach, 1994
467	NIB5455	Leyland Tiger TRCTL11/3RH	Duple Laser	C51F	1984	Ex Stagecoach, 1994
468	A663WSU	Leyland Tiger TRBTL11/2RP	Alexander TE	DP53F	1983	Ex Kelvin Central, 1993

491-499

		Volvo B6LE	Alexander ALX200	B36F	1996	

491	P491BRS	493	P493BRS	495	P495BRS	497	P497BRS	499	P499BRS
492	P492BRS	494	P494BRS	496	P496BRS	498	P498BRS		

501-512

		Dennis Dart 9.8SDL3017	Alexander Dash	B41F	1992	

501	J501FPS	504	J504FPS	507	J507FPS	509	J509FPS	511	J511FPS
502	J502FPS	505	J505FPS	508	J508FPS	510	J510FPS	512	J512FPS
503	J503FPS	506	J506FPS						

Displacing the Routemaster from Perth city services earlier in 1997 were fourteen of the new low-floor Volvo B6LE buses. Carrying suitable marketing lettering is 494, P494BRS. Following on from the 1996 order for 80 units with the Alexander ALX200 body, a further 70 similar examples are expected for the group during 1997. *Tony Wilson*

513-522

		Dennis Dart 9.8SDL3017		Alexander Dash		B40F	1993		
513	K101XHG	**515**	K103XHG	**517**	K105XHG	**519**	K107XHG	**521**	K109XHG
514	K102XHG	**516**	K104XHG	**518**	K106XHG	**520**	K108XHG	**522**	K110XHG

527-544

		Volvo B10M-62		Plaxton Premiére Interurban		DP51F	1994		
527	M527RSO	**531**	M531RSO	**535**	M535RSO	**539**	M539RSO	**542**	M542RSO
528	M528RSO	**532**	M532RSO	**536**	M536RSO	**540**	M540RSO	**543**	M543RSO
529	M529RSO	**533**	M533RSO	**537**	M537RSO	**541**	M541RSO	**544**	M544RSO
530	M530RSO	**534**	M534RSO	**538**	M538RSO				

545	1412NE	Volvo B10M-61	Van Hool Alizée	C53F	1986	Ex Hardie's Coaches, Aberchirder, 1994
546	TSV778	Volvo B10M-61	Van Hool Alizée	C53F	1986	Ex Hardie's Coaches, Aberchirder, 1994
547	TSV779	Volvo B10M-61	Van Hool Alizée	C53F	1987	Ex Rainworth Travel, 1992
548	TSV780	Volvo B10M-61	Van Hool Alizée	C53F	1987	Ex Shearings, 1991
549	TSV781	Volvo B10M-61	Van Hool Alizée	C53F	1987	Ex Shearings, 1991
550	CSU920	Volvo B10M-61	Van Hool Alizée	C53F	1987	Ex Rainworth Travel, 1992
551	CSU921	Volvo B10M-61	Van Hool Alizée	C53F	1987	Ex Shearings, 1991
552	CSU922	Volvo B10M-61	Van Hool Alizée	C53F	1987	Ex Shearings, 1991
553	CSU923	Volvo B10M-61	Van Hool Alizée	C53F	1987	Ex Shearings, 1991
554	F277WAF	Volvo B10M-61	Duple 320	C56F	1989	Ex Scotravel, Elgin, 1995
555	DDZ8844	Volvo B10M-61	Duple 320	C57F	1989	Ex Scotravel, Elgin, 1995
556	MIB7416	Volvo B10M-61	Plaxton Paramount 3500 III	C53F	1988	Ex Thos. Rowe, Muirkirk 1996
557	F424GGB	Volvo B10M-61	Plaxton Paramount 3200 III	C57F	1988	Ex Gray, Fochabers, 1996
558	UOT648	Volvo B10M-61	Van Hool Alizée	C53F	1988	Ex Eastons, Inverurie, 1996
559	OSK784	Volvo B10M-61	Duple 320	C53F	1988	Ex Eastons, Inverurie, 1996
560	XRC487	Volvo B10M-61	Van Hool Alizée	C49FT	1985	Ex MacLean, Buckie, 1997

561-570

		Volvo B10M-60		Plaxton Premiére Interurban		DP53F	1993	561/70 ex Stagecoach, 1994	
561	K561GSA	**563**	K563GSA	**565**	K565GSA	**567**	K567GSA	**569**	K569GSA
562	K562GSA	**564**	K564GSA	**566**	K566GSA	**568**	K568GSA	**570**	K570GSA

Soon to be the subject of a Corgi model, ten Volvo B10Ms with Van Hool Alizée bodywork are now used by Bluebird on their growing network of rural services. Photographed in Aberdeen was 549, TSV781 an example now allocated to Fyvie in Aberdeenshire. *Phillip Stephenson*

571-578

Volvo B10M-55   Alexander PS   B49F   1993   Ex Stagecoach, 1994

571	K571LTS	573	K573LTS	575	K575LTS	577	K577LTS	578	K578LTS
572	K572LTS	574	K574LTS	576	K576LTS			

579	L579JSA	Volvo B10M-60	Plaxton Premiére Interurban DP51F	1993
580	L580JSA	Volvo B10M-60	Plaxton Premiére Interurban DP51F	1993
581	L581JSA	Volvo B10M-60	Plaxton Premiére Interurban DP51F	1993
582	N582XSA	Volvo B10M-62	Plaxton Premiére Interurban DP51F	1996
583	N583XSA	Volvo B10M-62	Plaxton Premiére Interurban DP51F	1996
584	N584XSA	Volvo B10M-62	Plaxton Premiére Interurban DP51F	1996
585	L585JSA	Volvo B10M-60	Plaxton Premiére Interurban DP51F	1993
586	L586JSA	Volvo B10M-60	Plaxton Premiére Interurban DP51F	1993
587	L587JSA	Volvo B10M-60	Plaxton Premiére Interurban DP51F	1993
588	L588JSA	Volvo B10M-60	Plaxton Premiére Interurban DP51F	1993

589-598

Volvo B10M-55   Alexander PS   DP48F   1994

589	M589OSO	591	M591OSO	593	M593OSO	595	M595OSO	597	M597OSO
590	M590OSO	592	M592OSO	594	M594OSO	596	M596OSO	598	M598OSO

618	N618USS	Volvo B10M-62	Plaxton Expressliner 2	C44FT	1995
619	N619USS	Volvo B10M-62	Plaxton Expressliner 2	C44FT	1995
620	N620USS	Volvo B10M-62	Plaxton Expressliner 2	C44FT	1995
623	J455FSR	Volvo B10M-61	Plaxton Paramount 3500 III	C46FT	1991	Ex Express Travel, 1994
624	J456FSR	Volvo B10M-61	Plaxton Paramount 3500 III	C46FT	1992	Ex Speedlink, 1994
625	P625NSE	Volvo B10M-62	Plaxton Expressliner 2	C44FT	1997
626	P626NSE	Volvo B10M-62	Plaxton Expressliner 2	C44FT	1996

628-634

Volvo B10M-62   Plaxton Premiére Interurban DP51F   1996

628	N148XSA	630	N150XSA	632	N152XSA	633	N153XSA	634	N154XSA
629	N149XSA	631	N151XSA			

Bluebird Buses' 528, M528RSO is one of the 1994 intake of Interurban Volvo B10Ms. Seen at Kenmay bound for Aberdeen the vehicle displays both the Royal Arms and the banner proclaiming Bluebird Buses to be the Bus Company of the Year for 1996. *Iain Smart*

Stagecoach operations may retain veteran buses for use at Special events and services. One of the former Northern Scottish Albion Vikings is retained by Bluebird Buses as its 1111, GRS343E. *Phillip Stephenson*

Special event vehicles - traditional liveries

1101u	EDS50A	AEC Routemaster R2RH	Park Royal	H36/28R	1960	Ex Stagecoach, 1994
1102u	NSG636A	AEC Routemaster R2RH	Park Royal	H36/28R	1962	Ex Stagecoach, 1994
1105u	ALD968B	AEC Routemaster 2R2RH	Park Royal	H36/28R	1964	Ex Stagecoach, 1994
1106u	LDS201A	AEC Routemaster 2R2RH	Park Royal	H36/24R	1963	Ex Stagecoach, 1994
1107	490CLT	AEC Routemaster R2RH	Park Royal	H32/25R	1962	Ex Selkent, 1994
1109u	FES831W	Volvo B58-61	Duple Dominant IV	DP59F	1981	Ex Stagecoach, 1994
1110u	NMY643E	AEC Routemaster R2RH2	Park Royal	H32/24F	1967	Ex Kelvin Scottish, 1993
1111	GRS343E	Albion Viking VK43AL	Alexander Y	DP40F	1967	
1112	HDV639E	Bristol MW6G	Eastern Coach Works	C39F	1967	Ex preservation, 1996
1113u	HGM335E	Bristol FLF6G	Eastern Coach Works	H44/34F	1967	Ex Stagecoach, 1994
1114u	HFM561D	Bristol MW6G	Eastern Coach Works	C39F	1966	Ex preservation, 1996
1115	DGS625	Leyland Tiger PS1/2	McLennan	C39F	1951	Ex Stagecoach, 1994
1116u	LDS210A	AEC Routemaster R2RH	Park Royal	H36/28R	1962	Ex Stagecoach, 1994

Liveries: White, red, orange and blue (Stagecoach corporate); white (National Express) 618-24.

Previous Registrations:

126ASV	BMS511Y	KRS532V	HSA98V, CSU922
127ASV	BMS513Y	KRS682V	ORS107W, TSV719, PSO28W
128ASV	BMS515Y	L100JLB	L110JSA
1412NE	C325DND	LDS201A	607DYE
145CLT	-	LDS210A	245CLT
147YFM	D439XRS	LSK547	D437XRS
4585SC	-	LSK548	D438XRS
490CLT	From new	MHS4P	C464SSO
866NHT	ORS110W, TSV722, PSO32W	MHS5P	C465SSO
9492SC	TSO19X	MIB7416	F27LTO
A663WSU	A120GLS, WLT976	NIB4138	A45YAK
A940XGG	A507PST, GSU344	NIB5455	A46YAK
A941XGG	A505PST, GSU342	NSG636A	164CLT
A942XGG	A506PST, GSU343	NUF276	ORS108W, TSV720, PSO27W, OVL473
AAX589A	A216VWO	OSK784	E748JAY, A3KRT
AAX600A	A219VWO	PES190Y	VTY130Y, GSU341
AAX601A	A218VWO	RIB4309	A40XHE
AAX631A	A222VWO	TSV718	B328LSA
AKG162A	A223VWO	TSV719	B329LSA
AKG232A	A229VWO	TSV720	B330LSA
B291YSL	B209FFS, GSU343	TSV721	B331LSA
BSK756	E640BRS	TSV722	B332LSA
CSU920	D550MVR	TSV778	C330DND
CSU921	D551MVR	TSV779	D547MVR
CSU922	D552MVR	TSV780	D548MVR
CSU923	D553MVR	TSV781	D549MVR
D744BRS	D436XRS, BSK744	UOT648	E644UNE, LSK874
DGS625	From new	USK625	WLT980
DDZ8844	F27LTO	VLT272	ORS109W, TSV721, PSO31W, LSK528
EDS50A	WLT560	XRC487	From new
GSO1V	C471SSO	XSL596A	289CLT
HSR136W	ORS106W, TSV718, PSO27W	YTS820A	599CLT
HSK760	C110JCS		
KRS531V	HSA97V, CSU921		

BOWMAN

Bowman Coaches (Mull) Ltd, Scallastle, Craignure, Isle of Mull, North Ayrshire, PA65 6BA

TGD221R	Ford R1014	Plaxton Supreme III Express	C45F	1977	
UFT921T	Volvo B58-61	Plaxton Supreme III	C57F	1978	Ex Hay's Coaches, Huntly, 1995
HGA834T	Volvo B58-61	Plaxton Supreme IV	C53F	1979	Ex Hay's Coaches, Huntly, 1995
TSV677	Volvo B58-56	Plaxton Supreme IV	C53F	1979	Ex McDougall, Oban, 1995
TMA254V	Bedford YMT	Duple Dominant II	C53F	1980	Ex Hanmer, Wrexham, 1983
EBB588W	Volvo B58-56	Duple Dominant II Express	C53F	1980	Ex McDougall, Oban, 1995
RGD383W	Bedford YMT	Duple Dominant Express	C49F	1980	
A441JJC	Bedford YNT	Duple Laser	C53F	1983	Ex Royal Red, Llandudno, 1987
A985JJU	Leyland Tiger TRCTL11/3R	Duple Laser	C57F	1984	
A121XNH	DAF SB2300DHS585	Jonckheere Jubilee P50	C53FT	1984	Ex Nationwide, Lanark, 1989
B43OSB	Bedford YNT	Plaxton Paramount 3200 II	C53F	1985	
B494GBD	Volvo B10M-61	Jonckheere Jubilee	C51FT	1985	Ex Ellis, Wembley Park, 1995
B417CVH	DAF SB2300DHTD585	Plaxton Paramount 3200 II	C57F	1985	
D285XCX	DAF SB2300DHS585	Plaxton Paramount 3200 II	C53FT	1987	Ex Hardings, Redditch, 1990
D615MVR	Volvo B10M-61	Van Hool Alizée	C53F	1987	Ex Park's, Hamilton, 1992
F362MUT	Dennis Javelin 11SDA1906	Duple 320	C53F	1988	
PIJ5751	Volvo B10M-61	Plaxton Paramount 3500 III	C53F	1989	Ex Ambassador, Great Yarmouth, 1995

Previous Registrations:

B43OSB	B656OFP	PIJ5751	F105CCL	TSV677	AWB315T

Livery: Cream and red

Bluebird Buses' 022, 9492SC is the only one of the type in the fleet to have gained a personal numberplate. It is seen in County South Street in Perth where it is based along with all the other Eastern Coach Works-bodied Leyland Olympians currently in the fleet. *Tony Wilson*

BRIDGE

M McGibbons & A Tipping, Back Sneddon Street, Paisley, Renfrewshire, PA3 2DF

D283OOK	Freight Rover Sherpa	Carlyle	B18F	1987	Ex Phil Anslow Travel, Garndiffaith, 1994
D67TLV	Freight Rover Sherpa	Carlyle	B20F	1987	Ex Phil Anslow Travel, Garndiffaith, 1994
D68TLV	Freight Rover Sherpa	Carlyle	B20F	1987	Ex Phil Anslow Travel, Garndiffaith, 1994
D503MJA	Iveco Daily 49.10	Robin Hood City Nippy	B19F	1987	Ex GM Buses, 1992
D512MJA	Iveco Daily 49.10	Robin Hood City Nippy	B19F	1987	Ex GM Buses, 1992
D517MJA	Iveco Daily 49.10	Robin Hood City Nippy	B19F	1987	Ex GM Buses, 1992
D528MJA	Iveco Daily 49.10	Robin Hood City Nippy	B19F	1987	Ex GM Buses, 1992
D532MJA	Iveco Daily 49.10	Robin Hood City Nippy	B19F	1987	Ex GM Buses, 1992
E142VGG	Mercedes-Benz 709D	North West Coach Sales	C25F	1987	Ex Kean, Wemyss Bay, 1989
F906YWY	Mercedes-Benz 811D	Optare StarRider	B26F	1988	Ex Cowie South London, 1996
F920YWY	Mercedes-Benz 811D	Optare StarRider	B26F	1988	Ex Cowie South London, 1996
F34CWY	Mercedes-Benz 811D	Optare StarRider	B26F	1989	Ex Cowie Leaside, 1996
F46CWY	Mercedes-Benz 811D	Optare StarRider	B26F	1989	Ex Cowie South London, 1996
G917CLV	Mercedes-Benz 609D	North West Coach Sales	C24F	1989	
G967CLV	Mercedes-Benz 609D	North West Coach Sales	C24F	1989	
K95RGA	Mercedes-Benz 709D	Dormobile Routemaker	B29F	1993	
K96RGA	Mercedes-Benz 709D	Dormobile Routemaker	B29F	1993	

Livery: White and green

Passing Paisley Pizzaland while heading for Erskine, the location of an important road bridge over the Clyde estuary, is F920YWY of Bridge. One of four MetroRiders recently purchased from Cowie's London operations they help to remove earlier Freight Rover Sherpas from the fleet. *Andrew Jarosz*

The Scottish Bus Handbook

BRUCE COACHES

J Bruce, 11 Manse Road, Torbothie, Shotts, North Lanarkshire, ML7 5EL

ELG516K	Bedford SB5	Plaxton	C41F	1972	Ex Sharkey, Shotts, 1993
ASU512S	Volvo B58-56	Plaxton Supreme	C53F	1978	Ex Anderson, Lower Largo, 1997
K444GSM	Volvo B10M-60	Plaxton Paramount 3200 III	C53F	1982	Ex Mayne's, Buckie, 1997
357WMX	Volvo B10M-62	Van Hool Alizée	C49FT	1994	
L83XDS	Volvo B10M-60	Van Hool Alizée	C49FT	1994	
L531XUT	Volvo B10M-60	Jonckheere Deauville	C53F	1994	Ex Allisons Cs, Dunfermline, 1994
N549NYS	Volvo B10M-62	Van Hool Alizée	C49FT	1996	
N550NYS	Volvo B10M-62	Van Hool Alizée	C49FT	1996	
P240VGD	Volvo B10M-62	Van Hool Alizée	C49FT	1997	

Previous Registrations:
357WMX   L82XDS

Livery: White (David Urquhart Travel) 357WMX, L83XDS, L531XUT; white, grey and red (Londonliner) N549NYS, P240VGD; white (Caledonian Travel) N550NYS.

BRYANS of DENNY

W Bryans, 39 Sutherland Drive, Denny, FK6 5ER

GIL1685	Volvo B10M-61	Van Hool Alizée	C50FT	1988	Ex Mason, Bo'ness, 1995
H114YSU	Peugeot-Talbot Freeway	Talbot	B12FL	1990	Ex McDode, Uddinston, 1996
L836MWT	Optare MetroRider	Optare	B F	1993	Ex Optare demonstrator, 1995
L960KMS	Omni	Omni	B17F	1994	Ex Mitchell, Piean, 1994
L961KMS	Omni	Omni	B17F	1994	Ex Mitchell, Piean, 1994
M189RLS	Mercedes-Benz	TBP	DP22FL	1994	Ex Midland Bluebird, 1996
M283SMS	Optare MetroRider	Optare	B F	1995	
M597SSB	Dennis Dart 9.8DL	Plaxton Pointer	B35F	1995	Ex Stonehouse Coaches, 1996
P2WBC	Marshall Minibus	Marshall	B22FL	1996	

Previous Registrations:
GIL1685   E633UNE, LSK815

Livery: Red (L960/1JMS & M283SMS carry 'Easyboarder' lettering)

P2WBC is the latest addition to the fleet of Bruce Coaches. The Marshall integral product is seen in Falkirk on the tendered route E3, one of those marketed under the Easyboarder banner. *David Kat*

CLYDE COAST

Clyde Coast Coaches Ltd, 55 Montgomerie Street, Ardrossan, North Ayrshire, KA22 8HR

D5	SSN239S	Ailsa B55-10	Alexander AV	H44/35F	1977	Ex A1 Service, 1995
D6	UCS896S	Ailsa B55-10	Alexander AV	H44/35F	1978	Ex A1 Service, 1995
D7	SSN247S	Ailsa B55-10	Alexander AV	H44/31D	1977	Ex A1 Service, 1995
D8	SSN248S	Ailsa B55-10	Alexander AV	H44/31D	1977	Ex A1 Service, 1995
	ECS56V	Ailsa B55-10	Alexander AV	H44/35F	1979	Ex A1 Service, 1995
	RJI7976	Volvo B10M-61	Van Hool Alizée	C48FT	1984	Ex Marbill, Bath, 1995
	RJI6494	Volvo B10M-61	Van Hool Alizée	C49FT	1986	Ex Long's Coaches, Salsburgh, 1994
	1528RU	Mercedes-Benz 308D	PMT	M14	1989	Ex Mills, Baltasound, 1996
	RJI6395	Volvo B10M-61	Van Hool Alizée	C49FT	1989	Ex Park's, Hamilton, 1995
	RJI8711	Volvo B10M-60	Van Hool Alizée	C51FT	1990	Ex Meney, Saltcoats, 1997
	RJI7949	Volvo B10M-60	Van Hool Alizée	C49FT	1990	Ex Essex Coachways, Bow, 1996
	341AYF	Volvo B9M	Plaxton Paramount 3200	C35F	1990	Ex ?, 1997
	TJI6494	Volvo B9M	Plaxton Paramount 3200	C35F	1990	Ex ?, 1997
	TJI6494	Mercedes-Benz 811D	Dormobile Routemaker	B33F	1994	
	M310KRY	Toyota Coaster HZB50R	Caetano Optimo III	C21F	1995	
	RJI1890	Volvo B10M-62	Jonckheere Deauville	C53F	1996	
	RJI8712	Volvo B10M-62	Jonckheere Deauville	C49FT	1996	
	RJI8713	Volvo B10M-62	Jonckheere Deauville	C49FT	1996	
	P373XGG	Mercedes-Benz 711D	?	B25F	1996	
	P489TGA	Mercedes-Benz 611D	Onyx	C24FL	1996	

Previous Registrations:

1528RU	F296UEE	RJI6395	F765ENE, LSK506, F256MGB
341AYF	?	RJI8711	G164ECS
L906ANS	L855WDS, 341AYF	RJI8712	From new
RJI1890	N936RBC	RJI8713	From new
RJI7976	XRY278	TJI6494	?
RJI6494	C268LGA, WOI669	OHE265X, UCY629, YFJ65X.	
RJI7947	G875RNC	WOI669	

Livery: Blue; white and red (Clyde Coaster) F197ASD.

Jonckheere Deauville coachwork is shown on this Volvo B10M coach from the Clyde Coast fleet. RJI1890 was at rest in Blackpool when photographed complete with Clyde Coast's version of the Scottish red lion. Clyde Coast's bus operations have reduced somewhat in recent years. *Mark Bailey*

CLYDESIDE

Clydeside Buses Ltd, The Gatehouse, Porterfield Road, Renfrew, PA4 8JB

Depots: Pottery Street, Inchgreen, Greenock; Greenock Road, Inchinnan and Cochranemill Road, Johnstone

001	LAZ5847	Renault-Dodge S46	Northern Counties	B22F	1987	Ex North Western (Bee Line), 1996
002	LAZ4475	Renault-Dodge S46	Northern Counties	B22F	1987	Ex North Western (Bee Line), 1996
003	LAZ6739	Renault-Dodge S46	Northern Counties	B22F	1987	Ex North Western (Bee Line), 1996
136	N136YMS	Scania K113CRB	Van Hool Alizée	C53F	1996	
137	N137YMS	Scania K113CRB	Van Hool Alizée	C53F	1996	
138	N138YMS	Scania K113CRB	Van Hool Alizée	C53F	1996	
139	N139YMS	Scania K113CRB	Van Hool Alizée	C53F	1996	
140	MIL9320	Leyland Tiger TRCTL11/3R	Van Hool Alizée	C50FT	1984	Ex Pullman, Crofty, 1996

170-180 Leyland Tiger TRCLXC/2RH — Plaxton Paramount 3200 E — C49FT — 1984 — Ex Western Scottish, 1991

170	4225FM	**173**	407CLT	**176**	A879ASJ	**179**	54CLT	**180**	A848ASJ
172	WLT924	**175**	WLT956	**177**	WLT974				

201-208 Optare MetroRider — Optare — B29F — 1996

201	N201NHS	**203**	N203NHS	**205**	N201NHS	**207**	N207NHS	**208**	N208NHS
202	N202NHS	**204**	N204NHS	**206**	N201NHS				

211	D468PON	MCW MetroRider MF150/14	MCW	B23F	1987	Ex Darlington, 1995

212-216 MCW MetroRider MF150/38 — MCW — B25F — 1987 — Ex Darlington, 1995

212	E125KYW	**213**	E126KYW	**214**	E133KYW	**215**	E135KYW	**216**	E151KYW

217-227 Optare MetroRider — Optare — B29F — 1996

217	P217SGB	**219**	P219SGB	**221**	P221SGB	**224**	P224SGB	**226**	P226SGB
218	P218SGB	**220**	P220SGB	**223**	P223SGB	**225**	P225SGB	**227**	P227SGB

231	D168VRP	Mercedes-Benz L608D	Alexander AM	B20F	1986	Ex Crosville Cymru, 1996

232-236 Mercedes-Benz L608D — Reeve Burgess — DP19F — 1986 — Ex Midland, 1995

232	D202SKD	**233**	D203SKD	**234**	D204SKD	**235**	D205SKD	**236**	D206SKD

Cowie's Clydeside operation is now part of the Northern and Scottish Division. Many of the coaches in the fleet have gained index marks formerly on London Routemasters. Here we see 183, 407CLT, a Plaxton Paramount-bodied Leyland Tiger. *Phillip Stephenson*

As with several of the former British Bus operations, Clydeside took delivery of East Lancashire-bodied Scania buses. Shown here is 512, M112RMS one of five of the then new European design delivered in 1995. *Phillip Stephenson*

237	C707JMB	Mercedes-Benz L608D	Reeve Burgess	B20F	1986	Ex Midland, 1995
238	C708JMB	Mercedes-Benz L608D	Reeve Burgess	B20F	1986	Ex Midland, 1995
247	F760VNH	Mercedes-Benz 609D	Wadham Stringer Wessex	C21F	1989	Ex Cowan and Hamilton, Johnstone, 1995
248	H901GNC	Mercedes-Benz 609D	Made-to-Measure	C24F	1991	Ex Inverclyde, Port Glasgow, 1993
249	H902GNC	Mercedes-Benz 609D	Made-to-Measure	C24F	1991	Ex Inverclyde, Port Glasgow, 1993
250	J218HDS	Mercedes-Benz 709D	Carlyle	B29F	1992	Ex Inverclyde, Port Glasgow, 1993
251	L51LSG	Mercedes-Benz 709D	Plaxton Beaver	B25F	1993	
252	L52LSG	Mercedes-Benz 709D	Plaxton Beaver	B25F	1993	
253	L53LSG	Mercedes-Benz 709D	Plaxton Beaver	B25F	1993	
254	L54LSG	Mercedes-Benz 709D	Plaxton Beaver	B25F	1993	

255-265			Mercedes-Benz 711D		Plaxton Beaver		B25F		1994
255	L860LFS	258	L863LFS	260	L865LFS	262	L867LFS	264	L869LFS
256	L861LFS	259	L864LFS	261	L866LFS	263	L868LFS	265	L870LFS
257	L862LFS								

301	D261NCS	Renault-Dodge S56	Alexander AM	B25F	1987	Ex Western Scottish, 1991
318	D318SDS	Renault-Dodge S56	Alexander AM	B25F	1987	Ex Western Scottish, 1991
319	D319SDS	Renault-Dodge S56	Alexander AM	B25F	1987	Ex Western Scottish, 1991

Opposite, top: **The Optare MetroRider is still ordered my several of the former British Bus operations with Clydeside adding a further eighteen during 1996. Shown here is 220, P220SGB on service 80 to Glasgow Airport.** *Mark Bailey*
Opposite, bottom: Three body types can be found on the Scania saloons in the Clydeside fleet. Pictured while heading for Erskine is former Scania demonstrator 501, L588JSG. This vehicle carries the Northern Counties Paladin model shortly to be replaced at the Wigan assembly plant by the new Plaxton low-floor saloon. *Billy Nicol*

The Scottish Bus Handbook

Recent arrivals to the Clydeside fleet have been further examples of the Eastern Coach Works-designed double-deck coach built for National Bus Company. Captured in Paisley is 894, C454GKE once used on commuter services into London is may now be found undertaking similar work in Glasgow. *Murdoch Currie*

323-355

	Renault-Dodge S56		Alexander AM		B25F*	1987	Ex Western Scottish, 1991
							*354 is DP25F

323	E323WYS	329	E329WYS	336	E336WYS	343	E343WYS	350	E350WYS
324	E324WYS	330	E330WYS	337	E337WYS	344	E344WYS	351	E351WYS
325	E325WYS	331	E331WYS	338	E338WYS	345	E345WYS	353	E353WYS
326	E326WYS	332	E332WYS	339	E339WYS	348	E348WYS	354	E354WYS
327	E327WYS	334	E334WYS	342	E342WYS	349	E349WYS	355	E355WYS
328	E328WYS	335	E335WYS						

356	E810JSX	Renault-Dodge S56	Alexander AM	B25F	1987	Ex Fife Scottish, 1992
359	E813JSX	Renault-Dodge S56	Alexander AM	B25F	1987	Ex Fife Scottish, 1992

360-369

	Renault-Dodge S56		Reeve Burgess Beaver		B23F	1990	Ex Rider (York), 1992

360	G58RGG	362	G192NWY	364	G194NWY	366	G196NWY	369	G199NWY
361	G421MWY	363	G193NWY	365	G195NWY	367	G197NWY		

377	E101JPL	Renault-Dodge S56	Northen Counties	B25F	1988	Ex Londonlinks, 1995
378	E102JPL	Renault-Dodge S56	Northen Counties	B25F	1988	Ex Londonlinks, 1995
379	E103JPL	Renault-Dodge S56	Northen Counties	B25F	1988	Ex Londonlinks, 1995
380	E108JPL	Renault-Dodge S56	Northen Counties	B25F	1988	Ex Londonlinks, 1995
394	E494HHN	Renault-Dodge S56	Alexander AM	B25F	1987	Ex Yorkshire (Selby & District), 1995
397	E507HHN	Renault-Dodge S56	Alexander AM	B25F	1987	Ex Yorkshire (Selby & District), 1995
398	E508HHN	Renault-Dodge S56	Alexander AM	B25F	1987	Ex Yorkshire (Selby & District), 1995
401	M65FDS	Dennis Dart 9.8SDL3054	Plaxton Pointer	B40F	1995	
402	M67FDS	Dennis Dart 9.8SDL3054	Plaxton Pointer	B40F	1995	

The Scottish Bus Handbook

441-447

441-447		Volvo B6-9.9M		Alexander Dash		B40F	1994	

441	M841DDS	**443**	M843DDS	**445**	M845DDS	**446**	M846DDS	**447**	M847DDS
442	M842DDS	**444**	M844DDS						

No.	Reg	Chassis	Body	Type	Year	Notes
501	L588JSG	Scania L113CRL	Northern Counties Paladin	B51F	1994	Ex Scania demonstrator, 1995
502	M102RMS	Scania L113CRL	Northern Counties Paladin	B51F	1995	
503	M103RMS	Scania L113CRL	Northern Counties Paladin	B51F	1995	
504	M104RMS	Scania L113CRL	Alexander Strider	B51F	1995	
505	M105RMS	Scania L113CRL	Alexander Strider	B51F	1995	
506	M106RMS	Scania L113CRL	Alexander Strider	B51F	1995	
507	M107RMS	Scania L113CRL	Alexander Strider	B51F	1995	

508-513

508-513		Scania N113CRL		East Lancashire European		B45F*	1995	*509 is B51F

508	M108RMS	**509**	M109RMS	**510**	M110RMS	**512**	M112RMS	**513**	M113RMS

514-521

514-521		Scania L113CRL		East Lancashire European		B51F	1995	

514	M114RMS	**516**	M116RMS	**518**	M118RMS	**520**	M120RMS	**521**	M121RMS
515	M115RMS	**517**	M117RMS	**519**	M119RMS					

525	L25LSX	Scania N113CRL	East Lancashire European	B51F	1993	Ex Scania demonstrator, 1995

635-684

635-684		Leyland Leopard PSU3D/4R		Alexander AY		B53F	1977-78 Ex Western Scottish, 1991

635	TSJ35S	**639**	TSJ39S	**644**	TSJ44S	**652**	TSJ52S	**659**	TSJ59S
636	TSJ36S	**641**	TSJ41S	**647**	TSJ47S	**653**	TSJ53S	**660**	TSJ60S
637	TSJ37S	**642**	TSJ42S	**650**	TSJ50S	**654**	TSJ54S	**663**	TSJ63S
638	TSJ38S	**643**	TSJ43S	**651**	TSJ51S	**656**	TSJ56S	**684**	TSJ84S

691-727

691-727		Leyland Leopard PSU3E/4R		Alexander AY		B53F	1979 Ex Western Scottish, 1991

691	BSJ891T	**699**	BSJ899T	**705**	BSJ905T	**714**	BSJ914T	**722**	BSJ922T
693	BSJ893T	**700**	BSJ900T	**706**	BSJ906T	**716**	BSJ916T	**723**	BSJ923T
694	BSJ894T	**701**	BSJ901T	**707**	BSJ907T	**718**	BSJ918T	**725**	BSJ925T
695	BSJ890T	**702**	BSJ902T	**708**	BSJ908T	**719**	BSJ919T	**726**	BSJ926T
697	BSJ897T	**703**	BSJ903T	**712**	BSJ912T	**720**	BSJ920T	**727**	BSJ927T
698	BSJ898T	**704**	BSJ904T	**713**	BSJ913T	**721**	BSJ921T		

730-768

730-768		Leyland Leopard PSU3E/4R		Alexander AY		B53F	1980 Ex Western Scottish, 1991

730	WDS210V	**734**	GCS34V	**750**	GCS50V	**759**	GCS59V	**767**	GCS67V
731	GCS31V	**735**	GCS35V	**755**	GCS55V	**764**	GCS64V	**768**	GCS68V
732	GCS32V	**742**	GCS42V	**756**	GCS56V	**766**	GCS66V		

769	TSU642W	Leyland Leopard PSU3G/4R	Alexander AYS	B53F	1981	Ex East Midland, 1993
777	WCW312R	Leyland Leopard PSU3D/2R	Alexander AYS	B53F	1977	Ex Lancaster, 1993
779	WCW314R	Leyland Leopard PSU3D/2R	Alexander AYS	B53F	1977	Ex Lancaster, 1993
787	TSJ87S	Leyland Leopard PSU3D/4R	Alexander AY	B53F	1977	Ex Maidstone & District, 1996

788-798

788-798		Leyland Leopard PSU3E/4R		Alexander AY		B53F	1978 Ex Western Scottish, 1991

788	YCS88T	**791**	YCS91T	**796**	YCS96T	**797**	YCS97T	**798**	YCS98T
790	YCS90T	**794**	YCS94T						

801-805

801-805		Dennis Dart SLF		Plaxton Pointer		B37F	1996	

801	P801RWU	**802**	P802RWU	**803**	P803RWU	**804**	P804RWU	**805**	P805RWU

806-810

806-810		Dennis Dart SLF		Alexander ALX200		B40F	1997	

806	P806DBS	**807**	P807DBS	**808**	P808DBS	**809**	P809DBS	**810**	P810DBS

843	GTO303V	Leyland Fleetline FE30AGR	Northern Counties	H43/30F	1980	Ex Blue Bus (Derby), 1995
846	WDS212V	Leyland Fleetline FE30AGR	Northern Counties	H43/29F	1980	Ex Blue Bus (Derby), 1995
850	XRR50S	Leyland Fleetline FE30AGR	Northern Counties	H43/29F	1978	Ex City Rider (Derby), 1996
854	LMS154W	Leyland Fleetline FE30AGR	Alexander AD	H44/31F	1980	Ex Western Scottish, 1991
858	WDS216V	Leyland Fleetline FE30AGR	Northern Counties	H43/30F	1980	Ex City Rider (Derby), 1996
883	HDS83V	Leyland Fleetline FE30AGR	Alexander AD	H44/31F	1980	Ex Western Scottish, 1991
890	C450BKM	Leyland Olympian ONTL11/2R	Eastern Coach Works	CH45/28F	1985	Ex Northumbria, 1996
891	C451BKM	Leyland Olympian ONTL11/2R	Eastern Coach Works	CH45/28F	1985	Ex Northumbria, 1996
892	C452GKE	Leyland Olympian ONTL11/2RHSp	Eastern Coach Works	CH45/28F	1986	Ex Yorkshire (Selby & District), 1996
893	C214UPD	Leyland Olympian ONTL11/2RSp	Eastern Coach Works	CH45/28F	1985	Ex Northumbria, 1996
894	C454GKE	Leyland Olympian ONTL11/2RHSp	Eastern Coach Works	CH45/28F	1986	Ex Northumbria, 1996
895	YSU865	Leyland Olympian ONTL11/2R	Eastern Coach Works	CH45/28F	1983	Ex Maidstone & District, 1996
896	C453GKE	Leyland Olympian ONTL11/2RHSp	Eastern Coach Works	CH45/28F	1986	Ex Yorkshire (Selby & District), 1996
897	HSB874Y	Leyland Olympian ONTL11/2R	Eastern Coach Works (1985)	CH45/28F	1983	Ex Maidstone & District, 1996
898	GKE442Y	Leyland Olympian ONTL11/2R	Eastern Coach Works	CH45/28F	1983	Ex Maidstone & District, 1996
899	C449BKM	Leyland Olympian ONTL11/2R	Eastern Coach Works	CH45/28F	1985	Ex Northumbria, 1996
900	TPD106X	Leyland Olympian ONTL11/1R	Roe	H43/29F	1982	Ex Londonlinks, 1997
901	TPD130X	Leyland Olympian ONTL11/1R	Roe	H43/29F	1982	Ex Londonlinks, 1997
902	A147FPG	Leyland Olympian ONTL11/1R	Roe	H43/29F	1984	Ex Londonlinks, 1997
903	TPD116X	Leyland Olympian ONTL11/1R	Roe	H43/29F	1982	Ex Londonlinks, 1997
905	WSU475	Leyland Olympian ONTL11/2R	Eastern Coach Works	CH45/26F	1985	Ex Maidstone & District, 1996
906	YSU866	Leyland Olympian ONTL11/2R	Eastern Coach Works	CH45/28F	1983	Ex Maidstone & District, 1996
907	WSU476	Leyland Olympian ONTL11/2R	Eastern Coach Works	CH45/26F	1985	Ex Maidstone & District, 1996
921	CUL88V	Leyland Titan TNLXB2RR	Park Royal	H44/31F	1979	Ex Londonlinks, 1997
922	KYV372X	Leyland Titan TNLXB2RR	Leyland	H44/26F	1981	Ex Londonlinks, 1996
923	CUL143V	Leyland Titan TNLXB2RR	Park Royal	H44/26F	1980	Ex Londonlinks, 1996
924	CUL94V	Leyland Titan TNLXB2RR	Park Royal	H44/26F	1980	Ex Londonlinks, 1996
925	KYN285X	Leyland Titan TNLXB2RR	Leyland	H44/26F	1981	Ex Londonlinks, 1996
926	WYV60T	Leyland Titan TNLXB2RR	Park Royal	H44/26F	1979	Ex Londonlinks, 1996
927	CUL152V	Leyland Titan TNLXB2RR	Park Royal	H44/26F	1980	Ex Londonlinks, 1996
928	KYV408X	Leyland Titan TNLXB2RR	Leyland	H44/26F	1982	Ex Londonlinks, 1996
929	CUL139V	Leyland Titan TNLXB2RR	Park Royal	H44/26F	1980	Ex Londonlinks, 1996

Previous Registrations:

54CLT	A179UGB	WDS210V	GCS30V
407CLT	A173UGB	WDS212V	GTO46V
4225FM	A170UGB	WDS216V	GTO308V
A848ASJ	A180UGB, VLT234	WSU475	B446WKE
A879ASJ	A175UGB, VCS376, A806WSU, 32CLT	WSU476	B447WKE
G58RGG	G673NUA	WLT924	A176UGB
HSB874Y	GKE445Y, YSU867	WLT956	A177UGB
LAZ4475	D424NNA	WLT974	A186UGB
LAZ5847	D418NNA	YSU865	GKE443Y
LAZ6739	D428NNA	YSU866	GKE444Y
L588JSG	94D28205		
MIL9320	A383ROU, JEP417, KIB1767, A661AHB		

Livery: White, red and yellow; yellow and blue (Scottish Citylink) 136-40; white and red (Clyde Coaster) 804/5

Many of the Alexander Y-type buses that typify the former Scottish Bus Group fleets are still to be found in service, though many now carry new liveries. Seen in the yellow, white and red Clydeside livery is 727, BSJ927T.
Phillip Stephenson

H CRAWFORD

H Crawford Coaches Ltd, Shilford Mill, Neilston, Glasgow, G78 3BA

KBV139S	Leyland Leopard PSU3E/4R	Duple Dominant	C53F	1978	Ex A&S McLaughlin, Penwortham, 1994
LIW1926	Leyland Leopard PSU5C/4R	Duple Dominant II	C57F	1978	Ex Crowcroft, Monk Bretton, 1995
GPC777V	Leyland Leopard PSU3F/5R	Plaxton Supreme IV	C53F	1980	Ex Dorking Coaches, 1993
F254OFP	Volvo B10M-50	Alexander RV	DPH47/35F	1989	
J956LKO	Ford Transit VE6	Crystals	M12	1991	
K614OJR	Leyland-DAF 400	Crystals	M16	1992	
L266VUS	Scania K113CRB	Van Hool Alizée	C57F	1994	
L897RUF	Leyland-DAF 400	Crystals	M16	1994	
L906LFS	Mercedes-Benz 609D	Onyx	C24F	1994	
M68UWB	Leyland-DAF 400	Crystals	M16	1994	
M69UWB	Leyland-DAF 400	Crystals	M16	1994	
M268POS	Volvo B10M-62	Van Hool Alizée	C53FT	1994	
M269POS	Volvo B10M-62	Van Hool Alizée	C57F	1994	
M270POS	Volvo B10M-62	Van Hool Alizée	C53FT	1995	
M271POS	Volvo B10M-62	Van Hool Alizée	C53FT	1995	
M272POS	Volvo B10M-62	Jonckheere Deauville	C51FT	1995	
M274TSB	Volvo B10M-62	Van Hool Alizée	C53FT	1995	
M275TSB	Volvo B10M-62	Van Hool Alizée	C53FT	1995	
M133FGD	Volvo B9M	Van Hool Alizée	C36FT	1995	
N134HSD	Volvo B9M	Van Hool Alizée	C36FT	1996	
N276HSD	Volvo B10M-62	Van Hool Alizée	C53FT	1996	
N277HSD	Volvo B10M-62	Van Hool Alizée	C57F	1996	
P278VUS	Volvo B10M-62	Van Hool Alizée	C53FT	1997	
P279VUS	Volvo B10M-62	Van Hool Alizée	C53FT	1997	
P281VUS	Volvo B10M-62	Plaxton Première 350	C57F	1997	

Previous Registrations:

KBV139S	WRO431S, 799CVJ	LIW1926	XWX194S

Livery: White, red and maroon; yellow and blue (Scottish Citylink) M268POS, M275TSB.

Recent deliveries to H Crawford coaches are dominated by the Volvo B10M-61 with Van Hool Alizée bodywork. Pictured on a trip to Blackpool, M269POS is one of the 1994 delivery. The Alizée body styling has remained mostly unchanged for almost a decade yet still looks modern and fresh.
Paul Wigan

DART

Dart Buses Ltd, MacDowall Street, Paisley, Renfrewshire, PA..

402	C402VVN	Mercedes-Benz L608D	Reeve Burgess	B20F	1986	Ex United, 1996
421	C421VVN	Mercedes-Benz L608D	Reeve Burgess	B20F	1986	Ex Stott, Milnsbridge, 1996
422	C422VVN	Mercedes-Benz L608D	Reeve Burgess	B20F	1986	Ex United (Tees & District), 1996
427	C427VVN	Mercedes-Benz L608D	Reeve Burgess	B20F	1986	Ex Stott, Milnsbridge, 1996
430	C430VVN	Mercedes-Benz L608D	Reeve Burgess	B20F	1986	Ex Stott, Milnsbridge, 1996
434	C434VVN	Mercedes-Benz L608D	Reeve Burgess	B20F	1986	Ex Stott, Milnsbridge, 1996
442	C342VVN	Mercedes-Benz L608D	Reeve Burgess	B20F	1986	Ex Stott, Milnsbridge, 1996
449	C249OFE	Mercedes-Benz L608D	Reeve Burgess	B20F	1986	Ex RoadCar, 1996

501-513
| | | Mercedes-Benz L608D | Reeve Burgess | DP19F | 1986 | Ex Stagecoach Ribble, 1996 |

| 501 | D501RCK | **505** | D505RCK | **508** | D508RCK | **512** | D512RCK | **513** | D513RCK |
| 502 | D502RCK | | | | | | | | |

516	D516RCK	Mercedes-Benz L608D	Reeve Burgess	DP19F	1986	Ex McLaughlin, Penwortham, 1996
522	D502NWG	Mercedes-Benz L608D	Alexander AM	B20F	1986	Ex RoadCar, 1996
524	D524RCK	Mercedes-Benz L608D	Reeve Burgess	B20F	1986	Ex Mercury, Hoo, 1996
527	D507NWG	Mercedes-Benz L608D	Alexander AM	B20F	1986	Ex RoadCar, 1996
528	D508NWG	Mercedes-Benz L608D	Alexander AM	B20F	1986	Ex RoadCar, 1996
532	D212SKD	Mercedes-Benz L608D	Alexander AM	B20F	1986	Ex North Western, 1996
534	D214SKD	Mercedes-Benz L608D	Alexander AM	B20F	1986	Ex North Western, 1996

541-562
| | | Mercedes-Benz L608D | Reeve Burgess | B20F | 1986 | Ex Stagecoach Ribble, 1996 |

541	D541RCK	**546**	D546RCK	**551**	D551RCK	**553**	D553RCK	**555**	D555RCK
542	D542RCK	**548**	D548RCK	**552**	D552RCK	**554**	D554RCK	**562**	D562RCK
545	D545RCK								

Dart Buses has expanded the operations around Paisley and have recently expanded capacity with the introduction of Leyland National buses. Photographed at Buchanan bus station while working the X5 service to Linwood in April 1997 was RJI5343. *Malc McDonald*

Shown heading for Foxbar is 541, D541RCK a Mercedes-Benz L608D with Reeve Burgess bodywork originally new to Ribble now in the all-blue livery of Dart buses. Similar conversions by Alexander are also operated giving an interesting comparison of the two conversion models. *Murdoch Currie*

563	D563RCK	Mercedes-Benz L608D	Reeve Burgess	B20F	1986	Ex Sherratt, Cold Meece, 1996
564	D564RCK	Mercedes-Benz L608D	Reeve Burgess	B20F	1986	Ex Stagecoach Ribble, 1996
576	D226URG	Mercedes-Benz L608D	Alexander AM	DP19F	1986	Ex Go-Ahead, 1996
578	D228URG	Mercedes-Benz L608D	Alexander AM	DP19F	1986	Ex Go-Ahead, 1996
581	D231URG	Mercedes-Benz L608D	Alexander AM	DP19F	1986	Ex Go-Ahead, 1996
C1	VJI6961	Leyland Tiger TRCTL11/2R	Plaxton Supreme V Express	C53F	1982	Ex Go-Ahead (OK), 1997
C2	VJI6962	Leyland Tiger TRCTL11/2R	Plaxton Supreme V Express	C53F	1982	Ex Go-Ahead (OK), 1997
C3	VJI6963	Leyland Tiger TRCTL11/2R	Plaxton Supreme V Express	C53F	1982	Ex Go-Ahead (OK), 1997
M51	P151LSC	Mercedes-Benz 709D	Alexander Sprint	B29F	1996	
M52	P152LSC	Mercedes-Benz 709D	Alexander Sprint	B29F	1996	
N11	NIL5363	Leyland National 11351A/1R		B49F	1975	Ex Reading Buses, 1997
N12	NIL5364	Leyland National 11351A/1R		B49F	1978	Ex East Midland, 1997
N14	NIL5365	Leyland National 11351A/1R		B49F	1979	Ex East Midland, 1997
N15	NIL5366	Leyland National 11351A/1R		B49F	1978	Ex East Midland, 1997
N16	NIL5367	Leyland National 11351A/1R		B49F	1976	Ex Ebdons, Sidcup, 1997
N17	NIL5368	Leyland National 11351A/1R		B49F	1977	Ex East Midland, 1997
N18	NIL5369	Leyland National 11351A/1R		B49F	1977	Ex Eddie Brown, Helperby, 1997
N19	NIL5370	Leyland National 11351/1R		B49F	1975	Ex East Midland, 1997
N21	RJI5351	Leyland National 10351A/2R(Volvo)		DP42F	1977	Ex United, 1997
N22	NIL5371	Leyland National 10351A/1R		B41F	1977	Ex Eddie Brown, Helperby, 1997
N23	NIL5372	Leyland National 10351A/2R		B41F	1980	Ex East Midland, 1997
N24	NIL5373	Leyland National 10351A/2R		B36D	1977	Ex East Midland, 1997
N25	NIL5374	Leyland National 10351A/2R		B38D	1979	Ex East Midland, 1997
R91	E621BVK	Renault-Dodge S56	Alexander AM	B25F	1987	Ex Busways, 1996
R92	E622BVK	Renault-Dodge S56	Alexander AM	B25F	1987	Ex Busways, 1996
R93	E629BVK	Renault-Dodge S56	Alexander AM	B25F	1987	Ex Busways, 1996

Previous Registrations:

NIL5363	NRD145N	NIL5369	WGY597S	NIL5373	AYR322T
NIL5364	YKU77S	NIL5370	GOL398N	RJI5343	OJD871R
NIL5365	ABA25T	NIL5371	LDW362P	VJI6961	ONL953X
NIL5366	VKU79S	NIL5372	JAO477V	VJI6962	LFT3X
NIL5367	LPF602P	NIL5373	THX179S	VJI6963	LFT4X
NIL5368	RBU180R				

Livery: Blue and white

DAVIDSON BUSES

Davidson Buses Ltd, 14 Blackburn Road, Bathgate.

L703AGA	Mercedes-Benz 709D	WS Wessex II	B29F	1994	
M877DDS	Mercedes-Benz 811D	WS Wessex II	B33F	1994	
M277TSF	Omni	Omni	B F	1994	
M576TSG	Omni	Omni	B F	1994	
M415GUS	Mercedes-Benz 711D	WS Wessex II	B29F	1995	
N583WND	Mercedes-Benz 709D	Alexander Sprint	B27F	1995	Ex AA Buses, Ayr, 1996
N584WND	Mercedes-Benz 709D	Alexander Sprint	B27F	1995	Ex AA Buses, Ayr, 1996

Livery: Cream and green

L703AGA is one of five Mercedes-Benz minibuses operating for Davidson Buses of Bathgate. This vehicle carries WS Wessex bodywork, WS being the name of the coachbuilder to use the premises between Wadham Stringer and UVG, the current supplier. Davidson Buses' latest arrivals have come from the Ayrshire operation of AA Buses. *Phillip Stephenson*

DOCHERTY of IRVINE

H Tait, 40 Bank Street, Irvine, North Ayrshire, KA12 0LP

u	NTF9	Leyland Titan PD2/15	Leyland	H30/26R	1951	Ex Docherty, Irvine, 1995
u	BHN601B	Leyland Titan PD3/2	Alexander	H41/31F	1962	Ex A1 Service (Docherty), 1995
	PAG318H	Leyland Leopard PSU3A/4R	Plaxton Elite	C51F	1970	Ex Docherty, Irvine, 1995
	WAG513K	Leyland Leopard PSU3B/4R	Plaxton Elite II	C51F	1972	Ex Docherty, Irvine, 1995
	SCS384M	Volvo B58-56	Duple Dominant	C51F	1974	Ex Docherty, Irvine, 1995
	HCS260N	Volvo B58-56	Duple Dominant	C49F	1975	Ex Docherty, Irvine, 1995
w	NCS26P	Leyland Leopard PSU3C/4R	Duple Dominant	B51F	1976	Ex Docherty, Irvine, 1995
	NSP332R	Ailsa B55-10	Alexander AV	H44/31D	1976	Ex Docherty, Irvine, 1995
	5909D	Volvo B58-61	Plaxton Supreme III	C46FT	1978	Ex Docherty, Irvine, 1995
	ARC670T	Leyland Atlantean AN68A/1R	Northern Counties	H47/31D	1978	Ex City of Nottingham, 1996
	6491ED	Volvo B58-61	Duple Dominant II Express	C51F	1979	Ex Docherty, Irvine, 1995
	WTS269T	Ailsa B55-10	Alexander AV	H44/31D	1979	Ex Tayside, 1996
	WTS274T	Ailsa B55-10	Alexander AV	H44/31D	1979	Ex Tayside, 1996
	WTS277T	Ailsa B55-10	Alexander AV	H44/31D	1979	Ex Tayside, 1996
	AYR332T	Leyland National 10351A/2R (Volvo)		B36F	1979	Ex Docherty, Irvine, 1995
w	BUH205V	Leyland National 10351A/1R		B44F	1980	Ex Docherty, Irvine, 1995
	4151D	Volvo B58-61	Plaxton Viewmaster IV	C49FT	1981	Ex Docherty, Irvine, 1995
	RRA221X	Leyland National 2 NL116AL11/1R		B52F	1981	Ex City of Nottingham, 1996
	VST915	Volvo B10M-61	Van Hool Alizée	C49FT	1984	Ex Docherty, Irvine, 1995
	TSD285	Volvo Citybus B10M-50	Alexander RV	H47/31F	1985	Ex Docherty, Irvine, 1995
	2625ED	Volvo B9M	Caetano Algarve II	C41FT	1986	Ex Docherty, Irvine, 1995
	8614ED	Volvo B10M-61	Van Hool Alizée	C50FT	1987	Ex Docherty, Irvine, 1995
	E814JSX	Renault-Dodge S56	Alexander AM	DP25F	1987	Ex Docherty, Irvine, 1995
	WIA20	Volvo B9M	Caetano Algarve	C41FT	1988	Ex Docherty, Irvine, 1995
	H503KSJ	Mercedes-Benz 609D	Reeve Burgess	C23F	1991	Ex Docherty, Irvine, 1995
	EDO837	Volvo B10M-60	Van Hool Alizée	C49FT	1991	Ex Docherty, Irvine, 1995
	M711RVN	Mercedes-Benz 711D	Autobus Classique II	C24F	1995	Ex Mason, Bo'ness, 1995
	N814WSB	Mercedes-Benz 814D	Autobus Nouvelle	C27FT	1996	
	P878MSD	Mercedes-Benz 814D	Autobus Nouvelle	C24FT	1997	
		Bova FHD12.330	Bova Futura	C49FT	1997	

Previous Registrations:

2625ED	C645KDS	8614ED	D613MVR	TSD285	From new
4151D	MSD724W	BHN601B	TSD285	VST915	A849TDS
5909D	UCS897S	EDO837	H722YYS	WIA20	E979KJF
6491ED	CCS243T				

Livery: Cream

Docherty of Irvine operate a pair of Volvo B10Ms with Van Hool Alizée coachwork of which 8614ED is shown on a summer excursion to Blackpool. Two front-engined Leyland Titans remain in the fleet though these are currently out of use.
Paul Wigan

DOCHERTY'S MIDLAND COACHES

J & E Docherty, Priory Park, Auchterarder, Perthshire, PH3 1AE

B268KPF	Leyland Tiger TRCTL11/2RH	Plaxton Paramount 3200 E	C53F	1985	Ex Luton & District, 1992
913EWC	Volvo B10M-61	Plaxton Paramount 3200 III	C53F	1987	Ex Shearings, 1992
JD3164	Volvo B10M-61	Plaxton Paramount 3200 III	C53F	1987	Ex USSR Trade Delegation, 1992
TDR725	Volvo B10M-61	Van Hool Alizée	C53F	1988	Ex Park's, Hamilton, 1994
4488WD	Volvo B10M-61	Van Hool Alizée	C53F	1988	Ex Park's, Hamilton, 1994
2178ND	Volvo B10M-60	Plaxton Paramount 3500 III	C49FT	1989	Ex Park's, Hamilton, 1990
GSU378	Dennis Javelin 8.5SDL1903	Plaxton Paramount 3200 III	C35F	1989	
7119WD	Volvo B10M-60	Jonckheere Deauville P599	C53F	1993	Ex Park's, Hamilton, 1994
L6DMC	Mercedes-Benz 711D	Plaxton Beaver	C25F	1993	
8733CD	Volvo B10M-60	Jonckheere Deauville	C49FT	1994	
7067ED	Volvo B10M-62	Jonckheere Deauville	C49FT	1995	
N77JDS	Volvo B10M-62	Van Hool Alizée	C49FT	1996	
N167DSP	Mercedes-Benz 711D	Plaxton Beaver	C25F	1996	
P70JDS	Toyota Coaster HZB50R	Caetano Optimo III	C21F	1997	
P77JDS	Volvo B10M-62	Van Hool Alizée	C53F	1997	
P467JSP	LDV Convoy	LDV	M16	1997	

Previous Registrations:

2178ND	F989HGE	7119WD	K917RGE	GSU378	F407OSR		
4488WD	E638UNE, LSK831, E434CGA	8733CD	L117SSL	JD3164	248D334, E607KSP		
7067ED	M407XSL	913EWC	D573MVR	TDR725	E645UNE, LSK875		

Livery: White, black and grey

Docherty Midland Coaches operate a fleet liveried in white with black and grey relief. One of three Belgian-built Jonckheere Deauvilles is 8733CD parked here outside the depot in Auchterarder. In Britain, the Jonckheere products are imported by the Volvo dealer Yeates of Loughborough.
Bill Potter

FIFE SCOTTISH

Fife Scottish Omnibuses Ltd, Esplanade, Kirkcaldy, Fife, KY1 1SP

Depots : Methilhaven Road, Methil (Aberhill); Broad Street, Cowdenbeath; St Leonard's Street, Dunfermline; Flemington Road, Glenrothes; Esplanade, Kirkcaldy and City Road, St Andrews.

1-5			Mercedes-Benz 811D		Carlyle		B31F	1989-90 Ex Selkent, 1996		
1	F286KGK	2	H882LOX	3	H883LOX	4	H509AGC	5	H885LOX	

70-76			Mercedes-Benz 709D		Alexander Sprint		B25F	1994		
70	M770TFS	72	M772TFS	74	M774TFS	75	M775TFS	76	M776TFS	
71	M771TFS	73	M773TFS							

77	VLT77	Mercedes-Benz 811D	Reeve Burgess Beaver	B33F	1989	Ex Selkent, 1994
78	M778TFS	Mercedes-Benz 709D	Alexander Sprint	B25F	1994	
79	M779TFS	Mercedes-Benz 709D	Alexander Sprint	B25F	1994	
80	G280TSL	Mercedes-Benz 709D	Alexander Sprint	B23F	1990	Ex Bluebird, 1992
81	G281TSL	Mercedes-Benz 709D	Alexander Sprint	B23F	1990	Ex Bluebird, 1992
82	M780TFS	Mercedes-Benz 709D	Alexander Sprint	B25F	1994	

85-94			Mercedes-Benz 709D		Alexander Sprint		B25F	1993		
85	K485FFS	87	K487FFS	89	K489FFS	91	K491FFS	93	K493FFS	
86	K486FFS	88	K488FFS	90	K490FFS	92	K492FFS	94	K494FFS	

95	N95ALS	Mercedes-Benz 709D	Alexander Sprint	B25F	1996
96	N96ALS	Mercedes-Benz 709D	Alexander Sprint	B25F	1996
97	N97ALS	Mercedes-Benz 709D	Alexander Sprint	B25F	1996

The Jonckheere Mistral was introduced in 1996 displacing the Deauville design which had served the coachbuilder well in gaining exports to the British market. The Mistral design is gaining popularity in the rigid form though, so far, only the two bendi-buses for Stagecoach have been built in right-hand drive format. Pictured in Dunfermline is 561, N561SJF. *Tony Wilson*

Fife Scottish have now achieved an all-Mercedes-Benz minibus fleet following the arrival of five of the longer 811 type from Stagecoach Selkent. Pictured while heading for Methilhill is one of the 1993 delivery, 91, K491FFS. *Phillip Stephenson*

139-160 — Leyland Leopard PSU3F/4R* — Alexander AYS — B53F — 1980-81 *159/60 are PSU3G/4R

139	WFS139W	141	WFS141W	158	CSF158W	159	CSF159W	160	CSF160W
140	WFS140W	150	WFS150W						

180-189 — Leyland Leopard PSU3G/4R — Alexander AYS — B53F — 1982

180	PSX180Y	182	PSX182Y	184	PSX184Y	186	PSX186Y	188	PSX188Y
181	PSX181Y	183	PSX183Y	185	PSX185Y	187	PSX187Y	189	PSX189Y

200	XMS420Y	Leyland Leopard PSU3G/4R	Alexander AYS	DP49F	1982	Ex Ribble, 1992
261	CSF161W	Leyland Leopard PSU3G/4R	Alexander AYS	DP49F	1981	
262	CSF162W	Leyland Leopard PSU3G/4R	Alexander AYS	DP47F	1981	

264-269 — Leyland Leopard PSU3F/4R — Alexander AYS — DP49F — 1981

264	CSF164W	266	CSF166W	267	CSF167W	268	CSF168W	269	CSF169W
265	CSF165W								

270-279 — Leyland Leopard PSU3G/4R — Alexander AT — DP49F — 1982

270	NFS170Y	272	NFS172Y	274	NFS174Y	276	NFS176Y	278	NFS178Y
271	NFS171Y	273	NFS173Y	275	NFS175Y	277	NFS177Y	279	NFS179Y

290	RSC190Y	Leyland Leopard PSU3G/4R	Alexander AT	DP49F	1982
291	RSC191Y	Leyland Leopard PSU3G/4R	Alexander AT	DP49F	1982
292	RSC192Y	Leyland Leopard PSU3G/4R	Alexander AT	DP49F	1982
294	RSC194Y	Leyland Leopard PSU3G/4R	Alexander AT	DP49F	1982

In 1986 Fife took delivery of Alexander P-type bodywork on Leyland Tiger chassis. This rather-angular body soon took on the frontal styling already used by Alexander for its Singapore-assembled orders which then became known as the PS-type. Recently repainted, 422, D522DSX is seen in Dundee while operating to its base at St Andrews. *Paul Wigan*

301-310

								Volvo B10M-55		Alexander PS		B49F		1994

301	L301PSC	**303**	L303PSC	**305**	L305PSC	**307**	L307PSC	**309**	L309PSC
302	L302PSC	**304**	L304PSC	**306**	L306PSC	**308**	L308PSC	**310**	L310PSC

314-329

Volvo B10M-55   Alexander PS   B49F*   1995-96 *314/5 are DP48F

314	M314PKS	**318**	N318VMS	**321**	N321VMS	**324**	N324VMS	**327**	N327VMS
315	M315PKS	**319**	N319VMS	**322**	N322VMS	**325**	N325VMS	**328**	N328VMS
316	N316VMS	**320**	N320VMS	**323**	N323VMS	**326**	N326VMS	**329**	N329VMS
317	N317VMS								

412-419

Leyland Tiger TRCTL11/3RH   Alexander P   B61F   1986-87

412	D512CSF	**414**	D614ASG	**416**	D516DSX	**418**	D518DSX	**419**	D519DSX
413	D713CSC	**415**	D615ASG	**417**	D517DSX				

420-424

Leyland Tiger TRBTL11/2RH   Alexander P   B57F   1987

420	D520DSX	**421**	D521DSX	**422**	D522DSX	**423**	D523DSX	**424**	D524DSX

441	GSU341	Leyland Tiger TRCTL11/2RH	Alexander TC	C47F	1985	
442	GSU342	Leyland Tiger TRCTL11/2RH	Alexander TC	DP49F	1985	
444	GSU344	Leyland Tiger TRCTL11/2RH	Alexander TC	C47F	1985	
445	MSU445	Leyland Tiger TRCTL11/2RH	Alexander TC	C47F	1985	

466-470

Leyland Tiger TRBTL11/2R   Alexander TE   DP49F   1983   Ex Kelvin Central, 1989

466	MNS6Y	**467**	MNS7Y	**468**	MNS8Y	**469**	MNS9Y	**470**	MNS10Y

477	D277FAS	Leyland Tiger TRCTL11/3RH	Alexander TE	DP53F	1987	Ex Highland Scottish, 1987
478	D278FAS	Leyland Tiger TRCTL11/3RH	Alexander TE	DP53F	1987	Ex Highland Scottish, 1987
479	D279FAS	Leyland Tiger TRCTL11/3RH	Alexander TE	DP53F	1987	Ex Highland Scottish, 1987
499	MSU499	Leyland Tiger TRCTL11/3RZ	Duple 340	C48FT	1987	Ex Kelvin Central, 1990

The *Stagecoach Express* brand has sought out new markets and has gained a reputation for its quality of service. Pictured in its home town of Kirkcaldy is 568, P568MSX, one of five new rigid Interurban buses delivered during 1996 shortly after pair of Plaxton-bodied articulated examples.
Tony Wilson

503	GSU343	Volvo B10M-61	Van Hool Alizée	C46FT	1983	Ex Ribble (Hyndburn), 1996
504	IIL3504	Volvo B10M-61	Van Hool Alizée	C49FT	1988	Ex Rainworth Travel, 1993
506	IIL3506	Volvo B10M-61	Van Hool Alizée	C49FT	1988	Ex Rainworth Travel, 1993
512	M102CCD	Dennis Javelin 11SDL2133	Plaxton Premiere Interurban	DP47F	1994	Ex Stagecoach South, 1995
513	M103CCD	Dennis Javelin 11SDL2133	Plaxton Premiere Interurban	DP47F	1995	Ex Stagecoach South, 1995
514	M104CCD	Dennis Javelin 11SDL2133	Plaxton Premiere Interurban	DP47F	1995	Ex Stagecoach South, 1995

544-556   Volvo B10M-62   Plaxton Premiére Interurban   DP51F   1994

544	M944TSX	547	M947TSX	550	M950TSX	553	M953TSX	555	M955TSX
545	M945TSX	548	M948TSX	551	M951TSX	554	M954TSX	556	M956TSX
546	M946TSX	549	M949TSX	552	M952TSX				

561	N561SJF	Volvo B10MA-55	Jonckheere Mistral 35	AC72F	1996	
562	N562SJF	Volvo B10MA-55	Jonckheere Mistral 35	AC72F	1996	
563	P563MSX	Volvo B10MA-55	Plaxton Premiére Interurban	AC71F	1996	
564	P564MSX	Volvo B10MA-55	Plaxton Premiére Interurban	AC71F	1996	

565-569   Volvo B10M-62   Plaxton Premiére Interurban   DP51F   1996

565	P565MSX	566	P566MSX	567	P567MSX	568	P568MSX	569	P569MSX

570	P670EWB	Volvo B10MA-55	Plaxton Premiére Interurban	AC71F	1996	Ex East Midland (Grimsby), 1997
571	P671EWB	Volvo B10MA-55	Plaxton Premiére Interurban	AC71F	1997	

Opposite, top: **Twohundred** Volvo B6s were delivered to the Stagecoach group from the 1993 order of which 22 have now settled with the Fife Scottish operation. All carry the Alexander Dash body style as illustrated by 655, L655HKS seen leaving the bus station at Dunfermline.
Phillip Stephenson
Opposite, bottom: **Fifexpress** livery is seen on Plaxton Interurban 513, M103CCD, based on the Dennis Javelin chassis and one of three transferred to Fife from Stagecoach South when almost new.
Tony Wilson

At the start of 1997 the four bendi-buses at Fife were augmented by two of the Volvo B10MA buses destined for East Midland, one before it had entered service there. On a wet Spring day in 1997 570, P670LWB is seen departing Glasgow's Buchanan Street bus station for Kirkcaldy.
Billy Nicol

578-590 — Volvo B10M-60 — Plaxton Premiére Interurban — DP51F — 1993

578	L578HSG	581	L581HSG	584	L584HSG	587	L587HSG	589	L589HSG
579	L579HSG	582	L582HSG	585	L585HSG	588	L588HSG	590	L590HSG
580	L580HSG	583	L583HSG	586	L586HSG				

601-605 — Dennis Dart 9.8SDL3017 — Alexander Dash — B40F — 1992

601	K601ESH	602	K602ESH	603	K603ESH	604	K604ESH	605	K605ESH

606-613 — Dennis Dart SFD412 — Alexander Dash — B40F — 1996

606	P606CMS	608	P608CMS	610	P610CMS	612	P612CMS	613	P613CMS
607	P607CMS	609	P609CMS	611	P611CMS				

623-628 — Volvo B6-9.9M — Alexander Dash — B40F — 1993 Ex Ribble, 1994

623	L423MVV	625	L425MVV	626	L426MVV	627	L427MVV	628	L428MVV
624	L424MVV								

651-659 — Volvo B6-9.9M — Alexander Dash — B40F — 1993-94

651	L651HKS	653	L653HKS	655	L655HKS	657	L657HKS	659	L659HKS
652	L652HKS	654	L654HKS	656	L656HKS	658	L658HKS		

667	L267CCK	Volvo B6-9.9M	Alexander Dash	B40F	1993	Ex Ribble, 1994
668	L268CCK	Volvo B6-9.9M	Alexander Dash	B40F	1993	Ex Ribble, 1994
669	L269CCK	Volvo B6-9.9M	Alexander Dash	B40F	1993	Ex Ribble, 1994
670	M670SSX	Volvo B6-9.9M	Alexander Dash	B40F	1994	
671	M671SSX	Volvo B6-9.9M	Alexander Dash	B40F	1994	
672	M672SSX	Volvo B6-9.9M	Alexander Dash	B40F	1994	
673	M673SSX	Volvo B6-9.9M	Alexander Dash	B40F	1994	

Typifying the 1992 intake of Volvo Olympians is Fife Scottish 720, K720ASC seen here returning home to Dunfermline. *Tony Wilson*

701-725

Leyland Olympian ON2R50G13Z4 Alexander RL H47/32F 1992

701	J801WFS	704	J804WFS	707	J807WFS	720	K720ASC	723	K723ASC
702	J802WFS	705	J805WFS	718	K718ASC	721	K721ASC	724	K724ASC
703	J803WFS	706	J806WFS	719	K719ASC	722	K722ASC	725	K725ASC

737	G337KKW	Leyland Olympian ON2R56G13Z4	Alexander RL	DPH51/31F	1989	Ex East Midland, 1992
738	G338KKW	Leyland Olympian ON2R56G13Z4	Alexander RL	DPH51/31F	1989	Ex East Midland, 1992
758	A858SUL	Leyland Titan TNLXB2RR	Leyland	H44/30D	1983	Ex Selkent, 1997
760	KYV455X	Leyland Titan TNLXB2RR	Leyland	H44/24D	1981	Ex Selkent, 1997
761	RYK820Y	Leyland Titan TNLXB2RR	Leyland	H44/30D	1982	Ex Selkent, 1997
762	OHV801Y	Leyland Titan TNLXB2RR	Leyland	H44/30D	1981	Ex Selkent, 1997
765	A825SUL	Leyland Titan TNLXB2RR	Leyland	H44/30D	1983	Ex Selkent, 1997
766	A66THX	Leyland Titan TNLXB2RR	Leyland	H44/30F	1984	Ex Selkent, 1997
767	A607THV	Leyland Titan TNLXB2RR	Leyland	H44/30D	1984	Ex Selkent, 1997
784	B84WUV	Leyland Titan TNLXB2RR	Leyland	H44/30D	1985	Ex Selkent, 1997
797	B97WUV	Leyland Titan TNLXB2RR	Leyland	H44/30D	1985	Ex Selkent, 1997
816	LSX16P	Ailsa B55-10	Alexander AV	H44/35F	1975	
817	LSX17P	Ailsa B55-10	Alexander AV	H44/35F	1975	
832	LSX32P	Ailsa B55-10	Alexander AV	H44/35F	1975	
834	NSP334R	Ailsa B55-10	Alexander AV	H44/31D	1976	Ex Western Scottish (A1), 1995
836	NSP336R	Ailsa B55-10	Alexander AV	H44/31D	1976	Ex Western Scottish (A1), 1995

847-866

Ailsa B55-10 MkII Alexander AV H44/35F 1979

847	OSC47V	851	OSC51V	855	OSC55V	860	OSC60V	863	OSC63V
848	OSC48V	852	OSC52V	856	OSC56V	861	OSC61V	864	OSC64V
849	OSC49V	853	OSC53V	857	OSC57V	862	OSC62V	866	OSC66V
850	OSC50V	854	OSC54V						

Glenrothes is the depot represented by the letter G in the Fife Scottish fleet. It is also the location of this picture of Ailsa 834, NSP334R. This unit differs from the others in the fleet by being dual-doored and it joined the fleet in 1995 from the A1 operation of Western Buses. *Paul Wigan*

867-874

									Volvo B55-10 MkIII	Alexander RV	H44/37F	1984

867	A967YSX	869	A969YSX	871	A971YSX	873	A973YSX	874	A974YSX
868	A968YSX	870	A970YSX	872	A972YSX				

875	UFS875R	Ailsa B55-10	Alexander AV	H44/35F	1977
876	UFS876R	Ailsa B55-10	Alexander AV	H44/35F	1977
877	UFS877R	Ailsa B55-10	Alexander AV	H44/35F	1977
878	UFS878R	Ailsa B55-10	Alexander AV	H44/35F	1977

901-920

Volvo Citybus B10M-50   Alexander RV   DPH47/33F*   1985-87   908 ex Volvo demonstrator, 1986
*909/10 are DPH45/35F

901	C801USG	907	C807USG	910	E910KSG	915	C795USG	919	C799USG
905	C805USG	908	B108CCS	914	C794USG	918	C798USG	920	C800USG
906	C806USG	909	E909KSG						

940	F310MYJ	Volvo Citybus B10M-50	Northern Counties	DPH43/33F	1989	Ex Southdown, 1991
941	F311MYJ	Volvo Citybus B10M-50	Northern Counties	DPH43/33F	1989	Ex Southdown, 1991
942	F312MYJ	Volvo Citybus B10M-50	Northern Counties	DPH43/33F	1989	Ex Southdown, 1991

972-997

Volvo Citybus B10M-50   Alexander RV   H47/37F   1985-86

972	C802USG	979	B179FFS	984	B184FFS	988	C788USG	992	C792USG
973	C803USG	980	B180FFS	985	B185FFS	989	C789USG	993	C793USG
974	C804USG	981	B181FFS	986	B186FFS	990	C790USG	996	C796USG
977	B177FFS	982	B182FFS	987	C787USG	991	C791USG	997	C797USG
978	B178FFS	983	B183FFS						

1102	ABV669A	Leyland Atlantean PDR1/1	Metro Cammell	O44/31F	1961	Ex Cumberland, 1992
1107	UWV617S	Bristol VRT/SL3/6LXB	Eastern Coach Works	CO43/31F	1978	Ex Stagecoach South, 1994
1110w	OVV850R	Bristol VRT/SL3/501(6LX)	Eastern Coach Works	H43/31F	1976	Ex Stagecoach, 1994

Three former Southdown B10M Citybuses with Northern Counties bodywork were transferred to Fife in 1991 and joined a batch of Alexander-bodied examples. All are fitted with high-back seating and are used on *Fifexpress* services. Pictured in Anstruther is 940, F310MYJ. *Bill Potter*

1111	VTV167S	Bristol VRT/SL3/6LXB	Eastern Coach Works	H43/31F	1978	Ex Stagecoach, 1994
1112	RJT153R	Bristol VRT/SL3/6LXB	Eastern Coach Works	H43/31F	1977	Ex Stagecoach, 1994
1113	VPR487S	Bristol VRT/SL3/6LXB	Eastern Coach Works	H43/31F	1978	Ex Stagecoach, 1994
1114	XAP643S	Bristol VRT/SL3/6LXB	Eastern Coach Works	H43/31F	1978	Ex Stagecoach, 1994
1115	EWE204V	Bristol VRT/SL3/6LXB	Eastern Coach Works	H43/31F	1980	Ex East Midland, 1994
1116	HWG208W	Bristol VRT/SL3/6LXB	Eastern Coach Works	H43/31F	1980	Ex East Midland, 1994
1117w	RTH924S	Bristol VRT/SL3/6LXB	Eastern Coach Works	H43/31F	1977	Ex East Midland, 1994
1118	KWA217W	Bristol VRT/SL3/6LXC	Eastern Coach Works	H43/31F	1981	Ex East Midland, 1994
1119	KKY220W	Bristol VRT/SL3/6LXB	Eastern Coach Works	H43/31F	1981	Ex East Midland, 1994
1120	DWF198V	Bristol VRT/SL3/501	Eastern Coach Works	H43/31F	1980	Ex East Midland, 1994
1121	DWF199V	Bristol VRT/SL3/501	Eastern Coach Works	H43/31F	1980	Ex East Midland, 1994
1122	DWF200V	Bristol VRT/SL3/501	Eastern Coach Works	H43/31F	1980	Ex East Midland, 1994
1123	RVB973S	Bristol VRT/SL3/6LXB	Willowbrook	H43/31F	1978	Ex Stagecoach South, 1994
1124	RVB974S	Bristol VRT/SL3/6LXB	Willowbrook	H43/31F	1978	Ex Stagecoach South, 1994
1125	RVB978S	Bristol VRT/SL3/6LXB	Willowbrook	H43/31F	1978	Ex Stagecoach South, 1994
1126	TFN990T	Bristol VRT/SL3/6LXB	Willowbrook	H43/31F	1978	Ex Stagecoach South, 1994
1127	PRU917R	Bristol VRT/SL3/6LXB	Eastern Coach Works	H43/31F	1977	Ex Bluebird, 1994
1128	RPR716R	Bristol VRT/SL3/6LXB	Eastern Coach Works	H43/31F	1977	Ex Bluebird, 1994
1129w	WHH415S	Bristol VRT/SL3/501	Eastern Coach Works	H43/31F	1978	Ex Bluebird, 1994
1130w	PJJ16S	Bristol VRT/SL3/6LXB	Willowbrook	H43/31F	1977	Ex Stagecoach South, 1996
1136	LEO736Y	Leyland Atlantean AN68D/1R	Northern Counties	H43/32F	1983	Ex Ribble, 1995
1144w	SCN244S	Leyland Atlantean AN68A/2R	Alexander AL	H49/37F	1978	Ex Busways, 1995
1161w	SCN261S	Leyland Atlantean AN68A/2R	Alexander AL	H49/37F	1978	Ex Busways, 1995

Previous Registrations:

ABV669A	927GTA	H509AGC	H884LOX, WLT400
F286KGK	F430BOP, WLT491	IIL3504	E626UNE, GIL2967, E937XSB
GSU341	B207FFS	IIL3506	E624UNE, MIB658, E931XSB
GSU342	B208FFS	MSU445	B211FFS
GSU343	PGC522Y, 3402FM, SJI5407	MSU499	D319SGB
GSU344	B210FFS	VLT77	F396DHL

Livery: White, red, orange and blue (Stagecoach corporate); red (Fife traditional) 1102.

GALLOWAYS

J Galloway, 43 Whitecraigs Road, Harthill, South Lanarkshire, ML7 5SL

HCS787N	Leyland Leopard PSU3/3R	Alexander AYS	B53F	1975	Ex Whitelaw, Stonehouse, 1992
MSF126P	Leyland Leopard PSU3C/4R	Alexander AY	B53F	1975	Ex Lothian, 1991
MSF127P	Leyland Leopard PSU3C/4R	Alexander AY	B53F	1975	Ex Lothian, 1991
XSG70R	Leyland Leopard PSU3E/4R	Alexander AYS	B53F	1977	Ex Midland Scottish, 1992
CFS116S	Leyland Leopard PSU3E/4R	Duple Dominant I	C49F	1978	Ex Fife Scottish, 1993
ASP209T	Leyland Leopard PSU3E/4R	Duple Dominant I	C49F	1978	Ex Fife Scottish, 1993
WJM806T	Leyland Leopard PSU3E/4R	Plaxton Supreme III Express	C53F	1978	Ex Graham's, Paisley, 1990
MIB5088	Leyland Leopard PSU3G/4R	Willowbrook Warrior (1990)	B53F	1982	Ex Dunn Line, Nottingham, 1996
TJI3143	Volvo B10M-61	Plaxton Paramount 3200 III	C53F	1987	Ex Crawford, Neilston, 1990
TJI3142	Volvo B10M-60	Plaxton Paramount 3500 III	C50F	1989	Ex Wallace Arnold, 1993
TJI3141	Volvo B10M-60	Plaxton Paramount 3500 III	C53F	1989	Ex Britannia Travel, Telford, 1995
F256OFP	Volvo B10M-60	Duple 320	C57F	1989	Ex Crawford, Neilston, 1993
UJI2169	Volvo B10M-60	Plaxton Paramount 3500 III	C53F	1991	Ex Ambassador, Great Yarmouth, 1996
TJI3140	Volvo B10M-60	Plaxton Paramount 3500 III	C51FT	1992	Ex Bebb, Llantwit Fardre, 1995

Previous Registrations:

ASP209T	GSG134T, NSU134	TJI3142	F430DUG
MIB5088	CNH172X	TJI3143	E919EAY
TJI3140	J41VWO	UJI2169	H176EJU, TJI5402, H150VVG
TJI3141	F976HGE, NIW3546, F202GAW		

Livery: Red (buses); cream and red (coaches)

Alexander-bodied Leyland Leopard XSG70R was new to Fife Scottish and was then operated by Midland Bluebird before passing to Galloways of Harthill. It is seen in Bathgate in its red livery.
Murdoch Currie

GALSON MOTORS

Galson - Stornoway Motor Services Ltd, 1 Lower Barvas, Stornoway,
Isle of Lewis, HS2 0QZ

GS20	TAP288R	Leyland Leopard PSU3C/4R	Plaxton Supreme III	C44F	1976	Ex Rennie, Dunfermline, 1989
GS26	AGM688L	Leyland Leopard PSU3/3R	Alexander AY	B53F	1973	Ex Stagecoach, 1988
GS28	G900GWN	Ford Transit VE6	Ford	M14	1989	Ex Merlyns, Skewen, 1992
GS29	TRY51S	Leyland Leopard PSU5B/4R	Plaxton Supreme III	C57F	1978	Ex John Smith, Shotts, 1992
GS30	TTK248	Volvo B58-61	Plaxton Supreme IV	C53F	1981	Ex John Smith, Shotts, 1992
GS31	LWV269P	Leyland Leopard PSU3C/4R	Plaxton Supreme III	C53F	1976	Ex Rosemary, Terrington St Clement, 1993
GS32	XCC95V	Leyland Leopard PSU3E/4R	Plaxton Supreme IV Express	C53F	1980	Ex Hedon Silverwing, Hull 1994
GS33	YSV586	Leyland Leopard PSU3E/4R	Plaxton Supreme IV Express	C53F	1979	Ex Gardiner, Spennymoor, 1995
GS34	MAP351W	Leyland Leopard PSU3E/4R	Plaxton Supreme IV Express	C53F	1981	Ex Gardiner, Spennymoor, 1995
GS35	F291PAC	Ford Transit VE6	Dormobile	M16	1989	Ex Coventry CC, 1995
GS36	EGB63T	Leyland Leopard PSU3E/4R	Alexander AYS	B53F	1979	Ex KCB Network, 1995
GS37	EGB67T	Leyland Leopard PSU3E/4R	Alexander AYS	B53F	1979	Ex KCB Network, 1995
GS38	EGB74T	Leyland Leopard PSU3E/4R	Alexander AYS	B53F	1979	Ex KCB Network, 1995
GS39	EGB76T	Leyland Leopard PSU3E/4R	Alexander AYS	B53F	1979	Ex KCB Network, 1995
GS40	J144CYO	Ford Transit VE6	Readwheel	M16L	1991	Ex Voluntary Transport, Glenrothes, 1996
GS41	B294KPF	Leyland Tiger TRCTL11/3RH	Plaxton Paramount 3200 IIE	C51F	1985	Ex Andy James, Tetbury, 1996
GS42	M599GMR	Mercedes-Benz 811D	Autobus Classique II	B31F	1995	Ex Andy James, Tetbury, 1996
GS43	WPH119Y	Leyland Tiger TRCTL11/2R	Eastern Coach Works B51	C49F	1982	Ex Gilchrist, East Kilbride, 1996
GS44	LBZ6829	Volvo B10M-61	Plaxton Paramount 3500 III	C53F	1987	Ex Ross, Grantown-on-Spey, 1996
GS45	OJE533	Volvo B10M-61	Van Hool Alizée	C46FT	1983	Ex Weirs Tours, Clydebank, 1997

Previous Registrations:

LBZ6829	E551UHS	OJE533	From new	XCC95V	UFM267V, 794YKM
M599GMR	M33ARJ	TTK248	RLY889W	YSV586	JVF819V
TAP288R	OWV275R, 403DCD				

Livery: Yellow and cream

Galson Motors, based on the Isle of Lewis normally operates buses in a Yellow and cream livery. Pictured at the end of 1996, Leyland Leopard GS38, EGB74T, still carried the red of KCB Network. The bodywork is Alexander's AYS type. *Richard Walter*

GIBSON

James Gibson & Son, 16 Church Street, Moffat, Dumfries & Galloway, DG10 9HD

Depot : Mollingburn, Johnstone Bridge, Dumfries

JRB741N	Leyland Leopard PSU3C/4R	Duple Dominant E	DP53F	1975	Ex Graham's, Paisley, 1990
LWV268P	Leyland Leopard PSU3C/4R	Plaxton Supreme III	C46F	1976	Ex Rennie, Dunfermline, 1993
SDD137R	Leyland Leopard PSU3E/4R	Plaxton Supreme III	C53F	1977	Ex Holdcare, Peterlee, 1991
OPC37R	Bedford VAS5	Duple Dominant	C29F	1977	Ex Tuck, Chaldon, 1989
OJY573S	Volvo B58	Plaxton Viewmaster	C53F	1978	Acquired 1997.
GSU851T	Leyland Leopard PSU3C/3R	Alexander AT	DP49F	1979	Ex McColl, Balloch, 1994
GSU852T	Leyland Leopard PSU3C/3R	Alexander AT	DP49F	1979	Ex McColl, Balloch, 1994
GSU861T	Leyland Leopard PSU3C/3R	Alexander AYS	B53F	1979	Ex KCB Network, 1996
GSU862T	Leyland Leopard PSU3C/3R	Alexander AYS	B53F	1979	Ex KCB Network, 1996
GSU866T	Leyland Leopard PSU3C/3R	Alexander AYS	B53F	1979	Ex KCB Network, 1996
WCK126V	Leyland Leopard PSU3E/4R	Duple Dominant II Express	C49F	1979	Ex Lord, Blackpool, 1993
WCK129V	Leyland Leopard PSU3E/4R	Duple Dominant II Express	C49F	1979	Ex Lord, Blackpool, 1993
HIL7590	Volvo B10M-61	Van Hool Alizée	C53F	1982	
LIB5441	Van Hool T815	Van Hool Acron	C49FT	1983	Ex Beaton, Blantyre, 1990
HIL7589	Volvo B10M-61	Duple Caribbean	C51FT	1984	Ex Amport & District, Thruxton, 1988
HIL8028	Van Hool T815	Van Hool Alicron	C49FT	1985	
DSV711	Volvo B10M-61	Berkhof Esprite 350	C49FT	1985	Ex Compass Royston, Stockton, 1994
HIL8022	Volvo B10M-61	Ikarus Blue Danube	C49FT	1989	
WDZ4724	Volvo B10M-60	Van Hool Alizée	C50F	1993	Ex Wallace Arnold, 1997
OAZ9372	Volvo B10M-60	Van Hool Alizée	C50F	1993	Ex Wallace Arnold, 1997

Previous Registrations:

DSV711	From new	HIL8022	F155CSM	LIB5441	VVK200Y
HIL7589	A228LFX	HIL8028	B428MSW	PJI1825	D200HWR
HIL7590	CSM915X				

Livery: Red, maroon and orange

Gibsons of Moffat operate this Duple-bodied Leyland Leopard WCK126V. It is seen in Dumfries and carries the Dominant II Express body that was aimed at the grant-coach market whereby operators were subsidised if they purchased vehicles to certain specifications. The grant scheme was phased out during the early 1980s.
Murdoch Currie

GLEN COACHES

Glen Coaches Ltd, 8 McDougall Street, Port Glasgow, Renfrewshire, PA15 2TG

D389UGA	Volvo B10M-61	Van Hool Alizée	C53F	1987	Ex Allander Travel, Milngave, 1995
F546TMH	Volvo B10M-60	Van Hool Alizée	C53F	1989	Ex Turner, Bristol, 1994
F550TMH	Volvo B10M-60	Van Hool Alizée	C53F	1989	Ex Travellers, Hounslow, 1994
F553TMH	Volvo B10M-60	Van Hool Alizée	C53F	1989	Ex Travellers, Hounslow, 1994
L628AYS	Volvo B10M-62	Van Hool Alizée	C53F	1994	Ex Park's, Hamilton, 1996
L95GAX	Volvo B10M-62	Jonckheere Deauville 45	C51FT	1993	Ex Ralph's, Langley, 1996
M435ECS	Volvo B10M-62	Van Hool Alizée	C53F	1994	
M442ECS	Volvo B10M-62	Van Hool Alizée	C53F	1994	
M766WSC	Mercedes-Benz 814D	Plaxton Beaver	C33F	1995	
N140ESC	Mercedes-Benz 814D	Plaxton Beaver	C33F	1996	
P798KSF	Mercedes-Benz 814D	Plaxton Beaver	C33F	1996	
P583RGB	Mercedes-Benz 412D Sprinter	Adamson	M16	1996	
P390OFS	Mercedes-Benz 814D	Plaxton Beaver	C33F	1997	

Previous Registrations:

D389UGA	D562MVR, GIL1681, D695OSJ, 3786AT	M435ECS	KSK953
L628AYS	LSK481	M442ECS	KSK951

Livery: White and blue

Glen Coaches operate a modern fleet mostly comprising Van Hool Alizée-bodied Volvo B10Ms. The exceptions are Mercedes-Benz mini-coaches and P798KSF is a 33-seat Plaxton Beaver coach seen in Greenock while undertaking a private hire. *Murdoch Currie*

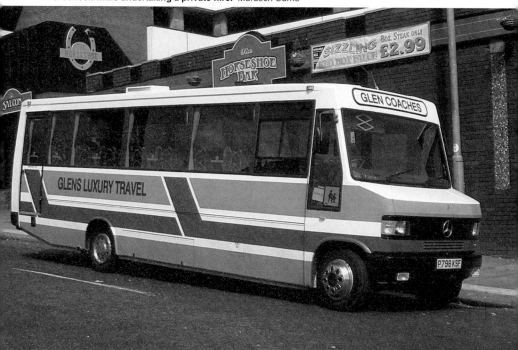

GOLDEN EAGLE

J, P & R Irvine, Muirhall Garage, 197 Main Street, Salsburgh,
Byshotts, North Lanarkshire, ML7 4LS

AUS417S	AEC Reliance 6U3ZR	Marshall	B51F	1978	
AUS418S	AEC Reliance 6U3ZR	Marshall	B51F	1978	
FDC409V	Leyland Leopard PSU3E/4R	Plaxton Supreme IV Express	DP55F	1979	Ex Kingston-upon-Hull, 1995
FDC410V	Leyland Leopard PSU3E/4R	Plaxton Supreme IV Express	DP55F	1979	Ex Kingston-upon-Hull, 1995
HPY421V	Leyland Leopard PSU3E/2R	Plaxton Supreme IV Express	DP53F	1980	Ex Cleveland Transit, 1995
UNS973W	Leyland Leopard PSU3E/4R	Duple Dominant	B55F	1981	
TIA6937	Volvo B10M-53	Plaxton Paramount 4000 II	CH54/13CT	1986	Ex Christie, Tullibody, 1993
JIL8561	Volvo B10M-61	Van Hool Alizée	C53F	1986	
JIL8562	Volvo B10M-61	Van Hool Alizée	C53FT	1988	
JIL8559	Volvo B10M-60	Van Hool Alizée	C53FT	1989	
JIL8553	Volvo B10M-60	Van Hool Alizée	C49FT	1990	Ex Whyte's, Newmachar, 1995
JIL8560	Volvo B10M-60	Van Hool Alizée	C53F	1992	
N985ODS	Volvo B10M-62	Van Hool Alizée	C53F	1996	

Previous Registrations:

JIL8553	G804DSS, HSK176, G341VSE	JIL8561	D864PGB
JIL8559	F235ESU	JIL8562	E129BSU
JIL8560	J39HSU	TIA6937	C740GOP

Livery: Red and cream (buses); white, red and gold (coaches); white N985ODS; white (Caledonian Travel) JIL8562

Now the oldest vehicle with Golden Eagle, AUS417S is a Marshall-bodied AEC Reliance and one of a pair that were new to the operation in 1978. Since the sale of their bus services Golden Eagle concentrate of contracts, holidays and private hire. *Paul Wigan*

GRAMPIAN

Grampian Regional Transport Ltd; Kirkpatrick of Deeside Ltd
395 King Street, Aberdeen, AB24 5RP
G E Mair Hire Services Ltd, St Peter Street, Aberdeen AB2 3HU

Depots : King Street, Aberdeen and Dee Street, Banchory.

1	K1GRT	Mercedes-Benz 0405G	Alexander Cityranger	AB60T	1992	
19	HRS262V	Leyland Atlantean AN68A/1R	Alexander AL	O45/29D	1980	
20	HRS271V	Leyland Atlantean AN68A/1R	Alexander AL	O45/29D	1980	
21	HRS278V	Leyland Atlantean AN68A/1R	Alexander AL	O45/29D	1980	
22	URS318X	Leyland Atlantean AN68C/1R	Alexander AL	O45/29D	1982	
23	YSO231T	Leyland Atlantean AN68A/1R	Alexander AL	O45/29D	1978	
25	CRG325C	Daimler CVG6	Alexander B	H37/29R	1965	
31	LSK570	MCW MetroRider MF154/26	MCW	C29F	1989	Ex Mair, Dyce, 1992
40	ESK955	Volvo B58-56	Duple Dominant II	C51F	1979	Ex Kirkpatrick, Banchory, 1991
41	ESK956	Volvo B10M-61	Plaxton Paramount 3200 III	C53F	1988	Ex Alexander's, Aberdeen, 1989
44	ESK957	Volvo B10M-61	Plaxton Paramount 3200 III	C57F	1988	Ex Alexander's, Aberdeen, 1989
47	LSK476	Dennis Javelin 8.5SDL1903	Duple 320	C35F	1989	Ex Dewar, Falkirk, 1992
49	LSK475	Leyland Tiger TRCL10/3ARZM	Plaxton 321	C53F	1990	Ex Dewar, Falkirk, 1992
52	PSU623	Leyland Tiger TRCLXC/3RH	Plaxton Paramount 3200 E	C53F	1986	
87	TSU651	Volvo B10M-60	Jonckheere Deauville P599	C51FT	1989	
92	J11GRT	Volvo B10M-60	Jonckheere Deauville P599	C49FT	1992	
93	K3GRT	Volvo B10M-60	Jonckheere Deauville P599	C49FT	1993	
94	K4GRT	Volvo B10M-60	Jonckheere Deauville P599	C47FT	1993	
96	P2GRT	Scania K113CRB	Irizar Century 12.35	C51FT	1997	
97	P4GRT	Scania K113CRB	Irizar Century 12.35	C51FT	1997	

101-110

		Leyland Olympian ONLXB/1R*	Alexander RH		H47/26D*	1984		*101-3 are H47/24D	
								*101-3/8 are ONLXB/1R(6LXCT)	

101	A101FSA	103	A103FSA	105	A105FSA	107	A107FSA	109	A109FSA
102	A102FSA	104	A104FSA	106	A106FSA	108	A108FSA	110	A110FSA

112-121

		Leyland Olympian ONLXB/1RV*	Alexander RH		H47/26D*	1985		*121 is H47/24D	
								*113/7/8/20/1 are ONLXB/1RV(6LXCT)	

112	B112MSO	114	B114MSO	116	B116MSO	118	B118MSO	120	B120MSO
113	B113MSO	115	B115MSO	117	B117MSO	119	B119MSO	121	B121MSO

122	E122DRS	Leyland Olympian ONCL10/2RZ	Alexander RH	DPH47/33F	1988	
123	E123DRS	Leyland Olympian ONCL10/2RZ	Alexander RH	DPH47/33F	1988	

All of Grampian's Leyland Olympians are now in the new version of fleet livery. No.110, A110FSA, wears standard bus livery, the vehicles with high-back seating carry the *Gold-Service* scheme. *Billy Nicol*

124-131

Leyland Olympian ONCL10/2RZ Alexander RH H49/29D 1988

| 124 | E124DRS | 126 | E126DRS | 128 | E128DRS | 130 | E130DRS | 131 | E131DRS |
| 125 | E125DRS | 127 | E127DRS | 129 | E129DRS | | | | |

201-206

Dennis Dart 9.8SDL3054 Alexander Dash B40F 1995-96

| 201 | N201VSA | 203 | N203VSA | 204 | N204VSA | 205 | N205VSA | 206 | N206VSA |
| 202 | N202VSA | | | | | | | | |

266-300

Leyland Atlantean AN68A/1R Alexander AL H45/29D 1980

266	HRS266V	274	HRS274V	281w	HSO281V	290w	HSO290V	296	LRS296W
267	HRS267V	275	HRS275V	283	HSO283V	292w	LRS292W	297	LRS297W
268	HRS268V	276u	HRS276V	286w	HSO286V	293	LRS293W	298	LRS298W
269	HRS269V	277u	HRS277V	287	HSO287V	294	LRS294W	299	LRS299W
273	HRS273V	279	HRS279V	289w	HSO289V	295	LRS295W	300	LRS300W

301-315

Leyland Atlantean AN68C/1R Alexander AL H45/29D 1981

301	NRS301W	304	NRS304W	307	NRS307W	310	NRS310W	313	NRS313W
302	NRS302W	305	NRS305W	308	NRS308W	311	NRS311W	314	NRS314W
303	NRS303W	306	NRS306W	309	NRS309W	312	NRS312W	315	NRS315W

316-330

Leyland Atlantean AN68C/1R Alexander AL H45/29D 1982

316	URS316X	320	URS320X	323	URS323X	326	URS326X	329	URS329X
317	URS317X	321	URS321X	324	URS324X	327	URS327X	330	URS330X
319	URS319X	322	URS322X	325	URS325X	328	URS328X		

331-345

Leyland Atlantean AN68D/1R Alexander AL H45/29D 1983

331	XSS331Y	334	XSS334Y	337	XSS337Y	340	XSS340Y	343	XSS343Y
332	XSS332Y	335	XSS335Y	338	XSS338Y	341	XSS341Y	344	XSS344Y
333	XSS333Y	336	XSS336Y	339	XSS339Y	342	XSS342Y	345	XSS345Y

401-409

Mercedes-Benz 709D Alexander Sprint B23F 1993

| 401 | K401HRS | 403 | K403HRS | 405 | K405HRS | 407 | K407HRS | 409 | K409HRS |
| 402 | K402HRS | 404 | K404HRS | 406 | K406HRS | 408 | K408HRS | | |

| 432 | 2GRT | MCW MetroRider MF150/10 | MCW | C23F | 1987 |
| 433 | TRS333 | MCW MetroRider MF150/10 | MCW | C23F | 1987 |

434-439

Mercedes-Benz 709D Reeve Burgess Beaver B23F 1991

| 434 | H34USO | 436 | H36USO | 437 | H37USO | 438 | H38USO | 439 | H39USO |
| 435 | H35USO | | | | | | | | |

440	E106JNH	Renault-Dodge S56	Alexander AM	DP23F	1987	Ex Northampton, 1994
441	E110JNH	Renault-Dodge S56	Alexander AM	DP23F	1988	Ex Northampton, 1994
442	E108JNH	Renault-Dodge S56	Alexander AM	DP23F	1988	Ex Mair's Coaches, 1994

501-514

Mercedes-Benz O405 Wright Cityranger B49F 1993

501	L501KSA	504	L504KSA	507	L507KSA	510	L510KSA	513	L513KSA
502	L502KSA	505	L505KSA	508	L508KSA	511	L511KSA	514	L514KSA
503	L503KSA	506	L506KSA	509	L509KSA	512	L512KSA		

515-524

Mercedes-Benz O405 Optare Prisma B49F 1995

| 515 | M1GRT | 517 | M517RSS | 519 | M519RSS | 521 | M521RSS | 523 | M523RSS |
| 516 | M516RSS | 518 | M518RSS | 520 | M520RSS | 522 | M522RSS | 524 | M524RSS |

525-549

Mercedes-Benz O405 Optare Prisma B47F* 1995-97 *525 is B49F

525	N525VSA	530	N530VSA	535	N535VSA	540	P540BSS	545	P545BSS
526	N526VSA	531	N531VSA	536	N536VSA	541	P541BSS	546	P546BSS
527	N527VSA	532	N532VSA	537	N537VSA	542	P542BSS	547	P547BSS
528	N528VSA	533	N533VSA	538	N538VSA	543	P543BSS	548	P548BSS
529	N529VSA	534	N534VSA	539	N539VSA	544	P544BSS	549	P549BSS

Mairs Coaches

702	PSU609	Volvo B10M-60	Plaxton Paramount 3500 III	C48FT	1989	Ex Wallace Arnold, 1992
703	PSU626	Volvo B10M-60	Plaxton Paramount 3500 III	C48FT	1989	Ex Clyde Coast, Ardrossan, 1992
704	PSU629	Volvo B10M-61	Van Hool Alizée	C53F	1984	
705	PSU628	Volvo B10M-61	Jonckheere Jubilee P599	C51FT	1987	Ex Buddens Skylark, Woodfalls, 1990
706	FSU333	Volvo B10M-60	Jonckheere Deauville P599	C51FT	1989	Ex Marbill, Beith, 1993
707	F326WCS	Mercedes-Benz 609D	Scott	C24F	1988	
708	F634JSO	Mercedes-Benz 609D	Made-to-Measure	C19F	1989	
709	F633JSO	Mercedes-Benz 609D	Made-to-Measure	C19F	1989	
710	K950HSA	Mercedes-Benz 609D	Made-to-Measure	C24F	1993	
711	FSU335	Mercedes-Benz L608D	Reeve Burgess	DP19F	1986	Ex Midland Bluebird, 1993
712	D532RCK	Mercedes-Benz L608D	Reeve Burgess	B20F	1986	Ex Midland Bluebird, 1993
713	LSK571	Mercedes-Benz L608D	Alexander AM	DP20F	1986	Ex Midland Bluebird, 1993
714	P20GRT	Scania L94	Irizar Inter-Century	C51FT	1997	
715	PSU968	Mercedes-Benz 609D	Scott	C22F	1990	
716	H193CVU	Mercedes-Benz 609D	Made-to-Measure	C24F	1990	
717	D232UHC	Mercedes-Benz L608D	Alexander AM	DP20F	1986	Ex Bluebird Northern, 1992
719	HSU955	Volvo B10M-61	Duple 340	C57F	1988	Ex Rider Group, 1996
720	PSU631	Volvo B10M-60	Jonckheere Jubilee P50	C53F	1985	Ex Buddens Skylark, Woodfalls, 1988
722	WSU460	Volvo B10M-61	Van Hool Alizée	C53F	1985	Ex Selwyn, Runcorn, 1994
723	HSO285V	Leyland Atlantean AN68A/1R	Alexander AL	H45/29D	1980	
724	HSO284V	Leyland Atlantean AN68A/1R	Alexander AL	H45/29D	1980	
727	HRS280V	Leyland Atlantean AN68A/1R	Alexander AL	H45/29D	1980	
728w	HSO61N	Leyland Leopard PSU4C/4R	Alexander AY	C45F	1975	
729w	ORS60R	Leyland Leopard PSU4C/4R	Alexander AY	C45F	1977	
731	J11AFC	Volvo B10M-60	Jonckheere Deauville P599	C49FT	1992	
732	737ABD	Volvo B10M-61	Jonckheere Deauville P599	C51FT	1988	
733	PSU627	Volvo B10M-61	Jonckheere Deauville P599	C51FT	1989	Ex River Valley, Sutton Valence, 1991
734	WSU447	Volvo B10M-60	Jonckheere Deauville P599	C51FT	1990	Ex Redwing, Camberwell, 1994
735	GSU390	Volvo B10M-61	Duple 340	C57F	1988	Ex Rider Group, 1996
736	131ASV	Volvo B10M-60	Van Hool Alizée	C55F	1990	Ex Henry Crawford, Neilston, 1993
737	K67HSA	Toyota Coaster HDB30R	Caetano Optimo II	C18F	1993	
738	L538XUT	Toyota Coaster HZB50R	Caetano Optimo III	C18F	1994	
739	LSK529	Dennis Javelin 8.5SDL1903	Plaxton Paramount 3200 III	C35F	1988	Ex Dewar, Falkirk, 1992
740	LSK530	Dennis Javelin 8.5SDL1903	Plaxton Paramount 3200 III	C35F	1988	Ex Dewar, Falkirk, 1992
741	XWL539	DAF MB230LB615	Plaxton Paramount 3500 III	C49FT	1992	Ex SMT, 1995

Grampian operate several routes under the Gold Service banner using vehicles in a dedicated livery. Shown operating service 16 to Cove is Optare-bodied Mercedes-Benz O405 number 527, N527VSA, from the 1996 delivery. *Billy Nicol*

742	JSV426	DAF SB3000DKV601	Van Hool Alizée	C49FT	1992	Ex SMT, 1995
743	D120NUS	Mercedes-Benz L708D	Alexander AM	B21F	1986	Ex Midland Bluebird, 1995

Kirkpatrick

904	LSK546	Mercedes-Benz L608D	Plaxton Mini Supreme	C20F	1985	Ex Epsom Coaches, 1990
905	781GRT	Leyland Tiger TRCLXC/2RH	Plaxton Paramount 3200 E	C49F	1986	
906	LSK527	Dennis Javelin 8.5SDL1903	Duple 320	C35F	1988	Ex Dewar, Falkirk, 1992
907	C103KDS	Mercedes-Benz L608D	Alexander AM	DP19F	1986	Ex Midland Bluebird, 1993
908w	C805SDY	Mercedes-Benz L608D	Alexander AM	DP19F	1986	Ex Midland Bluebird, 1993
909	D951VSS	Mercedes-Benz 307D	Devon Conversions	M12	1986	Ex Rigblast, Dyce, 1993
910	E467JSG	Renault-Dodge S56	Alexander AM	DP25F	1987	Ex SMT, 1994
911	LSU917	Leyland Tiger TRCTL11/2R	Plaxton Supreme V Express	C53F	1982	Ex Leicester Citybus, 1995
912	LSK573	Mercedes-Benz 609D	Scott	C24F	1988	
915	PSU624	Leyland Tiger TRCLXC/3RH	Plaxton Paramount 3200 E	C53F	1986	Ex Grampian, 1996
916	LSK572	Volvo B10M-61	Plaxton Paramount 3200 III	C57F	1988	

Previous Registrations:

2GRT	D32XSS	LSK571	D424UHC
131ASV	G260RNS	LSK572	F103HSO
737ABD	F950RNV	LSK573	F327WCS
781GRT	D55VSO	LSU917	YFJ17Y
ESK955	HSE696V	PSU609	F408DUG
ESK956	F101HSO	PSU623	D52VSO
ESK957	F104HSO	PSU624	D53VSO
FSU333	G845GNV	PSU626	F986HGE
FSU335	D517RCK	PSU627	F913YNV
GSU390	E407RWR	PSU628	D95BNV
HSU955	E406RWR	PSU629	B229LSO, 737ABD
JSV426	J812KHD	PSU631	B497CBD
K950HSA	K983XND	PSU968	D318VVV
LSK475	H154DJU	TRS333	D330VVV
LSK476	G166HMS	TSU651	F87CBD
LSK527	E151XHS	WSU447	FDF275T
LSK529	F739WMS	WSU447	G171RBD
LSK530	F369MUT	WSU460	B122DMA, SEL392
LSK546	C200HGF	WSU481	-
LSK570	F632JSA	XWL539	J795KHD

Livery: Ivory, green and gold; ivory, maroon, green and red (coaches); two-tone silver, maroon, green and red (Executive coaches); green (Aberdeen Corporation) 25, 79.

Opposite: **The main Grampian fleet numbers just short of 200 vehicles and provides services to the city of Aberdeen. Following the delivery of high quality buses from Wrights and Optare the latest arrivals are a batch of six Dennis Darts with Alexander Dash bodywork for the *Gold service* operation, as illustrated by 203, N203VSA seen in Union Street. The lower picture shows one of the Mercedes-Benz O405 buses with Wright Cityranger bodywork, Wrights building the body onto a chassis and front provided by Mercedes-Benz. Pictured with *Cityquick* lettering is 507, L507KSA.** *Billy Nicol/Paul Wigan*

Grampian, Kirkpatrick and Mairs Coaches remain separately managed though a new coach livery with common styling has been introduced, though the ticks of colour differs. Still part of the main Grampian fleet is open-top Atlantean 23, YSO231T pictured while running the Explorer service.
Bill Potter

GREATER GLASGOW

Strathclyde Buses Ltd
197 Victoria Road, Larkfield, Glasgow, G42 7AD

Depots :Connor Street, Airdrie; Glencryan Road, Cumbernauld; Great Western Road, Knightswood, Glasgow; Victoria Road, Larkfield, Glasgow; Tollcross Road, Parkhead, Glasgow; Hawthorn Street, Possilpark, Glasgow; Tinker's Lane, Motherwell and Cumbernauld Road, Stepps.

A2-39
Volvo-Ailsa B55-10 MkIII — Alexander RV — H44/35F — 1981

2	TGG378W	12	CSU220X	20	CSU228X	27	CSU235X	33	CSU241X
5	TGG381W	13	CSU221X	21	CSU229X	28	CSU236X	34	CSU242X
7	TGG383W	14	CSU222X	22	CSU230X	29	CSU237X	35	CSU243X
8	TGG384W	15	CSU223X	23	CSU231X	30	CSU238X	37	CSU245X
9	TGG385W	16	CSU224X	25	CSU233X	31	CSU239X	38	CSU246X
10	TGG386W	17	CSU225X	26	CSU234X	32	CSU240X	39	CSU247X
11	CSU219X	18	CSU226X						

A41-81
Volvo-Ailsa B55-10 MkIII — Alexander RV — H44/35F — 1982

41	KGG101Y	49	KGG109Y	60	KGG141Y	68	KGG128Y	75	KGG135Y
42	KGG102Y	50	KGG110Y	62	KGG122Y	69	KGG129Y	76	KGG136Y
43	KGG103Y	51	KGG111Y	63	KGG123Y	70	KGG130Y	77	KGG137Y
44	KGG104Y	52	KGG112Y	64	KGG124Y	71	KGG131Y	78	KGG138Y
45	KGG105Y	55	KGG115Y	65	KGG121Y	72	KGG132Y	79	KGG139Y
46	KGG106Y	56	KGG116Y	66	KGG126Y	73	KGG133Y	80	KGG140Y
47	KGG107Y	58	KGG118Y	67	KGG127Y	74	KGG134Y	81	KGG120Y
48	KGG108Y	59	KGG119Y						

A83-116
Volvo-Ailsa B55-10 MkIII — Alexander RV — H44/35F — 1983

83	OGG179Y	90	OGG186Y	100	A563SGA	106	A732PSU	111	A737PSU
85	OGG181Y	92	OGG188Y	101	A564SGA	107	A733PSU	113	A739PSU
86	OGG182Y	93	OGG189Y	103	A566SGA	108	A734PSU	114	A741PSU
87	OGG183Y	94	OGG190Y	104w	A567SGA	109	A735PSU	115	A742PSU
88	OGG184Y	95	OGG191Y	105	A568SGA	110	A736PSU	116	A743PSU
89	OGG185Y	99	A562SGA						

A117	A483UYS	Volvo-Ailsa B55-10 MkIII	Marshall	H44/35F	1984
A118	A484UYS	Volvo-Ailsa B55-10 MkIII	Marshall	H44/35F	1984

A119-133
Volvo-Ailsa B55-10 MkIII — Alexander RV — H44/35F — 1984

119	B999YUS	123	B24YYS	126	B27YYS	129	B30YYS	132	B33YYS
120	B21YYS	124	B25YYS	127	B28YYS	130	B31YYS	133	B34YYS
122	B23YYS	125	B26YYS	128	B29YYS				

AH1	ESU378X	Volvo-Ailsa Citybus B10M-50	Marshall	H47/39F	1982

AH2-6
Volvo Citybus B10M-50 — Alexander RV — H47/27F — 1984

2	A600TNS	3	A601TNS	4	A603TNS	5	A602TNS	6	A604TNS

AH7-76 — Volvo Citybus B10M-50 — Alexander RV — H47/37F — 1989

7	F89JYS	21	F793LSU	35	G283OGE	50	G298OGE	64	G692PNS
8	F90JYS	22	F794LSU	36	G284OGE	51	G299OGE	65	G693PNS
9	F91JYS	23	F795LSU	37	G285OGE	52	G300OGE	66	G694PNS
10	F92JYS	24	G409OGD	38	G286OGE	53	G301OGE	67	G695PNS
11	F93JYS	25	G410OGD	39	G287OGE	54	G302OGE	68	G696PNS
12	F94JYS	26	G411OGD	40	G288OGE	55	G303OGE	69	G697PNS
13	F95JYS	27	G412OGD	42	G290OGE	56	G304OGE	70	G698PNS
14	F96JYS	28	G413OGD	43	G291OGE	57	G685PNS	71	G699PNS
15	F97JYS	29	G414OGD	44	G292OGE	58	G686PNS	72	G700PNS
16	F98JYS	30	G415OGD	45	G293OGE	59	G687PNS	73	G701PNS
17	F99JYS	31	G416OGD	46	G294OGE	60	G688PNS	74	G702PNS
18	F790LSU	32	G280OGE	47	G295OGE	61	G689PNS	75	G703PNS
19	F791LSU	33	G281OGE	48	G296OGE	62	G690PNS	76	G704PNS
20	F792LSU	34	G282OGE	49	G297OGE	63	G691PNS		

AH77-101 — Volvo Citybus B10M-50 — Alexander RV — H47/37F — 1990

77	G521RDS	82	G526RDS	87	G531RDS	92	G536RDS	97	G541RDS
78	G522RDS	83	G527RDS	88	G532RDS	93	G537RDS	98	G542RDS
79	G523RDS	84	G528RDS	89	G533RDS	94	G538RDS	99	G543RDS
80	G524RDS	85	G529RDS	90	G534RDS	95	G539RDS	100	G544RDS
81	G525RDS	86	G530RDS	91	G535RDS	96	G540RDS	101	G545RDS

AS3	F384FYS	Volvo B10M-56	Plaxton Derwent	DP46F	1988	
AS4	F385FYS	Volvo B10M-56	Plaxton Derwent	DP46F	1988	
AS5	E31BTO	Volvo B10M-56	Plaxton Derwent	DP46F	1988	Ex Grahams, Paisley, 1990
AS6	C982KHS	Volvo B10M-61	Caetano Stagecoach	DP53F	1986	Ex Grahams, Paisley, 1990
AS7	C983KHS	Volvo B10M-61	Caetano Stagecoach	DP53F	1986	Ex Grahams, Paisley, 1990
AS8	C188RVV	Volvo B10M-61	Caetano Stagecoach	DP31DL	1986	Ex Grahams, Paisley, 1990

C9	JGE29T	Leyland Leopard PSU3E/4R	Duple Dominant II Express	C45FL	1979
C12	OGD660V	Leyland Leopard PSU3E/4R	Duple Dominant II Express	C51F	1980
C14	755SBH	MCW Metroliner CR126/4	MCW	C49FL	1983
C16	B200DGG	Leyland Tiger TRCLXC/2RH	Alexander TE	C49F	1985

CD91-95 — Dennis Dorchester SDA806 — Alexander TC — C47F — 1984

91	A206UYS	92	A202UYS	93	A203UYS	94	A204UYS	95	A205UYS

CD286-290 — Dennis Dorchester SDA806 — Alexander TE — C49F — 1984

286	A106UYS	287	A107UYS	288	A108UYS	289	A109UYS	290	A110UYS

CL134	PGA834V	Leyland Leopard PSU3F/4R	Alexander AT	C49F	1980	
CL135	PGA835V	Leyland Leopard PSU3F/4R	Alexander AT	C49F	1980	
CL136	PGA826V	Leyland Leopard PSU3F/4R	Alexander AT	C49F	1980	
CL139	PGA832V	Leyland Leopard PSU3F/4R	Alexander AT	C49F	1980	
CL158	WGB497W	Leyland Leopard PSU3G/4R	Duple Dominant II Express	C47F	1981	Ex Kelvin Scottish, 1989
CL161	RMS401W	Leyland Leopard PSU3G/4R	Alexander AT	C49F	1981	Ex Kelvin Scottish, 1989
CL162	RMS402W	Leyland Leopard PSU3G/4R	Alexander AT	B49F	1981	Ex Kelvin Scottish, 1989
CL178	NNH190Y	Leyland Leopard PSU5C/4R	Duple Dominant IV	C57F	1983	Ex Luton & District, 1991

CM274-281 — MCW Metrobus DR102/52 — Alexander RL — DPH45/33F — 1986

274	D674MHS	275	D675MHS	277	D677MHS	279	D679MHS	281	D681MHS

CO40	B697BPU	Leyland Olympian ONTL11/2RSp	Eastern Coach Works	CH45/28F	1985	Ex Northumbria, 1995
CO41	A102FPL	Leyland Olympian ONTL11/2R	Eastern Coach Works	CH45/28F	1985	Ex Northumbria, 1995

CO209-CO216 — Leyland Olympian ONLXB/1RH — Alexander RL — DPH47/27F — 1986

209	C809KHS	212	C802KHS	214	C804KHS	215	C805KHS	216	C806KHS
211	C801KHS	213	C803KHS						

CO244-CO249 — Leyland Olympian YN2RV18Z4 — Alexander Royale RL — DPH47/28F — 1994

244	M844DUS	246	M846DUS	247	M847DUS	248	M848DUS	249	M849DUS
245	M845DUS								

CS1	P25RFS	Scania K113CRB	Irizar Century 12.35	C51FT	1997	
CS2	P26RFS	Scania K113CRB	Irizar Century 12.35	C51FT	1997	
CT1	WLT760	Leyland Tiger TRCTL11/3R	Duple Dominant III	C46FT	1981	Ex Kelvin Scottish, 1989
CT8	WLT910	Leyland Tiger TRBTL11/2R	Duple Dominant II Express	C47F	1983	Ex Kelvin Scottish, 1989
CT9	WLT357	Leyland Tiger TRCTL11/2R	Plaxton Paramount 3200 E	C49F	1983	Ex Kelvin Scottish, 1989
CT10	WLT741	Leyland Tiger TRCTL11/2R	Plaxton Paramount 3200 E	C49F	1983	Ex Kelvin Scottish, 1989
CT12	WLT408	Leyland Tiger TRCTL11/2R	Plaxton Paramount 3200 E	C49F	1983	Ex Kelvin Scottish, 1989
CT13	WLT770	Leyland Tiger TRCTL11/3R	Plaxton Paramount 3200 E	C52F	1983	Ex Luton & District, 1991
CT14	WLT976	Leyland Tiger TRCTL11/3R	Plaxton Paramount 3200 E	C53F	1983	Ex Luton & District, 1991
CT15	KCB758	Leyland Tiger TRCTL11/3R	Plaxton Paramount 3200 E	C53F	1983	Ex Luton & District, 1991
CT16	BXI521	Leyland Tiger TRCTL11/3RH	Plaxton Paramount 3200 E	C50FT	1985	Ex Luton & District, 1991
CT28	WLT388	Leyland Tiger TRCTL11/3R	Plaxton Paramount 3200	C49F	1983	Ex Leyland demonstrator, 1984
CT29	A9KCB	Leyland Tiger TRBTL11/2RP	Alexander TE	C47F	1983	Ex Kelvin Scottish, 1989
CT30	C257SPC	Leyland Tiger TRCTL11/3RH	Duple 320	C53F	1986	Ex Munro, Uddingston, 1994
CT31	WLT677	Leyland Tiger TRCTL11/3RH	Duple Laser	C47FT	1984	Ex Kelvin Scottish, 1989
CT32	WLT678	Leyland Tiger TRCTL11/3RH	Duple Laser	C55F	1984	Ex Kelvin Scottish, 1989
CT99	CSU932	Leyland Tiger TRCTL11/3RH	Duple 320	C53F	1986	Ex Luton & District, 1992

CT202-207

Leyland Tiger TRBTL11/2R   Alexander AT   C49F   1982-83 Ex Kelvin Scottish, 1989

202	FGG602X	204	FGG604X	205	FGG605X	206	FGG601X	207	ALS104Y
203	FGG603X								

CT238	TPC108X	Leyland Tiger TRCTL11/2R	Eastern Coach Works	C51F	1982	Ex Irvine, Law, 1995
CT238	WPH116Y	Leyland Tiger TRCTL11/2R	Eastern Coach Works	C51F	1982	Ex Irvine, Law, 1995
CV1	H946DRJ	Volvo B10M-60	Plaxton Paramount 3500 III	C49FT	1991	On long-term hire, 1997
CV2	H947DRJ	Volvo B10M-60	Plaxton Paramount 3500 III	C49FT	1991	On long-term hire, 1997
CV3	H955DRJ	Volvo B10M-60	Plaxton Paramount 3500 III	C49FT	1991	On long-term hire, 1997

CV4-10

Volvo B10M-62   Plaxton Première 320   C53F   1997

CV4	P765XHS	CV6	P767XHS	CV8	P769XHS	CV9	P770XHS	CV10	P771XHS
CV5	P766XHS	CV7	P768XHS						

DM103   BLS672V   MCW Metrobus DR102/3   Alexander AD   H43/30F   1979

DM112-129

MCW Metrobus DR102/28*   Alexander RL   H45/33F   1982   *112 is DR104/5

112	CKS392X	119	ULS619X	126	ULS626X	127	ULS629X	129	TULS635X

DM133-150

MCW Metrobus DR102/33   Alexander RL   H45/33F   1983   DM138 was rebodied in 1985

133	BLS422Y	137	BLS428Y	142	BLS435Y	145	BLS439Y	148	BLS442Y
134	BLS425Y	138	BLS429Y	143	BLS436Y	146	BLS440Y	149	BLS444Y
135	BLS426Y	139	BLS430Y	144	BLS438Y	147	BLS441Y	150	BLS445Y
136	BLS427Y	140	BLS431Y						

DM151-167

MCW Metrobus DR102/39*   Alexander RL   H45/33F   1984   * DM162 is DR102/40
DM164-7 are DR102/47

151	A469GMS	154	A473GMS	157	A476GMS	160	B580MLS	165	B90PKS
152	A471GMS	155	A474GMS	158	A478GMS	162	B586MLS	166	B91PKS
153	A472GMS	156	A475GMS	159	B579MLS	164	B89PKS	167	B92PKS

DM168	G390OGD	MCW Metrobus DR102/72	MCW	H46/31F	1989	
GC1	SCK869	Leyland Tiger TRCTL11/2R	Duple Dominant IV	C53F	1980	Ex Whatman Papers, Maidstone, 1994

GLA23-30

Leyland Atlantean AN68A/2R   Alexander AL   H48/33F   1976-78 Ex Busways, 1993

23w	MVK520R	26	VCU305T	28	VCU308T	29	VCU311T	30	TVCU313T

GLA31	JVK240P	Leyland Atlantean AN68A/1R	Alexander AL	H45/31F	1976	Ex Busways, 1993
GLA33	MVK503R	Leyland Atlantean AN68A/2R	Alexander AL	H48/34F	1976	Ex Busways, 1993
GLA35	SCN272S	Leyland Atlantean AN68A/2R	Alexander AL	H49/37F	1978	Ex Busways, 1993
GLA36	UVK293T	Leyland Atlantean AN68A/2R	Alexander AL	H49/37F	1978	Ex Busways, 1993
GLO1	C807KHS	Leyland Olympian ONLXB/1RH	Alexander RL	DPH47/27F	1986	Ex Kelvin Central, 1993
GLO2	C808KHS	Leyland Olympian ONLXB/1RH	Alexander RL	DPH47/27F	1986	Ex Kelvin Central, 1993
GLO3	C810KHS	Leyland Olympian ONLXB/1RH	Alexander RL	DPH47/27F	1986	Ex Kelvin Central, 1993
GLO4	C113BTS	Leyland Olympian ONLXB/1RV	Alexander RL	H47/32F	1986	Ex Kelvin Central, 1993
GLO5	C114BTS	Leyland Olympian ONLXB/1RV	Alexander RL	H47/32F	1986	Ex Kelvin Central, 1993
GLO6	C115BTS	Leyland Olympian ONLXB/1RV	Alexander RL	H47/32F	1986	Ex Kelvin Central, 1993
GLOC7	C215UPD	Leyland Olympian ONTL11/2RSp	Eastern Coach Works	CH45/24F	1986	Ex Northumbria, 1993

1997 has the arrival of several types of bus for the Greater Glasgow operation. Pictured at Buchanan bus station in Glasgow is the first of a pair of Scania-Irizar coaches that are being used on express services of the Kelvin operation. CS1, P25RFS, is seen working service X5 to Abronhill, to the north of Cumbernauld. *Murdoch Currie*

The main type of vehicle being used on the recently introduced express services towards Cumbernauld is the Volvo B10M with Plaxton Première 320 bodywork. Illustrating the type is CV6, P767XHS on seen on service X3. In addition to the Kelvin name, First Express titles are also carried. *Nick Coleman*

| GM1 | E995WNS | MCW MetroRider MF151/8 | MCW | | B23F | 1987 | |
| GM2 | E996WNS | MCW MetroRider MF151/8 | MCW | | B23F | 1987 | |

GM3-7   MCW MetroRider MF150/55   MCW   B23F   1987

| 3 | E928XYS | 4 | E930XYS | 5 | E932XYS | 6 | E933XYS | 7 | E934XYS |

| GM8 | F238EDS | MCW MetroRider MF154/1 | MCW | | C28F | 1989 | |

GM9-15   MCW MetroRider MF150/55   MCW   B23F   1987

| 9 | E942XYS | 11 | E949XYS | 13 | E952XYS | 14 | E953XYS | 15 | E955XYS |
| 10 | E943XYS | 12 | E950XYS | | | | | | |

GM16	E201BNS	MCW MetroRider MF154/12	MCW		B33F	1988	
GM17	E203BNS	MCW MetroRider MF154/12	MCW		B33F	1988	
GM18	E929XYS	MCW MetroRider MF150/55	MCW		B23F	1987	
GM19	E931XYS	MCW MetroRider MF150/55	MCW		B23F	1987	
GM20	E939XYS	MCW MetroRider MF150/55	MCW		B23F	1987	
GM21	E314YDS	MCW MetroRider MF150/56	MCW		B21FL	1988	
GM22	E315YDS	MCW MetroRider MF150/56	MCW		B21FL	1988	
GM23	E937XYS	MCW MetroRider MF150/55	MCW		B23F	1987	
GM24	F345MGB	MCW MetroRider MF154/22	MCW		B25F	1989	Ex Dublin Bus, 1995
GM25	F290MGB	MCW MetroRider MF154/22	MCW		B25F	1989	Ex Dublin Bus, 1995
GM26	F301MGB	MCW MetroRider MF154/22	MCW		B25F	1989	Ex Dublin Bus, 1995
GM27	F347MGB	MCW MetroRider MF154/22	MCW		B25F	1989	Ex Dublin Bus, 1995
GM28	F303MGB	MCW MetroRider MF150/55	MCW		B25F	1988	Ex Dublin Bus, 1995
GM29	F302MGB	MCW MetroRider MF150/55	MCW		B25F	1989	Ex Dublin Bus, 1995
GM30	F111NPU	MCW MetroRider MF158/4	MCW		DP29F	1988	Ex Colchester, 1991
GM31	F201RVN	MCW MetroRider MF151/14	MCW		DP31F	1988	Ex The Eden, West Auckland, 1993
GM32	F203RVN	MCW MetroRider MF151/14	MCW		DP31F	1988	Ex The Eden, West Auckland, 1993

GM33-37   MCW MetroRider MF150/55   MCW   B23F   1987

| 33 | E940XYS | 34 | E941XYS | 35 | E945XYS | 36 | E948XYS | 37 | E951XYS |

GM38	E307YDS	MCW MetroRider MF150/56	MCW		B22FL	1988	
GM39	E311YDS	MCW MetroRider MF150/56	MCW		B22FL	1988	
GM40	E313YDS	MCW MetroRider MF150/56	MCW		B22FL	1988	

GM41-46   MCW MetroRider MF154/12   MCW   B33F   1988

| 41 | E179BNS | 43 | E181BNS | 44 | E182BNS | 45 | E183BNS | 46 | E184BNS |
| 42 | E180BNS | | | | | | | | |

| GM47 | D471UGA | MCW MetroRider MF150/39 | MCW | | B20F | 1987 | Ex Dublin Bus, 1995 |

GM48-62   MCW MetroRider MF154/12   MCW   B33F   1988

48	E187BNS	51	E191BNS	56	E200BNS	59	E206BNS	61	E208BNS
49	E188BNS	52	E192BNS	57	E202BNS	60	E207BNS	62	E209BNS
50	E190BNS	55	E199BNS	58	E205BNS				

GM63	H844UUA	Optare MetroRider	Optare		B29F	1991	Ex Optare demonstrator, 1991
GM64	F112NPU	MCW MetroRider MF158/3	MCW		B31F	1988	Ex Colchester, 1991
GM65	F113NPU	MCW MetroRider MF158/3	MCW		B31F	1988	Ex Colchester, 1991
GM66	F114NPU	MCW MetroRider MF158/3	MCW		B31F	1988	Ex Colchester, 1991
GM67	F115NPU	MCW MetroRider MF158/3	MCW		B31F	1988	Ex Colchester, 1991
GM68	H398SYG	Optare MetroRider MR03	Optare		B29F	1990	Ex Optare demonstrator, 1991
GM69	F344MGB	MCW MetroRider MF154/22	MCW		B20F	1988	Ex Dublin Bus, 1995
GM70	F346MGB	MCW MetroRider MF154/22	MCW		B20F	1988	Ex Dublin Bus, 1995
GM71	F343MGB	MCW MetroRider MF154/22	MCW		B20F	1988	Ex Dublin Bus, 1995
GM72	E195BNS	MCW MetroRider MF154/12	MCW		B33F	1988	
GM73	E196BNS	MCW MetroRider MF154/12	MCW		B33F	1988	
GM74	E197BNS	MCW MetroRider MF154/12	MCW		B33F	1988	
GM75	E310YDS	MCW MetroRider MF150/56	MCW		B13FL	1988	
GM76	E312YDS	MCW MetroRider MF150/56	MCW		B13FL	1988	
GM77	E316YDS	MCW MetroRider MF150/56	MCW		B13FL	1988	

The GCT name is being retained though the former Glasgow Corporation colours that were latterly used by GCT as seen here on MetroRider GM15, E955XYS are being replaced by the new livery. The vehicle was photographed in late April while heading for Rutherglen. *Mark Bailey*

LA538	VET606S	Leyland Atlantean AN68A/1R	Roe	H45/29F	1978	Ex Cedar Coaches, Bedford, 1995
LA539	CWG720V	Leyland Atlantean AN68A/1R	Alexander AL	H45/29F	1980	Ex Swift, Blaxton, 1995
LA540	CWG771V	Leyland Atlantean AN68A/1R	Roe	H45/29F	1980	Ex Mainline, 1995
LA541	CWG772V	Leyland Atlantean AN68A/1R	Roe	H45/29F	1980	Ex Mainline, 1995
LA542	JKW319W	Leyland Atlantean AN68B/1R	Marshall	H45/29F	1981	Ex Mainline, 1995
LA543	JKW329W	Leyland Atlantean AN68B/1R	Marshall	H45/29F	1981	Ex Mainline, 1995

LA544-51

		Leyland Atlantean AN68C/1R	Roe		H43/31F	1982	Ex Kingston-upon-Hull, 1995

544	WAG370X	546	WAG378X	548	WAG374X	550	WAG376X	551	WAG377X
545	WAG381X	547	WAG373X	549	WAG379X				

LA664	HGD870L	Leyland Atlantean AN68/1R	Alexander AL	H45/29F	1973
LA791	OYS188M	Leyland Atlantean AN68/1R	Alexander AL	H45/31F	1974

LA1034-1139

Leyland Atlantean AN68A/1R   Alexander AL   H45/31F   1976-77

1034	MDS697P	1106	TGE825R	1127	TGG742R	1130	TGG745R	1139	TGG754R
1049	MDS712P	1125	TGE840R	1129	TGG744R	1134	TGG749R		

LA1175-1250

Leyland Atlantean AN68A/1R   Alexander AL   H45/33F   1977-78

1175	UGG394R	1215	XUS586S	1225	XUS596S	1235	XUS606S	1246	XUS617S
1177	UGG396R	1216	XUS587S	1228	XUS599S	1236	XUS607S	1245	XUS616S
1179	UGG398R	1219	XUS590S	1230	XUS601S	1237	XUS608S	1247	XUS618S
1189	WUS567S	1221	XUS592S	1231	XUS602S	1239	XUS610S	1248	XUS619S
1192	WUS570S	1222	XUS593S	1232	XUS603S	1243	XUS614S	1249	XUS620S
1208	XUS579S	1223	XUS594S	1234	XUS605S	1244	XUS615S	1250	XUS621S
1212	XUS583S	1224	XUS595S						

LA1251-1350 Leyland Atlantean AN68A/1R Alexander AL H45/33F 1979-80

1251	FSU68T	1271	FSU88T	1291	FSU108T	1312	LSU369V	1332	LSU389V
1252	FSU69T	1272	FSU89T	1292	FSU109T	1313	LSU370V	1333	LSU390V
1253	FSU70T	1273	FSU90T	1293	FSU110T	1314	LSU371V	1334	LSU391V
1254	FSU71T	1274	FSU91T	1294	FSU111T	1315	LSU372V	1335	LSU392V
1255w	FSU72T	1275	FSU92T	1295	FSU112T	1316	LSU373V	1336	LSU393V
1256	FSU73T	1276	FSU93T	1296w	FSU113T	1317	LSU374V	1337	LSU394V
1257	FSU74T	1277	FSU94T	1297	FSU114T	1318	LSU375V	1338	LSU395V
1258	FSU75T	1278	FSU95T	1298	FSU115T	1319	LSU376V	1339	LSU396V
1259	FSU76T	1279	FSU96T	1299	FSU116T	1320	LSU377V	1340	LSU397V
1260	FSU77T	1280	FSU97T	1300	FSU117T	1321	LSU378V	1341	LSU398V
1261	FSU78T	1281	FSU98T	1301	FSU118T	1322	LSU379V	1342	LSU399V
1262	FSU79T	1282	FSU99T	1302	FSU119T	1323	LSU380V	1343	LSU400V
1263	FSU80T	1283	FSU100T	1303	FSU120T	1324	LSU381V	1344	LSU401V
1264	FSU81T	1284	FSU101T	1304	FSU121T	1325	LSU382V	1345	LSU402V
1265	FSU82T	1285	FSU102T	1305	FSU122T	1326	LSU383V	1346	LSU403V
1266	FSU83T	1286	FSU103T	1306	FSU123T	1328	LSU385V	1347	LSU404V
1267	FSU84T	1287	FSU104T	1307	FSU124T	1329	LSU386V	1348	LSU405V
1268	FSU85T	1288	FSU105T	1309	FSU126T	1330	LSU387V	1349	LSU406V
1269	FSU86T	1289	FSU106T	1310	FSU127T	1331	LSU388V	1350	LSU407V
1270	FSU87T	1290	FSU107T	1311	LSU368V				

LA1351-1449 Leyland Atlantean AN68A/1R Alexander AL H45/33F 1980-81

1351	RDS565W	1370	RDS549W	1389	RDS578W	1409	RDS598W	1432	SUS600W
1352	RDS566W	1371	RDS550W	1390	RDS579W	1410	RDS599W	1433	SUS601W
1353	RDS567W	1372	RDS551W	1391	RDS580W	1411	RDS600W	1434	SUS602W
1354	RDS568W	1373	RDS552W	1392	RDS581W	1412	RDS601W	1435	SUS603W
1355	RDS569W	1374	RDS553W	1393	RDS582W	1413	RDS602W	1436	SUS604W
1356	RDS570W	1375	RDS554W	1394	RDS583W	1414	RDS603W	1437	SUS605W
1357	RDS571W	1376	RDS555W	1395	RDS584W	1415	RDS604W	1438	SUS606W
1358	RDS572W	1377	RDS556W	1396	RDS585W	1416	RDS605W	1439	SUS607W
1359	RDS573W	1378	RDS557W	1397	RDS586W	1417	RDS606W	1440	UGB193W
1360	RDS574W	1379	RDS558W	1398	RDS587W	1418	RDS607W	1441	CUS296X
1361	RDS540W	1380	RDS559W	1399	RDS588W	1419	RDS608W	1442	CUS297X
1362	RDS541W	1381	RDS560W	1400	RDS589W	1420	RDS609W	1443	UGB196W
1363	RDS542W	1382	RDS561W	1402	RDS591W	1422	RDS611W	1444	CUS298X
1364	RDS543W	1383	RDS562W	1403	RDS592W	1424	RDS613W	1445	CUS299X
1365	RDS544W	1384	RDS563W	1404	RDS593W	1425	RDS614W	1446	CUS300X
1366	RDS545W	1385	RDS564W	1405	RDS594W	1426	RDS615W	1447	CUS301X
1367	RDS546W	1386	RDS575W	1406	RDS595W	1428	RDS617W	1448	CUS302X
1368	RDS547W	1387	RDS576W	1408	RDS597W	1429	RDS618W	1449	UGB202W
1369	RDS548W	1388	RDS577W						

LO2-10 Leyland Olympian ONLTL11/1R Roe H44/31F* 1981 *LO8 is H46/31F

2	CGG825X	6	CGG829X	8	CGG831X	9	CGG832X	10	CGG833X

LO12-16 Leyland Olympian ONTL11/1R Eastern Coach Works H46/31F 1982

12	CGG835X	13	CGG836X	14	CGG837X	15	CGG838X	16	CGG839X

LO17	ESU4X	Leyland Olympian ONTL11/1R	Alexander RH	H47/29F	1982
LO18	ESU5X	Leyland Olympian ONTL11/1R	Alexander RH	H47/29F	1982
LO19	ESU6X	Leyland Olympian ONTL11/1R	Alexander RH	H47/29F	1982
LO21	ESU8X	Leyland Olympian ONTL11/1R	Alexander RH	H47/29F	1982

LO22-46 Leyland Olympian ONTL11/1R* Eastern Coach Works H47/31F 1983 *LO30 has a Gardner engine

22	KGG142Y	29	KGG149Y	34	KGG154Y	39	KGG159Y	43	A372TGB
23	KGG143Y	30	KGG150Y	35	KGG155Y	40	KGG160Y	44	A373TGB
25	KGG145Y	31	KGG151Y	36	KGG156Y	41	KGG161Y	45	A374TGB
26	KGG146Y	32	KGG152Y	37	KGG157Y	42	A371TGB	46	A375TGB
27	KGG147Y	33	KGG153Y	38	KGG158Y				

LO48	J137FYS	Leyland Olympian ON2R50G13Z4	Leyland	H47/31F	1991
LO49	J138FYS	Leyland Olympian ON2R50G13Z4	Leyland	H47/31F	1991

Repaints into the new red colours of Greater Glasgow include some of the large numbers of Leyland Atlanteans. Representing the type is LA1395, RDS584W which was the first to be completed. It is seen at the Baillieston terminus of service 62. *Billy Nicol*

Now resplendent in its new colours is Leyland Olympian LO90, L190UNS. Delivered in 1993, this batch numbers 52 and forms the largest batch of the type. *Billy Nicol*

LO50-101   Leyland Olympian ON2R50C13V3   Alexander RL   H47/31F   1993

50	K350SDS	61	L161UNS	72	L172UNS	82	L182UNS	92	L192UNS
51	L551USU	62	L162UNS	73	L173UNS	83	L183UNS	93	L193UNS
52	L552USU	63	L163UNS	74	L174UNS	84	L184UNS	94	L194UNS
53	L553USU	64	L164UNS	75	L175UNS	85	L185UNS	95	L195UNS
54	L554USU	65	L165UNS	76	L176UNS	86	L186UNS	96	L196UNS
55	L155UNS	66	L166UNS	77	L177UNS	87	L187UNS	97	L197UNS
56	L156UNS	67	L167UNS	78	L178UNS	88	L188UNS	98	L198UNS
57	L157UNS	68	L168UNS	79	L179UNS	89	L189UNS	99	L199UNS
58	L158UNS	69	L169UNS	80	L180UNS	90	L190UNS	100	L202UNS
59	L159UNS	70	L170UNS	81	L181UNS	91	L191UNS	101	L201UNS
60	L160UNS	71	L171UNS						

LOC102	C448BKM	Leyland Olympian ONTL11/2RSp	Eastern Coach Works	CH45/28F	1985	Ex Northumbria, 1995	
LOC103	C212UPD	Leyland Olympian ONTL11/2RSp	Eastern Coach Works	CH45/28F	1985	Ex Northumbria, 1995	
LOC104	C213UPD	Leyland Olympian ONTL11/2RSp	Eastern Coach Works	CH45/28F	1985	Ex Northumbria, 1995	
LOC105	C211UPD	Leyland Olympian ONTL11/2RSp	Eastern Coach Works	CH45/28F	1985	Ex Northumbria, 1995	
LO111	ULS96X	Leyland Olympian ONLXB/1R	Eastern Coach Works	H45/32F	1982		
LO112	ULS97X	Leyland Olympian ONLXB/1R	Eastern Coach Works	H45/32F	1982		
LO113	ULS98X	Leyland Olympian ONLXB/1R	Eastern Coach Works	H45/32F	1982		
LO114	ULS99X	Leyland Olympian ONLXB/1R	Eastern Coach Works	H45/32F	1982		
LO115	ALS120Y	Leyland Olympian ONLXB/1R	Alexander RL	H45/32F	1983		
LO116	ALS121Y	Leyland Olympian ONLXB/1R	Alexander RL	H45/32F	1983		
LO117	ALS130Y	Leyland Olympian ONLXB/1R	Alexander RL	H45/32F	1983		
LO118	ALS131Y	Leyland Olympian ONLXB/1R	Alexander RL	H45/32F	1983		
LO119	C112BTS	Leyland Olympian ONLXB/1RV	Alexander RL	H47/32F	1986	Ex Strathtay, 1989	
LO123	A981FLS	Leyland Olympian ONLXB/1R	Alexander RL	H45/32F	1983	Ex Fife Scottish, 1989	
LO124	A982FLS	Leyland Olympian ONLXB/1R	Alexander RL	H45/32F	1983	Ex Fife Scottish, 1989	
LO125	A983FLS	Leyland Olympian ONLXB/1R	Alexander RL	H45/32F	1983	Ex Fife Scottish, 1989	
LO126	A984FLS	Leyland Olympian ONLXB/1R	Alexander RL	H45/32F	1983	Ex Fife Scottish, 1989	

M73	E308YDS	MCW MetroRider MF150/56	MCW	B13FL	1988	
M74	E309YDS	MCW MetroRider MF150/56	MCW	B15FL	1988	

MB1-5   MCW Metrobus DR101/5   MCW   H46/31F   1979

1	GGA750T	2	GGA751T	3	GGA752T	4	GGA753T	5	GGA754T

MB6-20   MCW Metrobus DR102/26   Alexander RH   H45/33F   1982

6	EUS101X	9	EUS104X	12	EUS107X	15	EUS110X	18	EUS113X
7	EUS102X	10	EUS105X	13	EUS108X	16	EUS111X	19	EUS114X
8	EUS103X	11	EUS106X	14	EUS109X	17	EUS112X	20	EUS115X

MB21-30   MCW Metrobus DR102/31   MCW   H46/31F   1983

21	KGG162Y	23	KGG164Y	25	KGG166Y	27	KGG168Y	29	KGG170Y
22	KGG163Y	24	KGG165Y	26	KGG167Y	28	KGG169Y	30	KGG171Y

MB31-43   MCW Metrobus DR102/36   MCW   H46/31F*   1983   *MB35 is H46/23FL

31	MUS309Y	34	MUS312Y	37	A731RNS	40	A734RNS	42	A736RNS
32	MUS310Y	35	MUS313Y	38	A732RNS	41	A735RNS	43	A737RNS
33	MUS311Y	36	A730RNS	39	A733RNS				

MB44	A738RNS	MCW Metrobus DR132/4	MCW	H46/31F	1983	
MB45	A739RNS	MCW Metrobus DR132/4	MCW	H46/31F	1983	

MB46-70   MCW Metrobus DR102/072   MCW   H46/31F*   1989   *MBC62-6 are DPH43/29F

46	G384OGD	51	G389OGD	56	G394OGD	61	G399OGD	66	G404OGD
47	G385OGD	52	G390OGD	57	G395OGD	62	G400OGD	67	G405OGD
48	G386OGD	53	G391OGD	58	G396OGD	63	G401OGD	68	G406OGD
49	G387OGD	54	G392OGD	59	G397OGD	64	G402OGD	69	G407OGD
50	G388OGD	55	G393OGD	60	G398OGD	65	G403OGD	70	G408OGD

Eight low floor East Lancashire Spryte-bodied Dennis Darts were delivered at the start of 1997 and carry GCT lettering. Pictured in Chambers Street, Clydeside. *Billy Nicol*

Strathclyde's Buses dual-sourced double-deck buses the early Leyland Olympians being delivered along-side MCW Metrobuses. The latter are concentrated at Possilpark depot which has not yet started repainting into the latest colours. *M E Lyons*

MD1-8

		Dennis Dart SLF		East Lancashire Spryte		B37F	1997		
1	P852VUS	3	P854VUS	5	P856VUS	7	P858VUS	8	P859VUS
2	P853VUS	4	P855VUS	6	P857VUS				

MD9	P860VUS	Dennis Dart SFD412	Plaxton Pointer	B40F	1997
MD10	P861VUS	Dennis Dart SFD412	Plaxton Pointer	B40F	1997

MD13-18

		Dennis Dart 9.8SDL3017		Alexander Dash		B41F	1992	Ex Stagecoach Scotland, 1992	
13	J513FPS	15	J515FPS	16	J516FPS	17	J517FPS	18	J518FPS
14	J514FPS								

MD19-28

		Dennis Dart SLF		Plaxton Pointer		B40F	1997		
19	P626WSU	21	P628WSU	23	P630WSU	25	P632WSU	27	P634WSU
20	P627WSU	22	P629WSU	24	P631WSU	26	P633WSU	28	P635WSU

MD29-43

		Dennis Dart SLF		UVG Urbanstar		B39F	1997		
29	P2UVG	32	P750WSU	35	P753WSU	38	P757WSU	41	P760WSU
30	P748WSU	33	P751WSU	36	P754WSU	39	P758WSU	42	P761WSU
31	P749WSU	34	P752WSU	37	P756WSU	40	P759WSU	43	P762WSU

MM35	D472UGA	MCW MetroRider MF150/39	MCW	B20F	1987	Ex Dublin Bus, 1995
MM36	D473UGA	MCW MetroRider MF150/39	MCW	B20F	1987	Ex Dublin Bus, 1995
MM37	D474UGA	MCW MetroRider MF150/39	MCW	B20F	1987	Ex Dublin Bus, 1995
MM38	D475UGA	MCW MetroRider MF150/39	MCW	B20F	1987	Ex Dublin Bus, 1995
MM39	E55LBK	MCW MetroRider MF150/70	MCW	B25F	1988	Ex Southampton, 1990
MM50	E935XYS	MCW MetroRider MF150/55	MCW	B23F	1987	Ex Clydeside 2000, 1995
MM53	E938XYS	MCW MetroRider MF150/55	MCW	B23F	1987	Ex Clydeside 2000, 1995
MM59	E944XYS	MCW MetroRider MF150/55	MCW	B23F	1987	Ex Clydeside 2000, 1995
MM62	E947XYS	MCW MetroRider MF150/55	MCW	B23F	1987	Ex Clydeside 2000, 1995
MM69	E954XYS	MCW MetroRider MF150/55	MCW	B23F	1987	Ex Clydeside 2000, 1995
MM71	E956XYS	MCW MetroRider MF150/55	MCW	B23F	1987	Ex Clydeside 2000, 1995
MM88	E185BNS	MCW MetroRider MF154/12	MCW	B33F	1988	
MM89	E186BNS	MCW MetroRider MF154/12	MCW	B33F	1988	
MM92	E189BNS	MCW MetroRider MF154/12	MCW	B33F	1988	
MM96	E193BNS	MCW MetroRider MF154/12	MCW	B33F	1988	
MM97	E194BNS	MCW MetroRider MF154/12	MCW	B33F	1988	
MM107	E204BNS	MCW MetroRider MF154/12	MCW	B33F	1988	

MV11	L81CNY	Volvo B6-9M	Marshall C33	DP36F	1994	Ex Bebb, Llantwit Fardre, 1997
MV12	L82CNY	Volvo B6-9M	Marshall C33	DP36F	1994	Ex Bebb, Llantwit Fardre, 1997
MV13	L85CNY	Volvo B6-9M	Marshall C33	DP36F	1994	Ex Bebb, Llantwit Fardre, 1997
MV14	L86CNY	Volvo B6-9M	Marshall C33	DP36F	1994	Ex Bebb, Llantwit Fardre, 1997
MV15	N103CKU	Volvo B6-9.9M	Alexander Dash	B40F	1995	Ex Mainline, 1997
MV16	N104CKU	Volvo B6-9.9M	Alexander Dash	B40F	1995	Ex Mainline, 1997

MV21-28

		Volvo B6-9.9M		Alexander Dash		B40F	1994	27/8 ex Loch Lomond Coaches, 1996	
21	L101WYS	23	L103WYS	25	L105XSU	27	M870DYS	28	M871DYS
22	L102WYS	24	L104WYS	26	L106XSU				

SD1-5

		Dennis Dorchester SDA804		Alexander TS		B53F	1983		
1	A101RGE	2	A102RGE	3	A103RGE	4	A104RGE	5	A105RGE

SL121	MHS39P	Leyland Leopard PSU3C/3R	Alexander AYS	B53F	1976	
SL127	GMS307S	Leyland Leopard PSU3E/4R	Alexander AYS	B53F	1978	Ex Midland Scottish, 1992
SL128	FSF728S	Leyland Leopard PSU3E/4R	Duple Dominant I	DP53F	1978	Ex Midland Bluebird, 1992
SL129	GMS298S	Leyland Leopard PSU3E/4R	Alexander AYS	B53F	1978	Ex Midland Bluebird, 1993
SL131	GMS281S	Leyland Leopard PSU3E/4R	Alexander AYS	B53F	1978	Ex Midland Scottish, 1992
SL132	YFS92S	Leyland Leopard PSU3E/4R	Alexander AYS	B53F	1977	Ex Fife Scottish, 1990
SL133	GMS304S	Leyland Leopard PSU3E/4R	Alexander AYS	B53F	1978	Ex Midland Bluebird, 1993

Opposite: **1997 has seen an influx of single deck buses from a variety of manufacturers. The upper picture shows one of SS9, one of four Scania L113CRLs with Wright Axcess-ultralow coachwork. Ten Alexander Strider-bodied Volvo B10Bs joined the Kelvin fleet in 1993. Pictured at Airdrie is SV309, L309VSU now carrying the new Kelvin livery.** *Billy Nicol*

The arrival of Dennis Darts for the Kelvin operation have seen the UVG batch placed into service on a new Kelvin route that duplicates the main service that Western Buses acquired from A1 Service. The Plaxton-bodied vehicles are normally found in the central area and are represented in this edition by MD25, P632WSU. *Nick Coleman*

SL137	WSU437S	Leyland Leopard PSU3C/3R	Alexander AYS	B53F	1977	
SL138	WSU438S	Leyland Leopard PSU3C/3R	Alexander AYS	B53F	1977	
SL140	WSU440S	Leyland Leopard PSU3C/3R	Alexander AYS	B53F	1977	
SL147	WSU447S	Leyland Leopard PSU3C/3R	Alexander AYS	B53F	1977	
SL152	YHS282S	Leyland Leopard PSU3E/4R	Duple Dominant E	DP55F	1977	Ex Midland Scottish, 1992
SL153	WSU453S	Leyland Leopard PSU3C/3R	Alexander AYS	B53F	1977	
SL155	GMS288S	Leyland Leopard PSU3E/4R	Alexander AYS	B53F	1978	
SL156	GMS290S	Leyland Leopard PSU3E/4R	Alexander AYS	B53F	1978	
SL157	GMS293S	Leyland Leopard PSU3E/4R	Alexander AYS	B53F	1978	
SL190	ULS317T	Leyland Leopard PSU3E/4R	Alexander AYS	B53F	1979	

SL240-246

Leyland Leopard PSU3F/4R   Alexander AYS   B53F   1981

| 240 | PUS150W | 242 | PUS152W | 244 | PUS154W | 245 | PUS155W | 246 | PUS156W |
| 241 | PUS151W | 243 | PUS153W | | | | | | |

SL247-257

Leyland Leopard PSU3G/4R   Alexander AYS   B53F   1981

247	TSU647W	250	TSU650W	252	TSU652W	254	TSU644W	256	TSU646W
248	TSU648W	251	TSU651W	253	TSU653W	255	TSU645W	257	TSU643W
549	TSU649W								

SL263-272

Leyland Leopard PSU3G/4R   Alexander AYS   B53F   1982-83

| 263 | LUS433Y | 265 | LUS435Y | 267 | LUS437Y | 269 | LUS439Y | 271 | LUS431Y |
| 264 | LUS434Y | 266 | LUS436Y | 268 | LUS438Y | 270 | LUS440Y | 272 | LUS432Y |

SN27	WBN467T	Leyland National 11351A/1R (Volvo)		B49F	1979	Ex Green, Kirkintilloch, 1993
SN38	MDS862V	Leyland National 2 NL116L11/1R (Volvo) E L Greenway (1994)	B49F	1980	
SN44	WAS769V	Leyland National 2 NL116L11/1R (Volvo)		B52F	1980	
SN50	YFS307W	Leyland National 2 NL116L11/1R (Volvo)		B52F	1980	
SN60	AST160W	Leyland National 2 NL116L11/1R (Volvo)		B49F	1981	
SN61	UFG50S	Leyland National 11351A/2R (Volvo)		B52F	1977	Ex Morrow, Glasgow, 1992

In 1995 Strathclyde Buses acquired the planned operations of Stagecoach Glasgow in a deal where Stagecoach acquired a 20% holding in the company. Subsequently that holding was sold to Firstbus who also acquired the remainder of the shares. Eighteen Volvo B10Ms expected to be operated by Stagecoach Glasgow were placed in service with Strathclyde. These are now receiving the new Greater Glasgow livery as illustrated by SV428, M428RRN seen at Enoch Square in Glasgow.
Murdoch Currie

SS1	H912HRO	Scania N113CRB	Plaxton Verde	B47F	1991	Ex Scania demonstrator, 1993
SS2	J113XSX	Scania N113CRB	Plaxton Verde	B51F	1992	Ex Scania demonstrator, 1993
SS3	TIB8511	Scania K93CRB	East Lancashire	DP51F	1993	
SS4	TIB8512	Scania K93CRB	East Lancashire	DP51F	1993	
SS5	TIB8513	Scania K93CRB	East Lancashire	DP51F	1993	
SS6	P106MFS	Scania L113CRL	Wright Axcess-ultralow	B47F	1996	
SS7	P107MFS	Scania L113CRL	Wright Axcess-ultralow	B47F	1996	
SS8	P108MFS	Scania L113CRL	Wright Axcess-ultralow	B47F	1996	
SS9	P109MFS	Scania L113CRL	Wright Axcess-ultralow	B47F	1996	

ST318-327

						Leyland Tiger TRBL11/2R		Alexander TS		B53F		1983	
318	OUS18Y	320	OUS20Y	322	OUS12Y	324	OUS14Y	326	OUS16Y
319	OUS19Y	321	OUS11Y	323	OUS13Y	325	OUS15Y	327	OUS17Y

ST333-398

Leyland Tiger TRBLXB/2RH Alexander TS B53F 1984-87

333	A33VDS	345	A25VDS	357	B257BYS	369	B249BYS	388	D373OSU
334	A34VDS	346	A26VDS	358	B258BYS	370	B250BYS	389	D374OSU
335	A35VDS	347	A27VDS	359	B259BYS	371	B251BYS	390	D375OSU
336	A36VDS	348	A28VDS	360	B260BYS	372	B252BYS	391	D376OSU
337	A37VDS	349	A29VDS	361	B261BYS	373	B241BYS	392	D377OSU
338	A38VDS	350	A30VDS	362	B262BYS	374	B242BYS	393	D378OSU
339	A39VDS	351	A31VDS	363	B263BYS	375	B243BYS	394	D379OSU
340	A40VDS	352	A32VDS	364	B244BYS	384	D369OSU	395	D380OSU
341	A21VDS	353	B253BYS	365	B245BYS	385	D370OSU	396	D381OSU
342	A22VDS	354	B254BYS	366	B246BYS	386	D371OSU	397	D382OSU
343	A23VDS	355	B255BYS	367	B247BYS	387	D372OSU	398	D383OSU
344	A24VDS	356	B256BYS	368	B248BYS				

SV301-310

Volvo B10B-58 Alexander Strider B51F 1993

301	L301VSU	303	L303VSU	305	L305VSU	307	L307VSU	309	L309VSU
302	L302VSU	304	L304VSU	306	L306VSU	308	L308VSU	310	L310VSU

SV401	LGE724Y	Volvo B58-56	Duple Dominant	B55F	1982	Ex McKenna, Uddingston, 1992
SV402	F706WCS	Volvo B10M-56	Duple Dominant	B53F	1988	Ex Golden Eagle, Salsburgh, 1994
SV409	G432UHS	Volvo B10M-55	Plaxton Derwent II	B55F	1990	Ex Golden Eagle, Salsburgh, 1994

SV411-428

Volvo B10M-55 Alexander PS DP48F 1994 Ex Stagecoach, 1995

411	M778PRS	415	M765PRS	419	M769PRS	423	M773PRS	426	M776PRS
412	M779PRS	416	M766PRS	420	M770PRS	424	M774PRS	427	M877PRS
413	M780PRS	417	M767PRS	421	M771PRS	425	M775PRS	428	M428RRN
414	M781PRS	418	M768PRS	422	M772PRS				

SV429-488

Volvo B10M-55 Alexander PS B49F 1995-96

429	N929LSU	441	N941LSU	453	N953LSU	465	N965LSU	477	N977LSU
430	N930LSU	442	N942LSU	454	N954LSU	466	N966LSU	478	N978LSU
431	N931LSU	443	N943LSU	455	N955LSU	467	N967LSU	479	N979LSU
432	N932LSU	444	N944LSU	456	N956LSU	468	N968LSU	480	N980LSU
433	N933LSU	445	N945LSU	457	N957LSU	469	N969LSU	481	N981LSU
434	N934LSU	446	N946LSU	458	N958LSU	470	N970LSU	482	N982LSU
435	N935LSU	447	N947LSU	459	N959LSU	471	N971LSU	483	N983LSU
436	N936LSU	448	N948LSU	460	N960LSU	472	N972LSU	484	N984LSU
437	N937LSU	449	N949LSU	461	N961LSU	473	N973LSU	485	N985LSU
438	N938LSU	450	N950LSU	462	N962LSU	474	N974LSU	486	N986LSU
439	N939LSU	451	N951LSU	463	N963LSU	475	N975LSU	487	N987LSU
440	N940LSU	452	N952LSU	464	N964LSU	476	N976LSU	488	N988LSU

SV489-518

Volvo B10M-55 Alexander PS B49F 1996

489	N89OGG	495	N95OGG	501	N121OGG	507	N127OGG	513	N133OGG
490	N190OGG	496	N96OGG	502	N122OGG	508	N128OGG	514	N134OGG
491	N91OGG	497	N97OGG	503	N123OGG	509	N129OGG	515	N135OGG
492	N92OGG	498	N98OGG	504	N124OGG	510	N130OGG	516	N136OGG
493	N93OGG	499	N199OGG	505	N125OGG	511	N131OGG	517	N137OGG
494	N94OGG	500	N120OGG	506	N126OGG	512	N132OGG	518	N138OGG

SV519-549

Volvo B10M-55 Alexander PS B49F 1996-97

519	P519PYS	526	P526PYS	532	P532TYS	538	P538TYS	544	P544TYS
520	P520PYS	527	P527PYS	533	P533TYS	539	P539TYS	545	P545TYS
521	P521PYS	528	P528PYS	534	P534TYS	540	P540TYS	546	P546TYS
522	P522PYS	529	P529PYS	535	P535TYS	541	P541TYS	547	P547TYS
523	P523PYS	530	P530PYS	536	P536TYS	542	P542TYS	548	P548TYS
524	P524PYS	531	P531TYS	537	P537TYS	543	P543TYS	549	P549TYS
525	P525PYS								

SV550	M10ULF	Volvo B10L	Alexander Ultra	B42F	1995	Ex Volvo demonstrator, 1996
SV551	M394MRW	Volvo B10L	Alexander Ultra	B44F	1995	Ex Volvo demonstrator, 1996
SV552	N141VDU	Volvo B10L	Alexander Ultra	B43F	1995	Ex Volvo demonstrator, 1996

SV553-558

Volvo B10L Wright Liberator B43F 1996

553	P188UNS	555	P190UNS	556	P191UNS	557	P192UNS	558	P193UNS
554	P189UNS								

SV559	P761XHS	Volvo B10L	Wright Liberator	B43F	1997
SV560	P762XHS	Volvo B10L	Wright Liberator	B43F	1997
SV561	P763XHS	Volvo B10L	Wright Liberator	B43F	1997
SV562	P764XHS	Volvo B10L	Wright Liberator	B43F	1997
SV563	P774XHS	Volvo B10BLE	Northen Counties	B43F	1997

VO1	M939EYS	Volvo Olympian YN2RV18V3	Alexander RH	H45/29F	1995
VO2	M940EYS	Volvo Olympian YN2RC16V3	Alexander RH	H45/29F	1995
VO3	M941EYS	Volvo Olympian YN2RC16V3	Northen Counties Palatine2	H47/30F	1995
VO4	M942EYS	Volvo Olympian YN2RC16V3	Northen Counties Palatine2	H47/30F	1995

More than a hundred and thirty Volvo B10Ms were taken into stock between 1995 and the start of 1997. Many of these have been allocated to Kelvin depots. One to arrive in the new colours was SV540, P540TYS, pictured in heavy rain in the Spring of 1997. *Billy Nicol*

VO27-33

				Volvo Olympian YN2RV18Z4		Alexander Royale RH		H45/29F		1994	
27	L827YGA	29	L829YGA	31	L831YGA	32	L832YGA	33	L833YGA
28	L828YGA	30	L830YGA						

VO34-43

				Volvo Olympian YN2RV18Z4		Alexander Royale RL		H47/32F		1994	
34	M834DUS	36	M836DUS	38	M838DUS	40	M840DUS	42	M842DUS
35	M835DUS	37	M837DUS	39	M839DUS	41	M841DUS	43	M843DUS

VO44-83

				Volvo Olympian YN2RV18V3		Alexander RL		H47/32F		1996	
44	N944SOS	52	N952SOS	60	N960SOS	68	N968SOS	76	P176TGD
45	N945SOS	53	N953SOS	61	N961SOS	69	N969SOS	77	P177TGD
46	N946SOS	54	N954SOS	62	N962SOS	70	N970SOS	78	P178TGD
47	N947SOS	55	N955SOS	63	N963SOS	71	N971SOS	79	P179TGD
48	N948SOS	56	N956SOS	64	N964SOS	72	N972SOS	80	P180TGD
49	N949SOS	57	N957SOS	65	N965SOS	73	N973SOS	81	P181TGD
50	N950SOS	58	N958SOS	66	N966SOS	74	P174TGD	82	P182TGD
51	N951SOS	59	N959SOS	67	N967SOS	75	P175TGD	83	P183TGD

VO84-103

				Volvo Olympian YN2RV18V3		Alexander RL		H47/32F		1996	
84	P184TGD	88	P188TGD	92	P192TGD	96	P196TGD	100	P201TGD
85	P185TGD	89	P189TGD	93	P193TGD	97	P197TGD	101	P202TGD
86	P186TGD	90	P190TGD	94	P194TGD	98	P198TGD	102	P203TGD
87	P187TGD	91	P191TGD	95	P195TGD	99	P199TGD	103	P204TGD

Sixty Alexander-bodied Volvo Olympians were delivered to Strathclyde Buses in 1996, and while the later ones, like VO99, P199TGD, were delivered in the new colours, many of the earlier type have now been repainted. Like most deliveries to the fleet in recent times, these buses feature electronic destination displays. *Billy Nicol*

VO104-153

		Volvo Olympian		Alexander RL		H47/32F	1997	
104	P585WSU	114	P595WSU	124	P606WSU	134	P616WSU	144
105	P586WSU	115	P596WSU	125	P607WSU	135	P617WSU	145
106	P587WSU	116	P597WSU	126	P608WSU	136	P618WSU	146
107	P588WSU	117	P598WSU	127	P609WSU	137	P619WSU	147
108	P589WSU	118	P599WSU	128	P610WSU	138	P620WSU	148
109	P590WSU	119	P601WSU	129	P611WSU	139	P621WSU	149
110	P591WSU	120	P602WSU	130	P612WSU	140	P622WSU	150
111	P592WSU	121	P603WSU	131	P613WSU	141	P623WSU	151
112	P593WSU	122	P604WSU	132	P614WSU	142	P624WSU	152
113	P594WSU	123	P605WSU	133	P615WSU	143	P625WSU	153

Previous Registrations:

755SBH	A741RNS	F301MGB	89-D-15	WLT357	TFS318Y
A9KCB	A119GLS, WLT770	F302MGB	89-D-12	WLT388	VTY131Y
BXI521	B287KPF	F303MGB	88-D-31371	WLT408	TFS321Y
CSU932	C259SPC	F343MGB	88-D-31235	WLT677	A125ESG
D471UGA	87-D-22542	F344MGB	88-D-31237	WLT678	A128ESG
D472UGA	87-D-22541	F345MGB	89-D-13	WLT741	TFS319Y, WLT371, PGE442Y
D473UGA	87-D-28222	F346MGB	88-D-31238	WLT760	BSG548W
D474UGA	87-D-28221	F347MGB	88-D-31372	WLT770	NBD106Y
D475UGA	87-D-28223	FSF728S	CFS112S, TSV612	WLT910	BLS106Y
F290MGB	89-D-14	KCB758	A104EPA	WLT976	NBD107Y
SCK869	UTV23V				

Livery: Red.

GREEN LINE

J Burns, 24 Glendower Way, Foxbar, Paisley, Renfrewshire, PA2 0TH

D304MHS	Renault-Dodge S56	Alexander AM	B21F	1986	Ex Puma, Erskine, 1996
D243NCS	Renault-Dodge S56	Alexander AM	B25F	1987	Ex Western, 1996
D831RYS	Renault-Dodge S56	Alexander AM	B25F	1987	Ex Darwen Minibus Services, 1996
E194HFV	Renault-Dodge S46	Northen Counties	B22F	1987	Ex Classic, Annfield Plain, 1996
E647DCK	Renault-Dodge S56	Dormobile	B25F	1987	Ex GMN, 1996
E152RNY	Freight Rover Sherpa	Carlyle Citybus 2	B20F	1987	Ex Dalybus, Eccles, 1995
E108LCW	Renault-Dodge S56	Northen Counties	B22F	1988	Ex Blackpool, 1996
E112LCW	Renault-Dodge S56	Northen Counties	B22F	1988	Ex Blackpool, 1996
F953CUA	Freight Rover Sherpa	Carlyle Citybus 2	B18F	1988	Ex Phil Anslow Travel, Garndiffaith, 1994
G144LRM	Mercedes-Benz 609D	Reeve Burgess Beaver	B20F	1989	Ex Glossopdale, Hyde, 1995
G145LRM	Mercedes-Benz 609D	Reeve Burgess Beaver	B20F	1989	Ex GMN, 1995
G180ORJ	Renault S56	Dormobile Routemaker	B25F	1989	Ex Bernard, New Mills, 1995

Livery: Green and white

Three of these Alexander-bodied Renault-Dodge S56s are in use for the Green Line operation based on Paisley. New to Kelvin Central D304MHS is seen in a livery of green and white with black window surrounds. The fleetname is features yellow shading only partly visible in this picture.
Phillip Stephenson

H-A-D COACHES

HAD Coaches Ltd, 34 Burnbrae Road, Shotts, North Lanarkshire, ML7 5DW

248FOU	Leyland Leopard PSU5A/4R	Plaxton Viewmaster	C57F	1976	Ex John Smith, Shotts, 1995
OSJ617R	Leyland Leopard PSU3C/3R	Alexander AY	B53F	1976	Ex Eadie Rentals, Cambuslang, 1994
RCS702R	Seddon Pennine 7	Alexander AT	C49F	1977	Ex Eadie Rentals, Cambuslang, 1994
FNS979S	Leyland Leopard PSU3E/3R	Plaxton Supreme III	C53F	1977	Ex Stuarts of Carluke, 1997
UJT366	Volvo B10M-61	Duple Goldliner IV	C57F	1981	Ex Stuarts of Carluke, 1995
B404NJF	Ford Transit 190	Rootes	B16F	1985	Ex Midland Fox, 1995
C452SJU	Ford Transit 190	Robin Hood	B16F	1985	Ex Midland Fox, 1995
F395DOA	Peugeot-Talbot Pullman	Talbot	B19FL	1989	Ex John Smith, Shotts, 1993
F466KDB	Mercedes-Benz 507D	Made-to-Measure	DP20F	1990	Ex John Morrow Coaches, Clydebank, 1995
J32NKJ	Ford Transit VE6	Ford	M14	1992	Ex Avis Rentals, 1993
CMS196	Mercedes-Benz 709D	Dormobile Routemaker	B25FL	1994	
L854WDS	Mercedes-Benz 709D	WS Wessex II	B18FL	1994	
L143XDS	Mercedes-Benz 709D	WS Wessex II	B18FL	1994	
L144XDS	Mercedes-Benz 709D	WS Wessex II	B18FL	1994	
L145XDS	Mercedes-Benz 709D	WS Wessex II	B18FL	1994	
L146XDS	Mercedes-Benz 709D	WS Wessex II	B18FL	1994	
OTB55	Volvo B10M-62	Van Hool Alizée	C53F	1994	Ex Park's, Hamilton, 1996
P2HAD	Volvo B10M-62	Plaxton Première 3.0	C53F	1997	
P3HAD	Volvo B10M-62	Plaxton Première 3.0	C53F	1997	

Previous Registrations:

248FOU	OVJ201R	OTB55	LSK830, L632AYS
CMS196	L972VGE	UJT366	CNS549X
FNS979S	VMJ959S, FSU374, USR325S, RIJ58		

Livery: White and silver

UJT366 is a Volvo B10M with Duple Goldliner bodywork seen here at Buchanan Street bus station operating for H-A-D Coaches in a white and silver livery. The unusual lines of the Goldliner IV were particularly favoured by Scottish Operators including the Scottish Bus Group. *Phillip Stephenson*

HARTE BUSES

P Harte, Unit 1, Ocean Terminal, Patrick Street, Greenock, Renfrewshire, PA16 8UU

IIB3728	Bedford YLQ	Plaxton Supreme IV	C45F	1980	Ex Ashton Coach Hire, Gourock, 1993
IIB5213	Mercedes-Benz 811D	Reeve Burgess Beaver	B25F	1989	Ex Reeve Burgess demonstrator, 1989
IIB7633	Mercedes-Benz 709D	Dormobile Routemaker	B29F	1992	
IIB6819	MAN 11.190	Optare Vecta	B40F	1994	Ex MAN demonstrator, 1995
M275FNS	Mercedes-Benz 811D	WS Wessex II	B33F	1995	
P938YSB	Mercedes-Benz 811D	Plaxton Beaver	B33F	1997	

Previous Registrations:

IIB3728	LUB970V	IIB6819	L822XMR
IIB5213	F158DKU	IIB7633	K664NGB

Named vehicles: IIB5213, *Solar Rider;* IIB6015, *Magic Rider;* IIB6819, *Mega Rider;* IIB7633, *Kool Rider;* M275FNS, *Sonic Rider.*

Livery: Brown, fawn and red

In comparison to minibuses, the Optare Vecta may seem large which may explain why IIB6819 of Harte Buses carries Mega Rider lettering. The MAN 11.180 was used for about a year by the chassis supplier for demonstration purposes before joining Harte Buses. *Phillip Stephenson*

HENDERSON TRAVEL

J, D & H Henderson, Unit 2, Whistleberry Industrial Estate, Hamilton, North Lanarkshire, ML3 OPR

LIW3462	Leyland Leopard PSU3B/4R	Willowbrook Warrior (1991)	B48F	1973	Ex Beak, Cosford, 1991
HCS818N	Leyland Leopard PSU3/3R	Alexander AYS	B53F	1975	Ex Northern Scottish, 1990
TSJ90S	Leyland Leopard PSU3E/4R	Alexander AY	B53F	1978	Ex Clydeside, 1996
C808SDY	Mercedes-Benz L608D	Alexander AM	B20F	1986	Ex Red & White, 1997
D556RCK	Mercedes-Benz L608D	Reeve Burgess	B20F	1986	Ex Avondale, Greenock, 1997
E635LSF	Mercedes-Benz 609D	Alexander AM	C25F	1988	
E504YSU	Mercedes-Benz 709D	Alexander AM	B25F	1988	Ex Caldwell, Greenock, 1989
E508YSU	Mercedes-Benz 609D	Alexander AM	B25F	1988	Ex Caldwell, Greenock, 1989
E766MSC	Mercedes-Benz 609D	Alexander AM	C25F	1988	Ex Wilson, Port Glasgow, 1989
E156XHS	Volvo B10M-56	Plaxton Derwent II	B54F	1988	Ex Hutchison, Overtown, 1995
E157XHS	Volvo B10M-56	Plaxton Derwent II	B54F	1988	Ex Hutchison, Overtown, 1991
F136KAO	Mercedes-Benz 609D	Reeve Burgess Beaver	B20F	1989	Ex A2B, Prenton, 1997
G109CSF	Mercedes-Benz 609D	Alexander AM	B25F	1989	
H897JCS	Mercedes-Benz 811D	Reeve Burgess Beaver	DP33F	1991	
J440UFS	Mercedes-Benz 709D	Alexander AM	DP25F	1991	
K657NGB	Mercedes-Benz 709D	Dormobile Routemaker	B29F	1992	
L25LSG	Mercedes-Benz 709D	Alexander Sprint	B25F	1993	
L833YDS	Volvo B6-50	Alexander Dash	B40F	1994	
L91NSF	Mercedes-Benz 709D	Alexander Sprint	B25F	1994	
L92NSF	Mercedes-Benz 709D	Alexander Sprint	B25F	1994	
M594RFS	Mercedes-Benz 709D	Alexander Sprint	B29F	1994	
M761GGE	Mercedes-Benz 709D	Alexander Sprint	B29F	1995	
N210ESF	Mercedes-Benz 711D	Alexander Sprint	B29F	1995	
P414MFS	Mercedes-Benz 711D	Alexander Sprint	B29F	1996	
P454MFS	Mercedes-Benz 711D	Alexander Sprint	B29F	1997	
P455MFS	Mercedes-Benz 711D	Alexander Sprint	B29F	1997	
P240OSF	Mercedes-Benz 711D	Alexander Sprint	B29F	1997	

Previous Registrations:
LIW3462   HHA196L, LIW2746

Livery: White and blue

Opposite: **Henderson Travel operate around Hamilton, and this takes the buses into East Kilbride. Representing the Henderson Travel fleet are two of the full-size buses. The upper picture shows Volvo B6 L833YDS which carries an Alexander Dash body and joined the fleet in 1994. Photographed at Hamilton rail interchange, LIW3462 is a Leyland Leopard rebodied in 1991 with a Willowbrook Warrior body.** *Malc McDonald/Murdoch Currie*

Henderson Travel's minibuses operate in an all-blue livery while on the larger vehicles while dominates the scheme. Pictured at the Pollock Centre in Glasgow, E504YSU, is one of two Alexander-bodied MB 709Ds that predate the Sprint style.
Murdoch Currie

HIGHLAND COUNTRY

Highland Country Buses Ltd, Farraline Park, Margaret Street, Inverness, Highland, IV1 1LT

A subsidiary of National Express plc

Depots : Myrtle Road, Aviemore; Ardgour Road, Caol; Inverlochy Road, Fort William; Kyle of Lochalsh; Park Road, Portree and Janet Street, Thurso; Wick. **Outstations** : numerous

B203	OSR203R	Bristol VRT/LL3/6LXB	Alexander AL	H49/36F	1975	Ex Highland Scottish, 1995
B644	RAN644R	Bristol VRT/SL3/6LXB	Eastern Coach Works	H43/34F	1977	Ex Highland Scottish, 1995
B645	RAN645R	Bristol VRT/SL3/6LXB	Eastern Coach Works	H43/34F	1977	Ex Highland Scottish, 1995

D313-327

		Leyland Fleetline FE30AGR	Eastern Coach Works	H43/32F	1978-79 Ex Highland Scottish, 1995

D313	SAS855T	D315	SAS857T	D321	UAS65T	D325	UAS69T	D327	UAS71T
D314	SAS856T	D319	UAS63T	D323	UAS67T	D326	UAS70T		

D376	BVR76T	Leyland Fleetline FE30AGR	Northern Counties	H43/32F	1979	Ex Highland Scottish, 1995
D591	YTE591V	Leyland Fleetline FE30AGR	Northern Counties	H43/32F	1979	Ex Highland Scottish, 1995

D920-930

		Daimler Fleetline CRG6LXB	Alexander AD	H44/31F	1976	Ex Highland Scottish, 1995

D920	SMS120P	D924	SMS124P	D925	SMS125P	D928	SMS128P	D930w	SMS130P
D923w	SMS123P						

F381	A260YEP	Leyland Olympian ONTL11/2R	Eastern Coach Works	CH45/28F	1984	Ex MTL (Merseybus), 1997
F382	B693BPU	Leyland Olympian ONTL11/2RSp	Eastern Coach Works	CH45/28F	1985	Ex MTL (Liverbus), 1997
L19	DSB119X	Leyland Leopard PSU3E/4R	Plaxton Supreme IV Express	C53F	1982	Ex West Coast Motors, Campbeltown, 1996
L109	GMS286S	Leyland Leopard PSU3E/4R	Alexander AYS	B53F	1978	Ex Highland Scottish, 1995
L117	LUA280V	Leyland Leopard PSU5D/4R	Plaxton Supreme IV	C55F	1980	Ex Highland Scottish, 1995
L118	DSB118X	Leyland Leopard PSU3E/4R	Plaxton Supreme IV Express	C53F	1982	Ex West Coast Motors, Campbeltown, 1996
L119	CFS119S	Leyland Leopard PSU3E/4R	Duple Dominant II Express	C49F	1978	Ex Gaelicbus, Ballachulish, 1996
L214	GSO79V	Leyland Leopard PSU3E/4R	Alexander AYS	B62F	1979	Ex Highland Scottish, 1995
L217	CAS511W	Leyland Leopard PSU3G/4R	Alexander AY	DP49F	1981	Ex Highland Scottish, 1995
L218	CAS512W	Leyland Leopard PSU3G/4R	Alexander AY	DP49F	1981	Ex Highland Scottish, 1995
L223	CAS517W	Leyland Leopard PSU3G/4R	Alexander AY	DP49F	1981	Ex Highland Scottish, 1995
L224	CAS518W	Leyland Leopard PSU3G/4R	Alexander AY	DP49F	1981	Ex Highland Scottish, 1995
L229	FAS374X	Leyland Leopard PSU3F/4R	Alexander AYS	B62F	1982	Ex Highland Scottish, 1995
L231	FAS376X	Leyland Leopard PSU3F/4R	Alexander AYS	B62F	1982	Ex Highland Scottish, 1995
L251	WFS152W	Leyland Leopard PSU3F/4R	Alexander AYS	B62F	1980	Ex Highland Scottish, 1995
L813	YSF83S	Leyland Leopard PSU3D/4R	Alexander AYS	B53F	1977	Ex Highland Scottish, 1995
L814	YSF104S	Leyland Leopard PSU3E/4R	Alexander AYS	B53F	1977	Ex Highland Scottish, 1995
L837	ULS337T	Leyland Leopard PSU3E/4R	Alexander AYS	B53F	1979	Ex Highland Scottish, 1995
L852	GCS52V	Leyland Leopard PSU3E/4R	Alexander AY	B53F	1980	Ex Highland Scottish, 1995
L867	XSG67R	Leyland Leopard PSU3E/4R	Alexander AYS	B53F	1977	Ex Highland Scottish, 1995
L868	XSG68R	Leyland Leopard PSU3E/4R	Alexander AYS	B53F	1977	Ex Highland Scottish, 1995
L869	XSG69R	Leyland Leopard PSU3E/4R	Alexander AYS	B53F	1977	Ex Highland Scottish, 1995
L872	LMS372W	Leyland Leopard PSU3F/4R	Alexander AYS	DP49F	1980	Ex Highland Scottish, 1995
L875	LMS375W	Leyland Leopard PSU3F/4R	Alexander AYS	DP49F	1980	Ex Highland Scottish, 1995

L876-896

		Leyland Leopard PSU3D/4R	Alexander AYS	B53F	1977	Ex Highland Scottish, 1995

L876	YSF76S	L878	YSF78S	L890	YSF90S	L891	YSF91S	L896	YSF96S

M1	P904DST	Optare MetroRider	Optare	B32F	1996	
M2	P905DST	Optare MetroRider	Optare	B32F	1996	
M3	P906DST	Optare MetroRider	Optare	B32F	1996	
M4	P907DST	Optare MetroRider	Optare	B32F	1996	

Since the last edition of this publication the Highland Omnibus fleet has been divided between Highland Country, a National Express subsidiary with operations that go well into The Highlands and Highland Scottish, now part of Rapsons with a depot in Inverness. Photographed in Thurso, Leyland Fleetline D327, UAS71T shows the Eastern Coach Works body style more common on the Bristol VR. *Murdoch Currie*

N8	NSK2727	Leyland National 11351A/1R (Volvo)		B50F	1979	Ex Gaelicbus, Ballachulish, 1996
N25	MIL9755	Leyland National 11351A/1R (Volvo)		DP45F	1977	Ex West Midlands Travel, 1996
N31	STJ31T	Leyland National 11351A/1R (Volvo)		B49F	1979	Ex West Midlands Travel, 1996
N34	STJ34T	Leyland National 11351A/1R (Volvo)		B49F	1979	Ex West Midlands Travel, 1996
N48	MIL9754	Leyland National 11351/1R/SC (Volvo)		B50F	1975	Ex West Midlands Travel, 1996
N56	TVP856S	Leyland National 11351A/1R (Volvo)		DP45F	1978	Ex West Midlands Travel, 1996
N62	TVP862S	Leyland National 11351A/1R (Volvo)		DP45F	1978	Ex West Midlands Travel, 1996
N64	TVP864S	Leyland National 11351A/1R (Volvo)		DP45F	1978	Ex West Midlands Travel, 1996
N65	TVP865S	Leyland National 11351A/1R (Volvo)		DP51F	1978	Ex West Midlands Travel, 1996
N476	MIL6675	Leyland National 11351/1R (Volvo)		B50F	1974	Ex Gaelicbus, Ballachulish, 1996
N503	MIL9752	Leyland National 11351/1R (Volvo)		B50F	1974	Ex Gaelicbus, Ballachulish, 1996
N516	MIL9753	Leyland National 11351/1R (Volvo)		B50F	1974	Ex Gaelicbus, Ballachulish, 1996
N830	MIL9756	Leyland National 11351A/1R (Volvo)		B50F	1977	Ex Gaelicbus, Ballachulish, 1996
P2	E434YSU	Mercedes-Benz 609D	Scott	C24F	1988	Ex Highland Scottish, 1995
P3	D153NON	Freight Rover Sherpa	Carlyle	B20F	1987	Ex Highland Scottish, 1995
P5	K504NST	Mercedes-Benz 811D	Wright NimBus	B31F	1993	Ex Highland Scottish, 1995
P6	L380PAS	Iveco TurboDaily 59.12	Marshall C31	B29F	1993	Ex Highland Scottish, 1995
P10	H810HVM	Mercedes-Benz 609D	Made-to-Measure	C26F	1991	Ex Martin, Spean Bridge, 1996
Q401	E401TBS	Renault-Dodge S56	Alexander AM	B25F	1988	Ex Highland Scottish, 1995
Q407	F951CSK	Renault-Dodge S56	?	B29F	1988	Ex Highland Scottish, 1995
SP1	JAZ9856	Scania K93CRB	Plaxton Paramount 3200 III	C49FT	1989	Ex Speedlink, 1996
SP2	JAZ9857	Scania K93CRB	Plaxton Paramount 3200 III	C53F	1990	Ex Speedlink, 1996
SP3	JAZ9858	Scania K93CRB	Plaxton Paramount 3200 III	C53F	1989	Ex Speedlink, 1996
SP4	JAZ9859	Scania K93CRB	Plaxton Paramount 3200 III	C53F	1989	Ex Speedlink, 1996
V112w	NSK267T	Volvo B58-61	Plaxton Supreme IV	C53F	1979	Ex Highland Scottish, 1995
V116	BYC789B	Volvo B58-61	Plaxton Supreme IV	C53F	1979	Ex Highland Scottish, 1995
V139w	TND139X	Volvo B58-61	Duple Dominant IV	C57F	1982	Ex Highland Scottish, 1995
V271	JAZ9851	Volvo B10M-61	Van Hool Alizée	C46FT	1981	Ex Highland Scottish, 1995
V474	JAZ9855	Volvo B10M-61	Plaxton Paramount 3200 II	C46FT	1983	Ex Highland Scottish, 1995
V557	BTU557W	Volvo B58-56	Plaxton Supreme IV	C53F	1981	Ex Highland Scottish, 1995
V640	JIL7640	Volvo B10M-61	Van Hool Alizée	C49FT	1981	Owned by Scottish Citylink Ltd

Fort William on the western coast of Scotland is now in the middle of Highland Country territory and is the location of one of its depots. Photographed in the town while preparing for a journey to Inverlochy is Mercedes-Benz P5, K504NST. The bodywork on this vehicle is by Wrights. *Murdoch Currie*

V641	G251VPK	Volvo B10M-60	Plaxton Paramount 3500 III	C46FT	1990	Ex Speedlink, 1997
V642	G252VPK	Volvo B10M-60	Plaxton Paramount 3500 III	C46FT	1990	Ex Speedlink, 1997
V643	G253VPK	Volvo B10M-60	Plaxton Paramount 3500 III	C46FT	1990	Ex Speedlink, 1997
V644	G254VPK	Volvo B10M-60	Plaxton Paramount 3500 III	C46FT	1990	Ex Speedlink, 1997
V645	G255VPK	Volvo B10M-60	Plaxton Paramount 3500 III	C46FT	1990	Ex Speedlink, 1997
V749	FHS749X	Volvo B10M-61	Duple Goldliner III	C49FT	1982	Ex Highland Scottish, 1995
V816	JAZ9852	Volvo B10M-61	Van Hool Alizée	C52FT	1988.	Ex Highland Scottish, 1995
V817	JAZ9853	Volvo B10M-61	Van Hool Alizée	C52FT	1988	Ex Highland Scottish, 1995
V883	JAZ9850	Volvo B10M-61	Van Hool Alizée	C52FT	1988	Ex Highland Scottish, 1995
V998	JAZ9854	Volvo B9M	Van Hool Alizée	C38FT	1988	Ex Martin, Spean Bridge, 1996
	603CYS	Bedford C5C1	Duple Vista	C29F	1961	Ex Highland Scottish, 1995

Previous Registrations:

A260YEP	a507GPC, A12MTL	JAZ9859	G804RNC
BTU557W	KKW804W, 798MMA	JIL7640	B322UNB, SPR124, B453GCB, MIW2418,
BYC789B	HGA832T		B838XWX, 357WMX
JAZ9850	A639EJS, 1983NT, A199PBS	MIL6675	ROK476M
JAZ9851	TGD767W, TRM144, MBS271W	MIL9752	TOE503N
JAZ9852	B216FJS	MIL9753	TOE516N
JAZ9853	B217FJS	MIL9754	LMB948P
JAZ9854	E477WUS, 4143AT, E998CGA	MIL9755	OOX825R
JAZ9855	FWT621Y, 353TPF, UCV206Y, ESK986, USK474Y	MIL9756	OOX830R
JAZ9856	F431GWG	NSK267T	CRS204T, 930GJF
JAZ9857	G780CFA	NSK272T	AOL8T
JAZ9858	G803RNC		

Livery: Blue, grey and red; yellow and blue (Highland Country) SP1-4, V271, V474, V816/7/83, V998; green (Gaelicbus) B165, D724, I119, N503/16, N830; red and cream (West Coast Motors) L19, L118.

Opposite top: **The latest arrivals with Highland Country are four the longer Optare MetroRiders which have commenced a new 'M' class of numbering as illustrated by M3, P906DST.** *Murdoch Currie*
Opposite bottom: **Painted in Scottish Citylink colours and Highland Country names is V816, JAZ9852 a Volvo B10M with Van Hool Alizée bodywork, one of three that transferred from Highland Scottish in 1995. New to Newtons of Dingwall it joined the Highland operation in 1985.** *Andrew Jarosz*

HUTCHISON

Hutchison Coaches (Overtown) Ltd, 5 Castlehill Road, Overtown,
Wishaw, North Lanarkshire, ML2 0QS

KSK931	Volvo B10M-61	Duple 340	C55F	1988
KSK932	Volvo B10M-61	Duple 340	C55F	1988
E648CHS	Volvo B10M-61	Duple 340	C55F	1988
F338VSD	Volvo B10M-56	Duple 300	B53F	1988
F339VSD	Volvo B10M-56	Duple 300	B53F	1988
F707WCS	Volvo B10M-56	Duple 300	B53F	1989
F708WCS	Volvo B10M-56	Duple 300	B53F	1989
F709WCS	Volvo B10M-56	Duple 300	B53F	1989
F771JYS	Volvo B10M-55	Duple 300	B53F	1989
F772JYS	Volvo B10M-55	Duple 300	B53F	1989
F773JYS	Volvo B10M-55	Duple 300	B53F	1989
F774JYS	Volvo B10M-55	Duple 300	B53F	1989
F775JYS	Volvo B10M-60	Duple 320	C59F	1989
F776JYS	Volvo B10M-60	Duple 320	C59F	1989
G456MGG	Dennis Dart 9SDL3002	Duple Dartline	B35F	1990
J17BUS	Volvo B10M-55	Duple 300	B53F	1992
J18BUS	Volvo B10M-55	Duple 300	B53F	1992
K15BUS	Volvo B10M-60	Plaxton Paramount 3200 III	C53F	1993
K16BUS	Volvo B10M-60	Plaxton Paramount 3200 III	C53F	1993
L684UYS	Volvo B10B-58	Northern Counties Paladin	B51F	1993
L685UYS	Volvo B10B-58	Northern Counties Paladin	B51F	1993
L23WGA	MAN 11.190	Optare Vecta	B42F	1993
L10BUS	Volvo B10M-62	Van Hool Alizée	C53F	1994
L11BUS	Volvo B10M-62	Van Hool Alizée	C53F	1994
L106YGD	MAN 11.190	Optare Vecta	B42F	1994
L670PWT	MAN 11.190	Optare Vecta	B40F	1994	Ex Essbee, Coatbridge, 1995
M679CSU	MAN 11.190	Optare Vecta	B42F	1994
PSV223	Volvo B10M-62	Van Hool Alizée	C55F	1995
TSV497	Volvo B10M-62	Van Hool Alizée	C52F	1995
XSV229	Volvo B10M-62	Van Hool Alizée	C52F	1995
XUF456	Volvo B10M-62	Van Hool Alizée	C55F	1995
M867FSU	MAN 11.190	Optare Vecta	B42F	1995
M868FSU	MAN 11.190	Optare Vecta	B42F	1995
N608OGE	MAN 11.190	Optare Vecta	B42F	1996
P995RHS	MAN 11.190	Optare Vecta	B42F	1996
KSK930	Volvo B10M-62	Van Hool Alizée	C48DLT	1996
KSK933	Volvo B10M-62	Van Hool Alizée	C53F	1996
KSK934	Volvo B10M-62	Van Hool Alizée	C53F	1996
P502VUS	Volvo B10M-62	Van Hool Alizée	C53F	1997
P503VUS	Volvo B10M-62	Van Hool Alizée	C53F	1997
P504VUS	Volvo B10M-62	Van Hool Alizée	C53F	1997
P505VUS	Dennis Javelin	Marcopolo Explorer 2	C53F	1997
P506VUS	Dennis Javelin	Marcopolo Explorer 2	C53F	1997
P507VUS	Volvo B10M-62	Plaxton Première 320	C57F	1997
P508VUS	Volvo B10M-62	Plaxton Première 320	C57F	1997
P203CGA	Volkswagon Transporter	Volkswagon	M10	1997
HCO514	Optare Excel	Optare	B40F	1997

Previous Registrations:

E648CHS	TE154XHS, KSK933	KSK931	E152XHS	TSV497	From new
H558YYS	G439NGE	KSK932	E153XHS	XSV229	From new
HCO514	From new	PSV223	From new	XUF456	From new

Livery: Blue and cream; silver and red or white red and blue (Scottish Pullman coaches); white (David Urquhart Travel) L8/9BUS, KSK933, P505/6VUS; white (Caledonia Travel) XSV229, KSK934.

Opposite: **Representing the Hutchison fleet are two examples from different aspects of the operation. The upper picture illustrates the silver-based Super Pullman livery used for the coach fleet. XSV229 is one of twelve Van Hool Alizée-bodied Volvo coaches and is seen at the depot. The latest arrival in the bus fleet is Buggy Bus HCO514, an Optare Excel integral which entered the fleet earlier this year. Painted in the service bus livery it has carried the private index mark from new.** *Mark Bailey*

IRVINES OF LAW

P & I Irvine, Lawmuir Road Garage, Law, Carluke, South Lanarkshire, ML8 5JB

Reg	Chassis	Body	Type	Year	History
NAH136P	Bristol VRT/SL3/6LXB	Eastern Coach Works	H43/31F	1976	Ex MK Metro, 1996
MEL556P	Bristol VRT/SL3/6LX	Eastern Coach Works	H43/31F	1976	Ex MK Metro, 1996
NJT34P	Bristol VRT/SL3/6LX	Eastern Coach Works	H43/31F	1976	Ex MK Metro, 1996
JOV778P	Ailsa B55-10	Alexander AV	H44/35F	1976	Ex Scutt, Owston Ferry, 1997
ULS324T	Leyland Leopard PSU3E/4R	Alexander AYS	B53F	1979	Ex Oban & District, 1996
TYS268W	Dennis Dominator DD137B	Alexander RL	H45/34F	1981	Ex Delta, Kirkby-in-Ashfield, 1996
MIL5980	Leyland Tiger TRCTL11/3R	Duple 320	C53F	1986	Ex Powner Travel, Burbage, 1996
C760CWX	MCW Metroliner DR130/26	MCW	CH57/22FT	1986	Ex Bailey, Sutton-in-Ashfield, 1997
JIL5281	Bova FHD12.280	Bova Futura	C49FT	1986	Ex Birss, Balmedie, 1997
HJI380	Leyland Tiger TRCTL11/3RZ	Duple 320	C53FT	1987	Ex Dorset Travel Services, 1993
RJI4578	Van Hool T815H	Van Hool Alizée	C53F	1988	Ex Emmerson Coaches, Immingham, 1997
F450FDB	Leyland Tiger TRCTL11/3ARZ	Duple 320	C57F	1989	Ex Hamilton of Uxbridge, 1996
790CVD	Dennis Javelin 12SDA1916	Plaxton Paramount 3200 III	C53F	1989	Ex Lewis', Pailton, 1996
G82KUB	Mercedes-Benz 811D	Optare StarRider	B26F	1989	Ex Metroline, 1997
G83KUB	Mercedes-Benz 811D	Optare StarRider	B26F	1989	Ex Metroline, 1997
G87KUB	Mercedes-Benz 811D	Optare StarRider	B26F	1989	Ex Metroline, 1997
N791SJU	Dennis Javelin 12SDA2136	Marcopolo Explorer	C53F	1996	
N792SJU	Dennis Javelin 12SDA2136	Marcopolo Explorer	C53F	1996	
P316UHS	Dennis Javelin 12SDA2136	Marcopolo Explorer 2	C50FT	1996	
P885USU	Dennis Javelin 12SDA2136	Marcopolo Explorer 2	C53F	1996	

Previous Registrations:

790CVD	F621SAY	MIL5980	C766DYO, 917DBO, C415YRF
HJI380	D24NWO	RJI4578	E446MMM
JIL5281	1716WW, C894URS		

Livery: Red and cream; white (David Urquhart Travel); N791/2SJU.

Blackpool had featured in the plans of Scottish holidaymakers for several decades with thousands heading for the Lancashire resort during Glasgow Fortnight. While the numbers have diminished the resort still sees many visitors. Pictured on the promenade is Leyland Tiger F450FDB of Irvine's of Law. The Duple 320 bodywork is one of two of the type currently in the fleet. *Paul Wigan*

KEENAN OF AYR

John Keenan & Sons (Darwin Garage) Ltd, Coalhall, South Ayrshire, KA6 6ND

Reg	Chassis	Body	Seats	Year	History
STG476Y	Leyland Leopard PSU3/4R	Plaxton P'mount 3200 (1983)	C53F	1967	Ex Parfitt's, Rhymney Bridge, 1993
THB541Y	Leyland Leopard PSU3/4R	Plaxton P'mount 3200 (1983)	C53F	1968	Ex Parfitt's, Rhymney Bridge, 1993
HGD894L	Leyland Atlantean AN68/1R	Alexander AL	H45/29F	1973	Ex Strathclyde PTE, 1984
RAX804M	Leyland Leopard PSU3B/4R	Plaxton Bustler (1988)	B55F	1974	Ex Parfitt's, Rhymney Bridge, 1994
SBA202R	Bedford VAS5	Plaxton Supreme III	C29F	1977	Ex Lowden, Sunniside, 1982
HGD214T	Leyland Atlantean AN68A/1R	Alexander AL	H45/33F	1979	Ex Graham's, Paisley, 1990
BNC957T	Leyland Atlantean AN68A/1R	Park Royal	H43/32F	1979	Ex GM Buses, 1993
BTE208V	Leyland Leopard PSU3E/4R	Duple Dominant II Express	DP51F	1980	Ex Southend, 1990
MPL125W	Leyland Leopard PSU3E/4R	Duple Dominant IV Express	C53F	1981	Ex South Yorkshire's Transport, 1991
MPL137W	Leyland Leopard PSU3E/4R	Duple Dominant IV Express	C53F	1981	Ex South Yorkshire's Transport, 1991
B145FCS	Mercedes-Benz L608D	PMT Hanbridge	C19F	1984	
AEF91A	DAF MB200DKFL600	Duple Laser 2	C57F	1985	Ex Southend, 1993
YIJ3053	DAF MB200DKFL600	Duple Laser 2	C57F	1985	Ex Southend, 1993
TJI1328	Volvo B10M-61	Plaxton Paramount 3500 II	C53F	1985	Ex Clynnog & Trefor, Trefor, 1995
A1VOL	Volvo B10M-61	Plaxton Paramount 3500 II	C53F	1986	Ex Stonehouse Coaches, 1995
246AJF	Volvo B10M-61	Van Hool Alizée	C53F	1986	Ex Epsom Coaches, 1996
OJD11R	Mercedes-Benz 609D	Whittaker Europa	C21F	1989	Ex Whittaker demonstrator, 1989

Previous Registrations:

A1VOL	C176LWB, UBM880, C411SSB, UBM880, C799SSB, SJI1977		
246AJF	C331DND	STG476Y	ECK880E
AEF91A	B252CVX	THB541Y	MNW332F
B145FCS	B410BSJ, 246AJF	TJI1328	C486HAK, C484HAK, XSU653.
OJD11R	G881KKY	YIJ3053	B253CVX

Livery: White, yellow, orange and red

Photographed while loading passengers in Burns Statue Square in Ayr, Keenan's BNC957T is a Park Royal-bodied Leyland Atlantean new to Greater Manchester. A further vehicle from the same batch is currently operated by near-by Western Buses. *Malc McDonald*

LRT LOTHIAN

Lothian Region Transport plc, 1/4 Shrub Place, Edinburgh, EH7 4PA

Depots: Annandale Street, Edinburgh; Longstone Road, Edinburgh; Seafield Road East, Edinburgh;
Tappins depot, Didcot and James Street, York

| 14 | BFS14L | Leyland Atlantean AN68/1R | Alexander AL | O45/33F | 1973 | |

20-25

| | | Leyland Atlantean AN68C/1R | Alexander AL | PO45/31F | 1981 | *23 is H45/31F |

20	GSC660X	22	GSC662X	23	GSC663X	24	GSC664X	25	GSC665X
21	GSC661X								

34-50

| | | Leyland Atlantean AN68/1R | Alexander AL | O45/33F | 1973 |

34	BFS34L	41	BFS41L	43	BFS43L	45	BFS45L	49	BFS49L
39	BFS39L	42	BFS42L	44	BFS44L	48	BFS48L	50	BFS50L
40	BFS40L								

51w	USX51V	Leyland Leopard PSU3F/4R	Duple Dominant II Express	C53F	1980
53	USX53V	Leyland Leopard PSU3F/4R	Duple Dominant II Express	C53F	1980
54	USX54V	Leyland Leopard PSU3F/4R	Duple Dominant II Express	C53F	1980
55	PSC55Y	Leyland Tiger TRCTL11/2R	Duple Dominant II	C49F	1982
56	PSC56Y	Leyland Tiger TRCTL11/2R	Duple Dominant II	C49F	1982
57	PSC57Y	Leyland Tiger TRCTL11/2R	Duple Dominant II	C49F	1982
58	PSC58Y	Leyland Tiger TRCTL11/2R	Duple Dominant II	C49F	1982
59	A59AFS	Leyland Tiger TRCTL11/3RH	Duple Caribbean	C51F	1983
60	A60AFS	Leyland Tiger TRCTL11/3RH	Duple Caribbean	C51F	1983
61	B61GSC	Leyland Tiger TRCTL11/3RH	Duple Laser 2	C53F	1984
62	B62GSC	Leyland Tiger TRCTL11/3RH	Duple Laser 2	C53F	1984
63	C63PSG	Leyland Tiger TRCTL11/3RH	Duple Laser 2	C53F	1985
64	C64PSG	Leyland Tiger TRCTL11/3RH	Duple Laser 2	C53F	1985
65	D65BSC	Leyland Tiger TRCTL11/3RH	Duple 340	C55F	1986
66	D66BSC	Leyland Tiger TRCTL11/3RH	Duple 340	C55F	1986
67	G67DFS	Leyland Tiger TRCL10/3ARZA	Plaxton Paramount 3500 III	C53F	1989
68	G68DFS	Leyland Tiger TRCL10/3ARZA	Plaxton Paramount 3500 III	C53F	1989
70	L70LRT	Toyota Coaster HDB30R	Caetano Optimo II	C21F	1993
71	H71NFS	Leyland Tiger TRCL10/3ARZA	Plaxton Paramount 3500 III	C53F	1991

Opposite, top: **The Airline service linking Edinburgh with its airport at Turnhouse is operated by Leyland Olympians 366-371 and white Volvo Olympians 431-3. Pictured here in the special livery for the service is 367, F367WSC.** *Mark Bailey*
Opposite, bottom: The latest arrivals with LRT Lothian are a further batch of Volvo Olympians with Alexander Royale bodywork. Commencing from number 251, they are similar to the 1996 batch illustrated here by 426, P426KSX. The picture captures the arrangement of DiPTAC hand rails featured on this batch. *Richard Walter*

LRT Lothian operate open-top services in Oxford and Cambridge as well as Edinburgh. Here we see one from Scotland's capital city as 42, BFS42L is seen travelling along Princes Street.
Murdoch Currie

On extended loan from Volvo, L456JCK has been numbered 156 by LRT Lothian for the duration of its stay, working from the Marine garage until the end of April 1997 when it moved to Central. This vehicle is a Volvo B10L that has been fitted with Säffle bodywork to their 2000 design. Säffle is a subsidiary of Volvo and is based in Sweden. Further vehicles to this design are being built by Alexanders, the majority being sold to operators in Ireland. *Richard Walter*

72	H72NFS	Leyland Tiger TRCL10/3ARZA	Plaxton Paramount 3500 III	C53F	1991
73	L73NSX	Dennis Javelin 12SDA2136	Caetano Algarve II	C53F	1994
74	N74BFS	Dennis Javelin 12SDA2136	Caetano Algarve II	C53F	1995
75	N75CSX	Dennis Javelin 12SDA2136	Caetano Algarve II	C53F	1995
76	P76KSC	Dennis Javelin 12SDA2136	Caetano Algarve II	C53F	1996
78	P78OSC	Dennis Javelin 12SDA2136	Caetano Algarve II	C53F	1997

102	KSX102X	Leyland National 2 NL116AL11/2R		B45D	1982
103	KSX103X	Leyland National 2 NL116AL11/2R		B45D	1982
104	KSX104X	Leyland National 2 NL116AL11/2R		B45D	1982
105	KSX105X	Leyland National 2 NL116AL11/2R		B45D	1982
106	TFS106Y	Leyland National 2 NL116TL11/2R		B45D	1983
107	TFS107Y	Leyland National 2 NL116TL11/2R		B45D	1983
108	A108CFS	Leyland National 2 NL116TL11/2R		B45D	1984
109	A109CFS	Leyland National 2 NL116TL11/2R		B45D	1984

112-123

Dennis Dart 9SDL3016 · Alexander Dash · B35F · 1992

112	K112CSG	115	K115CSG	118	K118CSG	120	K120CSG	122	K122CSG
113	K113CSG	116	K116CSG	119	K119CSG	121	K121CSG	123	K123CSG
114	K114CSG	117	K117CSG						

138-149

Leyland National 2 NL116TL11/2R · B45D · 1985

138	B138KSF	141	B141KSF	144	B144KSF	146	B146KSF	148	B148KSF
139	B139KSF	142	B142KSF	145	B145KSF	147	B147KSF	149	B149KSF
140	B140KSF	143	B143KSF						

156	L456JCK	Volvo B10L	Säffle	B40D	1994	On evaluation from Volvo

177-188

Leyland Lynx LX2R11C15Z4S · Leyland Lynx 2 · B43D · 1991

177	H177OSG	180	H180OSG	183	H183OSG	185	H185OSG	187	H187OSG
178	H178OSG	181	H181OSG	184	H184OSG	186	H186OSG	188	H188OSG
179	H179OSG	182	H182OSG						

Volvo

201-234

Leyland Olympian YN2RZ16Z4   Alexander RH   H51/30D   1995

201	M201VSX	208	M208VSX	215	M215VSX	223	M223VSX	229	M229VSX
202	M202VSX	209	M209VSX	216	M216VSX	224	M224VSX	230	M230VSX
203	M203VSX	210	M210VSX	217	M217VSX	225	M225VSX	231	M231VSX
204	M204VSX	211	M211VSX	218	M218VSX	226	M226VSX	232	M232VSX
205	M205VSX	212	M212VSX	219	M219VSX	227	M227VSX	233	M233VSX
206	M206VSX	213	M213VSX	220	M220VSX	228	M228VSX	234	M234VSX
207	M207VSX	214	M214VSX	221	M221VSX				

248	NSX248T	Leyland Leopard PSU3E/4R	Duple Dominant I	C53F	1979
249	NSX249T	Leyland Leopard PSU3E/4R	Duple Dominant I	C53F	1979
250	NSX250T	Leyland Leopard PSU3E/4R	Duple Dominant I	C53F	1979

251-285

Volvo Olympian   Alexander Royale   H51/30D   1997

251	P251PSX	258	P258PSX	265	P265PSX	272	P272PSX	279	P279PSX
252	P252PSX	259	P259PSX	266	P266PSX	273	P273PSX	281	P281PSX
253	P253PSX	260	P260PSX	267	P267PSX	274	P274PSX	282	P282PSX
254	P254PSX	261	P261PSX	268	P268PSX	275	P275PSX	283	P283PSX
255	P255PSX	262	P262PSX	269	P269PSX	276	P276PSX	284	P284PSX
256	P256PSX	263	P263PSX	270	P270PSX	277	P277PSX	285	P285PSX
257	P257PSX	264	P264PSX	271	P271PSX	278	P278PSX		

300-335

Leyland Olympian ONCL10/2RZ Alexander RH   H51/30D   1988

300	E300MSG	308	E308MSG	315	E315MSG	322	E322MSG	329	E329MSG
301	E301MSG	309	E309MSG	316	E316MSG	323	E323MSG	330	E330MSG
302	E302MSG	310	E310MSG	317	E317MSG	324	E324MSG	331	E331MSG
303	E303MSG	311	E311MSG	318	E318MSG	325	E325MSG	332	E332MSG
304	E304MSG	312	E312MSG	319	E319MSG	326	E326MSG	333	E333MSG
305	E305MSG	313	E313MSG	320	E320MSG	327	E327MSG	334	E334MSG
306	E306MSG	314	E314MSG	321	E321MSG	328	E328MSG	335	E335MSG
307	E307MSG								

336-365

Leyland Olympian ONCL10/2RZ Alexander RH   H51/30D   1989

336	G336CSG	342	G342CSG	348	F348WSC	354	F354WSC	360	F360WSC
337	G337CSG	343	G343CSG	349	F349WSC	355	F355WSC	361	F361WSC
338	G338CSG	344	G344CSG	350	F350WSC	356	F356WSC	362	F362WSC
339	G339CSG	345	G345CSG	351	F351WSC	357	F357WSC	363	F363WSC
340	G340CSG	346	F346WSC	352	F352WSC	358	F358WSC	364	F364WSC
341	G341CSG	347	F347WSC	353	F353WSC	359	F359WSC	365	F365WSC

366-371

Leyland Olympian ONCL10/2RZ Alexander RH   DPH47/31F   1989

366	F366WSC	368	F368WSC	369	F369WSC	370	F370WSC	371	F371WSC
367	F367WSC								

401-430

Volvo Olympian   Alexander Royale   H51/30D   1996

401	N401GSX	407	N407GSX	413	P413KSX	419	P419KSX	425	P425KSX
402	N402GSX	408	P408KSX	414	P414KSX	420	P420KSX	426	P426KSX
403	N403GSX	409	P409KSX	415	P415KSX	421	P421KSX	427	P427KSX
404	N404GSX	410	P410KSX	416	P416KSX	422	P422KSX	428	P428KSX
405	N405GSX	411	P411KSX	417	P417KSX	423	P423KSX	429	P429KSX
406	N406GSX	412	P412KSX	418	P418KSX	424	P424KSX	430	P430KSX

431	P431KSX	Volvo Olympian	Alexander Royale	DP47/30F	1996
432	P432KSX	Volvo Olympian	Alexander Royale	DP47/30F	1996
433	P433KSX	Volvo Olympian	Alexander Royale	DP47/30F	1996
443	GFS443N	Leyland Atlantean AN68/1R	Alexander AL	PO45/33F	1975
447	GFS447N	Leyland Atlantean AN68/1R	Alexander AL	PO45/33F	1975
448	GFS448N	Leyland Atlantean AN68/1R	Alexander AL	PO45/33F	1975
477	MSF477P	Leyland Atlantean AN68A/1R	Alexander AL	PO45/33F	1976

579-598 Leyland Atlantean AN68A/1R Alexander AL H45/30D* 1979 *583 is O45/33F

579w	JSX579T	**589**	JSX589T	**591**	JSX591T	**595**	JSX595T	**597**	JSX597T
583	JSX583T	**590**	JSX590T	**594**	JSX594T	**596**	JSX596T	**598**	JSX598T

601-620 Leyland Atlantean AN68A/1R Alexander AL H45/30D* 1979 *583 is O45/33F

601	OSC601V	**605**	OSC605V	**609**	OSC609V	**613**	OSC613V	**617**	OSC617V
602	OSC602V	**606**	OSC606V	**610**	OSC610V	**614**	OSC614V	**618**	OSC618V
603	OSC603V	**607**	OSC607V	**611**	OSC611V	**615**	OSC615V	**619**	OSC619V
604	OSC604V	**608**	OSC608V	**612**	OSC612V	**616**	OSC616V	**620**	OSC620V

621-659 Leyland Atlantean AN68C/1R Alexander AL H45/30D 1981

621	GSC621X	**629**	GSC629X	**637**	GSC637X	**645**	GSC645X	**653**	GSC653X
622	GSC622X	**630**	GSC630X	**638**	GSC638X	**646**	GSC646X	**654**	GSC654X
623	GSC623X	**631**	GSC631X	**639**	GSC639X	**647**	GSC647X	**655**	GSC655X
624	GSC624X	**632**	GSC632X	**640**	GSC640X	**648**	GSC648X	**656**	GSC656X
625	GSC625X	**633**	GSC633X	**641**	GSC641X	**649**	GSC649X	**657**	GSC657X
626	GSC626X	**634**	GSC634X	**642**	GSC642X	**650**	GSC650X	**658**	GSC658X
627	GSC627X	**635**	GSC635X	**643**	GSC643X	**651**	GSC651X	**659**	GSC659X
628	GSC628X	**636**	GSC636X	**644**	GSC644X	**652**	GSC652X		

667 GSC667X Leyland Olympian ONTL11/1R Alexander RH H47/28D 1982

668-702 Leyland Olympian ONTL11/2R Eastern Coach Works H50/31D 1982-83

668	OFS668Y	**675**	OFS675Y	**682**	OFS682Y	**689**	OFS689Y	**696**	OFS696Y
669	OFS669Y	**676**	OFS676Y	**683**	OFS683Y	**690**	OFS690Y	**697**	OFS697Y
670	OFS670Y	**677**	OFS677Y	**684**	OFS684Y	**691**	OFS691Y	**698**	OFS698Y
671	OFS671Y	**678**	OFS678Y	**685**	OFS685Y	**692**	OFS692Y	**699**	OFS699Y
672	OFS672Y	**679**	OFS679Y	**686**	OFS686Y	**693**	OFS693Y	**700**	OFS700Y
673	OFS673Y	**680**	OFS680Y	**687**	OFS687Y	**694**	OFS694Y	**701**	OFS701Y
674	OFS674Y	**681**	OFS681Y	**688**	OFS688Y	**695**	OFS695Y	**702**	OFS702Y

703-736 Leyland Olympian ONTL11/2R Eastern Coach Works H51/32D 1983

703	A703YFS	**710**	A710YFS	**717**	A717YFS	**724**	A724YFS	**731**	A731YFS
704	A704YFS	**711**	A711YFS	**718**	A718YFS	**725**	A725YFS	**732**	A732YFS
705	A705YFS	**712**	A712YFS	**719**	A719YFS	**726**	A726YFS	**733**	A733YFS
706	A706YFS	**713**	A713YFS	**720**	A720YFS	**727**	A727YFS	**734**	A734YFS
707	A707YFS	**714**	A714YFS	**721**	A721YFS	**728**	A728YFS	**735**	A735YFS
708	A708YFS	**715**	A715YFS	**722**	A722YFS	**729**	A729YFS	**736**	A736YFS
709	A709YFS	**716**	A716YFS	**723**	A723YFS	**730**	A730YFS		

LRT Lothian, 431, P431KSX is seen on Airport service wearing the mainly white livery. The final three of the 1996 order differ from the main batch in having only the front single door and being fitted with high-back seating, both visible in this picture. *Tony Wilson*

In the early eighties Lothian purchased a total product from Leyland. This used the Olympian chassis with Eastern Coach Works bodies. Almost a hundred of this combination operate for LRT Lothian represented here by 742, B742GSC from the Central garage in Edinburgh. *Richard Walter*

737-769
Leyland Olympian ONTL11/2R Eastern Coach Works H51/32D 1984

737	B737GSC	744	B744GSC	751	B751GSC	758	B758GSC	764	B764GSC
738	B738GSC	745	B745GSC	752	B752GSC	759	B759GSC	765	B765GSC
739	B739GSC	746	B746GSC	753	B753GSC	760	B760GSC	766	B766GSC
740	B740GSC	747	B747GSC	754	B754GSC	761	B761GSC	767	B767GSC
741	B741GSC	748	B748GSC	755	B755GSC	762	B762GSC	768	B768GSC
742	B742GSC	749	B749GSC	756	B756GSC	763	B763GSC	769	B769GSC
743	B743GSC	750	B750GSC	757	B757GSC				

770-794
Leyland Olympian ONTL11/2R Eastern Coach Works H51/32D 1985-86

770	C770SFS	775	C775SFS	780	C780SFS	785	C785SFS	790	C790SFS
771	C771SFS	776	C776SFS	781	C781SFS	786	C786SFS	791	C791SFS
772	C772SFS	777	C777SFS	782	C782SFS	787	C787SFS	792	C792SFS
773	C773SFS	778	C778SFS	783	C783SFS	788	C788SFS	793	C793SFS
774	C774SFS	779	C779SFS	784	C784SFS	789	C789SFS	794	C794SFS

800-835
Leyland Olympian ON2R56C13Z4 Alexander RH H51/30D 1990

800	G800GSX	808	G808GSX	815	G815GSX	822	G822GSX	829	G829GSX
801	G801GSX	809	G809GSX	816	G816GSX	823	G823GSX	830	G830GSX
802	G802GSX	810	G810GSX	817	G817GSX	824	G824GSX	831	G831GSX
803	G803GSX	811	G811GSX	818	G818GSX	825	G825GSX	832	G832GSX
804	G804GSX	812	G812GSX	819	G819GSX	826	G826GSX	833	G833GSX
805	G805GSX	813	G813GSX	820	G820GSX	827	G827GSX	834	G834GSX
806	G806GSX	814	G814GSX	821	G821GSX	828	G828GSX	835	G835GSX
807	G807GSX							

836-871   Leyland Olympian ON2R56C13Z4   Alexander RH   H51/30D   1991

836	J836TSC	844	J844TSC	851	J851TSC	858	J858TSC	865	J865TSC
837	J837TSC	845	J845TSC	852	J852TSC	859	J859TSC	866	J866TSC
838	J838TSC	846	J846TSC	853	J853TSC	860	J860TSC	867	J867TSC
839	J839TSC	847	J847TSC	854	J854TSC	861	J861TSC	868	J868TSC
840	J840TSC	848	J848TSC	855	J855TSC	862	J862TSC	869	J869TSC
841	J841TSC	849	J849TSC	856	J856TSC	863	J863TSC	870	J870TSC
842	J842TSC	850	J850TSC	857	J857TSC	864	J864TSC	871	J871TSC
843	J843TSC								

872-894   Leyland Olympian ON2R56C13Z4   Alexander RH   H51/30D   1992-93

872	K872CSF	877	K877CSF	882	K882CSF	886	K886CSF	891	K891CSF
873	K873CSF	878	K878CSF	883	K883CSF	887	K887CSF	892	K892CSF
874	K874CSF	879	K879CSF	884	K884CSF	889	K889CSF	893	K893CSF
875	K875CSF	880	K880CSF	885	K885CSF	890	K890CSF	894	K894CSF
876	K876CSF	881	K881CSF						

911-942   Leyland Atlantean AN68/1R   Alexander AL   O45/33F   1974

911	OFS911M	925	OSF925M	928	OSF928M	939	OSF939M	942	OSF942M
912	OFS912M								

950-983   Volvo Olympian YN2RC16Z4   Alexander RH   H51/30D   1994

950	L950MSC	957	L957MSC	964	L964MSC	971	L971MSC	978	L978MSC
951	L951MSC	958	L958MSC	965	L965MSC	972	L972MSC	979	L979MSC
952	L952MSC	959	L959MSC	966	L966MSC	973	L973MSC	980	L980MSC
953	L953MSC	960	L960MSC	967	L967MSC	974	L974MSC	981	L981MSC
954	L954MSC	961	L961MSC	968	L968MSC	975	L975MSC	982	L982MSC
955	L955MSC	962	L962MSC	969	L969MSC	976	L976MSC	983	L983MSC
956	L956MSC	963	L963MSC	970	L970MSC	977	L977MSC		

Named vehicles: 14, *The Oxford Student*; 20, *Granta Star*, 21 *Fenland Star*, 22 *Cambridge Star*, 23, *Pictish Star*, 24 *Anglian Star*, 25, *Eastern Star*, 34, *The Oxford Graduate*, 39, *Dunedin Star*, 40, *Edinburgh Star*, 41, *Scottish Star*, 42, *Lothian Star*, 43, *Lowland Star*, 44, *Gaelic Star*, 45, *Celtic Star*, 48, *The Oxford Professor*, 49, *The Oxford Don*; 50, *The Oxford Blue*; 443, *Norman Star*, 447, *Holyrood Star*, 448, *Waverley Star*, 477, *Ebor Star*, 583, *Caledonian Star*, 911, *English Star*, 912, *Viking Star*, 925, *Roman Star*, 928, *Saxon Star*, 939, *The Oxford Bulldog*; 942, *Pentland Star*.

Livery: Madder and white (buses); black and white (coaches and double-decks with high-back seating); white, blue and black (open-top vehicles); dual blue (Airport service 100); The Cambridge Classic Tour: 20-2/4/5; The Oxford Classic Tour: 12, 34, 48-50, 939; The York Classic Tour; 53, 443, 477, 596-8, 911/2/25/8.

The majority of LRT Lothian's Volvo Olympians have the Alexander Royale body style that features large wrap-round windscreens. When fitted onto the longer Olympian chassis a small centrally-positioned window is added as seen on this picture of 403, N403GSX, taken as the vehicle turns onto Princes Street. *Tony Wilson*

LOWLAND / SMT

Lowland Omnibuses Ltd, 14-16 Eskbank Road, Dalkeith, Midlothian, EH22 1HH

Depots : Eskbank Road, Dalkeith; Duke Street, Galashiels; Dovecot Street, Hawick; Roxburgh Street, Kelso; The Mall, Musselburgh; Tantallon Road, North Berwick and Innerleithen Road, Peebles. **Outstations:** Tweedmouth Trading Estate, Berwick and Castlegate, Jedburgh.

18w	158ASV	Leyland National 11351A/1R		B52F	1978	Ex Lothian Transit, 1996
19	GSX869T	Leyland National 11351A/1R		B52F	1978	Ex Eastern Scottish, 1985
20	RFS580V	Leyland National 2 NL116L11/1R		B52F	1980	Ex Midland Bluebird, 1996
73	P173DMS	Mercedes-Benz O405	Optare Prisma	DP49F	1997	
74	P174DMS	Mercedes-Benz O405	Optare Prisma	DP49F	1997	
109w	FFS9X	Leyland Tiger TRCTL11/3R	Duple Goldliner IV	C50FT	1982	Ex Eastern Scottish, 1988
187	487GFR	AEC Reliance 2U3RA	Harrington Grenadier	C34F	1964	Owned by Prestige Tours
214	P214NSC	Dennis Dart SLF SFD...	Plaxton Pointer	B38F	1997	
215	P215NSC	Dennis Dart SLF SFD...	Plaxton Pointer	B38F	1997	
301	J301ASH	Leyland Tiger TR2R56V16Z4	Alexander Q	DP49F	1991	
302	J302ASH	Leyland Tiger TR2R56V16Z4	Alexander Q	DP49F	1991	
303	J303ASH	Leyland Tiger TR2R56V16Z4	Alexander Q	DP49F	1991	
304	J304ASH	Leyland Tiger TR2R56V16Z4	Alexander Q	DP49F	1991	
311	PSF311Y	Leyland Tiger TRBTL11/2R	Alexander AT	C49F	1982	Ex SMT, 1996
312	PSU322	Leyland Tiger TRBTL11/2R	Alexander AT	C49F	1982	Ex SMT, 1996
313	PSF313Y	Leyland Tiger TRBTL11/2R	Alexander AT	C49F	1982	Ex Eastern Scottish, 1985
314	PSF314Y	Leyland Tiger TRBTL11/2R	Alexander AT	C49F	1982	Ex Eastern Scottish, 1985
315	PSF315Y	Leyland Tiger TRBTL11/2R	Alexander AI	C49F	1982	Ex Eastern Scottish, 1985
316	PSF316Y	Leyland Tiger TRBTL11/2R	Alexander AT	C49F	1982	Ex Eastern Scottish, 1985
318w	PSU318	Leyland Tiger TRCTL11/3R	Duple Goldliner III	C50F	1982	Ex Eastern Scottish, 1988
319w	PSU319	Leyland Tiger TRCTL11/3R	Duple Goldliner III	C49FT	1982	Ex Kelvin Scottish, 1988

320-327		Leyland Tiger TRBTL11/2RP	Alexander TE	C49F	1983	Ex Eastern Scottish, 1985 320/21 ex SMT, 1996

320	A328BSC	322	A322BSC	324	A324BSC	326	A326BSC	327	A327BSC
321	A329BSC	323	A323BSC	325	A325BSC		

328	D328DKS	Leyland Tiger TRBTL11/2RH	Alexander TE	C49F	1987	
329	D329DKS	Leyland Tiger TRBTL11/2RH	Alexander TE	C49F	1987	
330	D330DKS	Leyland Tiger TRBTL11/2RH	Alexander TE	C49F	1987	

At the turn of 1997 Lothian/SMT renumbered its fleet into a common series with Midland Bluebird with each company managing part of the former SMT operation. When photographed Lowland SSX607V was numbered 7, but has since been numbered 1607. It is seen in Berwick.
Tony Wilson

Four low-floor Scania buses joined the Lowland fleet in 1996 and these carry Wright Axcess-ultralow bodywork fitted with high-back seating. Photographed in Galashiels en route for Hawick is 503, P503XSH. *Tony Wilson*

331	A20SMT	Leyland Tiger TRCTL11/2R	Plaxton Paramount 3200 E	C49F	1984	Ex SMT, 1996
336	WSV136	Leyland Tiger TRCTL11/2RH	Plaxton Paramount 3200 II	C49F	1985	Ex SMT, 1996
337	WSV137	Leyland Tiger TRCTL11/2RH	Plaxton Paramount 3200 II	C49F	1985	Ex SMT, 1996
338	WSV138	Leyland Tiger TRCTL11/2RH	Plaxton Paramount 3200 II	C49F	1985	Ex SMT, 1996
342	A12SMT	Leyland Tiger TRCTL11/2R	Plaxton Paramount 3200 II E	C53F	1985	Ex Ian Glass, Haddington, 1991
349	D349ESC	Leyland Tiger TRBTL11/2RP	Alexander TE	C49F	1987	Ex SMT, 1996
350	D350ESC	Leyland Tiger TRBTL11/2RP	Alexander TE	C49F	1987	Ex SMT, 1996
351	D351ESC	Leyland Tiger TRBTL11/2RP	Alexander TE	C49F	1987	Ex SMT, 1996
366	JFS166X	Leyland Tiger TRCTL11/3R	Plaxton Supreme V	C51F	1982	Ex Ian Glass, Haddington, 1991
370	PSU320	Leyland Royal Tiger B50	Roe Doyen	C44FT	1984	Ex Eastern Scottish, 1989
371	PSU321	Leyland Royal Tiger B50	Roe Doyen	C44FT	1984	Ex Eastern Scottish, 1988
376	D276FAS	Leyland Tiger TRCTL11/3RH	Alexander TE	C53F	1987	Ex Highland Scottish, 1987
388	KSU388	Leyland Tiger TRCTL11/3RH	Duple 340	C46FT	1987	Ex Kelvin Scottish, 1989
389	BSS76	Leyland Tiger TRCTL11/3R	Jonckheere Jubilee	C51FT	1984	Ex Ian Glass, Haddington, 1991
390	KSU390	Leyland Tiger TRCTL11/2R	Plaxton Paramount 3200 E	C49F	1983	Ex Eastern Scottish, 1985
391	KSU391	Leyland Tiger TRCLXC/2RH	Plaxton Paramount 3200 E	C49F	1984	Ex Western Scottish, 1986
392	KSU392	Leyland Tiger TRCTL11/2RH	Plaxton Paramount 3200 II	C49F	1985	Ex Eastern Scottish, 1985
393	KSU393	Leyland Tiger TRCTL11/2RH	Plaxton Paramount 3200 II	C49F	1985	Ex Eastern Scottish, 1985
394	KSU394	Leyland Tiger TRCTL11/2RH	Plaxton Paramount 3200 III	C48FTL	1987	
401	NUD801W	Leyland Leopard PSU3F/4R	Duple Dominant II	C55F	1981	Ex Lothian Transit, 1994
407	FFS7X	Leyland Leopard PSU3E/4R	Plaxton Supreme IV	C53F	1982	Ex Ian Glass, Haddington, 1991
501	M151PKS	Scania N113CRL	Wright Pathfinder	DP49F	1995	
502	M152PKS	Scania N113CRL	Wright Pathfinder	DP49F	1995	
503	P503XSH	Scania L113CRL	Wright Axcess-ultralow	DP47F	1996	
504	P504XSH	Scania L113CRL	Wright Axcess-ultralow	DP47F	1996	
505	P505XSH	Scania L113CRL	Wright Axcess-ultralow	DP47F	1996	
506	P506XSH	Scania L113CRL	Wright Axcess-ultralow	DP47F	1996	
675	K175YVC	Mercedes-Benz 811D	Wright NimBus	B33F	1993	Ex Lothian Transit, 1996

Early 1997 saw several vehicles exchanged between Midland Scottish and Lowland, particularly the former SMT buses. Now with Lowland are six East Lancashire-bodied Leyland Olympians represented here by 948, A78RRP. *Mark Bailey*

742	DSA242T	Leyland Atlantean AN68A/1R	Alexander AL	H45/29D	1979	Ex Grampian, 1996	
745	DSA245T	Leyland Atlantean AN68A/1R	Alexander AL	H45/29D	1979	Ex Grampian, 1996	
749	DSA249T	Leyland Atlantean AN68A/1R	Alexander AL	H45/34F	1979	Ex Midland Bluebird, 1996	
750	DSA250T	Leyland Atlantean AN68A/1R	Alexander AL	H45/29D	1979	Ex Grampian, 1996	
751	DSA251T	Leyland Atlantean AN68A/1R	Alexander AL	H45/34F	1979	Ex Grampian, 1996	
763	HRS263V	Leyland Atlantean AN68A/1R	Alexander AL	H45/29D	1980	Ex Grampian, 1996	
916	ALS116Y	Leyland Olympian ONLXB/1R	Alexander RL	H45/32F	1983	Ex Eastern Scottish, 1985	
919	ALS119Y	Leyland Olympian ONLXB/1R	Alexander RL	H45/32F	1983	Ex SMT, 1996	
937	A137BSC	Leyland Olympian ONLXB/1R	Alexander RL	H45/32F	1984	Ex SMT, 1996	
942	A142BSC	Leyland Olympian ONLXB/1R	Alexander RL	H45/32F	1984	Ex SMT, 1996	
943	A143BSC	Leyland Olympian ONLXB/1R	Alexander RL	DPH45/29F	1984	Ex Eastern Scottish, 1985	

945-950

		Leyland Olympian ONLXB/1R	East Lancashire	H47/32F	1984	Ex Midland Bluebird, 1997	
945	A81RRP	**947**	A77RRP	**948**	A78RRP	**949** A79RRP	**950** A80RRP
946	A82RRP						

951	D901CSH	Leyland Olympian ONTL11/1RH	Alexander RL	DPH43/27F	1987		
952	D902CSH	Leyland Olympian ONTL11/1RH	Alexander RL	DPH43/27F	1987		
959	B159KSC	Leyland Olympian ONTL11/1RH	Alexander RL	H45/32F	1985	Ex Eastern Scottish, 1985	
960	B160KSC	Leyland Olympian ONTL11/1RH	Alexander RL	H45/32F	1985	Ex Eastern Scottish, 1986	
988w	VAO488Y	Leyland Titan TNTL11/1RF	Leyland	H48/31F	1982	Ex Ian Glass, Haddington, 1991	

1023-1047

		Ailsa B55-10		Alexander AV	H44/35F	1978	Ex SMT, 1996
1023	CSG773S	**1026**	CSG776S	**1036** TSJ596S	**1040** TSJ600S	**1044** BGG254S	
1024	CSG774S	**1033**	TSJ593S	**1039** TSJ599S	**1042** BGG252S	**1047** BGG257S	

After the arrival of some Renault-Dodges the minibus requirement for Lowland has been met by the Optare MetroRider of which twenty-one are now in service. No 1535, L725JKS was photographed while working a local service in Galashiels. Five new MetroRiders with extra luggage compartments are on order for the recently re-gained *Border Courier* contract. *Tony Wilson*

1049-1058

	Volvo B55-10 MkIII	Alexander RV	H44/37F	1984	Ex SMT, 1996	

1049	B149GSC	1051	B151GSC	1053	B153GSC	1055	B155GSC	1057	B157GSC
1050	B150GSC	1052	B152GSC	1054	B154GSC	1056	B156GSC	1058	B158GSC

1076-1095

Volvo B55-10 MkIII · Alexander RV · H44/35F · 1981 · Ex SMT, 1996

1076	HSF76X	1081	HSF81X	1085	HSF85X	1088	HSF88X	1093	HSF93X
1077	HSF77X	1082	HSF82X	1086	HSF86X	1091	HSF91X	1094	HSF94X
1078	HSF78X	1083	HSF83X	1087	HSF87X	1092	HSF92X	1095	HSF95X
1080	HSF80X	1084	HSF84X						

1169-1173

Volvo Citybus B10M-50 · Alexander RV · H44/37F · 1985 · Ex SMT, 1996

1169	B169KSC	1170	B170KSC	1171	B171KSC	1172	B172KSC	1173	B173KSC

1187	E187HSF	Volvo Citybus B10M-50	Alexander RV	DPH45/35F	1987	Ex SMT, 1996
1188	E188HSF	Volvo Citybus B10M-50	Alexander RV	DPH45/35F	1987	Ex SMT, 1996
1189	E189HSF	Volvo Citybus B10M-50	Alexander RV	DPH45/35F	1987	Ex SMT, 1996
1190	E190HSF	Volvo Citybus B10M-50	Alexander RV	DPH45/35F	1987	Ex SMT, 1996
1402	D402ASF	Renault-Dodge S56	Alexander AM	B21F	1986	Ex SMT, 1995
1403w	D403ASF	Renault-Dodge S56	Alexander AM	B21F	1986	Ex SMT, 1995
1420	D420ASF	Renault-Dodge S56	Alexander AM	B16FL	1986	Ex SMT, 1996

1421-1430

Renault-Dodge S56 · Alexander AM · B25F* · 1987-88 *1426 is DP25F

1421	D751DSH	1423	D753DSH	1425	D755DSH	1426	E756GSH	1430	D750DSH
1422	D752DSH	1424	D754DSH						

Opposite: **Two photographs with contrasting age differences from the SMT operation are illustrated here. The upper picture shows 214, P214NSC, one of a pair of low floor Dennis Darts to join the fleet during 1997. Both carry Plaxton's Pointer bodywork.**
Lowland inherited many of the Seddon Pennine products and is now the principal operator of the type in the country. The lower picture is of 1650, YSG650W seen here with Alexander AYS-type bodywork. *Tony Wilson/Mark Bailey*

1434	E434JSG	Renault-Dodge S56	Alexander AM	B25F	1987	Ex SMT, 1995	
1435	E435JSG	Renault-Dodge S56	Alexander AM	B25F	1987	Ex SMT, 1995	
1458	E458JSG	Renault-Dodge S56	Alexander AM	DP25F	1987	Ex SMT, 1996	
1471	H471OSC	Renault S75	Reeve Burgess Beaver	B31F	1991	Ex SMT, 1995	
1472	H472OSC	Renault S75	Reeve Burgess Beaver	B31F	1991	Ex SMT, 1995	
1476	H476OSC	Renault S75	Reeve Burgess Beaver	B31F	1991	Ex SMT, 1995	

1503-1514

Optare MetroRider   Optare   B31F   1992   Ex SMT, 1996

1503	J503WSX	1505	J505WSX	1507	J507WSX	1509	J509WSX	1514	K514BSX
1504	J504WSX	1506	J506WSX	1508	J508WSX		

1518-1522

Optare MetroRider   Optare   B31F   1994   Ex SMT, 1996

1518	L518KSX	1519	L519KSX	1520	L520KSX	1521	L521KSX	1522	L522KSX

1530-1537

Optare MetroRider   Optare   DP32F*   1994   *1530-2 are B32F

1530	L720JKS	1532	L722JKS	1534	L724JKS	1536	L726JKS	1537	L727JKS
1531	L721JKS	1533	L723JKS	1535	L725JKS		

1538-1542

Optare MetroRider   Optare   B22F   1997

1538	P	1539	P	1540		1541		1542	

1601	RSX591V	Seddon Pennine 7	Alexander AYS	B53F	1979	Ex SMT, 1996

1602-1630

Seddon Pennine 7   Alexander AYS   B53F*   1979-80 Ex SMT, 1996
1602/4/7/10/8 are B60F; 1603/6 are DP49F; 1602/3/5-7/10 ex Eastern Scottish 1985

1602	SSX602V	1606	SSX606V	1612	SSX612V	1620	SSX620V	1628	SSX628V
1603	SSX603V	1607	SSX607V	1613	SSX613V	1621	SSX621V	1629	SSX629V
1604	SSX604V	1609	SSX609V	1618	SSX618V	1622	SSX622V	1630	SSX630V
1605	SSX605V	1610	SSX610V	1619	SSX619V	1627	SSX627V		

1631-1659

Seddon Pennine 7   Alexander AYS   B53F*   1979-80 Ex SMT, 1996
*1631-4 are B60F; 1631/9 ex Eastern Scottish 1985; 1632/7/8/54 ex Midland Bluebird 1996-97

1631	YSG631W	1635	YSG635W	1639	YSG639W	1645	YSG645W	1655	YSG655W
1632	YSG632W	1636	YSG636W	1640	YSG640W	1647	YSG647W	1658	YSG658W
1633	YSG633W	1637	YSG637W	1642	YSG642W	1650	YSG650W	1659	YSG659W
1634	YSG634W	1638	YSG638W	1643	YSG643W	1654	YSG654W		

1663	VFS324V	Seddon Pennine 7	Plaxton Supreme IV Express	C49F	1979	Ex Eastern Scottish, 1985
1664	VFS432V	Seddon Pennine 7	Alexander AT	C45F	1979	Ex SBG Engineering, 1990
1665	DSD965V	Seddon Pennine 7	Alexander AT	C49F	1979	Ex SBG Engineering, 1990
1666	DSD958V	Seddon Pennine 7	Alexander AT	C49F	1979	Ex SBG Engineering, 1990
1668	ESF571W	Seddon Pennine 7	Plaxton Supreme IV Express	C45F	1981	Ex Kelvin Scottish, 1986
1670	NFS984T	Seddon Pennine 7	Plaxton Supreme IV Express	C49F	1979	Ex Lothian Transit, 1994

A single Leyland Swift is operated by Lothian on its border services. Pictured in Peebles, 1715, G715OSH carries bodywork by Reeve Burgess to the Harrier design. As can be seen in the picture, this example is fitted with a coach door rather than the folding-leaf door option. *Tony Wilson*

1676	LSC936T	Seddon Pennine 7	Alexander AYS	DP49F	1982	Ex SMT, 1996
1678	LSC938T	Seddon Pennine 7	Alexander AYS	B53F	1982	Ex Midland Bluebird, 1996
1683	JFS983X	Seddon Pennine 7	Alexander AYS	B49F	1982	Ex Midland Bluebird, 1997
1684	JFS984X	Seddon Pennine 7	Alexander AYS	B53F	1982	Ex Eastern Scottish, 1985
1685	JFS985X	Seddon Pennine 7	Alexander AYS	DP49F	1982	Ex Eastern Scottish, 1985
1686	JFS986X	Seddon Pennine 7	Alexander AYS	B53F	1982	Ex Eastern Scottish, 1985
1687	SSX597V	Seddon Pennine 7	Alexander AYS	B60F	1982	Ex Eastern Scottish, 1985
1688	JSF928T	Seddon Pennine 7	Alexander AT	C49F	1979	Ex Eastern Scottish, 1985
1689	JSF929T	Seddon Pennine 7	Alexander AT	C49F	1979	Ex Eastern Scottish, 1985
1692	CSG792S	Seddon Pennine 7	Plaxton Supreme III Express	C49F	1978	Ex Eastern Scottish, 1985
1694	CSG794S	Seddon Pennine 7	Plaxton Supreme III Express	C45F	1978	Ex Eastern Scottish, 1990
1698	SSC108P	Seddon Pennine 7	Alexander AT	C24DL	1976	Ex Midland Bluebird, 1996
1699	GSX899T	Seddon Pennine 7	Alexander AT	C49F	1978	Ex Eastern Scottish, 1985
1715	G715OSH	Leyland Swift LBM6T/1RS	Reeve Burgess Harrier	C29F	1989	
1739	M399OMS	Omni	Omni Citizen	B16FL	1994	Ex SMT, 1996
1749	H649USH	Ford Transit VE6	Deansgate	M15	1991	Ex Grieve, Hawick, 1994
1851	OSG71V	Leyland Fleetline FE30AGR	Eastern Coach Works	H43/32F	1979	Ex Eastern Scottish, 1985
1853w	OSG53V	Leyland Fleetline FE30AGR	Eastern Coach Works	H43/32F	1979	Ex SMT, 1995
1854	GSC854T	Leyland Fleetline FE30AGR	Eastern Coach Works	H43/32F	1978	Ex Eastern Scottish, 1985
1884	TYS264W	Dennis Dominator DD137B	Alexander RL	H45/34F	1981	Ex Central Scottish, 1987
1885	TYS255W	Dennis Dominator DD135B	Alexander RL	H45/34F	1981	Ex Central Scottish, 1987
1890	MDL650R	Bristol VRT/SL3/6LXB	Eastern Coach Works	H43/31F	1976	Ex Southern Vectis, 1990
1895	NDL655R	Bristol VRT/SL3/6LXB	Eastern Coach Works	H43/31F	1977	Ex Southern Vectis, 1991
1896	NDL656R	Bristol VRT/SL3/6LXB	Eastern Coach Works	H43/31F	1977	Ex Southern Vectis, 1991

2101-2105

		Scania K113CRB		Plaxton Paramount 3500 III	C49FT*	1990	*Seating varies

2101	PSU316	2102	LAT662	2103	PSU317	2104	PSU314	2105	PSU315

2106	M106PKS	Scania K113CRB	Van Hool Alizée	C49FT	1995	
2107	N107VKS	Scania K113CRB	Van Hool Alizée	C49FT	1996	
2201	KEX532	Volvo B58-61	Plaxton Viewmaster IV Exp	C50FT	1981	Ex Lothian Transit, 1994
2304	VXI8734	DAF MB200DKFL600	Duple Caribbean 2	C51F	1986	Ex Ian Glass, Haddington, 1991
2307	ESX257	DAF MB200DKTL600	Van Hool Alizée	C46FT	1982	Ex Ian Glass, Haddington, 1991
2309	KSU389	DAF SB2300DHS585	Smit Euroliner	C53F	1985	Ex Ian Glass, Haddington, 1991
2310	FFS10X	DAF MB200DKTL600	Plaxton Supreme VI	C57F	1982	Ex Shanks, Galashiels, 1992
2427	KBZ3627	Dennis Javelin 12SDA1907	Duple 320	C53F	1988	Ex Ian Glass, Haddington, 1991
2428	KBZ3628	Dennis Javelin 8.5SDL1903	Duple 320	C35F	1988	Ex Ian Glass, Haddington, 1991
2429	KBZ3629	Dennis Javelin 12SDA1907	Duple 320	C53F	1989	Ex Ian Glass, Haddington, 1991

Previous Registrations:

158ASV	OLS805T	NSC702X	FFS10X
487GFR	From new	PLS536W	ASH1W
A12SMT	B267KPF	PSU314	H104TSH
A20SMT	A331BSC	PSU315	H105TSH
BSS76	A678DSF	PSU316	G101RSH
ESF571W	DSC975W, PSU318	PSU317	H103TSH
ESX257	WFR612Y	PSU318	MSC557X, KSU388, NSC411X
FFS7X	MVK332X	PSU319	MSC552X, WLT741, HGD741X, PSU319, NSC413X
FFS9X	PSF559Y, KSU389	PSU320	A562BSX
FFS10X	VTT14X, LAT662	PSU321	A563BSX
KBZ3627	E888MSX	PSU322	PSF322Y
KBZ3628	E900MSX	RSX84J	RXA51J, PSU314
KBZ3629	F777UFS	VFS324V	OSF963V, PSU315
KEX532	GOP730W, PBC453	VFS414V	USX969V, PXI8935
KSU388	D320RNS	VFS423V	USX971V, PSU316
KSU389	B88KSF	VFS432V	DSD933V, PSU319
KSU390	TFS317Y	VSU715	A124ESG
KSU391	A185UGB	VXI8734	C700USC
KSU392	B342RLS	WSV136	B336RLS
KSU393	B343RLS	WSV137	B337RLS
KSU394	D501CSH	WSV138	B338RLS
LAT662	G102RSH		
NFS984T	LSC950T, PSU322		

Livery: Yellow and green (Lowland); cream and green (SMT); ivory, blue and orange (Ian Glass); blue and yellow (Scottish Citylink) 2101/2; metallic green (Prestige Tours) 2105-7.

MacEWAN'S COACH SERVICES

J N MacEwan, Johnfield, Amisfield, Dumfries & Galloway, DG1 3LS

GFM882	Bristol L6A	Eastern Coach Works	B35F	1948	Ex Philp, Dunfermline, 1990
GRS114E	Leyland Atlantean PDR1/1	Alexander A	O43/34F	1967	Ex Grampian, 1996
TMU847Y	Leyland Leopard PSU3E/4R	Duple Dominant IV (1983)	C53F	1972	Ex Reynolds Diplomat, Bushey, 1994
GGV47N	Bristol LH6L	Plaxton Elite III Express	C43F	1974	Ex driving school, Liverpool, 1995
LHL247P	Leyland Leopard PSU3C/4R	Alexander AT	DP49F	1976	Ex Peacock, Dumfries, 1995
MFR126P	Leyland Leopard PSU4C/2R	Alexander AYS	B45F	1976	Ex Edinburgh Transport, 1996
PTT71R	Bristol LH6L	Plaxton Supreme III Express	C43F	1976	Ex Bedlington, Ashington, 1994
SFJ124R	Bristol LH6L	Plaxton Supreme III Express	C43F	1977	Ex Bedlington, Ashington, 1994
OHY789R	Leyland Leopard PSU3D/4R	Plaxton Supreme III Express	C51F	1977	Ex Dickson, Dumfries, 1991
TPJ67S	Bristol LHS6L	Eastern Coach Works	B35F	1977	Ex Moffat & Williamson, Gauldry, 1994
YPL83T	AEC Reliance 6U2R	Duple Dominant II Express	C49F	1979	Ex Morse, Stillington, 1995
AHN391T	Leyland Leopard PSU3E/4R	Plaxton Supreme III Express	C53F	1979	Ex Reynolds, Watford, 1995
PGA833V	Leyland Leopard PSU3F/4R	Alexander AT	C49F	1980	Ex KCB Network, 1996
LFJ848W	Bristol LHS6L	Eastern Coach Works	B35F	1980	Ex Moffat & Williamson, Gauldry, 1994
LFJ849W	Bristol LHS6L	Eastern Coach Works	B35F	1980	Ex Golden Coaches, Llandow, 1995
LFJ850W	Bristol LHS6L	Eastern Coach Works	B35F	1980	Ex Moffat & Williamson, Gauldry, 1994
LPY458W	Leyland Leopard PSU3E/4R	Duple Dominant	B55F	1981	Ex South Lancashire, St Helens, 1997
PNW344W	Leyland Leopard PSU3F/4R	Plaxton Supreme IV	C46F	1981	Ex Rosemary, Terrington St Clements, 1992
RIB9362	Leyland Tiger TRCTL11/3R	Duple	C53F	1981	Ex Knotty Bus, Chesterton, 1996
JDE189X	Leyland Tiger TRCTL11/2R	Duple	C53F	1982	Ex Bakers, Enstone, 1996
WEX828X	Leyland Leopard PSU3G/4R	Eastern Coach Works B51	DP47F	1982	Ex Fitzcharles, Grangemouth, 1993
XPW879X	Leyland Leopard PSU3G/4R	Eastern Coach Works B51	DP47F	1982	Ex Fitzcharles, Grangemouth, 1993
VUD29X	Leyland Leopard PSU3G/4R	Eastern Coach Works B51	DP49F	1982	Ex Fitzcharles, Grangemouth, 1993
841FAT	Leyland Tiger TRCTL11/3R	Plaxton Paramount 3500	C49FT	1983	Ex Monks European, Leigh, 1992
A907LWU	Leyland Tiger TRCTL11/3R	Plaxton Paramount 3200 E	C44FT	1983	Ex Dorset Travel Services, 1992
D513RTT	Leyland Royal Tiger RT	Van Hool Alizée	C53F	1986	Ex Sapphire of London, 1993
E165TWO	Freight Rover Sherpa	Carlyle Citybus 2	B20F	1988	Ex Hamilton, Uxbridge, 1993
E187UKG	Freight Rover Sherpa	Carlyle Citybus 2	B20F	1988	Ex Red & White, 1994
E188UKG	Freight Rover Sherpa	Carlyle Citybus 2	B20F	1988	Ex Red & White, 1994
E191UKG	Freight Rover Sherpa	Carlyle Citybus 2	B20F	1988	Ex National Welsh, 1991
E192UKG	Freight Rover Sherpa	Carlyle Citybus 2	B20F	1988	Ex Williams, Runcorn, 1993
E193UKG	Freight Rover Sherpa	Carlyle Citybus 2	B20F	1988	Ex National Welsh, 1991
E194UKG	Freight Rover Sherpa	Carlyle Citybus 2	B20F	1988	Ex Williams, Runcorn, 1993
F747TRE	Freight Rover Sherpa	PMT Bursley	DP16F	1989	Ex Rainbow Bus Co, Dunkerswell, 1990
G401MFV	Hestair-Duple SDA1512	Duple 425	C53FT	1990	Ex Ashton, St Helens, 1997
H512YCX	DAF SB220LC500	Optare Delta	DP48F	1991	Ex K Line, Huddersfield, 1997
J882UNA	Mercedes-Benz 709D	Plaxton Beaver	B23F	1991	Ex Jim Stones, Leigh, 1997
K477SSM	Mercedes-Benz 709D	Dormobile Routemaker	B29F	1993	
K478SSM	Mercedes-Benz 709D	Dormobile Routemaker	B29F	1993	
K877DSG	Mercedes-Benz 814D	Plaxton Beaver	C33F	1993	Ex Glen Coaches, Port Glasgow, 1996
L676VSM	Mercedes-Benz 709D	Dormobile Routemaker	B29F	1993	
L677VSM	Mercedes-Benz 709D	Dormobile Routemaker	B29F	1993	
M804ASM	Mercedes-Benz 814D	Autobus Classique 2	C33F	1995	
M578BSM	Mercedes-Benz 709D	Alexander Sprint	B29F	1995	
M62DSJ	Bova FHD12.330	Bova Futura	C53F	1995	Ex Stonehouse Coaches, 1997
N117FSM	Scania K113CRB	Van Hool Alizée	C49FT	1996	
N209FSM	Mercedes-Benz 709D	Plaxton Beaver	B29F	1996	
N210FSM	Mercedes-Benz 709D	Plaxton Beaver	B29F	1996	
N703FSM	Ford Transit VE6	Crystals Challenger	B20F	1996	
N704FSM	Ford Transit VE6	Crystals Challenger	B20F	1996	
N705FSM	Ford Transit VE6	Crystals Challenger	B20F	1996	
N706FSM	Ford Transit VE6	Crystals Challenger	B20F	1996	
N885FSM	Bova FLC12.280	Bova Futura Club	C53F	1996	
P151KSM	Mercedes-Benz O405	Optare Prisma	B47F	1996	
P152KSM	Mercedes-Benz O405	Optare Prisma	B47F	1996	
P153KSM	Mercedes-Benz O405	Optare Prisma	B47F	1996	

Previous Registrations:

841FAT	EFR755Y	RIB9362	KHG185W, 2174PH
D513RTT	D39HMT	TMU847Y	JRK622K

Opposite: **McEwan's Coach Services have recently been awarded the Scottish Borders RailLink Service for which they have purchased three new Optare Prisma buses. The upper picture shows Leyland Leopard XPW879X while the new Prisma is P153KSM.** *Mark Bailey/Tony Wilson*

McGILL'S

McGill's Bus Service Ltd, 3 Muriel Street, Barrhead, Glasgow, G78 1QE

P	GVD47	Guy Arab III	Duple	H31/26R	1950	Ex Hutchison, Overtown, 1952
w	VYJ893	AEC Routemaster R2RH(Iveco)	Park Royal	H36/28R	1959	Ex London Buses, 1994
	TDS611R	Leyland National 11351A/1R		B52F	1977	
	XYS596S	Leyland National 11351A/1R		B52F	1978	
	DYS636T	Leyland National 11351A/1R		B52F	1978	
	AAK112T	Leyland National 10351B/1R		B44F	1979	Ex Somerbus, Paulton, 1989
w	GGE171T	Leyland National 10351A/1R		B41F	1979	Ex Strathclyde's Transport, 1986
	KRS536V	Leyland National 2 NL106L11/1R		B44F	1980	Ex Northern Scottish, 1991
	KKG109W	Leyland National 2 NL116AL11/1R		B52F	1981	Ex Edmunds, Rassau, 1986
	UGE388W	Leyland National 2 NL116AL11/1R		B52F	1981	
	UGE389W	Leyland National 2 NL116AL11/1R		B52F	1981	
	BHS206X	Leyland National 2 NL116AL11/1R		B52F	1981	
	BHS207X	Leyland National 2 NL116AL11/1R		B52F	1981	
	B724AGD	Leyland National 2 NL116TL11/1R		B52F	1984	
	B725AGD	Leyland National 2 NL116HLXCT/1R		B52F	1985	
	C263FGG	Leyland National 2 NL116HLXCT/1R		B52F	1986	
	C264FGG	Leyland National 2 NL116HLXCT/1R		B52F	1986	
	D614BCK	Iveco Daily 49.10	Robin Hood City Nippy	B21F	1987	Ex Rennies, Dumfermline, 1994
	H733HWK	Leyland Lynx LX2R11C15Z4S	Leyland Lynx 2	B51F	1990	Ex VL Bus demonstrator, 1991
	K91RGA	Mercedes-Benz 709D	Dormobile Routemaker	B25F	1993	Ex Rowe, Muirkirk, 1995
	K92RGA	Mercedes-Benz 709D	Dormobile Routemaker	B25F	1993	Ex Rowe, Muirkirk, 1995
	K945SGG	Mercedes-Benz 709D	Dormobile Routemaker	B29F	1993	
	K946SGG	Dennis Dart 9SDL3011	Plaxton Pointer	B35F	1993	
	K947SGG	Dennis Dart 9SDL3011	Plaxton Pointer	B35F	1993	
	L705AGA	Mercedes-Benz 709D	WS Wessex II	B29F	1994	
	N439GHG	Dennis Dart 9SDL	Northern Counties Paladin	B39F	1995	
	N440GHG	Dennis Dart 9SDL	Northern Counties Paladin	B39F	1995	
	N473MUS	Dennis Dart 9SDL	Northern Counties Paladin	B39F	1995	
	N474MUS	Dennis Dart 9SDL	Northern Counties Paladin	B39F	1995	

Previous Registrations:
KRS536V GSO2V   VYJ893   VLT89

Livery: Grey and red

Opposite, top: **For the centenary of McGills services in 1994 a AEC Routemaster which had been refurbished and re-engined with an Iveco unit joined the fleet from London buses. Photographed in service, VYJ893 illustrates the former fleet-name style.** *Malc McDonald* **Six Dennis Darts four with Northern Counties bodywork and two with Plaxton bodies, now operate with McGills. Pictured in heavy rain at Paisley (right) is N439GHG while in much more pleasant weather, K946SGG is seen in colour.** *Malc McDonald/ Phillip Stephenson*

MACKIES

J L Mackie, 32 Glasshouse Loan, Alloa, The Clackmannanshire, FK10 1DM

YMS85R	Leyland Leopard PSU5A/4R	Plaxton Supreme III	C55F	1977	Ex Kings of Dunblane, 1992
FXI8035	Leyland Leopard PSU3E/4R	Willowbrook Warrior (1989)	B51F	1977	Ex Devon General, 1986
NSC822X	Bova EL26/581	Bova Europa	C53F	1981	
SL8417	Ward Dalesman	Plaxton Paramount 3200	C53F	1983	
SL8207	Leyland Tiger TRCTL11/3R	Plaxton Paramount 3500	C53F	1985	
D122FLS	Leyland Lynx LX563TL11FR1	Leyland Lynx	B49F	1986	
D634BBV	Leyland Lynx LX112L10ZR1	Leyland Lynx	B51F	1987	Ex Leyland demonstrator, 1988
D107NDW	Leyland Lynx LX112TL11ZR1R	Leyland Lynx	B51F	1987	Ex Merthyr Tydfil, 1989
D112NDW	Leyland Lynx LX112TL11ZR1R	Leyland Lynx	B51F	1987	Ex Merthyr Tydfil, 1989
YFS438	Dennis Javelin 8.5SDA1915	Duple 320	C35F	1989	
J498VMS	Ward Dalesman	Willowbrook Crusader	C53F	1991	
SL8852	Dennis Javelin 8.5SDA1926	Plaxton Paramount 3200 III	C35F	1992	
PFG362	Volvo B10M-60	Van Hool Alizée	C53FT	1992	Ex Hutchison, Overtown, 1997
YBL526	Volvo B10M-60	Van Hool Alizée	C57FT	1992	Ex Hutchison, Overtown, 1997
K620DMS	Volvo B10M-60	Van Hool Alizée	C53F	1993	
L424LLS	Volvo B10M-62	Van Hool Alizée	C53F	1994	
XSV270	Volvo B9M	Van Hool Alizée	C38F	1995	
P736FMS	Dennis Dart SLF SFD...	UVG UrbanStar	B43F	1997	
P737FMS	Dennis Dart SLF SFD...	UVG UrbanStar	B43F	1997	
P738FMS	Dennis Dart SLF SFD...	UVG UrbanStar	B43F	1997	
P739FMS	Dennis Dart SLF SFD...	UVG UrbanStar	B43F	1997	

Previous Registrations:

FXI8035	SAD131R	SL8207	From new	YBL526	J20BUS
NSC822X	PFG362	SL8417	CLS709Y,YFS438,WCS785Y	XSV270	From new
PFG362	J19BUS	SL8852	J867YLS	YFS438	From new

Livery: White, brown and beige

J J McMENEMY

J McMenemy Co Ltd, Central Garage, 2 Princess Street, Ardrossan,
North Ayrshire, KA22 8BP

ASD31T	Leyland Atlantean AN68A/1R	Alexander AL	H45/33F	1979	Ex A1 Service (McMenemy), 1995
A10EBM	Volvo B10M-61	Van Hool Alizée	C49FT	1988	Ex Meney, Saltcoats, 1996
F678LGG	Volvo B10M-61	Plaxton Paramount 3200 III	C53F	1989	Ex Southern Coaches, Barrhead, 1997
NBZ2604	Volvo B10M-60	Plaxton Paramount 3500 III	C53F	1989	Ex A1 Service (McMenemy), 1995

Previous Registrations:

A10EBM	E660UWU	NBZ2604	G169LET

Mackie's of Alloa have built an interesting fleet that includes two Ward Dalesman chassis, four Leyland Lynx and three of the latest UrbanStar bodies from UVG. The buses operate around the new authority of The Clackmannanshire which encompasses parts of former Stirlingshire. Illustrating the fleet we see P737FMS, one of the UrbanStars on a Dennis Dart heading for Tillicoultry while the lower picture shows YFS438, a short version of the Dennis Javelin here fitted with a Duple 320 body. It is seen outside Balmoral Castle. *David Kat/British Bus Publishing*

MARBILL

Marbill Coach Services Ltd, 1 Acacia Drive, Beith, East Ayrshire, KA15 1DA

Depot : Yard No2 Mains Road, Beith.

FJY912E	Leyland Atlantean PDR1/1	Metro Cammell	H43/32F	1967	Ex Plymouth, 1986
LKP381P	Ailsa B55-10	Alexander AV	H44/35F	1975	Ex A1 (J McMenemy), Ayr, 1994
PAU200R	Daimler Fleetline CRG6LX	Northern Counties	H47/33F	1976	Ex Dunnet, Keiss, 1990
OUC57R	Leyland Fleetline FE30GR	MCW	H44/32F	1976	Ex Marshall, Ballieston, 1993
NOC380R	Leyland Fleetline FE30ALR	Alexander AL	H43/33F	1976	Ex A1 (McKinnon), Ayr, 1994
OSJ616R	Leyland Leopard PSU3C/4R	Alexander AY	B53F	1976	Ex Loch Lomond Coaches, 1994
NOC458R	Leyland Fleetline FE30AGR	MCW	H44/33F	1977	Ex A1 (McKinnon), Ayr, 1994
RJA801R	Leyland Atlantean AN68A/1R	Park Royal	H43/32F	1977	Ex Western Buses, 1996
YMS705R	Ailsa B55-10	Alexander AV	H44/35F	1977	Ex KCB Network, 1996
YMS712R	Ailsa B55-10	Alexander AV	H44/35F	1977	Ex KCB Network, 1996
VCD296S	Leyland Leopard PSU3E/4R	Duple Dominant I	C47F	1978	Ex Kelvin Central, 1993
WSU448S	Leyland Leopard PSU3C/4R	Alexander AYS	B53F	1977	Ex Loch Lomond Coaches, 1996
CFM88S	Leyland Fleetline FE30AGR	Northern Counties	H43/29F	1978	Ex Clynnog & Trefor, Trefor, 1994
XSJ646T	Leyland Fleetline FE30AGR	Northern Counties	H44/31F	1978	Ex Western, 1993
GSU831T	Leyland Leopard PSU3E/4R	Alexander AYS	B53F	1979	Ex Loch Lomond Coaches, 1996
GSU832T	Leyland Leopard PSU3E/4R	Alexander AYS	B53F	1979	Ex Loch Lomond Coaches, 1996
LHS741V	Ailsa B55-10 MkII	Alexander AV	H44/35F	1979	Ex KCB Network, 1995
LHS747V	Ailsa B55-10 MkII	Alexander AV	H44/35F	1979	Ex KCB Network, 1995
LHS751V	Ailsa B55-10 MkII	Alexander AV	H44/35F	1979	Ex KCB Network, 1995
ECS57V	Ailsa B55-10 MkII	Alexander AV	H44/35F	1979	Ex A1 Service (McMenemy), 1995
ECS883V	Leyland Fleetline FE30AGR	Northern Counties	H44/31F	1979	Ex Western Buses, 1996
ECS885V	Leyland Fleetline FE30AGR	Northern Counties	H44/31F	1979	Ex Western Buses, 1996
XRY278	Ford R1014	Duple Dominant II Express	C35F	1980	Ex Eagle Coaches, Stevenston, 1996
BJI6863	Volvo B10M-61	Van Hool Alizée	C53F	1987	Ex Park's, Hamilton, 1992
GJI625	Volvo B10M-61	Van Hool Alizée	C53F	1987	Ex Park's, Hamilton, 1992

Marbill comprises a mixed operation of executive coaches and contract buses from their base in East Ayrshire. Representing the former is LJI978, one of eight Volvo B10M s in the fleet fitted with Van Hool Alizée coachwork. The vehicle was carrying in previous mark of K713TSO when pictured with a full load heading for Blackpool's Illuminations. *Paul Wigan*

The Volvo marque features in the double-deck fleet through half a dozen Alexander-bodied Ailsas. All bar one came from KCB Network, the exception is ECS57V which came from McMenemy's part of the A1 Service operation and was one of the vehicles retained by the operator when the services passed to Western Buses. *Billy Nicol*

GJI926	Volvo B10M-61	Van Hool Alizée	C53F	1988	Ex Park's, Hamilton, 1995
HJI565	Volvo B10M-61	Van Hool Alizée	C53F	1988	Ex Park's, Hamilton, 1995
H884LSD	Volvo B10M-60	Van Hool Alizée	C48FT	1990	Ex Allander Travel, Milngavie, 1997
AJI8353	Mercedes-Benz 609D	Made-to-Measure	C24F	1992	
LJI978	Volvo B10M-60	Van Hool Alizée	C53F	1993	
TIW572S	Volvo B10M-62	Van Hool Alizée	C53F	1994	Ex Allander Travel, Milngavie, 1997
L850WDS	Mercedes-Benz 811D	WS Wessex II	B28FL	1994	
L851WDS	Mercedes-Benz 811D	WS Wessex II	B28FL	1994	
L852WDS	Mercedes-Benz 811D	WS Wessex II	B28FL	1994	
L857WDS	Mercedes-Benz 811D	Dormobile Routemaker	B33F	1994	
M988CYS	Mercedes-Benz 709D	WS Wessex II	B28FL	1994	
M481CSD	Volvo B10M-62	Van Hool Alizée	C55F	1995	
2154K	Volvo B10M-62	Van Hool Alizée	C55F	1995	
M760GGE	Volvo B10M-62	Van Hool Alizée	C55F	1995	
N797FSD	Mercedes-Benz 709D	WS Wessex II	B16FL	1995	
N798FSD	Mercedes-Benz 709D	WS Wessex II	B16FL	1995	
N799FSD	Mercedes-Benz 709D	WS Wessex II	B16FL	1995	
N801FSD	Mercedes-Benz 709D	WS Wessex II	B16FL	1995	
N207GCS	Mercedes-Benz 709D	WS Wessex II	B16FL	1995	
N208GCS	Mercedes-Benz 709D	WS Wessex II	B16FL	1995	
N992KUS	Ford Transit VE6	Deansgate	M8	1995	
N993KUS	Mercedes-Benz 410D	Deansgate	M16	1995	
P553KSD	Dennis Javelin 12SDA2136	Plaxton Première 320	C57F	1996	
P554KSD	Dennis Javelin 12SDA2136	Plaxton Première 320	C57F	1996	

Previous Registrations:

AJI8353	K667NGB	H884LSD	2154K, H103XNS, 9446AT
2154K	M482CSD	HJI565	E639UNE, LSK832, E958CGA
BJI6863	D564MVR, GIL1683, D781OSJ	LJI978	K713TSD
F499MGD	F158XSJ, LJI978	TIW5725	LSK839, L634AYS, XAT11X, L786ANS
GJI625	D566MVR, GIL1685, D812OSJ	XRY278	NLP60V
GJI926	E641UNE, LSK871, E959CGA		

Livery: Orange, gold and black

MAYNES

G Mayne, Cluny Garage, Buckie, Aberdeenshire, AB56 1PS

PUF249M	Ford R1114	Duple Dominant	C49F	1974	Ex Bluebird Buses, 1996
ESE353T	Bedford YMT	Duple Dominant II	C53F	1979	Ex Bluebird Buses, 1996
YSU989	Ford R1014	Plaxton Supreme IV	C35F	1980	Ex DC Minicoaches, Glenmavis, 1996
YSU990	MAN 16-280	Berkhof Esprite 350	C53F	1986	Ex Beaton, Blantyre, 1996
E123RAX	Freight Rover Sherpa	Carlyle Citybus 2	B20F	1987	Ex Fishers, Bronington, 1997
F888XOE	Freight Rover Sherpa	Carlyle Citybus 2	B20F	1988	Ex Merry Hill, Oldbury, 1996
F680LGG	Toyota Coaster HB31R	Caetano Optimo	C21F	1989	Ex Steele's Cs, Stevenston, 1996
G270GKG	Freight Rover Sherpa	Carlyle Citybus 2	B20F	1990	Ex Merry Hill, Oldbury, 1996
H724LOL	Freight Rover Sherpa	Carlyle Citybus 2	B20F	1990	Ex Anderson, Castleford, 1996
J24VWO	Volvo B10M-60	Plaxton Paramount 3500 III	C501T	1992	Ex Garnett, Tindale Crescent, 1997
L210RST	Mercedes-Benz 410D	Autobus Classique	M16	1993	
M222GSM	Volvo B10M-62	Jonckheere Deauville	C51F	1995	
M444GSM	Volvo B10M-62	Jonckheere Deauville	C53F	1995	
M500GSM	Scania K113CRB	Van Hool Alizée	C F	1995	
M555GSM	Dennis Javelin 12SDA2131	Berkhof Excellence 1000	C53F	1995	
M777GSM	Dennis Javelin 12SDA2131	Berkhof Excellence 1000	C53F	1995	
N240WDO	Mercedes-Benz 814D	Autobus Classique 2	C23F	1995	
N460KMW	Mercedes-Benz 814D	Autobus Classique 2	C33F	1995	
N500GSM	Scania K113CRB	Van Hool Alizée	C49F	1996	
N550GFS	Scania K113CRB	Van Hool Alizée	C51F	1996	
N588GBW	Volvo B10M-62	Caetano Algarve II	C51FT	1996	Ex Maidstone & District, 1997
N888GSM	Toyota Coaster HZB50R	Caetano Optimo III	C21F	1996	
N999GSM	Toyota Coaster HZB50R	Caetano Optimo III	C21F	1996	
P500GSM	Volvo B10M-62	Van Hool Alizée	C57F	1996	
P555GSM	Volvo B10M-62	Van Hool Alizée	C57F	1996	
P222GSM	Volvo B10M-62	Berkhof Axial	C51FT	1997	
P GSM	Volvo B10M-62	Berkhof Axial	C51FT	1997	

Previous Registrations:

YSU989	RMB405V	YSU990	C44KHS

Livery: White, blue and gold

Maynes of Buchie principally operate coaches on extended tours. Pictured on one of these in Blackpool was one of three Scania K113s in the fleet, all of which are fitted with Van Hool Alizée bodywork.
David Donati Collection

MIDLAND BLUEBIRD / SMT

Midland Bluebird Ltd, Carmuirs House, 300 Stirling Road, Larbert, Stirlingshire, FK5 3NJ

Depots: Dunmore Street, Balfron; Cowie Road, Bannockburn; Westfield Avenue, Edinburgh; Stirling Road, Larbert; High Street, Linlithgow; Almondvale, Livingston and Centrex Vehicle Training, Deans, Livingston;

26	DMS26V	Leyland National 2 NL116L11/1R		B49F	1980	
29	NLS981W	Leyland National 2 NL116L11/1R		B52F	1980	
32	NLS984W	Leyland National 2 NL116L11/1R		B52F	1980	
51	K473EDT	Mercedes-Benz O405	Alexander Cityranger	B51F	1992	Ex Mercedes-Benz demonstrator, 1993

52-57		Mercedes-Benz O405	Wright Cityranger	B51F	1993	
52	L552GMS	54	L554GMS	55	L555GMS	56	L556GMS	57	L557GMS
53	L553GMS					

58	L140MAK	Mercedes-Benz O405	Wright Cityranger	B51F	1994	Ex Mercedes-Benz demonstrator, 1995

61-70		Mercedes-Benz O405	Optare Prisma	B49F	1995	Ex SMT, 1996
61	N61CSC	63	N63CSC	65	N65CSC	67	N67CSC	69	N69CSC
62	N62CSC	64	N64CSC	66	N66CSC	68	N68CSC	70	N70CSC

71	P171DMS	Mercedes-Benz O405	Optare Prisma	DP49F	1997	
72	P172DMS	Mercedes-Benz O405	Optare Prisma	DP49F	1997	
77	P877YKS	Mercedes-Benz O405	Optare Prisma	DP49F	1997	
78	P878YKS	Mercedes-Benz O405	Optare Prisma	DP49F	1997	
79	P879YKS	Mercedes-Benz O405	Optare Prisma	DP49F	1997	
101	FSU381	Leyland Tiger TRBTL11/2R	Alexander AT	DP49F	1983	
102	FSU382	Leyland Tiger TRBTL11/2R	Alexander AT	DP49F	1983	
103	FSU383	Leyland Tiger TRBTL11/2R	Alexander AT	DP49F	1983	
105	FSU380	Leyland Tiger TRBTL11/2R	Alexander AT	DP49F	1983	
107	101ASV	Leyland Tiger TRBTL11/2R	Duple Dominant II Express	C49F	1983	Ex Kelvin Scottish, 1986
108	FSU308	Leyland Tiger TRBTL11/2R	Duple Dominant II Express	C47F	1983	Ex Kelvin Scottish, 1986
114	FSU334	Leyland Tiger TRBTL11/2R	Alexander TE	C46F	1983	
116	SSU816	Leyland Tiger TRBTL11/2RP	Alexander TC	C47F	1983	
117	BSV807	Leyland Tiger TRBTL11/2RP	Alexander TC	C42DL	1983	Ex Kelvin Scottish, 1988
118	7881UA	Leyland Tiger TRBTL11/2RP	Alexander TC	C42DL	1983	
121	SSU821	Leyland Tiger TRCTL11/3RH	Duple Caribbean	C51F	1984	
129	SSU859	Leyland Tiger TRCTL11/3RH	Duple Laser	C46FT	1984	
130	693AFU	Leyland Tiger TRCTL11/3RH	Duple Laser	C51FT	1984	
131	SSU831	Leyland Tiger TRCTL11/3RH	Duple Laser 2	C46FT	1985	
132	SSU837	Leyland Tiger TRCTL11/3RH	Duple Laser 2	C46FT	1985	
136	SSU897	Leyland Tiger TRCLXC/2RH	Plaxton Paramount 3200 E	C49F	1984	Ex Clydeside Scottish, 1985
138	OVT798	Leyland Tiger TRCLXC/2RH	Plaxton Paramount 3200 E	C49F	1984	Ex Western Scottish, 1986
139	119ASV	Leyland Tiger TRCTL11/3R	Duple Goldliner IV	C53F	1982	Ex Western Scottish, 1986

141-145		Leyland Tiger TRCTL11/3RH	Duple 340	C49FT	1987	
141	SSU841	142	SSU857	143	KSU834	144	FSV634	145	156ASV

147	SSU827	Leyland Tiger TRCTL11/3R	Duple Goldliner IV	C53F	1982	Ex Kelvin Scottish, 1988
148	SSU861	Leyland Tiger TRCTL11/3R	Duple Goldliner IV	C53F	1982	Ex Kelvin Scottish, 1988
149	SSU829	Leyland Tiger TRCTL11/3R	Duple Goldliner III	C53F	1982	Ex Kelvin Scottish, 1988
150	WSU487	Leyland Tiger TRCTL11/3R	Plaxton Paramount 3200 E	C53F	1983	Ex Grampian, 1991
151	WSU489	Leyland Tiger TRCTL11/3R	Plaxton Paramount 3200 E	C53F	1983	Ex Grampian, 1991
152	GSU338	Leyland Tiger TRCTL11/3R	Plaxton Paramount 3200 E	C57F	1983	Ex Grampian, 1991
153	GSU339	Leyland Tiger TRCTL11/3R	Plaxton Paramount 3200 E	C57F	1983	Ex Grampian, 1991
154	PSU625	Leyland Tiger TRCLXC/2RH	Plaxton Paramount 3200 E	C53F	1986	Ex Grampian, 1991
155	PSU622	Leyland Tiger TRCLXC/2RH	Plaxton Paramount 3200 E	C53F	1986	Ex Grampian, 1991
156	WSU479	Leyland Tiger TRCTL11/3RH	Plaxton Paramount 3200 E	C48FT	1984	Ex Grampian, 1993
157	YJF16Y	Leyland Tiger TRCTL11/2R	Plaxton Supreme V Express	C53F	1982	Ex Leicester Citybus, 1995
158	ANK316X	Leyland Tiger TRCTL11/3R	Plaxton Supreme IV	C57F	1982	Ex Kings of Dunblane, 1995
159	FNM868Y	Leyland Tiger TRCTL11/2R	Plaxton Supreme V	C53F	1983	Ex Kings of Dunblane, 1995

The higher cost of the Mercedes-Benz O405 units in comparison to British-built products have restricted the numbers in use. Joint ventures with Alexander, Wright and Optare where the chassis-cowl is fitted with local bodywork have seen limited numbers of O405 buses in use on the higher quality services. Pictured in Bannockburn while heading for Stirling University is one with Wright bodywork, 55, L555GMS. *Paul Wigan*

160	D591MVR	Leyland Tiger TRCTL11/3RZ	Plaxton Paramount 3200 III	C53F	1987	Ex Kings of Dunblane, 1995
161	D599MVR	Leyland Tiger TRCTL11/3RZ	Plaxton Paramount 3200 III	C53F	1987	Ex Kings of Dunblane, 1995
162	E60MMT	Leyland Tiger TRCTL11/3RZ	Duple 340	C55F	1987	Ex Kings of Dunblane, 1995
163	F716SML	Leyland Tiger TRCL10/3ARZA	Duple 340	C55F	1989	Ex Kings of Dunblane, 1995
164	H838SLS	Leyland Tiger TRCL10/3ARZA	Plaxton Paramount 3500 III	C53F	1991	Ex Kings of Dunblane, 1995

201-213

| | | Dennis Dart SLF SFD212 | Plaxton Pointer | B38F | 1996-97 |

201	P201NSC	204	P204NSC	207	P207NSC	210	P210NSC	212	P212NSC
202	P202NSC	205	P205NSC	208	P208NSC	211	P211NSC	213	P213NSC
203	P203NSC	206	P206NSC	209	P209NSC				

332	WSV135	Leyland Tiger TRCTL11/2RH	Plaxton Paramount 3200 E	C49F	1984	Ex SMT, 1996
333	WSV140	Leyland Tiger TRCTL11/2R	Plaxton Paramount 3200 E	C49F	1984	Ex SMT, 1996
335	A13SMT	Leyland Tiger TRCTL11/2RH	Plaxton Paramount 3200 II	C49F	1985	Ex SMT, 1996
339	A9SMT	Leyland Tiger TRCTL11/2RH	Plaxton Paramount 3200 II	C49F	1985	Ex SMT, 1996
340	A10SMT	Leyland Tiger TRCTL11/2RH	Plaxton Paramount 3200 II	C49F	1985	Ex SMT, 1996
341	A14SMT	Leyland Tiger TRCTL11/2RH	Plaxton Paramount 3200 II	C49F	1985	Ex SMT, 1996
345	A15SMT	Leyland Tiger TRCTL11/3RH	Duple 340	C53F	1987	Ex SMT, 1996
346	A16SMT	Leyland Tiger TRCTL11/3RH	Duple 340	C53F	1987	Ex SMT, 1996
347	A17SMT	Leyland Tiger TRCTL11/3RH	Duple 340	C53F	1987	Ex SMT, 1996
348	A18SMT	Leyland Tiger TRCTL11/3RH	Duple 340	C53F	1987	Ex SMT, 1996
400	RMS400W	Leyland Leopard PSU3G/4R	Alexander AT	DP49F	1981	

403-412

| | | Leyland Leopard PSU3G/4R | Alexander AYS | DP49F* | 1982 | *410/1 are B53F |

| 403 | TMS403X | 408 | TMS408X | 410 | TMS410X | 411 | TMS411X | 412 | TMS412X |

413	ULS713X	Leyland Leopard PSU3G/4R	Alexander AT	DP49F	1982	
414	ULS714X	Leyland Leopard PSU3G/4R	Alexander AT	DP49F	1982	
416	ULS716X	Leyland Leopard PSU3G/4R	Alexander AT	DP49F	1982	
417	ULS717X	Leyland Leopard PSU3G/4R	Alexander AT	DP49F	1982	
419	WFS154W	Leyland Leopard PSU3F/4R	Alexander AYS	B53F	1980	Ex Alexander (Fife), 1982

The Leyland Leopard still provides good service for many Scottish operators. Seen working the Stirling-Glasgow service of Midland Bluebird is their 468, HSU273, with Plaxton Supreme body. It is one of a pair retro-fitted with TL11 engines. *Les Peters*

421	XMS421Y	Leyland Leopard PSU3G/4R	Alexander AYS	DP49F	1982	
425	XMS425Y	Leyland Leopard PSU3G/4R	Alexander AYS	DP49F	1982	
438	ULS338T	Leyland Leopard PSU3E/4R	Alexander AYS	B53F	1979	
441	DLS351V	Leyland Leopard PSU3E/4R	Alexander AYS	B53F	1979	
442	DLS352V	Leyland Leopard PSU3E/4R	Alexander AYS	B53F	1979	
451	GSO80V	Leyland Leopard PSU3E/4R	Alexander AYS	B53F	1980	Ex Fife Scottish, 1988
454	WFS146W	Leyland Leopard PSU3F/4R	Alexander AYS	B53F	1980	Ex Fife Scottish, 1988
455	WFS143W	Leyland Leopard PSU3F/4R	Alexander AYS	B53F	1980	Ex Fife Scottish, 1988
456	WFS144W	Leyland Leopard PSU3F/4R	Alexander AYS	B53F	1980	Ex Fife Scottish, 1988
457	CSF155W	Leyland Leopard PSU3F/4R	Alexander AYS	B53F	1981	Ex Fife Scottish, 1988
462	EMS362V	Leyland Leopard PSU3E/4R	Alexander AT	DP49F	1980	
463	EMS363V	Leyland Leopard PSU3E/4R	Alexander AT	DP49F	1980	
466	EMS366V	Leyland Leopard PSU3E/4R	Alexander AT	DP49F	1980	Ex Kelvin Scottish, 1985
467	HSU247	Leyland Leopard PSU5D/4R(TL11) Plaxton Supreme IV	C53F	1981	Ex Grampian, 1991
468	HSU273	Leyland Leopard PSU5D/4R(TL11) Plaxton Supreme IV	C53F	1981	Ex Grampian, 1991

474-486

	Leyland Leopard PSU3F/4R	Alexander AYS	B53F*	1980	*478 is DP49F

474	LMS374W	477	LMS377W	479	LMS379W	482	LMS382W	486	LMS386W
476	LMS376W	478	LMS378W	481	LMS381W	484	LMS384W		

493	FSU318	Leyland Leopard PSU3G/4R	Duple Dominant II Express	C49F	1981
498	RMS398W	Leyland Leopard PSU3G/4R	Alexander AT	DP49F	1981
499	RMS399W	Leyland Leopard PSU3G/4R	Alexander AT	DP49F	1981

551-566

	Scania N113CRB	Wright Endurance	B49F	1994

551	L551HMS	555	L555HMS	558	L558JLS	561	L561JLS	564	L564JLS
552	L552HMS	556	L556HMS	559	L559JLS	562	L562JLS	565	L565JLS
553	L553HMS	557	L557JLS	560	L60HMS	563	L563JLS	566	L566JLS
554	L554HMS								

567-574

Scania N113CRL — Wright Pathfinder — B49F — 1995

567	M567RMS	569	M569RMS	571	M571RMS	573	N573VMS	574	N574VMS
568	M568RMS	570	M570RMS	572	N572VMS				

575	P575DMS	Scania L113CRL	Wright Axcess-ultralow	DP47F	1996	
576	P576DMS	Scania L113CRL	Wright Axcess-ultralow	DP47F	1996	
577	P577DMS	Scania L113CRL	Wright Axcess-ultralow	DP47F	1996	
578	P578DMS	Scania L113CRL	Wright Axcess-ultralow	DP47F	1996	
604	C812SDY	Mercedes-Benz L608D	Alexander AM	B20F	1986	Ex Bluebird, 1992
606	C821SDY	Mercedes-Benz L608D	Alexander AM	B20F	1986	Ex Bluebird, 1992
607	D226UHC	Mercedes-Benz L608D	Alexander AM	B20F	1986	Ex Bluebird, 1992
608	D227UHC	Mercedes-Benz L608D	Alexander AM	B20F	1986	Ex Bluebird, 1992
609	D229UHC	Mercedes-Benz L608D	Alexander AM	B20F	1986	Ex Bluebird, 1992
622	C102KDS	Mercedes-Benz L608D	Alexander AM	B21F	1986	Ex Kelvin Scottish, 1987
625	H925PMS	Mercedes-Benz 709D	Reeve Burgess Beaver	B25F	1990	
626	H926PMS	Mercedes-Benz 709D	Reeve Burgess Beaver	B25F	1990	

632-641

Mercedes-Benz 709D — Alexander AM — B25F* — 1991 — *637-641 are DP23F

632	H972RSG	634	H974RSG	636	H976RSG	638	J775WLS	640	J778WLS
633	H973RSG	635	H975RSG	637	J774WLS	639	J776WLS	641	J779WLS

642	J310XLS	Mercedes-Benz 711D	Reeve Burgess Beaver	C25F	1992	Ex Kings of Dunblane, 1995

651-659

Mercedes-Benz 709D — Alexander AM — B25F — 1993

651	K651DLS	653	K653DLS	655	K655DLS	657	K657DLS	659	K659DLS
652	K652DLS	654	K654DLS	656	K656DLS	658	K658DLS		

686-690

Mercedes-Benz 711D — Alexander Sprint — B25F — 1995

686	N686WLS	687	N687WLS	688	N688WLS	689	N689WLS	690	N690WLS

701-717

Leyland Atlantean AN68A/1R — Alexander AL — H45/29D* — 1977-78 Ex Grampian, 1991-95
*701/4 are H45/34F and ex SMT, 1996; 715/7 are H45/31F; 716 is O45/31F and is owned by Stirling Council

701	ORS201R	704	ORS204R	708	ORS208R	711	ORS211R	716	ORS216R
702	ORS202R	705	ORS205R	709	ORS209R	715	ORS215R	717	ORS217R
703	ORS203R								

718-727

Leyland Atlantean AN68A/1R — Alexander AL — H45/29D* — 1977-78 Ex Grampian, 1991-95
*719/20/3 are H45/31F; 724/6 are H45/34F and ex SMT, 1996

718	XSA218S	720	XSA220S	723	XSA223S	725	XSA225S	727	XSA227S
719	XSA219S	721	XSA221S	724	XSA224S	726	XSA226S		

733-737

Leyland Atlantean AN68A/1R — Alexander AL — H45/34F — 1978 Ex SMT, 1996
*737 is H45/29D and ex Grampian, 1996

733	YSO233T	734	YSO234T	735	YSO235T	736	YSO236T	737	YSO237T

738-757

Leyland Atlantean AN68A/1R — Alexander AL — H45/29D* — 1978-79 Ex Grampian, 1996
*744/8 ex SMT, 1996; *744/8/56/7 are H45/34F

738	DSA238T	744	DSA244T	748	DSA248T	756	DSA256T	757	DSA257T
743	DSA243T	747	DSA247T						

761	HRS261V	Leyland Altantean AN68A/1R	Alexander AL	H45/34F	1980	Ex Grampian, 1996
765	HRS265V	Leyland Altantean AN68A/1R	Alexander AL	O45/34F	1980	Ex Grampian, 1997
788	HRS288V	Leyland Altantean AN68A/1R	Alexander AL	H45/34F	1980	Ex Grampian, 1997

800-807

MCW Metrobus DR132/6 — Alexander RL — H45/33F — 1985 — 800-4 ex Kelvin Central, 1990

800	B100PKS	802	B102PKS	804	B104PKS	806	B106PKS	807	B88PKS
801	B101PKS	803	B103PKS	805	B105PKS				

808-813

MCW Metrobus DR102/52 — Alexander RL — H45/33F* — 1986 — *812/3 are DPH45/33F

808	D108ELS	810	D110ELS	811	D111ELS	812	143ASV	813	110ASV
809	D109ELS								

814	HSU301	MCW Metrobus DR132/9	Alexander RL	DPH45/33F	1986	
815	D115ELS	MCW Metrobus DR132/9	Alexander RL	DPH45/33F	1986	
816	D116ELS	MCW Metrobus DR132/9	Alexander RL	DPH45/33F	1986	

817-821

MCW Metrobus DR132/10 — Alexander RL — DPH47/33F — 1987

817	365UMY	818	VXU444	819	WLT724	820	TSV612	821	E209JKS

830-834

MCW Metrobus DR102/28 — Alexander RL — H45/33F — 1982 — 831-4 ex Kelvin Central, 1989

830	ULS630X	831	ULS620X	832w	ULS622X	833	ULS623X	834	ULS624X

840	ULS640X	MCW Metrobus DR104/10	Alexander RL	H45/33F	1982	Ex KCB Network, 1996
843	ULS643X	MCW Metrobus DR104/10	Alexander RL	H45/33F	1982	
859	BLS437Y	MCW Metrobus DR102/33	Alexander RL	H45/33F	1983	
868	BLS446Y	MCW Metrobus DR102/33	Alexander RL	H45/33F	1983	
870	A470GMS	MCW Metrobus DR102/39	Alexander RL	H45/33F	1984	
877	A477GMS	MCW Metrobus DR102/39	Alexander RL	H45/33F	1984	
881	B581MLS	MCW Metrobus DR102/39	Alexander RL	H45/33F	1984	
882	B582MLS	MCW Metrobus DR102/39	Alexander RL	H45/33F	1984	
883	B583MLS	MCW Metrobus DR132/2	Alexander RL	H45/33F	1984	
884	B584MLS	MCW Metrobus DR132/2	Alexander RL	H45/33F	1984	Ex Kelvin Central, 1990
885	B585MLS	MCW Metrobus DR102/40	Alexander RL	H45/33F	1984	
887	B587MLS	MCW Metrobus DR132/3	Alexander RL	H45/33F	1984	Ex Kelvin Central, 1990
888	B588MLS	MCW Metrobus DR132/3	Alexander RL	H45/33F	1984	
893	B93PKS	MCW Metrobus DR102/47	Alexander RL	H45/33F	1984	Ex Kelvin Central, 1990
894	B94PKS	MCW Metrobus DR102/47	Alexander RL	H45/33F	1984	
895	B95PKS	MCW Metrobus DR102/47	Alexander RL	H45/33F	1984	
896	B96PKS	MCW Metrobus DR102/47	Alexander RL	H45/33F	1984	
898	B98PKS	MCW Metrobus DR132/6	Alexander RL	H45/33F	1985	
899	B99PKS	MCW Metrobus DR132/6	Alexander RL	H45/33F	1985	

900-915

Leyland Olympian ONLXB/1R — Eastern Coach Works — H45/32F* — 1982 — Ex SMT, 1996
*901-4 are DPH45/32F

900	ULS100X	904	ULS104X	907	ULS107X	910	ULS110X	913	ULS113X
901	ULS101X	905	ULS105X	908	ULS108X	911	ULS111X	914	ULS114X
902	ULS102X	906	ULS106X	909	ULS109X	912	ULS112X	915	ULS115X
903	ULS103X								

917-941

Leyland Olympian ONLXB/1R — Alexander RL — H45/32F — 1983-84 Ex SMT, 1996

917	ALS117Y	924	ALS124Y	928	ALS128Y	934	ALS134Y	939	A139BSC
918	ALS118Y	925	ALS125Y	929	ALS129Y	935	ALS135Y	940	A140BSC
922	ALS122Y	926	ALS126Y	932	ALS132Y	936	A136BSC	941	A141BSC
923	ALS123Y	927	ALS127Y	933	ALS133Y	938	A138BSC		

Allocated fleet number 716, OSR216R is currently owned by Stirlingshire council and is operated by Midland Bluebird on Heritage tours of Stirling. painted in a livery of red with yellow relief, It is seen in that city during the 1996 season.
Tony Wilson

961	B161KSC	Leyland Olympian ONTL11/1R	Alexander RL	H45/32F	1985	Ex SMT, 1996		
962	B162KSC	Leyland Olympian ONTL11/1R	Alexander RL	H45/32F	1985	Ex SMT, 1996		
963	B163KSC	Leyland Olympian ONTL11/1R	Alexander RL	H45/32F	1985	Ex SMT, 1996		

1201-1212 — Volvo B10B-58 — Alexander Strider — B51F — 1993 — Ex SMT, 1996

1201	L201KFS	1204	L204KSX	1207	L207KSX	1209	L209KSX	1211	L211KSX
1202	L202KFS	1205	L205KSX	1208	L208KSX	1210	L210KSX	1212	L212KSX
1203	L203KSX	1206	L206KSX						

1213	L213KSX	Volvo B10B-58	Wright Endurance	B51F	1993	Ex SMT, 1996

1431-1470 — Renault-Dodge S56 — Alexander AM — B25F* — 1987 — Ex SMT, 1996
*1466/8-70 are DP25F

1431	E431JSG	1439	E439JSG	1450	E450JSG	1456	E456JSG	1463	E463JSG
1432	E432JSG	1441	E441JSG	1451	E451JSG	1459	E459JSG	1466	E466JSG
1433	E433JSG	1442	E442JSG	1453	E453JSG	1460	E460JSG	1468	E468JSG
1436	E436JSG	1447	E447JSG	1454	E454JSG	1461	E461JSG	1469	E469JSG
1437	E437JSG	1449	E449JSG	1455	E455JSG	1462	E462JSG	1470	E470JSG

1473-1502 — Renault S75 — Reeve Burgess Beaver — B31F — 1991 — Ex SMT, 1994-96

1473	H473OSC	1481	H481OSC	1487	H487OSC	1492	H492OSC	1497	H497OSC
1474	H474OSC	1482	H482OSC	1488	H488OSC	1493	H493OSC	1498	H498OSC
1475	H475OSC	1483	H483OSC	1489	H489OSC	1494	H494OSC	1499	H499OSC
1477	H477OSC	1484	H484OSC	1490	H490OSC	1495	H495OSC	1501	H501OSC
1478	H478OSC	1485	H485OSC	1491	H491OSC	1496	H496OSC	1502	H502OSC
1479	H479OSC	1486	H486OSC						

1510-1527 — Optare MetroRider — Optare — B31F* — 1992-94 Ex SMT, 1995-96; 1523 is B25FL

1510	J510WSX	1513	K513BSX	1517	K517BSX	1524	L524KSX	1526	L526KSX
1511	J511WSX	1515	K515BSX	1523	L523KSX	1525	L525KSX	1527	L527KSX
1512	J512WSX	1516	K516BSX						

1528	M284SMS	Optare MetroRider	Optare	DP25F	1995	Owned by Central RC

1608-1660 — Seddon Pennine 7 — Alexander AYS — B53F* — 1979-80 Ex SMT, 1996, 1625 ex Midland, 1997
*1608/60 are DP49F

1608	SSX608V	1625	SSX625V	1656	YSG656W	1657	YSG657W	1660w	YSG660W
1624	SSX624V	1646	YSG646W						

Opposite: **Two single-deck buses represent the changes that are taking place in the fleet. Midland Bluebird provide the vehicles for part of the former SMT operation and these retain their green and cream livery. The upper picture shows 1207, one of twelve Volvo B10Bs with Alexander's Strider bodywork that were new to SMT while the lower picture shows one the 1997 delivery of Dennis Darts, all of which are allocated to the Westfield depot. Interesting comparisons may be made with the Lowland vehicle, for positions of fleet numbers etc.** *Mark Bailey/Tony Wilson*

The pride of thirteen Leyland Lions are all based at Livingston depot from where 1982 was working when photographed arriving in Bathgate.
Paul Wigan

1680	JFS980X	Seddon Pennine 7	Alexander AYS	B53F	1982	Ex SMT, 1996
1681	JFS981X	Seddon Pennine 7	Alexander AYS	B53F	1982	Ex SMT, 1996
1682	JFS982X	Seddon Pennine 7	Alexander AYS	B53F	1982	Ex SMT, 1996
1696	GSX896T	Seddon Pennine 7	Alexander AT	C49F	1978	Ex SMT, 1996
1697	GSX897T	Seddon Pennine 7	Alexander AT	C49F	1978	Ex SMT, 1996
1723	AWG623	AEC Regal	Alexander	C31F	1947	Ex preservation, 1986
1748	G601OSH	Ford Transit VE6	Dormobile	M16	1989	Ex Lowland, 1997
1861	GSC861T	Leyland Fleetline FE30AGR	Eastern Coach Works	H43/32F	1978	Ex SMT, 1996
1865	OSG65V	Leyland Fleetline FE30AGR	Eastern Coach Works	H43/32F	1979	Ex SMT, 1996
1871	OSG71V	Leyland Fleetline FE30AGR	Eastern Coach Works	H43/32F	1979	Ex SMT, 1996

1974-1986

	Leyland Lion LDTL11/2R	Alexander RH	DPH49/37F*	1986-87 Ex SMT, 1996

*1980/4-6 are DPH45/35F; 1976/7 are DPH45/37F

1974	C174VSF	1977	C177VSF	1980	C180VSF	1983	C183VSF	1985	D185ESC
1975	C175VSF	1978	C178VSF	1981	C181VSF	1984	D184ESC	1986	D186ESC
1976	C176VSF	1979	C179VSF	1982	C182VSF				

2202	692FFC	Volvo B10M-61	Jonckheere Jubilee P599	C51FT	1989	Ex Laing, Thornton Heath, 1991
2203	TSU682	Volvo B10M-61	Jonckheere Jubilee P599	C51FT	1989	Ex Grampian, 1992
2204	ESK958	Volvo B10M-61	Plaxton Paramount 3200 III	C48FT	1989	Ex Grampian, 1992
2205	FSU315	Volvo B10M-60	Plaxton Paramount 3200 III	C46FT	1989	Ex Wallace Arnold, 1993
2207	144ASV	Volvo B10M-60	Jonckheere Deauville P599	C51FT	1989	Ex Redwing, Camberwell, 1994
2208	K924RGE	Volvo B10M-60	Jonckheere Deauville P599	C51FT	1993	Ex Park's, 1995
2308	F608HGO	DAF				
2315	F615HGO	DAF				
2337	K537RGX	DAF				
2408	J8SMT	Dennis Javelin 12SDA1929	Plaxton Paramount 3200 III	C53F	1992	Ex SMT, 1996
2409	L109OSX	Dennis Javelin 12SDA2131	Plaxton Premiére 320	C53F	1994	Ex SMT, 1996
2410	L110OSX	Dennis Javelin 12SDA2131	Plaxton Premiére 320	C53F	1994	Ex SMT, 1996
2419	A19SMT	Dennis Javelin 12SDA1907	Duple 320	C53FT	1988	Ex SMT, 1996

Previous Registrations:-

101ASV	BLS107Y	FSV634	D144HMS
110ASV	D113ELS	GSU338	ERF72Y, 4327PL, FEH778Y
119ASV	SSJ132Y	GSU339	ERF73Y, 8636PL, FEH780Y
143ASV	D112ELS	HSU247	LPN355W
144ASV	G170RBD	HSU273	LPN357W, 411DCD, OUF51W
156ASV	D145HMS, 692FFC, D625GSG	HSU301	D114ELS
365UMY	E617NLS	J8SMT	J864WSC
692FFC	F914YNV	KSU834	D143HMS
693AFU	A130ESG	OVT798	A184UGB
7881UA	A118GLS	PSU622	D51VSO
A9SMT	B339RLS	PSU625	D54VSO
A10SMT	B340RLS	SSU816	A116GLS
A13SMT	B335RLS, GCS245, WSV144	SSU821	A121ESG
A14SMT	B341RLS	SSU827	MSC554X, WLT770, HGD711X
A15SMT	D345ESC	SSU829	MSC553X, WLT760, HGD745X
A16SMT	D346ESC	SSU831	B131PMS
A17SMT	D347ESC	SSU837	B132PMS
A18SMT	D348ESC	SSU841	D141HMS
A19SMT	F250OFP	SSU857	D142HMS
AWG623	From new	SSU859	A129ESG, 692FFC
BSV807	A117GLS, WLT415, A253WYS	SSU861	MSC555X
E209JKS	E621NLS, 373GRT	SSU897	A168UGB
ESK958	F105SSE	TSU682	F912YNV
FSU302	RMS397W	TSV612	E620NLS
FSU308	BLS108Y	VXU444	E618NLS, FSU309, E771PSG
FSU315	F412DUG	WLT724	E619NLS
FSU318	RMS393W, FSU303	WSU479	A75JFA
FSU334	BMS514Y	WSU487	A21GBC
FSU380	ALS105Y	WSU489	A22GBC
FSU381	ALS101Y	WSV135	A332BSC
FSU382	ALS102Y	WSV140	A330BSC
FSU383	ALS103Y		

Livery: Cream and blue (Midland Bluebird); cream and green (SMT); yellow and blue (Scottish Citylink) 141-4, 2204/8, 2408-10; blue and gold (Bluebird Executive) 2202/7, 2419; white and blue (Kings of Dunblane) 158-64, 642; white (National Express) 2203/5; red (Easyboarder) 1528; red (Stirling Council) 716; white, pink and green (West Express) 335/40.

MOFFAT & WILLIAMSON

Moffat & Williamson Ltd, Main Road, Gauldry, Fife, DD6 8RQ

Depots : Main Road, Gauldry and Boston Road, Glenrothes.

VNB169L	Leyland Atlantean AN68/1R	Park Royal	H43/32F	1973	Ex Skills, Nottingham, 1988
GUA380N	Bristol VRT/SL2/6LX	Eastern Coach Works	H43/33F	1974	Ex Devon General, 1987
MTV762P	Leyland Leopard PSU3C/4R	Duple Dominant E	DP53F	1976	Ex Nottingham, 1989
MOD572P	Bristol VRT/SL3/6LXB	Eastern Coach Works	H43/33F	1976	Ex Devon General, 1987
MES228P	Leyland Leopard PSU3C/4R	Plaxton Supreme III	C53F	1976	Ex Kings of Dunblane, 1986
SWW299R	Bristol VRT/SL3/6LXB	Eastern Coach Works	H43/34F	1976	Ex York City & District, 1989
YBW606R	Bristol VRT/SL3/6LXB	Eastern Coach Works	H43/34F	1976	Ex Thames Transit, 1989
VDV123S	Bristol VRT/SL3/6LXB	Eastern Coach Works	H43/33F	1978	Ex Devon General, 1989
GMS301S	Leyland Leopard PSU3E/4R	Alexander AYS	B51F	1978	Ex Kelvin Scottish, 1988
HUP760T	Bristol VRT/SL3/6LXB	Eastern Coach Works	H43/34F	1978	Ex United, 1992
YBK335V	Leyland Atlantean AN68A/1R	Alexander AL	H45/34F	1979	Ex Thames Transit, 1991
YBK336V	Leyland Atlantean AN68A/1R	Alexander AL	H45/34F	1979	Ex Thames Transit, 1991
YBK337V	Leyland Atlantean AN68A/1R	Alexander AL	H45/32F	1979	Ex Thames Transit, 1991
YBK338V	Leyland Atlantean AN68A/1R	Alexander AL	H45/28D	1979	Ex Thames Transit, 1991
YBK339V	Leyland Atlantean AN68A/1R	Alexander AL	H45/32F	1979	Ex Thames Transit, 1991
YBK340V	Leyland Atlantean AN68A/1R	Alexander AL	H45/32F	1979	Ex Thames Transit, 1991
YBK341V	Leyland Atlantean AN68A/1R	Alexander AL	H45/34F	1979	Ex Thames Transit, 1991
YBK342V	Leyland Atlantean AN68A/1R	Alexander AL	H45/32F	1979	Ex Thames Transit, 1991
YBK343V	Leyland Atlantean AN68A/1R	Alexander AL	H45/28D	1979	Ex Thames Transit, 1991
YBK344V	Leyland Atlantean AN68A/1R	Alexander AL	H45/28D	1979	Ex Thames Transit, 1991
CWG694V	Leyland Atlantean AN68A/1R	Alexander AL	H45/33F	1979	Ex Enterprise & Silver Dawn, 1992
TYS270W	Dennis Dominator DD137B	Alexander RL	H45/34F	1981	Ex KCB Network, 1995
OJI8324	Ford R1014	Plaxton Supreme IV	C35F	1981	Ex Stott, Milnsbridge, 1994
FGE423X	Dennis Dominator DD137B	Alexander RL	H45/34F	1982	Ex KCB Network, 1995
FGE426X	Dennis Dominator DD137B	Alexander RL	H45/34F	1982	Ex KCB Network, 1995
MSL281X	Dennis Dominator DD137B	Alexander RL	H45/34F	1982	Ex KCB Network, 1995
BSK790	Leyland Tiger TRCTL11/3RZ	Plaxton Paramount 3500 II	C57F	1985	Ex Shearings, 1989
BSK791	Leyland Tiger TRCTL11/3RZ	Plaxton Paramount 3500 II	C57F	1985	Ex Longstaff, Amble, 1995
B459WTC	Ford Transit 190	Dormobile	B16F	1985	Ex Aberfeld Motors, 1997
C339RPE	Ford Transit 190	Dormobile	B16F	1986	Ex Western Omni, 1997
D971TKC	Renault-Dodge S56	Northern Counties	B22F	1987	Ex Merseybus, 1992
FSU393	Leyland Tiger TRCTL11/3RZ	Van Hool Alizée	C53F	1987	Ex Travellers, Hounslow, 1990
FSU395	Leyland Tiger TRCTL11/3RZ	Van Hool Alizée	C53F	1987	Ex Travellers, Hounslow, 1990
FSU375	Volvo B10M-61	Plaxton Paramount 3500 III	C53F	1987	Ex Winterbourne Pioneer, 1992
E179UWF	Renault-Dodge S56	Reeve Burgess Beaver	B25F	1987	Ex Mainline, 1992
E431YHL	Mercedes-Benz 709D	Reeve Burgess Beaver	B25F	1988	Ex Your Bus, Alcester, 1992

St Andrews is the setting for this picture of Moffat & Williamson's D971TKC a Northern Counties-bodied Renault-Dodge S56 purchased from Merseybus in 1992.
Mark Bailey

119

GMS301S is a Leyland Leopard with an Alexander Y-type body that has been extensively refurbished using a set of PS-type front panels. *Murdoch Currie*

Moffat & Williamson have secured many school contracts on which double-deck buses are needed. To meet this requirement several Leyland Atlanteans were obtained from the Portsmouth operations of Thames Transit, and one of these, YBK336V is seen at the Glenrothes base. *David Cove*

Two of Moffat & Williamson's coaches were parked at Blackpool for the annual excursions to the Illuminations that are supported particularly well by both Scots and Lancastrians. FSU375 is a Volvo B10M with Plaxton Paramount bodywork. *Paul Wigan*

E596JSP	Mercedes-Benz 609D	Reeve Burgess Beaver	C23F	1988	
FSU374	Leyland Tiger TRCTL11/3ARZ	Plaxton Paramount 3500 III	C57F	1988	Ex Armchair, Brentford, 1993
FSV598	Volvo B10M-53	Plaxton Paramount 4000 III	CH55/12CT	1989	Ex Bailey's Cs, Sutton-in-Ashfield, 1995
G731FSC	Iveco Daily 49.10	Carlyle Dailybus 2	B24F	1990	
G315TKO	Iveco Daily 49.10	Dormobile	B25F	1990	Ex Dormobile, Folkestone, 1990
FSU371	Mercedes-Benz 811D	Reeve Burgess Beaver	C25F	1990	
FSU372	Leyland Tiger TRCL10/3ARZM	Plaxton Paramount 3500 III	C49F	1990	Ex Fishwick, 1994
FSU394	Leyland Tiger TRCL10/3ARZM	Plaxton Paramount 3500 III	C49F	1990	Ex Fishwick, 1994
BSK789	Volvo B10M-60	Van Hool Alizée	C49FT	1990	Ex Fishwick, Leyland, 1995
J437MDB	Leyland-DAF 400	Made-to-Measure	M16	1991	
121ASV	Leyland Tiger TRCL10/3ARZM	Plaxton 321	C53F	1992	Ex Bebb, Llantwit Fardre, 1994
122ASV	Leyland Tiger TRCL10/3ARZM	Plaxton 321	C53F	1992	Ex Bebb, Llantwit Fardre, 1994
YBK159	Auwaeter Neoplan N122/3	Auwaeter Skyliner	CH61/18CT	1992	Ex Durham Travel, 1997
K825HUM	Volvo B10M-60	Van Hool Alizée	C49FT	1993	Ex Wallace Arnold, 1996
K828HUM	Volvo B10M-60	Jonckheere Deauville 45	C53F	1993	Ex Wallace Arnold, 1997
K831HUM	Volvo B10M-60	Jonckheere Deauville 45	C53F	1993	Ex Wallace Arnold, 1997
M341WSL	Mercedes-Benz 711D	Plaxton Beaver	C25F	1994	
M975WES	Mercedes-Benz 709D	Plaxton Beaver	B25F	1995	
M498XSP	Mercedes-Benz 709D	Plaxton Beaver	B27F	1995	
N860DSP	Volvo B10M-62	Plaxton Première 320	C53F	1996	
N861DSP	Volvo B10M-62	Plaxton Première 350	C49F	1996	
N659ESN	Volvo B10M-62	Plaxton Première 350	C49F	1996	

Previous Registrations:

121ASV	J28UNY	FSU375	E565UHS
122ASV	J29UNY	FSU393	D233HMT
BSK789	G23MHG	FSU394	G25MHG
BSK790	B509UNB	FSU395	D231HMT
BSK791	B497UNB	FSV598	F707COA
C239CES	C358FVU, FSU372	MES228P	TLS735P, 122ASV, 121ASV
FSU371	G318UES	MSL281X	FGE432X, WLT367
FSU372	G24MHG	OJI8324	NMC66X
FSU374	E997NMK	YBK159	J2DTS

Livery: Brown and cream; white (David Urquhart Travel) N860/1DSP; white (NST Travel) K825HUM

MORRISON'S OF CASTLETOWN

D B Morrison, 12 Traill Street, Castletown, Highland, KW14 8UG

Depot: Mossy Garage, Castletown.

	HRC102C	Leyland Tiger Cub PSUC1/1	Alexander Y	C41F	1965	Ex Trent, 1981
	JMC281N	AEC Reliance 6U3ZR	Plaxton Elite III	C45F	1975	Ex Weller, Midhurst, 1983
	AUJ735T	Bedford YMT	Duple Dominant II	C53F	1979	Ex Gordon, Dornoch, 1989
w	YFB7V	Bedford YMT	Duple Dominant II	C53F	1979	Ex Central, Keighley, 1985
	OFA990	Volvo B10M-60	Van Hool Alizée	C46FT	1982	Ex Skye-ways, Kyle, 1993
	A103EBC	DAF MB200DKFL600	Plaxton Paramount 3500	C48FT	1983	Ex Bydand, Ardersier, 1991
	NFL881	Volvo B10M-61	Van Hool Alizée	C49FT	1985	Ex Skye-ways, Kyle, 1993
	RIB8035	Volvo B10M-61	Van Hool Alizée	C49FT	1985	Ex Weir's Tours, Clydebank, 1997
	GSU375	Albion Equipment Co Puma	Van Hool Alizée	C28FT	1985	Ex Black Cat, Leyton, 1993
	D120DWP	Iveco Daily 49.10	Robin Hood City Nippy	B21F	1987	Ex Bromyard Bus Company, 1992
	E431LDL	Toyota Coaster HB31R	Caetano Optimo	C21F	1988	Ex Cheyne, Turriff, 1996
	G964SFT	Toyota Coaster HB31R	Caetano Optimo	C18F	1989	Ex UKAEA, Dounreay, 1994
	P454SSK	Mercedes-Benz Sprinter 412D	Onyx	M16	1997	

Previous Registrations:

D120DWP	D536MJA, ENM1T	GSU375	B629MSF
E431LDL	E251MRV, HBZ4683	RIB8035	B471UNB, XTW359, B450GCB

Livery: Yellow, red and maroon

Photographed in Inverness at the end of its run from Glasgow is Morrison's only DAF, A103EBC. This vehicles carries one the early Plaxton Paramount 3500 bodies. *Andrew Jarosz*

MUNRO'S OF JEDBURGH

JH, JR & WJ Munro, Oakvale Garage, Bongate, Jedburgh, Scottish Borders, TD8 6DU

XSH464V	Bedford YMQ	Plaxton Supreme IV Express	C45F	1980	Ex Nichol, Hawick, 1990
ESK834	Volvo B10M-61	Plaxton Paramount 3200 III	C53F	1987	Ex Shearings, 1992
ESK847	Leyland Tiger TRCTL11/3ARZ	Plaxton Paramount 3200 III	C53F	1988	
F439KSH	Freight Rover Sherpa	Deansgate	M16	1988	
J200BCS	Mercedes-Benz 709D	Made-to-Measure	C19F	1992	
J400BCS	Mercedes-Benz 811D	Autobus Classique	DP25F	1992	
J500BCS	Mercedes-Benz 709D	Made-to-Measure	C19F	1992	
L196MHL	Leyland-DAF 400	Autobus Classique	M16	1993	
M901NKS	Mercedes-Benz 814D	Plaxton Beaver	C33F	1994	

Previous Registrations:

ESK834	D572MVR	ESK847	E375HSH

Livery: Red and white

Seen in a red, gold and black livery is Munro's XSH464V. This Bedford chassis carries a Plaxton Supreme V body built to the express style. It is seen at its home base in Jedburgh. Until 1997 Munro's operated the Border Courier contract but this has now passed to Lowland. *Tony Wilson*

OBAN & DISTRICT

Oban & District Buses Ltd, Soroba Lane, Oban, Argyll & Bute, PA34 4HX

w	GMS308S	Leyland Leopard PSU3E/4R	Alexander AYS	B53F	1978	Ex Midland Bluebird, 1992
	EGB62T	Leyland Leopard PSU3C/3R	Alexander AYS	B53F	1979	Ex KCB Network, 1995
	GSU848T	Leyland Leopard PSU3C/3R	Alexander AYS	B53F	1979	Ex KCB Network, 1995
	DLS349V	Leyland Leopard PSU3E/4R	Alexander AYS	B53F	1979	Ex Midland Bluebird, 1995
	DLS350V	Leyland Leopard PSU3E/4R	Alexander AYS	B53F	1979	Ex Midland Bluebird, 1995
	LMS380W	Leyland Leopard PSU3F/4R	Alexander AYS	B60F	1980	Ex Midland Bluebird, 1992
	WFS145W	Leyland Leopard PSU3F/4R	Alexander AYS	B53F	1980	Ex Midland Bluebird, 1992
	WFS151W	Leyland Leopard PSU3F/4R	Alexander AYS	B60F	1980	Ex Midland Bluebird, 1992
	CAS519W	Leyland Leopard PSU3G/4R	Alexander AY	C49F	1981	Ex Midland Bluebird, 1992
	CAS520W	Leyland Leopard PSU3G/4R	Alexander AY	C49F	1981	Ex Midland Bluebird, 1992
	CSF157W	Leyland Leopard PSU3G/4R	Alexander AYS	B53F	1981	Ex Midland Bluebird, 1992
	MSL275X	Leyland Leopard PSU3G/4R	Plaxton Supreme V Express	C53F	1982	Ex Tayside, 1995
	FSU319	Leyland Leopard PSU3G/4R	Plaxton Supreme V Express	C53F	1982	Ex Tayside, 1996
	SSU851	Leyland Leopard PSU3G/4R	Plaxton Supreme V Express	C53F	1982	Ex Tayside, 1995
	MSL278X	Leyland Leopard PSU3G/4R	Plaxton Supreme V Express	C53F	1982	Ex Tayside, 1996
	109ASV	Leyland Tiger TRBTL11/2R	Duple Dominant II	C47F	1983	Ex Midland Bluebird, 1992
	SSU727	Leyland Tiger TRCLXC/2RH	Plaxton Paramount 3200 E	C49F	1984	Ex Midland Bluebird, 1992
	D428ASF	Renault-Dodge S56	Alexander AM	B21F	1986	Ex SMT, 1995
	F67RFS	MCW MetroRider MF150/102	MCW	DP25F	1988	Ex Fife Scottish, 1996
	F69RFS	MCW MetroRider MF150/102	MCW	DP25F	1988	Ex Fife Scottish, 1996
	F790PSN	MCW MetroRider MF150/102	MCW	DP25F	1988	Ex Fife Scottish, 1996
u	L263AAG	Leyland-DAF 400	Onyx	DP16F	1994	Ex van, 1994
	L264AAG	Leyland-DAF 400	Onyx	DP16F	1994	Ex van, 1994
	L502YGD	Leyland-DAF 400	Onyx	DP16F	1994	Ex van, 1994
	L142XDS	Leyland-DAF 400	Dormobile	B20F	1994	Ex Wynter-M, Irvine, 1996
	N101WSB	Dennis Dart 9.8SDL3054	Alexander Dash	B40F	1996	
	N202WSB	Dennis Dart 9.8SDL3054	Alexander Dash	B40F	1996	

Previous Registrations:

109ASV	BLS109Y	MSL278X	KES303X, 2133PL
F790PSN	F70RFS, MSU463	SSU727	A169UGB
FSU319	KES305X, 7017PF, MSL276X	SSU851	KES302X, 2741AP, MSL277X
MSL275X	KES304X, 5414PH		

Livery: Blue and cream

Opposite: **When the Oban operation of Midland Bluebird was separated the majority of the fleet was Leyland Leopards with Alexander bodywork on the buses. One of these, CSF157W is seen in the upper picture. The lower picture shows the latest arrival, an Alexander-bodied Dennis Dart. N202WSB is one of a pair supplied in 1996 and seen at the main bus stand in Oban.**
Malc McDonald/
Andrew Jarosz

Photographed in Fort William is Oban & District's MSL276X, a Leyland Leopard with Plaxton Supreme coachwork.
Murdoch Currie

ORION AUTOBUS

D&M Sassarini, 33 Ryan Road, Wemyss Bay, North Ayrshire

D403SGS	Freight Rover Sherpa	Carlyle	B18F	1987	Ex Ely, Woodston, 1996
E153UKR	Iveco Daily 49.10	Robin Hood City Nippy	B23F	1987	Ex Stagecoach South (East Kent), 1996
E156UKR	Iveco Daily 49.10	Robin Hood City Nippy	B23F	1987	Ex Stagecoach South (East Kent), 1996
E162UKR	Iveco Daily 49.10	Robin Hood City Nippy	B23F	1987	Ex Stagecoach South (East Kent), 1996
E168UKR	Iveco Daily 49.10	Robin Hood City Nippy	B23F	1987	Ex Stagecoach South (East Kent), 1996
G271GKG	Freight Rover Sherpa	Carlyle Citybus 2	B20F	1989	Ex Merry Hill, Oldbury, 1996
G273HBO	Freight Rover Sherpa	Carlyle Citybus 2	B20F	1989	Ex Merry Hill, Oldbury, 1996

Livery: Yellow and white

New to East Kent Iveco Daily E156UKR seen here with its Robin Hood City Nippy body. Four of this type are now with the minibus operations of Orion Autobus which commenced services in 1996. *Andrew Jarosz*

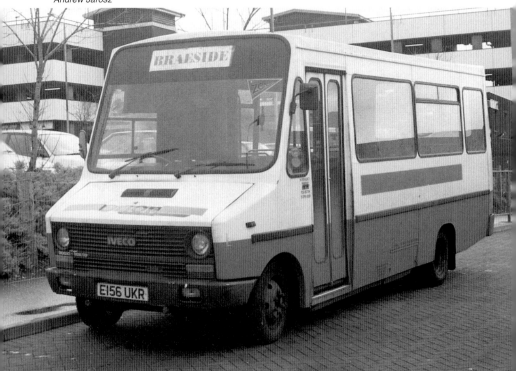

OWENS COACHES

A S Owen & A Owen, Bailside Farm, Chapelhall, North Lanarkshire, ML6 8QP

A824ASJ	Quest VM	Plaxton Paramount 3200	C53F	1984	Ex Doyle, Enniskerry, 1996
XKW870	Volvo B10M-61	Caetano Algarve	C51FT	1985	Ex McCormick, Airdrie, 1996
F551TMH	Volvo B10M-60	Van Hool Alizée	C53F	1989	Ex Travellers, Hounslow, 1994
F555TMH	Volvo B10M-60	Van Hool Alizée	C53F	1989	Ex Travellers, Hounslow, 1994
P771BJF	Dennis Javelin	Caetano Porto	C57F	1997	
P779BJF	Dennis Javelin	Caetano Algarve II	C F	1997	

Previous Registrations:

A824ASJ   A822LEL, 84-MO-341   XKW870   C136GSD

Livery: Blue and yellow (Scottish Citylink) F551TMH, P771BJF.

Caetano Algarve bodywork is shown here on a Volvo B10M chassis registered XKW870 with Owens Coaches. It is seen in Scottish Citylink livery, and was displaced from that duty with the arrival of the first Caetano Porto in Scotland, P771BJF, earlier this year. *Paul Wigan*

PARK'S

Park's of Hamilton (Coach Hirers) Ltd, 20 Bothwell Road, Hamilton,
North Lanarkshire, ML3 0AY

Depots : Bothwell Road, Hamilton and Forrest Street, Blantyre.

MBZ7159	Auwaerter Neoplan N122/3	Auwaerter Skyliner	CH57/20CT	1989	Ex Trathens, Plymouth, 1996
LSK481	Auwaerter Neoplan N122/3	Auwaerter Skyliner	CH57/20CT	1991	Ex Trathens, Plymouth, 1996
LSK483	Auwaerter Neoplan N122/3	Auwaerter Skyliner	CH57/20CT	1991	Ex Trathens, Plymouth, 1996
H544DVM	Volvo B10M-60	Plaxton Paramount 3500 III	C49FT	1991	Ex Shearings, 1995
H949DRJ	Volvo B10M-60	Plaxton Paramount 3500 III	C49FT	1991	Ex Shearings, 1995
H952DRJ	Volvo B10M-60	Plaxton Paramount 3500 III	C49FT	1991	Ex Shearings, 1995
H956DRJ	Volvo B10M-60	Plaxton Paramount 3500 III	C49FT	1991	Ex Shearings, 1995
J301FSR	Auwaerter Neoplan N122/3	Auwaerter Skyliner	CH57/20CT	1992	Ex Trathens, Plymouth, 1996
J450NTT	Auwaerter Neoplan N122/3	Auwaerter Skyliner	CH57/20CT	1992	Ex Trathens, Plymouth, 1997

	Volvo B10M-62		Van Hool Alizée		C53F		1995		
T	LSK495	T	LSK499	T	LSK503	C	LSK507	C	LSK511
T	LSK496	T	LSK500	C	LSK504	C	LSK508	C	LSK512
T	LSK497	T	LSK501	C	LSK505	C	LSK509	C	LSK513
T	LSK498	T	LSK502	C	LSK506	C	LSK510	C	LSK514

	Volvo B10M-62		Van Hool Alizée		C44FT		1995		
NE	N311BYA	Volvo B10M-62		Van Hool Alizée	C44FT	1995	Ex Trathens, Plymouth, 1996
NE	N312BYA	Volvo B10M-62		Van Hool Alizée	C44FT	1995	Ex Trathens, Plymouth, 1996
NE	N313BYA	Volvo B10M-62		Van Hool Alizée	C44FT	1995	Ex Trathens, Plymouth, 1996
NE	N314BYA	Volvo B10M-62		Van Hool Alizée	C44FT	1995	Ex Trathens, Plymouth, 1997

	Volvo B10M-62		Jonckheere Deauville		C53F		1996		
SC	N802NHS	SC	N804NHS	SC	N805NHS	SC	N806NHS	SC	N807NHS
SC	N803NHS								

	Volvo B10M-62		Van Hool Alizée		C53F		1996		
P	KSK951	P	KSK953	P	KSK981	P	KSK983	P	KSK985
P	KSK952	P	KSK980	P	KSK982	P	KSK984	P	KSK986

	Volvo B10M-62		Van Hool Alizée		C53F		1996		
DU	HSK641	DU	HSK645	DU	HSK648	NB	LSK830	C	LSK835
DU	HSK642	DU	HSK646	DU	HSK649	NB	LSK831	C	LSK839
DU	HSK643	DU	HSK644	DU	HSK647	DU	HSK650	C	LSK844
DU	HSK644								

	Volvo B10M-62		Van Hool Alizée		C53F		1997		
	HSK651		HSK655		HSK659	P	KSK950	P	KSK978
	HSK652		HSK656		HSK660	P	KSK954	P	KSK979
	HSK653		HSK657	P	KSK948	P	KSK976	P	LSK444
	HSK654		HSK658	P	KSK949	P	KSK977	P	LSK555

Previous Registrations:

KSK951	LSK444	LSK953	KSK950	LSK483	H982GDV
KSK952	LSK555	LSK481	H981GDV	MBZ7159	F626CWJ

Livery: White, grey and red (Park's of Hamilton) P; yellow & blue (Scottish Citylink) SC; orange/blue/yellow (Trafalgar) T; white, red and blue (Nuclear Bus) NB; white (National Express) NE; white (Caledonian) C; white (David Urquhart Travel) DU or white.

Opposite: **The fleet of modern coaches operated by Park's of Hamilton feeds many, almost new, vehicles to many other operators listed in this book. Most of the fleet are liveried for specific contracts though the upper picture shows KSK948 in the company's colours. All the single-deck coaches are Volvo products and, bar four purchased from Shearings, feature coachwork from the two Belgian suppliers, Van Hool and Jonckheere. The lower picture shows one of six Jonckheere Deauville models that work on Scottish Citylink services.** *Paul Wigan/Les Peters*

PATERSON'S

Thomas Paterson & Brown Ltd, 51 Holmhead, Kilbirnie, North Ayrshire, KA25 6BS

EAG980D	Daimler Fleetline CRG6LX	Alexander D	H44/31F	1966	Ex A1 Service (Murray), 1979
OSD720H	Ford R192	Plaxton Panorama Elite	C45F	1970	
TAG516M	Volvo B58-56	Duple Dominant Express	C53F	1974	
GEU368N	Leyland National 10351/1R		B44F	1974	Ex Badgerline, 1986
LGA14P	Ford R1014	Plaxton Supreme III Express	C45F	1975	
JOV739P	Ailsa B55-10	Alexander AV	H44/35F	1976	Ex London Buses, 1991
JOV769P	Ailsa B55-10	Alexander AV	H44/35F	1976	Ex London Buses, 1991
SFV428P	Leyland Atlantean AN68/1R	Eastern Coach Works	H43/31F	1976	Ex North Western, 1996
YBW600R	Bristol VRT/SL3/6LXB	Eastern Coach Works	H43/31F	1976	Ex Moffat & Williamson, Gauldry, 1994
TPU70R	Leyland Atlantean AN68/1R	Eastern Coach Works	H43/31F	1977	Ex North Western, 1996
SDA617S	Leyland Fleetline FE30AGR	Park Royal	H43/33F	1977	Ex Waddell, Lochwinnoch, 1991
SSN253S	Ailsa B55-10	Alexander AV	H44/31D	1977	Ex Tayside, 1994
SSN255S	Ailsa B55-10	Alexander AV	H44/31D	1978	Ex Tayside, 1995
WTS258T	Ailsa B55-10	Alexander AV	H44/31D	1979	Ex Tayside, 1994
ESJ526V	Volvo B58-61	Duple Dominant II	C52F	1979	
ESJ527V	Volvo B58-56	Duple Dominant II	C53F	1979	
GSD271V	Volvo B58-56	Duple Dominant II Express	C53F	1980	
LCS317W	Leyland National 2 NL106L11/1R		B44F	1980	
LCS624W	Leyland National 2 NL106L11/1R		B44F	1980	
USV809	Volvo B58-61	Plaxton Supreme IV	C55F	1981	Ex Dodsworth, Boroughbridge, 1986
USV810	Volvo B58-61	Plaxton Supreme IV	C55F	1981	Ex Dodsworth, Boroughbridge, 1986
RGD968W	Volvo B58-61	Van Hool Alizée	C52F	1981	
TIB4022	Volvo B10M-61	Van Hool Alizée	C53F	1982	
D116TFT	Freight Rover Sherpa	Carlyle	B20F	1986	Ex Amberline, 1993
E591UHS	Volvo B10M-61	Plaxton Paramount 3500 III	C53F	1988	Ex Park's, Hamilton, 1989
F687ONR	Volvo B10M-60	Van Hool Alizée	C49FT	1989	
A20SAM	Volvo B10M-60	Plaxton Paramount 3500 III	C51F	1992	
SIB8045	Volvo B10M-60	Van Hool Alizée	C53F	1993	
N93HSJ	Volvo B10M-62	Van Hool Alizée	C49FT	1996	
N94HSJ	Volvo B10M-62	Van Hool Alizée	C49FT	1996	

Previous Registrations:

SIB8045	From new		USV809	HBT325W
TIB4022	FGB740X		USV810	BNP5W

Livery: Cream and red; metallic grey, pink and green (DA Tours) F687ONR, A20SAM, N93/4HSJ.

Paterson's operate a mixed fleet of vehicles from their base in Ayrshire. The double deck buses are represented by Leyland, Daimler, Bristol and Ailsa marques while the coaches are mostly modern Volvo B10Ms. The latest pair of coaches are in DA Tours livery and are seen together when new. N93HSJ and N94HSJ are Volvo B10Ms with Van Hool Alizée bodies.
Earnest Barnett

PUMA COACHES

A Morrin, 16 Rashie Burn, North Barr, Erskine, Renfrewshire, PA8 6DT

Depot : Yorkhill Quay, Glasgow

	D248NCS	Renault-Dodge S56	Alexander AM	B25F	1987	Ex Western (A1 Service), 1996
	D254NCS	Renault-Dodge S56	Alexander AM	B25F	1987	Ex Western Buses, 1996
	D301SDS	Renault-Dodge S56	Alexander AM	DP25F	1987	Ex Western Buses, 1996
	E809JSX	Renault-Dodge S56	Alexander AM	B25F	1987	Ex Fife Scottish, 1995
	E614FRN	MCW MetroRider MF150/42	MCW	B25F	1987	Ex Stott, Milnsbridge, 1997
261	F61RFS	MCW MetroRider MF150/98	MCW	B25F	1988	Ex Hall, Kennoway, 1996
266	F66RFS	MCW MetroRider MF150/98	MCW	B25F	1988	Ex Fife Scottish, 1996
268	F68RFS	MCW MetroRider MF150/98	MCW	DP25F	1988	Ex Fife Scottish, 1996

Livery: White, red, yellow and black.

Puma compete with Greater Glasgow on the south-side of the city and employ two types of minibus, the Renault-Dodge S56 with Alexander bodywork and the MCW MetroRider. One of three of the latter that were new to Fife Scottish is 268, F68RFS. *Billy Nicol*

RAPSON / HIGHLAND SCOTTISH

Rapson's Coaches Ltd, 1 Seafield Road, Inverness, IV1 1TN
Highland Scottish Omnibuses Ltd, 1 Seafield Road, Inverness, IV1 1TN

Depots : Unit 2, Industrial Estate, Alness; Seafield Road, Inverness.

Rapson's

MBS281W	Volvo B58-61	Van Hool Alizée	C49FT	1981	Ex Rapson, Brora, 1985
USK500Y	Volvo B10M-61	Jonckheee Jubilee P90	CH48/9FT	1983	Ex Rapson, Brora, 1985
9637EL	Volvo B10M-61	Van Hool Alizée	C46FT	1983	Ex Carnell, Sheffield, 1986
162EKH	Volvo B10M-61	Jonckheere Jubilee P90	CH47/10FT	1984	Ex Rapson, Brora, 1985
GAZ4632	Volvo B10M-61	Plaxton Paramount 3500	C51FT	1984	Ex Mason, Bo'ness, 1996
ESK930	Volvo B10M-61	Plaxton Paramount 3500 II	C48FT	1986	Ex Wallace Arnold, 1991
ESK932	Volvo B10M-61	Plaxton Paramount 3500 II	C48FT	1986	Ex Wallace Arnold, 1991
ESK934	Volvo B10M-61	Plaxton Paramount 3500 II	C50F	1986	Ex Wallace Arnold, 1991
ESK985	Volvo B10M-60	Plaxton Premiére 350 (1993)	C46FT	1989	
3692NT	Volvo B10M-60	Plaxton Paramount 3500 III	C48FT	1989	Ex Highland Country, 1995
Fxxxxxx	Volvo B10M-61	Plaxton Paramount 3500 III	C47FT	1989	Ex Express Travel, 1993
2080NT	Volvo B10M-60	Plaxton Paramount 3500 III	C48FT	1989	Ex Wallace Arnold, 1993
G261UAS	Volvo B10M-60	Plaxton Paramount 3500 III	C46FT	1989	
G262UAS	Volvo B10M-60	Plaxton Paramount 3500 III	C49FT	1989	
4234NT	Volvo B10M-60	Plaxton Paramount 3500 III	C49FT	1990	
NJS246	Volvo B10M-60	Van Hool Alizée	C46FT	1990	Ex Wallace Arnold, 1995
ESK981	Volvo B10M-60	Plaxton Paramount 3500 III	C48FT	1991	Ex Wallace Arnold, 1995
ESK986	Volvo B10M-62	Plaxton Expressliner 2	C46FT	1993	
L592RST	Volvo B10M-62	Plaxton Expressliner 2	C46FT	1993	
L845RST	Volvo B10M-60	Van Hool Alizée	C44FT	1993	
ESK983	Volvo B10M-62	Plaxton Premiére 350	C49FT	1995	
N139YST	Volvo B10M-62	Plaxton Expressliner 2	C46FT	1995	
N905AAS	Volvo B10M-62	Plaxton Expressliner 2	C46FT	1995	
N906AAS	Volvo B10M-62	Plaxton Expressliner 2	C46FT	1995	
N764CAS	Volvo B10M-62	Plaxton Expressliner 2	C46FT	1996	
P491FAS	Volvo B10M-62	Plaxton Expressliner 2	C46FT	1997	
P492FAS	Volvo B10M-62	Plaxton Expressliner 2	C46FT	1997	
P648FST	Volvo B10M-62	Jonckheere Mistral 50	C43F	1997	
P649FST	Volvo B10M-62	Plaxton Expressliner 2	C46FT	1997	

Highland Bus & Coach

P1	E911AFM	Mercedes-Benz 609D	PMT	C24F	1988	Ex Whitelaw, Stonehouce, 1080
P4	D154NON	Freight Rover Sherpa	Carlyle	B20F	1987	Ex Bournemouth, 1989
P8	M487WAS	Mercedes-Benz 811D	Alexander Sprint	B33F	1995	
P9	M623WAS	Mercedes-Benz 811D	Alexander Sprint	B33F	1995	
	M485VST	Toyota Coaster HZB50R	Caetano Optimo III	C21F	1995	
D51	NAL51P	Leyland Fleetline FE30AGR	Alexander AD	H44/34F	1976	Ex Carterton Coaches, 1992
L108	GMS300S	Leyland Leopard PSU3E/4R	Alexander AYS	B53F	1978	Ex Midland Scottish, 1992
D111	ULS659T	Leyland Fleetline FE30AGR	Eastern Coach Works	H43/32F	1979	Ex Midland Scottish, 1993
L213	GSO78V	Leyland Leopard PSU3E/4R	Alexander AYS	B62F	1979	Ex Alexander (Northern), 1981
L219	CAS513W	Leyland Leopard PSU3G/4R	Alexander AY	DP49F	1981	
L220	CAS514W	Leyland Leopard PSU3G/4R	Alexander AY	DP49F	1981	
L221	CAS515W	Leyland Leopard PSU3G/4R	Alexander AY	DP49F	1981	
L222	CAS516W	Leyland Leopard PSU3G/4R	Alexander AY	DP49F	1981	
L227	FAS372X	Leyland Leopard PSU3G/4R	Alexander AYS	B62F	1982	
L228	FAS373X	Leyland Leopard PSU3F/4R	Alexander AYS	B62F	1982	
L230	FAS375X	Leyland Leopard PSU3F/4R	Alexander AYS	B62F	1982	
L252	WFS153W	Leyland Leopard PSU3F/4R	Alexander AYS	B62F	1980	Ex Alexander (Fife), 1983

Opposite: **The latest Highland livery is illustrated here in both small and large formats. Working on minibus operations in Nairn is P8, M487WAS, a Mercedes-Benz 811 with Alexander Sprint bodywork. The lower picture shows D322, UAS66T, an Eastern Coach Works-bodied Leyland Fleetline that was new to the Highland Scottish operation in 1979.** *Malc McDonald/Robert Edworthy*

Rapson's have several workings on the Scottish Citylink network, part of National Express operation. Pictured working the 969 service to Aberdeen is G262UAS, a Volvo B10M-61 with Plaxton Paramount bodywork. *Phillip Stephenson*

D316	SAS858T	Leyland Fleetline FE30AGR	Eastern Coach Works	H43/32F	1978	
D317	SAS859T	Leyland Fleetline FE30AGR	Eastern Coach Works	H43/32F	1978	
D318	SAS860T	Leyland Fleetline FE30AGR	Eastern Coach Works	H43/32F	1978	
D320	UAS64T	Leyland Fleetline FE30AGR	Eastern Coach Works	H43/32F	1979	
D322	UAS66T	Leyland Fleetline FE30AGR	Eastern Coach Works	H43/32F	1979	
D324	UAS68T	Leyland Fleetline FE30AGR	Eastern Coach Works	H43/32F	1979	
D326	MGP226L	Bristol VRT/SL6G	Eastern Coach Works	H39/31F	1973	Ex Dept of Transport, Harmondsworth, 1987
	DWH696W	Leyland Fleetline FE30AGR	Northern Counties	H43/32F	1980	Ex Dunnet, Keiss, 1992
Q404	E404TBS	Renault-Dodge S56	Alexander AM	B25F	1988	
Q405	E405TBS	Renault-Dodge S56	Alexander AM	B25F	1988	
Q406	C185XSK	Renault-Dodge S56	Reeve Burgess	C21F	1985	Ex Highland Country, 1997
L803	LMS383W	Leyland Leopard PSU3F/4R	Alexander AYS	B53F	1980	Ex Kelvin Scottish, 1986
L833	ULS333T	Leyland Leopard PSU3E/4R	Alexander AYS	B53F	1979	Ex Kelvin Scottish, 1986
L836	GCS36V	Leyland Leopard PSU3E/4R	Alexander AY	B53F	1980	Ex Clydeside Scottish, 1988
L843	GCS43V	Leyland Leopard PSU3E/4R	Alexander AY	B53F	1980	Ex Clydeside Scottish, 1988
L857	DLS357V	Leyland Leopard PSU3E/4R	Alexander AYS	B53F	1979	Ex Kelvin Scottish, 1986
L863	GCS63V	Leyland Leopard PSU3E/4R	Alexander AY	B53F	1980	Ex Clydeside Scottish, 1988
L873	LMS373W	Leyland Leopard PSU3F/4R	Alexander AYS	B53F	1980	Ex Kelvin Scottish, 1986
L877	YSF7/S	Leyland Leopard PSU3D/4R	Alexander AYS	B60F	1977	
Z882	A182UGB	Leyland Tiger TRCLXC/2RH	Plaxton Paramount 3200 E	C49F	1984	Ex Western Scottish, 1986
L884	YSF84S	Leyland Leopard PSU3D/4R	Alexander AYS	B62F	1977	Ex Fife Scottish, 1988
L893	YSF103S	Leyland Leopard PSU3E/4R	Alexander AYS	B53F	1977	Ex Fife Scottish, 1988
L894	YSF94S	Leyland Leopard PSU3E/4R	Alexander AYS	B53F	1977	Ex Fife Scottish, 1990
L895	YSF95S	Leyland Leopard PSU3D/4R	Alexander AYS	B53F	1977	Ex Fife Scottish, 1990

Previous Registrations:

162EKH	B22FJS	ESK981	H625UWR
2080NT	F426DUG	ESK983	M488WAS
318DHR	C330FSU, ESK983	ESK985	G260UAS, 318DHR
3692NT	F401DUG, 8665WA, F963GUB	ESK986	L591RST
4234NT	G542LWU	Fxxxxxx	F306URU, ESK985
9637EL	WWA47Y	GAZ4632	A157PXR
ESK930	C110DWR	MBS281W	CST390W, TOI9785, LIJ595
ESK932	C112DWR	NJS246	H619UWR
ESK934	C115DWR	USK500Y	448GWL

Livery: Cream, red and yellow; yellow and blue (Scottish Citylink); white (National Express); cream and red (Rapson's Coaches).

RENNIE'S

Rennie's of Dunfermline Ltd, Wellwood, Dunfermline, Fife, KY12 0PY

KSA179P	Leyland Atlantean AN68/1R	Alexander AL	H45/29D	1976	Ex Grampian, 1988
PHH409R	Bristol VRT/SL3/501	Eastern Coach Works	H43/31F	1976	Ex Bluebird, 1993
PEX386R	Bristol VRT/SL3/6LXB	Eastern Coach Works	H43/31F	1976	Ex Cambus, 1997
OYJ64R	Leyland Atlantean AN68A/1R	East Lancashire	H44/29D	1977	Ex Brighton, 1987
RUS326R	Leyland Atlantean AN68A/1R	Alexander AL	H45/31F	1976	Ex Strathclyde's Buses, 1989
RUS327R	Leyland Atlantean AN68A/1R	Alexander AL	H45/31F	1976	Ex Strathclyde's Buses, 1989
RUS330R	Leyland Atlantean AN68A/1R	Alexander AL	H45/31F	1976	Ex Strathclyde's Buses, 1989
RUS331R	Leyland Atlantean AN68A/1R	Alexander AL	H45/31F	1976	Ex Strathclyde's Buses, 1989
TGG760R	Leyland Atlantean AN68A/1R	Alexander AL	H45/31F	1977	Ex Strathclyde's Buses, 1989
URB160S	Bristol VRT/SL3/6LXB	Eastern Coach Works	H43/31F	1977	Ex Bluebird, 1993
WHH414S	Bristol VRT/SL3/501	Eastern Coach Works	H43/31F	1978	Ex Bluebird, 1993
OEM782S	Leyland Atlantean AN68/1R	MCW	H43/32F	1978	Ex Merseybus, 1993
OEM792S	Leyland Atlantean AN68/1R	MCW	H43/32F	1978	Ex Merseybus, 1993
OEM801S	Leyland Atlantean AN68/1R	MCW	H43/32F	1978	Ex Merseybus, 1993
OEM802S	Leyland Atlantean AN68/1R	MCW	H43/32F	1978	Ex Merseybus, 1993
XAK912T	Bristol VRT/SL3/501	Eastern Coach Works	H43/31F	1979	Ex RoadCar, 1994
XAK915T	Bristol VRT/SL3/501	Eastern Coach Works	H43/31F	1979	Ex RoadCar, 1994
JMB398T	Bristol VRT/SL3/6LXB	Eastern Coach Works	H43/31F	1979	Ex Midland, 1994
DEX213T	Bristol VRT/SL3/6LXB	Eastern Coach Works	H43/31F	1979	Ex Cambus, 1997
CJH118V	Bristol VRT/SL3/6LXB	Eastern Coach Works	H43/31F	1980	Ex Reading Buses, 1995
CJH122V	Bristol VRT/SL3/6LXB	Eastern Coach Works	DPH39/27F	1980	Ex Beeline, 1995
CJH126V	Bristol VRT/SL3/6LXB	Eastern Coach Works	DPH41/25F	1980	Ex Reading Buses, 1995
GGM77W	Bristol VRT/SL3/6LXB	Eastern Coach Works	H43/31F	1980	Ex Reading Buses, 1995
GGM78W	Bristol VRT/SL3/6LXB	Eastern Coach Works	H43/31F	1980	Ex Reading Buses, 1995
GGM79W	Bristol VRT/SL3/6LXB	Eastern Coach Works	H43/31F	1980	Ex Reading Buses, 1995
DBV31W	Bristol VRT/SL3/6LXB	Eastern Coach Works	H43/31F	1980	Ex Stagecoach Midland Red, 1996
GTX740W	Bristol VRT/SL3/501	Eastern Coach Works	H43/31F	1980	Ex London & Country, 1995
WTU471W	Bristol VRT/SL3/6LXB	Eastern Coach Works	H43/31F	1980	Ex Midland, 1994
KSD99W	Volvo-Ailsa B55-10	Alexander AV	H44/35F	1980	Ex Clydeside 2000, 1993
KSD100W	Volvo-Ailsa B55-10	Alexander AV	H44/35F	1980	Ex Clydeside 2000, 1993
YMB515W	Bristol VRT/SL3/6LXB	Eastern Coach Works	H43/31F	1981	Ex Midland, 1994
CJJ678W	Bristol VRT/SL3/6LXB	Eastern Coach Works	H43/31F	1981	Ex Stagecoach South, 1996
GIL8469	Volvo B10M-61	Duple Goldliner IV	C46FT	1982	Ex Western, 1995
HIL6811	Leyland Tiger TRCTL11/3R	Plaxton Paramount 3500	C48FT	1983	Ex Alder Valley, 1991
HIL6812	Leyland Tiger TRCTL11/3R	Plaxton Paramount 3500	C48FT	1983	Ex Alder Valley, 1991
XSA5Y	Volvo B57	Alexander AYS	B51F	1983	Ex Bluebird, 1994
A471HNC	Dennis Falcon V	Northern Counties	H47/37F	1984	Ex Stagecoach Manchester, 1997
A472HNC	Dennis Falcon V	Northern Counties	H47/37F	1984	Ex Stagecoach Manchester, 1997
A473HNC	Dennis Falcon V	Northern Counties	H47/37F	1984	Ex Stagecoach Manchester, 1997
LSK478	Leyland Tiger TRCTL11/3RZ	Duple Caribbean	C53F	1984	Ex Bluebird, 1993
LSK479	Leyland Tiger TRCTL11/3RZ	Duple Caribbean	C53F	1984	Ex Bluebird, 1993
439BUS	DAF SB2300DHS585	Plaxton Paramount 3200	C53F	1984	Ex Metroline (Brents), 1996
C461JCP	DAF SB2300DHTD585	Plaxton Paramount 3200 II	C53F	1984	Ex Metroline (Brents), 1996
GDZ3363	Volvo B10M-61	Berkhof Emperor 395	CH48/12FT	1985	Ex Marbill, Beith, 1992
D35DNH	Iveco Daily 49.10	Robin Hood City Nippy	B19F	1987	Ex United Counties, 1993
D726YBV	Iveco Daily 49.10	Robin Hood City Nippy	B19F	1987	Ex United Counties, 1993
XCD108	Volvo B10M-61	Jonckheere Jubilee	C49FT	1985	Ex Sussex International, Worthing, 1995
TJI1687	Aüwaerter Neoplan N722/3	Plaxton Paramount 4000 II	CH53/18CT	1986	Ex Dunn-Line, Nottingham, 1994
PIJ601	Aüwaerter Neoplan N722/3	Plaxton Paramount 4000 II	CH53/18CT	1986	Ex Hedingham & District, 1995
PIB9211	Volvo B10M-61	Jonckheere Jubilee	C51FT	1988	Ex Croydon Circuit Coaches, 1991
NXX451	Volvo B10M-61	Ikarus Blue Danube	C49FT	1989	Ex Abbott, Stockton, 1996
PIW2891	Mercedes-Benz 609D	Crystals	C24F	1990	Ex B's Coaches, Lochgelly, 1994
L447OSC	Iveco Daily 49.10	Jubilee Charter	C19F	1994	
N250CSG	Iveco Daily 49.10	Jubilee Charter	C19F	1994	
N944MGG	Mercedes-Benz 811D	Mellor	C25F	1995	

Wellwood depot is the location of Eastern Coach Works-bodied Bristol VR JMB398T. This body was available in three heights, the highbridge version (4.46m), the most common version (4.20m) and a low version at 4.12m. This latter was supplied to PMT and National Welsh while the former most notable went to Ribble, Northen and London Country. *Paul Wigan*

N680GSC	Volvo B10M-62	Jonckheere Deauville	C55F	1996
N681GSC	Volvo B10M-62	Jonckheere Deauville	C55F	1996
P387ARY	Iveco 95.E18	Indcar	C31FT	1997
P388ARY	Iveco 95.E18	Indcar	C33F	1997
P389ARY	Iveco 95.E18	Indcar	C33F	1997
P152FBC	Iveco EuroRider 391.12	Beulas Staeygo 35	C49FT	1997
P153FBC	Iveco EuroRider 391.12	Beulas Staeygo 35	C49FT	1997
P154FBC	Iveco EuroRider 391.12	Beulas Staeygo 35	C49FT	1997

Previous Registrations:

439BUS	A991JJU	LSK479	A166TGE
E418JKS	E743TCS, 439BUS	NXX451	F418LNL
GDZ3303	B188CGA, WLT546, B552EGG	PIB9211	E698NNH
GIL8469	GGE130X, ESU435, TOS720X	PIJ601	WCY701, C357KEP
HIL6811	YPJ204Y	PIW2891	H567NSF, MIB4830, H770RSC
HIL6812	YPJ205Y	RJI5720	G170LET
IIW8815	F805COJ, 191WHW, F835FOS	TJI1687	C179KHG, A3BOB, C687RRR
LSK478	A165TGE	XCD108	C406LRP

Livery: Blue and white

Opposite: The Rennies fleet principally operate contract services and quality coaches from their base in Dunfermline. Many coaches and double-deck buses are employed on school contracts and illustrated here are former Alder Valley HIL6811, a Leyland Tiger with Plaxton Paramount bodywork and Bristol VR DBV31W which came north from Stagecoach Midland Red in 1996. The latest arrivals with Rennies are the three Dennis Falcon double-decks that were latterly with Stagecoach Manchester and were part of GM Buses experimental fleet. *Paul Wigan*

RIDDLER

C W & G Riddler, Carnie Loan, Arbroath, Angus, DD11 4DS

HSU273N	Ford R1014	Plaxton Elite III	C45F	1975	Ex Rudd, Methlick, 1988
OKK154	Volvo B58-56	Plaxton Viewmaster III	C49F	1977	Ex Prentice Westwood, East Calder, 1996
FGG572T	Ford R1114	Duple Dominant II	C53F	1978	Ex Bean, Brechin, 1993
DNK403T	Ford R1114	Duple Dominant II Express	C35F	1979	Ex Walker, Garelochhead, 1992
VSX490V	DAF MB200DKTL600	Plaxton Supreme IV	C53F	1980	Ex Mackie, Alloa, 1985
IIL3477	Volvo B10M-61	Plaxton Paramount 3500	C49FT	1984	Ex Smith, Bold Heath, 1993
IIL3478	Volvo B10M-61	Plaxton Paramount 3500	C49FT	1984	Ex Smith, Bold Heath, 1993
NEG322	Volvo B10M-61	Van Hool Alizée	C50FT	1984	Ex Cotter, Glasgow, 1987
4504RU	Volvo B10M-61	Plaxton Paramount 3500 III	C53F	1987	Ex Clyde Coast, Ardrossan, 1992
YSV904	Volvo B10M-61	Plaxton Paramount 3500 III	C53F	1987	Ex Clyde Coast, Ardrossan, 1992
E987BDS	Volvo B10M-61	Plaxton Paramount 3500 III	C57F	1988	Ex MacPhail, Newarthill, 1993
E100LBC	Volvo B10M-61	Duple 320	C55F	1988	Ex Marshall, Baillieston, 1993
J799FTS	Dennis Javelin 12SDA1919	Plaxton Paramount 3200 III	C57F	1992	
J400SOU	Volvo B10M-60	Van Hool Alizée	C52FT	1992	Ex Southern Coaches, Barrhead, 1996
K222GSM	Volvo B10M-60	Plaxton Paramount 3200 III	C53F	1992	Ex Maynes, Buckie, 1996
L630AYS	Volvo B10M-62	Van Hool Alizée	C53F	1994	Ex Park's, Hamilton, 1996

Previous Registrations:

4504RU	D804SGB	OKK154	TGD994R
IIL3477	4085RU, A561MEH	NEG322	From new
IIL3478	6322RU, A562MEH	VSX490V	FLS734V, SL8417
J400SOU	J868JNS	YSV904	D806SGB
L630AYS	LSK824		

Livery: White and blue

Rowe's Bus and Coach Services K776AFS, an Alexander Sprint-bodied Mercedes-Benz 811D into the fleet in 1994 and subsequently purchased four further Mercedes-Benz minibuses. It is seen in Dalmellington en route for Cumnock. *Murdoch Currie*

ROWE'S

G, A, T & G Rowe, Townhead Garage, 151 Main Street, Muirkirk, East Ayrshire, KA18 3QS

TSN576M	Leyland Leopard PSU3E/4R	Plaxton Elite III	C50F	1974	Ex Tudhope Coaches, Kilmarnock, 1997
LWB383P	Ailsa B55-10	Van Hool McArdle	H44/31D	1976	Ex Tudhope Coaches, Kilmarnock, 1997
KHG193T	Leyland Atlantean AN68A/1R	East Lancashire	H45/33D	1978	Ex Tudhope Coaches, Kilmarnock, 1997
LUA268V	Ford R1114	Plaxton Supreme IV	C53F	1980	Ex Tudhope Coaches, Kilmarnock, 1997
OEX798W	Leyland Leopard PSU3E/4R	Willowbrook 003	DP49F	1980	Ex Vanguard, Bedworth, 1991
KSD90W	Volvo B55-10	Alexander AV	H44/35F	1980	Ex Tudhope Coaches, Kilmarnock, 1997
KSD93W	Volvo B55-10	Alexander AV	H44/35F	1980	Ex Tudhope Coaches, Kilmarnock, 1997
KSD103W	Volvo B55-10	Alexander AV	H44/35F	1980	Ex Tudhope Coaches, Kilmarnock, 1997
KSD110W	Volvo B55-10	Alexander AV	H44/35F	1980	Ex Tudhope Coaches, Kilmarnock, 1997
KSD112W	Volvo B55-10	Alexander AV	H44/35F	1980	Ex Tudhope Coaches, Kilmarnock, 1997
MSL64X	Leyland Tiger TRCTL11/3R	Plaxton Supreme VI	C51F	1982	Ex JJ Travel, Coatbridge, 1996
CSO387Y	Leyland Tiger TRCTL11/2R	Duple Dominant II Express	C47F	1983	Ex Busways, 1995
CSO388Y	Leyland Tiger TRCTL11/2R	Duple Dominant II Express	C47F	1983	Ex Busways, 1995
A23PGS	Bedford YNT	Wright Contour	C51F	1984	Ex Tudhope Coaches, Kilmarnock, 1997
B521YTC	Volvo B10M-61	Plaxton Paramount 3200 II	C57F	1985	Ex Tudhope Coaches, Kilmarnock, 1997
DJU704	Leyland Tiger TRCTL11/3RH	Duple Caribbean	C44FT	1985	Ex SMT, 1995
D358CBC	Mercedes-Benz O303/15R	Mercedes-Benz	C53F	1987	Ex Shire Coaches, St Albans, 1996
F425ENB	Mazda E2200	Made-to-Measure	M14	1988	Ex Grangeburn, Motherwell, 1991
F44CTX	Leyland Tiger TRCTL11/3ARZ	Duple 320	C61F	1989	Ex Tudhope Coaches, Kilmarnock, 1997
F47LRA	Volvo B10M-60	Plaxton Paramount 3200 III	C57F	1989	Ex Tudhope Coaches, Kilmarnock, 1997
K776AFS	Mercedes-Benz 811D	Alexander Sprint	B31F	1992	Ex Stonehouse Minicoaches, 1994
L704AGA	Mercedes-Benz 811D	WS Wessex II	B24FL	1994	
N851ASF	Mercedes-Benz 709D	Alexander Sprint	B29F	1995	
N852ASF	Mercedes-Benz 709D	Alexander Sprint	B29F	1995	
N983ESD	Ford Transit VE6	Ford	M14	1995	Ex Tudhope Coaches, Kilmarnock, 1997
P799KSF	Mercedes-Benz 709D	Alexander Sprint	B29F	1996	

Previous Registrations:

B521YTC	432CYA	DJU704	B567LSC
CSO387Y	ASA11Y, TSV781	MSL64X	FGD824X, 913EWC
CSO388Y	ASA7Y, TSV777	TSN576M	PHA301M, YFC736

Livery: Brown and orange

Recently withdrawn from the Rowe's fleet is Leyland Leopard VUD30X seen on service to Muirkirk, a Strathclyde's Buses tendered service.
Murdoch Currie

ROYAL MAIL POST BUS

9100116	G470UHS	Land Rover 90	Post Office	4-seat	1990
9730264	G881PAO	Ford Escort Estate		4-seat	1990
0100072	J436GDS	Land Rover 90	Post Office	4-seat	1991
0100081	H657CST	Land Rover 90	Post Office	4-seat	1991
0100082	H658CST	Land Rover 90	Post Office	4-seat	1991

0750104-114 Leyland-DAF 200   Post Office   M11   1990-91

0750104 J544FSU	0750110 J549FSU	0750111 J550FSU	0750113 J282EST	0750114 J305EST
0750105 J545FSU				

0750112 J306EST   Leyland-DAF 400   Post Office   M16   1991

1750007-71 Leyland-DAF 200   Post Office   M11   1991-92

1750007 J962VSG	1750019 J625FAS	1750030 J832VSF	1750040 J658AAO	1750063 J590ESL
1750009 J153USF	1750020 J626FAS	1750032 J834VSF	1750041 J659AAO	1750064 J474FRS
1750012 J165USF	1750022 J627FAS	1750033 J831VSF	1750044 J660AAO	1750065 J601ESL
1750013 J154USF	1750024 J	1750034 J833VSF	1750048 J633AAO	1750066 J475FRS
1750014 J330EST	1750025 J166VSF	1750035 J382HYS	1750053 J661AAO	1750069 J470FRS
1750015 J622FAS	1750026 J203VSF	1750036 J383HYS	1750059 J473FSR	1750070 J476FRS
1750016 J621FAS	1750027 J221VSF	1750038 J656AAO	1750062 J472FSR	1750071 J
1750018 J624FAS	1750028 J841VSF	1750039 J657AAO		

Opposite: **Postbuses still form a major transport link for the rural communities of Scotland. In Scotland, as in England and Wales, the operation is mostly conducted with 11-seat versions of the normal LDV mailvan, though the 1990 examples are shortly to be replaced by new LDV Convoy models. Shown here are Land Rover 2770020, L908JSF at Ballater and 1750069, J470FRS, at Callander.** *British Bus Publishing/Murdoch Currie*

Photographed outside Blackwaterfoot Post Office on the Isle of Arran is Leyland DAF 200 3750006, M754TSF. *Tony Wilson*

1760002-25 — Peugeot 405 Estate — 4-seat 1992

1760002 J641FAS	1760008 J974VSG	1760013 J643FAS	1760019 J657ASO	1760022 J408HYS
1760003 J961VSG	1760009 J970VSG	1760014 J642FAS	1760020 J381HYS	1760023 J471ASO
1760004 J969VSG	1760010 J971VSG	1760015 J963VSG	1760021 J756ASO	1760025 H912FDU
1760005 J975VSG	1760011 J972VSG	1760016 J973VSG		

1770100-105 — Land Rover 90 — Post Office — 4-seat 1992

1770100 J478FSR	1770102 J480FSR	1770103 J481FSR	1770104 J482FSR	1770105 J483FSR
1770101 J479FSR				

2750004 K242BSG	Leyland DAF 400	Post Office	M14	1993
2750005 K241BSG	Leyland DAF 400	Post Office	M14	1993
2750006 XXI7400	Leyland DAF 400	Post Office	M14	1993
2750037 K265DSG	Leyland DAF 400	Post Office	M14	1993
2750039 K275DSG	Leyland DAF 400	Post Office	M15	1993

2760004-14 — Peugeot 405 Estate — 4-seat 1993-94

2760004 J902WFS	2760007 K253BSG	2760010 K422BSG	2760012 K424BSG	2760016 K409BSG
2760006 J979WFS	2760008 J48XSC	2760011 K423BSG	2760014 K426BSG	

2770015-32 — Land Rover 90 — Post Office — 4-seat 1993-94

2770015 K408BSG	2770019 L907JSF	2770023 K256BSG	2770027 K259BSG	2770030 K262BSG
2770016 K409BSG	2770020 L908JSF	2770024 K257BSG	2770028 K279BSG	2770031 K263BSG
2770017 K390BSG	2770022 K261BSG	2770026 K258BSG	2770029 K331BSG	2770032 K392BSG
2770018 K931BSG				

3750005 M753TSF	Leyland DAF 200	Post Office	M11	1994
3750006 M754TSF	Leyland DAF 200	Post Office	M11	1994
3750007 M21LYV	Leyland DAF 200	Post Office	M11	1994
3760002 L232LSC	Peugeot 405 Estate		4-seat	1994
4750003 M229WSG	Leyland DAF 200	Post Office	M11	1995
4750004 M853TSF	Leyland DAF 200	Post Office	M11	1995
4760001 M709VSC	Peugeot 405 Estate		4-seat	1995
5750005 N226GSC	Leyland DAF 200	Post Office	M10	1996
5750006 N447CSG	Leyland DAF 400	Post Office	M15	1996
5750008 ?	Leyland DAF 200	Post Office	M10	1996
5750011 P59KSK	Leyland DAF 400	Post Office	M15	1996
5750012 N948GSG	Leyland DAF 400	Post Office	M15	1996

5760003-30 — Ford Sierra Estate — 4-seat 1996

5760003 M702XSG	5760010 N408CSG	5760015 N418CSF	5760021 N553FSC	5760026 ?
5760007 N413CSG	5760011 N409CSG	5760016 N451FSC	5760022 N554FSC	5760027 N455FSC
5760006 N407CSG	5760012 N410CSG	5760017 N436FSC	5760023 N558FSC	5760028 N456FSC
5760008 N414CSG	5760013 N411CSG	5760018 N439FSC	5760024 N452FSC	5760029 N457FSC
5760009 N415CSG	5760014 N412CSG	5760020 N552FSC	5760025 N453FSC	5760030 N437FSC

6760002-14 — Ford Sierra Estate — 4-seat 1996-97

6760002 P572NSC	6760006 P576NSC	6760010 P465NSC	6760015 P580NSC	6760018 P549NSC
6760003 P573NSC	6760007 P438NSC	6760011 P466NSC	6760016 P581NSC	6760019 P550NSC
6760004 P574NSC	6760008 P463NSC	6760013 P	6760017 P582NSC	6760025 P583NSC
6760005 P575NSC	6760009 P464NSC	6760014 P579NSC		

Livery: Post Office red and yellow

SCOTTISH TRAVEL

Flosshaul Ltd, 32 Glenside Road, Port Glasgow, Inverclyde, PA14 ???

C518TJF	Ford Transit	Rootes	B16F	1986	Ex Wilson's Coaches, Gourock, 1996
D23WNH	Iveco Daily 49.10	Robin Hood City Nippy	B19F	1986	Ex Wilson's Coaches, Gourock, 1996
D33BVV	Iveco Daily 49.10	Robin Hood City Nippy	B23F	1987	Ex Wilson's Coaches, Gourock, 1997
D126NUS	Mercedes-Benz L608D	Alexander AM	B21F	1986	Ex Dennis's Coaches, Dukinfield, 1996
D950UDY	Mercedes-Benz L608D	Alexander AM	B20F	1986	Ex Dennis's Coaches, Dukinfield, 1996
D957UDY	Mercedes-Benz L608D	Reeve Burgess	B20F	1986	Ex Dennis's Coaches, Dukinfield, 1996
D93VCC	Mercedes-Benz L608D	Reeve Burgess	B20F	1987	Ex Dennis's Coaches, Dukinfield, 1996
D95VCC	Mercedes-Benz L608D	Reeve Burgess	B20F	1987	Ex Dennis's Coaches, Dukinfield, 1996
D97VCC	Mercedes-Benz L608D	Reeve Burgess	B20F	1987	Ex Dennis's Coaches, Dukinfield, 1996
E477RAV	Mercedes-Benz 609D	Reeve Burgess Beaver	DP25F	1988	Ex Westside, Gourock, 1996
F281GNB	Mercedes-Benz 609D	Made-to-Measure	C24F	1988	Ex Westside, Gourock, 1996
F125HGD	Mercedes-Benz 609D	North West Coach Sales	C23F	1989	Ex Wilson's Coaches, Gourock, 1996
J913HGD	Mercedes-Benz 709D	Dormobile Routemaker	B29F	1991	Ex Westside, Gourock, 1996
K202OHS	Mercedes-Benz 709D	Dormobile Routemaker	B29F	1993	Ex Westside, Gourock, 1996
K203OHS	Mercedes-Benz 709D	Dormobile Routemaker	B29F	1993	Ex Westside, Gourock, 1996
K204OHS	Mercedes-Benz 709D	Dormobile Routemaker	B29F	1993	Ex Westside, Gourock, 1996

Livery: White

Scottish Travel operate minibuses and are based at Port Glasgow. Most of the vehicles are Mercedes-Benz, the L608D units coming to the fleet from Dennis's Coaches based in Tameside, Manchester. Pictured here is an L608D converted by Alexander, D126NUS which was one a batch new to Kelvin in 1986. *Andrew Jarosz*

SHALDER

Shalder Coaches Ltd, Lower Scord, Scalloway, Shetland, ZE1 0UQ

S	719CEL	Volvo B58-56	Plaxton Elite III	C53F	1973	Ex Bagnall, Swadlincote, 1987
O	PUX705M	Bedford YRT	Duple Dominant Express	C53F	1974	Ex Peace, Kirkwall, 1984
O	GBS84N	Bedford YRQ	Duple Dominant Express	C45F	1974	Ex Peace, Kirkwall, 1984
S	MGG396P	Bedford YRQ	Duple Dominant Express	C53F	1975	Ex Leask, Lerwick, 1987
S	GPS730P	Bedford YRT	Duple Dominant Express	C53F	1975	
S	GPS714P	Bedford YRQ	Duple Dominant Express	C45F	1976	Ex Peace, Kirkwall, 1984
O	GPS715P	Bedford YRQ	Duple Dominant Express	C45F	1976	Ex Peace, Kirkwall, 1984
S	RNP957P	Volvo B58-61	Plaxton Supreme III Express	C53F	1976	Ex McPhillips, Armadale, 1987
S	FSU331	Volvo B58-56	Caetano	C53F	1977	Ex Peace, Kirkwall, 1984
S	USE500R	Bedford YMT	Duple Dominant	C53F	1977	Ex Bolts, Lerwick, 1988
O	CLC976T	Ford A0609	Moseley Faro	C25F	1978	Ex Peace, Kirkwall, 1984
S	CSE122T	Bedford YLQ	Plaxton Supreme III	C45F	1978	Ex Stonehouse Coaches, 1995
S	KPS701T	Bedford YLQ	Plaxton Supreme IV Express	C45F	1979	Ex Leask & Silver, Lerwick, 1993
S	LPS210T	Bedford YLQ	Duple Dominant II	C45F	1979	Ex Bolts, Lerwick, 1988
S	LPS850V	Volvo B58-56	Plaxton Supreme II Express	C53F	1979	
S	LPS963V	Bedford YLQ	Duple Dominant II Express	C45F	1979	Ex Bolts, Lerwick, 1988
O	CMT871V	Bedford YMT	Unicar	C53F	1979	Ex Don, Dunmow, 1984
O	CMT882V	Bedford YMT	Unicar	C53F	1979	Ex Rennie, Dunfermline, 1986
O	FUJ905V	Bedford YMT	Duple Dominant II	C53F	1980	Ex Mayne's, Buckie, 1994
S	MPS666V	Volvo B58-56	Plaxton Supreme IV Express	C53F	1980	
S	FSU718	Volvo B58-56	Duple Dominant II Express	C53F	1980	
S	PVS20W	Bedford YLQ	Duple Dominant II	C35F	1980	Ex Turner, Huyton, 1987
S	OPS899X	Volvo B58-56	Duple Dominant III	C53F	1982	
O	THB420Y	Bedford YNT	Plaxton Paramount 3200	C53F	1983	Ex Capitol, Cwmbran, 1993
S	THB424Y	Bedford YNT	Plaxton Paramount 3200	C53F	1983	Ex Capitol, Cwmbran, 1993
S	JIL5809	Bedford YMP	Plaxton Paramount 3200	C45F	1983	Ex Evans, Tregaron, 1996
O	A343SPS	Fiat 60F10	Caetano Beja	C18F	1983	Ex Bolts, Lerwick, 1988
O	A416SPS	Bedford YNT	Plaxton Paramount 3200	C53F	1983	Ex Bolts, Lerwick, 1988
O	B509YAT	Bedford YNT	Plaxton Paramount 3200 II	C53F	1985	Ex Wimco, Mitcham, 1994
O	C771FBH	Bedford YNV	Duple 320	C57F	1985	Ex Evans, Tregaron, 1996
S	C319CVU	Mercedes-Benz L307D	Imperial	M12	1986	Ex Anderson, Lower Largo, 1992
S	D31XSS	MCW MetroRider MF150/10	MCW	C23F	1987	Ex Grampian, 1988
S	D982NJS	Mercedes-Benz 609D	Made-to-Measure	C27F	1987	Ex Gordon, Dornoch, 1994
S	D660XPS	Volvo B10M-61	Duple 320	C57F	1987	
S	D181TSB	Volvo B10M-61	Plaxton Paramount 3200 III	C57F	1988	Ex West Coast Motors, 1993
S	D426JDB	Ford Transit	Made-to-Measure	M12	1988	Ex Bolts, Lerwick, 1988
S	E566MAC	Peugeot-Talbot Pullman	Talbot	B22F	1988	Ex Roberts, Deiniolen, 1990
S	E630MAC	Peugeot-Talbot Pullman	Talbot	B22F	1988	Ex Peugeot-Talbot demonstrator, 1991
S	E609YPS	Mercedes-Benz 811D	Reeve Burgess Beaver	C29F	1988	Ex Jamieson, Cullivoe, 1993
S	F828APS	Volvo B10M-60	Plaxton Paramount 3200 III	C57F	1989	
S	F469WFX	Volvo B10M-60	Plaxton Paramount 3200 III	C57F	1989	Ex Excelsior, 1989
S	F938TVC	Peugeot-Talbot Pullman	Talbot	B22F	1989	Ex Mitchell, Plean, 1991
S	G192SCH	MCW MetroRider MF154/2	MCW	C26F	1990	Ex Dunn-Line, Nottingham, 1992
S	H410DPS	Volvo B10M-60	Plaxton Paramount 3200 III	C57F	1990	
S	J75FPS	Volvo B10M-60	Plaxton Paramount 3200 III	C57F	1991	

Previous Registrations:

719CEL	KEG771L	FSU718	MPS970W
FSU331	WDU693S	JIL5809	XVN501Y

Livery: Black and white

Shuttle Buses' yellow and white livery is now a familiar sight around Kilwinning where the operator provides minibus services. Above is J609KGB, one a pair with Dormobile Routemaker bodywork delivered new in 1992. The lower picture shows one of the smaller minibuses, Ford Transit E689WKJ, and one of four of the type which are fitted with the Dormobile product constructed for Ford.
Phillip Stephenson

SHUTTLE BUSES

Shuttle Buses Ltd, Caledonia House, Longford Avenue, Kilwinning, Ayrshire, KA13 6EX

	Reg	Chassis	Body	Seating	Year	History
	NLE515	AEC Regal IV 9821LT	Metro-Cammell	B38F	1953	Ex Hughes, Castle Douglas (caravan), 1992
	UJI8218	Leyland Atlantean AN68A/2R	Alexander AL	H49/37F	1978	Ex Busways, 1996
	THX642S	Leyland Fleetline FE30ALR	Park Royal	H44/27D	1978	Ex Midland Fox, 1995
	DAZ8290	Leyland Leopard PSU3F/4R	Alexander AT	C49F	1980	Ex Western, 1994
	WNH51W	Bedford YMQ	Lex Maxeta	B37F	1981	Ex Boyd, Loans, 1993
	VJI3001	Mercedes-Benz L608D	Reeve Burgess	B20F	1987	Ex Western, 1996
	HIL3188	Leyland Olympian ONTL11/2RH	East Lancashire	CH47/31F	1987	Ex Rhondda, 1996
w	E644DCK	Renault-Dodge S56	Dormobile	B25F	1987	Ex Western (A1 Service), 1996
	E689WKJ	Ford Transit VE6	Dormobile	B20F	1988	Ex Berry, Stockton, 1993
	F88GGC	Mercedes-Benz 811D	Robin Hood	C29F	1989	Ex R&I Tours, Park Royal, 1995
	G188GSG	Ford Transit VE6	Dormobile	B20F	1990	
	G831RDS	Ford Transit VE6	Dormobile	B20F	1990	
	G737PGA	Ford Transit VE6	Dormobile	C20F	1989	Ex Wynter-M, Irvine, 1994
	H124YGG	Mercedes-Benz 709D	Dormobile Routemaker	B29F	1990	Ex Bridge Coaches, Paisley, 1997
	H667AGD	Mercedes-Benz 709D	Dormobile Routemaker	B29F	1991	Ex Bridge Coaches, Paisley, 1997
	J607KGB	Mercedes-Benz 709D	Dormobile Routemaker	B29F	1992	
	J609KGB	Mercedes-Benz 709D	Dormobile Routemaker	B29F	1992	
	J216XKY	Mercedes-Benz 709D	Alexander Sprint	B25F	1991	Ex Reg's, Hertford, 1995
	J217XKY	Mercedes-Benz 709D	Alexander Sprint	B25F	1991	Ex Reg's, Hertford, 1995
	K770AFS	Mercedes-Benz 814D	Plaxton Beaver	C33F	1992	Ex White Star, Neilston, 1996
	L917UGA	Mercedes-Benz 709D	Dormobile Routemaker	B29F	1993	
	N2SBL	Mercedes-Benz 709D	Alexander Sprint	B29F	1996	

Previous Registrations:

DAZ8290	PGA829V	HIL3188	D888YHG	UJI8218	SCN271S

Livery: White and yellow

The Shuttle Buses fleet also contains WNH51W, an example of the Lex Mexeta body seen passing through Irvine. This early attempt at the midi bus was based on a Bedford YMQ chassis. *Malc McDonald*

SILVER COACH LINES

Silver Coach Lines Ltd, 81 Salamander Street, Leith, Edinburgh, EH6 7JZ

PSU610	Kässbohrer Setra S210HDI	Kässbohrer	C28FT	1989
PSU611	Kässbohrer Setra S210HDI	Kässbohrer	C28FT	1989
PSU612	Kässbohrer Setra S210HDI	Kässbohrer	C35F	1989
PSU613	Kässbohrer Setra S210HDI	Kässbohrer	C35F	1989
PSU614	Kässbohrer Setra S215HD	Kässbohrer Tornado	C49FT	1989
PSU615	Kässbohrer Setra S215HD	Kässbohrer Tornado	C49FT	1989
PSU616	Kässbohrer Setra S215HD	Kässbohrer Tornado	C49FT	1989
PSU617	Kässbohrer Setra S215HD	Kässbohrer Tornado	C49FT	1989
PSU618	Kässbohrer Setra S215HD	Kässbohrer Tornado	C49FT	1989
PSU698	Kässbohrer Setra S215HD	Kässbohrer Tornado	C49FT	1989
N122RJF	Toyota Coaster HZB50R	Caetano Optimo III	C18F	1996
N123RJF	Toyota Coaster HZB50R	Caetano Optimo III	C18F	1996
N124RJF	Toyota Coaster HZB50R	Caetano Optimo III	C18F	1996
P825PSG	Toyota Coaster B850R	Caetano Optimo IV	C18F	1997
P550XTL	Kässbohrer Setra S250	Kässbohrer	C48FT	1997
P551XTL	Kässbohrer Setra S250	Kässbohrer	C48FT	1997
P552XTL	Kässbohrer Setra S250	Kässbohrer	C48FT	1997
P	Kässbohrer Setra S250	Kässbohrer	C46FT	1997
P	Kässbohrer Setra S250	Kässbohrer	C46FT	1997
P	Kässbohrer Setra S250	Kässbohrer	C46FT	1997

Previous Registrations:
PSU marks were all from new; the 1997 Setras will be registered PSU615-7/9-21 in late 1997.

Livery: White, blue and orange

The 9.3m long Kässbohrer Setra S210 forms a high quality minicoach, through the numbers licensed in Britain are few. Four operate with Silver Coach Lines and PSU613 is seen taking a break during a tour. The fox emblem carried by the fleet derives from this operators former identity as Silver Fox of Edinburgh. *Robert Edworthy*

SILVER FOX

Silver Fox Coaches Ltd, Tower Garage, 67 Ferry Road, Renfrew, Glasgow, PA4 8SH

VML5G	Leyland Atlantean PDR2/1	Park Royal	H47/32D	1968	Ex Leukaemia Unit Fund, Edinburgh, 1987
JOV756P	Ailsa B55-10	Alexander AV	H44/35F	1976	Ex London Buses, 1992
JOV784P	Ailsa B55-10	Alexander AV	H44/35F	1976	Ex London Buses, 1992
NPG266W	Bedford YNT	Plaxton Supreme IV	C53F	1981	Ex Kevan, Erskine, 1996
NVY148	Volvo B10M-61	Van Hool Alizée	C50FT	1984	Ex Cotter, Glasgow, 1987
E145VGG	Mercedes-Benz 609D	North West Coach Sales	C24F	1987	Ex McMillan, Thornliebank, 1996
JIL5280	Bova FHD12.280	Bova Futura	C49FT	1988	Ex Whyte's Coaches, Newmachar, 1994
JIL4386	Volvo B10M-60	Van Hool Alizée	C49FT	1990	Ex Hutchinson, Overtown, 1995
H721YYS	Volvo B10M-60	Van Hool Alizée	C49FT	1991	Ex Hutchinson, Overtown, 1995
K265SSD	Volvo B10M-60	Jonckheere Deauville	C53FT	1992	Ex H Crawford, Neilston, 1995
K813EET	Bova FHD12.290	Bova Futura	C53F	1993	Ex Bruce Coaches, Shotts, 1996
P69PSB	Bova FHD12.330	Bova Futura	C49FT	1997	

Previous Registrations:

JIL4386	G370GCV	JIL5280	E953CSS	NVY148	From new

Livery: Red and silver (coaches); red (buses).

The attractive lines of the Jonckheere Deauville are illustrated in this view of Silver Fox K265SSD, seenlettered for CIE Tours. In 1996 an eventual replacement for the Deauville, the Mistral, was announced with the first examples now entering service although the Deauville remains available. *Paul Wigan*

SLAEMUIR COACHES

S Mc L McPherson, 13 Westray Avenue, Park Farm, Port Glasgow,
Argyle & Bute, PA14 6AX

D134NUS	Mercedes-Benz L608D	Alexander AM	B21F	1986	Ex Thanet Bus, Ramsgate, 1995
D139NUS	Mercedes-Benz L608D	Alexander AM	B21F	1986	Ex Thanet Bus, Ramsgate, 1995
E39OMS	Mercedes-Benz 709D	Alexander AM	C24F	1987	Ex Roadrunner Coaches, Gourock, 1995
E506YSU	Mercedes-Benz 709D	Alexander Sprint	B25F	1988	Ex Crainey's Coaches, Kilsyth, 1995
E324OSC	Mercedes-Benz 709D	Alexander Sprint	C25F	1988	Ex Green, Kirkintilloch, 1990
E974VWY	Mercedes-Benz 609D	Reeve Burgess	C25F	1988	Ex Cropper, Kirkstall, 1993
G733PGA	Mercedes-Benz 709D	PMT	C25F	1989	
J716USF	Mercedes-Benz 709D	Alexander Sprint	DP25F	1991	Ex Avondale Coaches, Greenock, 1995
K886UDB	Mercedes-Benz 709D	Plaxton Beaver	B29F	1993	Ex Davidson Buses, Whitburn, 1996
L637DNA	Mercedes-Benz 709D	Marshall C19	B27F	1994	Ex AA, Ayr, 1996
N943MGG	Mercedes-Benz 709D	Marshall C19	B29F	1994	Ex Argyle Bus (Ashton), Port Glasgow, 1997
N34GSX	Mercedes-Benz 709D	Alexander Sprint	B29F	1996	

Livery: Pale blue and navy.

Sleamuir Coaches is a further minibus operation to have become established to the west of Glasgow, in this case solely employing on Mercedes-Benz models. Seen here in the mostly pale-blue livery is E506YSU, a 709D type with Alexander Sprint bodywork. It was photographed passing through Greenock bus station. *Malc McDonald*

SKYE-WAYS

Clan Garage (Kyle) Ltd, Ferry Pier, Kyle of Lochalsh, Highland, IV40 8AF

Reg	Chassis	Body	Seats	Year	History
VHV109G	AEC Reliance 6MU3R	Plaxton Panorama Elite	C45C	1969	Ex Glenton Tours, Nunhead, 1976
BAN115H	AEC Reliance 6MU3R	Plaxton Panorama Elite	C34C	1970	Ex Glenton Tours, Nunhead, 1977
ANV775J	Bristol VRT/SL6G	Eastern Coach Works	H39/31F	1971	Ex United Counties, 1989
TME134M	AEC Reliance 6MU4R	Plaxton Elite III	C38C	1974	Ex Glenton Tours, Nunhead, 1981
LSO82P	Ford A0609	Alexander AS	B27F	1976	Ex Munro, Ardelve, 1990
KKV698V	Volvo B58-61	Plaxton Supreme IV	C57F	1980	Ex Peace, Kirkwall, 1996
A842ASJ	Volvo B10M-61	Van Hool Alizée	C49FT	1984	Ex Gilchrist, East Kilbride, 1996
D460BEO	Renault-Dodge S56	East Lancashire	B22F	1986	Ex Hampshire Bus, 1992
D21SAO	Renault-Dodge S56	Reeve Burgess	B23F	1986	Ex Hampshire Bus, 1992
E208JST	Renault Master T35D	Coachwork Conversions	M12	1988	
F782UJS	Volvo B10M-60	Van Hool Alizée	C51FT	1989	
G454TST	Volvo B10M-60	Van Hool Alizée	C51FT	1989	
G761WAS	Volvo B10M-60	Van Hool Alizée	C49FT	1990	
G811WST	Volvo B10M-60	Van Hool Alizée	C52FT	1990	
H258AAS	Volvo B10M-60	Van Hool Alizée	C51FT	1990	
J11SKY	Volvo B10M-60	Van Hool Alizée	C55F	1992	
K5SKY	Volvo B10M-60	Van Hool Alizée	C49FT	1993	
K7SKY	Van Hool T815	Van Hool Alicron	C53F	1993	
M8SKY	Volvo B10M-62	Van Hool Alizée	C53F	1994	
L2SKY	LDV 400	LDV	M16	1995	Ex Kennings Self-Drive, 1997
M6SKY	Mercedes-Benz 0405	Optare Prisma	B49F	1995	Ex Optare demonstrator, 1996
M933LPM	LDV 400	LDV	M16	1995	Ex Kennings Self-Drive, 1996
M134SKY	Volvo B10M-62	Van Hool Alizée	C51F	1995	
M135SKY	Volvo B10M-62	Van Hool Alizée	C51F	1995	

1996 saw the arrival with Skye-Ways of a Mercedes-Benz O405 with Optare Prisma bodywork. Carrying the Select index mark N4SKY it is seen at Flodigarry, the terminus of its service from the island's capital, Portree. *Murdoch Currie*

In addition to the, now standard, Volvo B10Ms with Van Hool Alizée bodywork, the 1993 deliveries included an integral Van Hool, the T815, here with a taller Alicron body. It is seen at Fort William in May 1997. *Murdoch Currie*

N1SKY	Volvo B10M-62	Van Hool Alizée	C53F	1996
N4SKY	Mercedes-Benz 0405	Optare Prisma	B51F	1996
12EWO	Bova FHD12.330	Bova Futura	C49FT	1997

Previous Registrations:

12EWO	From new	M8SKY	M925SYG
A842ASJ	A608UGD, GIL7364, GIL3575	NCC745	From new
L2SKY	M607GGB	NFB892	-

Livery: Blue

The ferry between Kyle of Lochalsh and Kyleakin was replaced by a road bridge during 1996. Based at the former end of the road is Skye-Ways depot where Bristol VR ANV775J is seen carrying the alternative fleetname, Clan Coaches.
Robert Edworthy

SOUTHERN COACHES

Southern Coaches (NM) Ltd, Lochlibo Road, Barrhead, Glasgow, G78 1LF

H290XNS	Volvo B10M-60	Van Hool Alizée	C53F	1990	
J100SOU	DAF MB230LT615	Van Hool Alizée	C51FT	1992	
K200SOU	Volvo B10M-60	Plaxton Paramount 3200 III	C53F	1992	
K300SOU	Volvo B10M-60	Plaxton Paramount 3200 III	C53F	1993	
K600SOU	Volvo B10M-60	Jonckheere Deauville P599	C53F	1993	Ex Park's, Hamilton, 1994
L80SOU	Toyota Coaster HZB50R	Caetano Optimo III	C18F	1994	
L500SOU	Volvo B10M-62	Van Hool Alizée	C55F	1994	
M700SOU	Volvo B10M-62	Van Hool Alizée	C55F	1995	
M800SOU	Volvo B10M-62	Plaxton Première 320	C57F	1995	
M900SOU	Volvo B10M-62	Plaxton Première 320	C53F	1995	
N2SOU	Toyota Coaster HZB50R	Caetano Optimo III	C18F	1996	
N6SOU	Volvo B9M	Van Hool Alizée	C38FT	1996	
N10SOU	Volvo B10M-62	Van Hool Alizée	C51F	1996	
N30SOU	Volvo B9M	Van Hool Alizée	C38FT	1996	
N400SOU	Volvo B10M-62	Plaxton Première 320	C57F	1996	
P20SOU	Volvo B10M-62	Van Hool Alizée	C55F	1997	
P50SOU	Volvo B10M-62	Plaxton Première 320	C53F	1997	
P60SOU	Volvo B10M-62	Plaxton Première 320	C53F	1997	
P70SOU	DAF DE33WSSB3000	Ikarus Blue Danube	C57F	1997	

Previous Registrations:
K600SOU   K909RGE

Livery: Cream, blue and orange

The cream, blue and orange livery of Southern Coaches and their a fine collection of personal index marks with all bar one vehicle now carrying SOU plates certainly helps the fleet stand out from the crowd. Pictured here is Plaxton Première 320 N400SOU. *Paul Wigan*

SPA MOTORS

N R M D&S MacArthur, Kinettas, Strathpeffer, Highland, IV14 9BH

ATA563L	Bristol VRT/SL2/6G	Eastern Coach Works	H43/32F	1973	Ex East Yorkshire, 1989
UWY62L	Bristol VRT/SL2/6G	Eastern Coach Works	H39/31F	1973	Ex West Yorkshire, 1989
OWR552M	Bristol VRT/SL2/6G	Eastern Coach Works	H43/31F	1974	Ex York City & District, 1989
RHK402M	Volvo B58-56	Plaxton Elite III	C49F	1974	Ex Harris, Grays, 1983
RHK403M	Volvo B58-56	Plaxton Elite III	C49F	1974	Ex Harris, Grays, 1983
RCH155R	Bristol VRT/SL3/6LXB	Eastern Coach Works	H43/27D	1976	Ex Southend, 1992
RYG386R	Bristol VRT/SL3/6LXB	Eastern Coach Works	H43/31F	1976	Ex Southend, 1992
BYD93B	Volvo B58-56	Duple Dominant II	C50FT	1979	Ex hHi-Lite, Lye, 1994
OTU971V	Volvo B58-61	Plaxton Supreme IV	C48F	1979	Ex Cotswold Courier, Cheltenham, 1988
WSH433V	Volvo B58-61	Plaxton Supreme IV	C53F	1980	Ex Austin, Earlston, 1985
PYB464	Volvo B58-56	Jonckheere Bermuda	C49FT	1981	Ex Irvine, Law, 1985
XIB9829	Volvo B10M-61	Jonckheere Bermuda	C49FT	1981	Ex Selwyns, Runcorn, 1988
VEL374	Volvo B10M-61	Van Hool Alizée	C50FT	1983	Ex Munro, Uddingston, 1993
JIL3391	Volvo B10M-61	Jonckheere Jubilee P50	C49F	1983	Ex Antler, Rugeley, 1988
OIB3519	Volvo B10M-61	Van Hool Alizée	C55F	1987	Ex R P Coaches, Ludgershall, 1993
GIL3316	Iveco 315-8	Caetano Algarve	C28F	1987	Ex Marshall's, Leighton Buzzard, 1994
E40OMS	Mercedes-Benz 709D	Alexander AM	DP25F	1987	Ex MacKenzie, Achiltibuie, 1993
ALZ2485	DAF MB230LB615	Van Hool Alizée	C51FT	1988	Ex Longworth, Warton, 1990
MAZ6509	Volvo B10M-61	Van Hool Alizée	C51F	1988	Ex Epsom Coaches, 1995
F790UJS	Dennis Javelin 12SDA1907	Duple 320	C57F	1989	
F791UJS	Dennis Javelin 12SDA1907	Duple 320	C57F	1989	
F294GNB	Mercedes-Benz 811D	Made-to-Measure	C24F	1989	Ex Cadger, Balmedie, 1993
G71PYS	Ford Transit VE6	Scott	M15	1989	Ex Parklands, Newton Mearns, 1993
H881EEA	Ford Transit VE6	Ford	M14	1991	Ex NBTS, Birmingham, 1996
L984AJU	Toyota Coaster HZB50R	Caetano Optimo III	C21F	1994	
P550MSF	Mercedes-Benz 814D	Plaxton Beaver	C33F	1996	

Previous Registrations:

ALZ2485	E631KCX	JIL3391	ONV647Y, 3085EL, CHN587Y		PYB464 RAY3W
BYD93B	RJS518V	MAZ6509	E515YGC	VEL374	MSU614Y
GIL3316	E700GNH	OIB3519	D108HLJ	XIB9829	WTU771W

Livery: White and orange

Pictured in Inverness is PYB464 of Spa Coaches. The Volvo B58 carries Jonckheere Bermuda body work, one of two with this style in the fleet. *Andrew Jarosz*

STAGECOACH GLASGOW

Stagecoach Glasgow Ltd, Dunblane Street, Glasgow, G4 0HJ

Depots : Dunblane Street, Culcaddens and Blochairn

035-046		Mercedes-Benz L608D		Reeve Burgess		B20F	1986-87 Ex Cumberland, 1997		
37	D37UAO	39	D39UAO	42	D42UAO	43	D43UAO	46	D46UAO
38	D38UAO								

051-058		Mercedes-Benz L608D		Reeve Burgess		B20F	1986	Ex Cumberland, 1997	
051	D531RCK	053	D530RCK	054	D534RCK	055	D525RCK	058	D558RCK
052	D520RCK								

080	C80OCW	Mercedes-Benz L608D	Reeve Burgess	B20F	1986	Ex Ribble (B&P), 1997
081	D81UFV	Mercedes-Benz L608D	Sparshatts	B20F	1986	Ex Ribble (B&P), 1997
082	D82UFV	Mercedes-Benz L608D	Sparshatts	B20F	1986	Ex Ribble (B&P), 1997
083	D83UFV	Mercedes-Benz L608D	Sparshatts	B20F	1986	Ex Ribble (B&P), 1997

201-232		Mercedes-Benz L608D		Alexander AM		B21F	1986	Ex Kelvin Scottish, 1987	
201	C101KDS	207	D107NUS	213	D113NUS	226	D136NUS	231	D131NUS
204	C104KDS	208	D108NUS	218	D118NUS	230	D130NUS		

233	C594SHC	Mercedes-Benz L608D	PMT Hanbridge	B20F	1986	Ex Western Buses, 1997

361-386		Volvo B6LE		Alexander ALX200		B40F	1997		
361	P361DSA	367	P367DSA	372	P372DSA	377	P377DSA	382	P382DSA
362	P362DSA	368	P368DSA	373	P373DSA	378	P378DSA	383	P383DSA
363	P363DSA	369	P369DSA	374	P374DSA	379	P379DSA	384	P384DSA
364	P364DSA	370	P370DSA	375	P375DSA	380	P380DSA	385	P385DSA
365	P365DSA	371	P371DSA	376	P376DSA	381	P381DSA	386	P386DSA
366	P366DSA								

520-530		Volvo B10M-55		Northern Counties Paladin		DP48F	1997	On loan from Stagecoach Manchester	
520	P877MNE	523	P883MNE	525	P885MNE	527	P889MNE	529	P893MNE
521	P878MNE	524	P884MNE	526	P886MNE	528	P891MNE	530	P894MNE
522	P881MNE								

Livery: White, blue, orange and red (Stagecoach corporate)

The Scottish Bus Handbook

Stagecoach Glasgow planned to commence services in 1994, but just as the operation began the routes and some vehicles went to Strathclyde's Buses as part of a deal that gave Stagecoach a 20% stake in Strathclyde's Buses. Stagecoach later sold that holding on instructions following a MMC report, FirstBus being the purchaser. The Stagecoach Glasgow operators licence, however, remained dormant until 1997 when the unit commenced operations with new low-floor Volvo B6s on routes that provided new links between the centre of Glasgow and its suburbs. The initial batch of vehicles carry Alexander ALX200 bodies as illustrated by 376, P376DSA and these have been joined, pending the arrival of the next order of PS-type Volvo B10Ms, with Northern Counties examples diverted from Stagecoach Manchester. From this batch, 52, P878MNE is seen in Easterhouse on the first day of new service X19. *Murdoch Currie*

STEELES COACHES

R B Steele Ltd, Portland Place, Stevenston, North Ayrshire, KA20 3NN

GFS410N	Leyland Atlantean AN68/1R	Alexander AL	H45/30D	1975	Ex A1 Service (Steele), 1995
MVK508R	Leyland Atlantean AN68A/2R	Alexander AL	H48/33F	1976	Ex Grangeburn, Motherwell, 1996
ATV672T	Leyland Atlantean AN68A/1R	Northern Counties	H47/31D	1978	Ex City of Nottingham, 1996
ASD30T	Leyland Atlantean AN68A/1R	Alexander AL	H45/33F	1979	Ex Keenan, Coalhall, 1996
DSD55V	Leyland Atlantean AN68A/1R	Roe	H43/34F	1979	Ex A1 Service (Steele), 1995
NIW8920	Volvo B10M-61	Van Hool Alizée	C53F	1985	Ex A1 Service (Steele), 1995
N107GSJ	Mercedes-Benz 814D	Plaxton Beaver	C33F	1996	

Previous Registrations:
NIW8920   B312UNB

Livery:

STEVENSON MOTOR COMPANY

T A Hill, Glencairn Street, Stevenston, North Ayrshire, KA20 3BU

LKP384P	Ailsa B55-10	Alexander AV	H44/35F	1975	Ex A1 Service (Hill), 1995
JOV783P	Ailsa B55-10	Alexander AV	H44/35F	1976	Ex A1 Service (Meney), 1995
WTS270T	Ailsa B55-10	Alexander AV	H44/31D	1979	Ex Tayside, 1996
WTS271T	Ailsa B55-10	Alexander AV	H44/31D	1979	Ex Tayside, 1996
ASD32T	Ailsa B55-10 MkII	Alexander AV	H44/35F	1979	Ex A1 Service (Hill), 1995
CSL604V	Ailsa B55-10 MkII	Alexander AV	H44/34F	1980	Ex Tayside, 1996
CSL605V	Ailsa B55-10 MkII	Alexander AV	H44/34F	1980	Ex Tayside, 1996
CSL613V	Ailsa B55-10 MkII	Alexander AV	H44/34F	1980	Ex Tayside, 1996
F253MGB	Volvo B10M-61	Van Hool Alizée	C49FT	1989	Ex Park's, Hamilton, 1995

Previous Registrations:
F253MGB   F764ENE, LSK505

Livery: Blue

Four Plaxton Derwent buses fulfill the large bus requirement for Stokes of Lanark who are based in Carstairs. All are based on the Leyland Tiger bus chassis and pictured in that town is F343GUS.
Mark Bailey

STOKES

William Stokes & Sons Ltd, 22 Carstairs Road, Carstairs, South Lanarkshire, ML11 8QD

EGA609T	Leyland Leopard PSU3E/4R	Duple Dominant II Express	C53F	1978	
HGE51T	Leyland Leopard PSU3E/4R	Plaxton Supreme IV Express	C53F	1979	
ESU815X	Bristol LHS6L	Plaxton Supreme V Express	C33F	1982	
HSB703Y	Leyland Tiger TRCTL11/2R	Plaxton Paramount 3200 E	C49F	1983	
MSU300Y	Leyland Tiger TRCTL11/2R	Duple Dominant II Express	C53F	1983	
A386XOS	Leyland Tiger TRCTL11/2R	Duple Laser Express	C53F	1983	
B186YUS	Mercedes-Benz L307D	Reeve Burgess	M12	1984	
WSU209	Leyland Tiger TRCTL11/3RH	Van Hool Alizée	C53F	1986	
WSU557	Volvo B10M-61	Van Hool Alizée.	C53F	1986	Ex Shearings, 1992
WSU864	Van Hool T815	Van Hool Alicron	C53F	1987	Ex Clarke's of London, 1987
F479FGE	Leyland Tiger TRBTL11/2RP	Plaxton Derwent	B54F	1988	
F480FGE	Leyland Tiger TRBTL11/2RP	Plaxton Derwent	B54F	1988	
F343GUS	Leyland Tiger TRBTL11/2RP	Plaxton Derwent	B54F	1988	
F344GUS	Leyland Tiger TRBTL11/2RP	Plaxton Derwent	B54F	1988	
WSU857	Volvo B10M-60	Van Hool Alizée	C53F	1989	Ex Skye-ways, Kyle, 1994
WSU859	Volvo B10M-60	Ikarus Dlue Danube	C49FT	1989	
WSU860	Dennis Javelin 8.5SDA1915	Plaxton Paramount 3200 III	C32FT	1989	Ex Green, Kirkintilloch, 1990
WSU858	Volvo B10M-60	Van Hool Alizée	C53FT	1990	Ex H Crawford, Neilston, 1994
H716LOL	Mercedes-Benz 811D	Carlyle	B33F	1990	
H717LOL	Mercedes-Benz 811D	Carlyle	B33F	1990	
H718LOL	Mercedes-Benz 811D	Carlyle	B33F	1990	
H719LOL	Mercedes-Benz 811D	Carlyle	B33F	1990	
WSU871	Van Hool T815	Van Hool Alicron	C53F	1991	
L292USU	Dennis Dart 9SDL3021	Plaxton Pointer	B35F	1993	
L293USU	Dennis Dart 9SDL3021	Plaxton Pointer	B35F	1993	
N753LSU	Volvo B6-9.9M	Alexander Dash	B40F	1995	
N971MGG	Volvo B6-9.9M	Alexander Dash	B40F	1995	

Previous Registrations:

A386XOS	A846TDS, WSU858	WSU858	H262XDS
HSB703Y	MSU299Y, WSU857	WSU859	G586KKU
WSU209	C180EME	WSU860	G850VAY
WSU557	C334DND, ESU117, C430GVM	WSU864	D298HMT
WSU857	G93PGB	WSU871	H290TDT

Livery: Red and cream; white (David Urquhart Travel) WSU871

Photographed in Durham, Stokes' WSU860, is an 8.5 metre Dennis Javelin with Plaxton Paramount bodywork. Four midibuses operate for Stoke on services in South Lanarkshire, two Dennis-Plaxton Pointer and two Volvo-Alexander Dash. *Tony Wilson*

STONEHOUSE COACHES

N Collison, 48 New Street, Stonehouse, South Lanarkshire, ML9 3LT

UMB985	Leyland Leopard PSU3C/4R	Plaxton Supreme III	C38C	1977	Ex Smith, Carstairs, 1992
E571UKK	Ford Transit VE6	Dormobile	M10L	1988	Ex Walsall MBC, 1996
UBM880	Leyland Swift LBM6T/2RS	Reeve Burgess	B39F	1989	Ex County of Avon, 1994
G257VJD	Peugeot-Talbot Freeway	Talbot	DP12FL	1990	Ex LB Hillingdon, 1997
G260VJD	Peugeot-Talbot Freeway	Talbot	DP12FL	1990	Ex LB Hillingdon, 1997
G360PNN	Ford Transit VE6	Leicester-Carriage Builders	M16L	1990	Ex Nottinghamshire CC, 1997
H26KSD	Leyland-DAF 400	Leyland-DAF	M16	1991	Ex Drummond, Cleland, 1997
H185WVH	Iveco Daily 49.10	Mellor	M6L	1991	Ex Singh, Huddersfield, 1996
J968KGB	Ford Transit VE6	Deansgate	M12	1992	Ex private owner, 1995
A1GRL	Ford Transit VE6	Ford	M15	1992	Ex private owner, 1994
K1GRL	Ford Transit VE6	Ford	M11	1993	Ex private owner, 1996
M598RFS	Mercedes-Benz 814D	Plaxton Beaver	C33F	1994	Ex Glasgow Rangers FC, 1996
M510JRY	Mercedes-Benz 814D	Dormobile Routemaker	C33F	1995	
OFA590	Volvo B10M-62	Jonckheere Deauville 45	C53F	1995	Ex Park's, Hamilton, 1996
M597SSB	Dennis Dart 9.8SDL3031	Plaxton Pointer	B31F	1995	Ex Stewart, Inverinan, 1996
M63DSJ	Bova FHD12.330	Bova Futura	C53F	1995	Ex Silver Choice, East Kilbride, 1997
N301FSG	Scania K113TRB	Irizar Century 12.37	C49FT	1996	Ex Silver Choice, East Kilbride, 1997
N1BUS	Volvo B10M-62	Jonckheere Deauville 45	C51F	1996	
N5BUS	Mercedes-Benz 811D	Marshall	B33F	1996	
P166LSC	Mercedes-Benz 609D	Onyx	C24F	1996	
P612RGB	Mercedes-Benz 609D	Adamson	DP24F	1996	
P991TGB	Mercedes-Benz 711D	Adamson	DP24F	1996	
P3BUS	Volvo B10M-62	Jonckheere Mistral	C51F	1997	

Previous Registrations:

A1GRL	J929OCS	OFA590	KSK983, M988HHS	UMB985	PYT155R
K1GRL	K626DMS	UBM880	F36TMP		

Livery: White (David Urquhart Travel) LNN590, N1BUS

Adamson's service bus bodywork is seen on P199TGB, a Mercedes-Benz 711D which is fitted with high-back seating for additional comfort. Though there is no destination blind, the vehicle is frequently found on school contract work. *Earnest Barnett*

STRATHTAY BUSES

Strathtay Scottish Omnibuses Ltd, Seagate, Dundee, Angus, DD1 2HR
James Meffan Ltd, Parkend, Kirriemuir, Angus, DD8 4PD

Subsidiaries of Yorkshire Traction Co Ltd
Depots :Elliot Industrial Estate, Arbroath; Haugh Road, Blairgowrie; Seagate, Dundee; Prior Road, Forfar; Parkhead, Kirriemuir
(Meffan); Rossie Island Road, Montrose.

104	WLT921	Mercedes-Benz L608D	Reeve Burgess	DP10FL	1983	Ex Scottish Council for Spastics, 1988
105	GYS77X	Mercedes-Benz L508D	Pilcher Greene	DP9FL	1982	Ex Jewish Assn for Handicapped, 1989

106-118

		Renault-Dodge S56	Dormobile Routemaker	B25F	1989	

106	G889FJW	110	G893FJW	112	G895FJW	114w	G897FJW	117	G900FJW
108	G891FJW	111	G894FJW	113	G896FJW	116	G899FJW	118	G901FJW
109	G892FJW								

126w	D568VBV	Freight Rover Sherpa	Dormobile	B16F	1986	Ex RoadCar, 1991
128	VLT217	Mercedes-Benz 609D	PMT	C19F	1988	Ex Shearings, 1991
134	C241OFE	Mercedes-Benz L608D	Reeve Burgess	DP19F	1986	Ex RoadCar, 1994
135	C240OFE	Mercedes-Benz L608D	Reeve Burgess	DP19F	1986	Ex RoadCar, 1995
136	G438NGE	Mercedes-Benz L507D	Scott	M10L	1989	Ex Jackson, Invergowrie, 1994
137	G754RVJ	Leyland-DAF 400	Careline	M9L	1989	Ex Jackson, Invergowrie, 1994
138	D250WTY	Mercedes-Benz 609D	Devcoplan	C8FL	1987	Ex Durham CC, 1994
139	E122HLK	Renault-Dodge S46	Robin Hood	B8FL	1988	Ex LB Bromley, 1994
140	E124HLK	Renault-Dodge S46	Robin Hood	B8FL	1988	Ex LB Bromley, 1994
142	C242OFE	Mercedes-Benz L608D	Reeve Burgess	B20F	1986	Ex RoadCar, 1995
143	C243OFE	Mercedes-Benz L608D	Reeve Burgess	B20F	1986	Ex RoadCar, 1995
144	C244OFE	Mercedes-Benz L608D	Reeve Burgess	B20F	1986	Ex RoadCar, 1995
145	F748MSC	Mercedes-Benz 709D	Alexander AM	B25F	1988	Ex Town Fliers, St Helens, 1996
146	IIB6015	Mercedes-Benz 709D	Reeve Burgess Beaver	B25F	1988	Ex Avondale Coaches, Greenock, 1996
148	N148DSL	Optare MetroRider MR35	Optare	DP25F	1996	
149	N149DSL	Optare MetroRider MR35	Optare	DP25F	1996	
150	N150DSL	Optare MetroRider MR35	Optare	DP25F	1996	
151	N151DSL	Optare MetroRider MR35	Optare	DP25F	1996	
202	J235LLK	Renault S75	Plaxton Beaver	B31F	1991	Ex London Buses, 1992
203	G291KWY	Renault S75	Reeve Burgess Beaver	DP33F	1989	Ex Harrogate & District, 1993
204	G293MWU	Renault S75	Reeve Burgess Beaver	DP31F	1990	Ex Harrogate & District, 1993
205	G292KWY	Renault S75	Reeve Burgess Beaver	DP31F	1989	Ex Harrogate & District, 1993
209	G892WML	Renault S75	Reeve Burgess Beaver	B31F	1989	Ex London Buses, 1994
210	G893WML	Renault S75	Reeve Burgess Beaver	B31F	1989	Ex London Buses, 1994

Strathtay Buses have chosen the Dennis Dart for its new deliveries of midi-size buses, though three body-builders are represented. The first to arrive carried Wright bodywork and these were followed by four Northern Counties Paladins. One of these is 308, N308DSL, seen in Dundee. The lastest arrivals are bodied by East Lancashire with their Spyte design.
Malc McDonald

301-305 | Dennis Dart 9.8SDL3017 | Wright Handy-bus | B39F | 1993

301	K301MSN	302	K302MSN	303	K303MSN	304	K304MSN	305	K305MSN

306	M306XSN	Dennis Dart 9.8SDL3054	Northern Counties Paladin	B39F	1995
307	M307XSN	Dennis Dart 9.8SDL3054	Northern Counties Paladin	B39F	1995
308	N308DSL	Dennis Dart 9.8SDL3054	Northern Counties Paladin	B39F	1996
309	N309DSL	Dennis Dart 9.8SDL3054	Northern Counties Paladin	B39F	1996
310	P310HSN	Dennis Dart SLF SFD212	East Lancashire Spryte	B39F	1996
311	P311HSN	Dennis Dart SLF SFD212	East Lancashire Spryte	B39F	1996
312	P312	Dennis Dart SLF SFD212	East Lancashire Spryte	B39F	1997
313	P313	Dennis Dart SLF SFD212	East Lancashire Spryte	B39F	1997

401	K401JSR	Volvo B10M-60	Plaxton Paramount 3200 III	C49FT	1992	
402	K402JSR	Volvo B10M-60	Plaxton Paramount 3200 III	C49FT	1992	
403	WLT610	Volvo B10M-61	Plaxton Paramount 3500 III	C48FT	1988	Ex Yorkshire Traction, 1996
406	VLT183	Leyland Tiger TRBTL11/2R	Duple Dominant II Express	C45F	1983	Ex Midland Scottish, 1985
407	VLT298	Leyland Tiger TRBTL11/2R	Alexander TE	C49F	1983	Ex Midland Scottish, 1985
408	FSU309	Leyland Tiger TRCTL11/3RH	Duple Laser	C55F	1984	Ex Midland Scottish, 1985
409	VLT93	Leyland Tiger TRCTL11/3R	Duple Laser	C55F	1984	Ex Midland Scottish, 1985
410	VLT45	Leyland Tiger TRCTL11/3RH	Duple Laser 2	C57F	1985	Ex Midland Scottish, 1985
411	WLT917	Leyland Tiger TRCTL11/2RP	Alexander TE	C47F	1985	Ex Northern Scottish, 1985
412	WLT427	Leyland Tiger TRCTL11/2RP	Alexander TE	C47F	1985	Ex Northern Scottish, 1985
416	WLT743	Leyland Tiger TRCTL11/3R	East Lancashire (1992)	DP57F	1982	Ex Northern Scottish, 1985
417	821DYE	Leyland Tiger TRCTL11/3R	East Lancashire (1992)	DP57F	1981	Ex Kelvin Scottish, 1986
418	415VYA	Leyland Tiger TRCTL11/3RH	Alexander TC	C55F	1987	

419-423 | Leyland Tiger TRCLXC/2RH | Alexander TE | C49F | 1985 | Ex Kelvin Central, 1989

419	HSK765	420	HSK766	421	HSK791	422	HSK792	423	WLT784

425	WLT943	Leyland Tiger TRCTL11/3RZH	Duple 340	C49FT	1987	Ex Kelvin Scottish, 1990
426	365DXU	Leyland Tiger TRCTL11/3RZH	Duple 340	C49FT	1987	Ex Kelvin Scottish, 1990
451	R451	Volvo B10M-62	Plaxton Première 320	C53F	1997	
452	R452	Volvo B10M-62	Plaxton Première 320	C53F	1997	
453	R453	Volvo B10M-62	Plaxton Première 320	C53F	1997	
501	A112ESA	Leyland Tiger TRBTL11/2R	Alexander P	B52F	1983	Ex Northern Scottish, 1987
502	A113ESA	Leyland Tiger TRBTL11/2R	Alexander P	B52F	1983	Ex Northern Scottish, 1987
503	A114ESA	Leyland Tiger TRBTL11/2R	Alexander P	B52F	1983	Ex Northern Scottish, 1987
504	A115ESA	Leyland Tiger TRBTL11/2R	Alexander P	B52F	1983	Ex Northern Scottish, 1987
521	670CLT	Leyland Leopard PSU3D/4R	Alexander AT	C49F	1978	Ex Midland Scottish, 1985
523	VOH640	Leyland Leopard PSU3E/4R	Alexander AT	C49F	1979	Ex Northern Scottish, 1985
524	XNR453	Leyland Leopard PSU3E/4R	Alexander AT	C49F	1979	Ex Northern Scottish, 1985
526	YSV318	Leyland Leopard PSU3E/4R	Alexander AT	C49F	1979	Ex Northern Scottish, 1985
528w	ASP97T	Leyland Leopard PSU3E/4R	Duple Dominant I	C49F	1979	Ex Northern Scottish, 1985
534	866PYC	Leyland Leopard PSU3F/4R	Alexander AT	C49F	1980	Ex Northern Scottish, 1985

535-543 | Leyland Leopard PSU3E/4R* | Alexander AYS | B53F | 1980-82 Ex Northern Scottish, 1985
*539-43 are PSU3G/4R

535	GSO85V	538	GSO88V	540	XSS40Y	542	XSS42Y	543	XSS43Y
536	GSO86V	539	XSS39Y	541	XSS41Y	542		543	

544	LMS385W	Leyland Leopard PSU3F/4R	Alexander AYS	DP49F	1980	Ex Midland Scottish, 1985
545	TMS409X	Leyland Leopard PSU3G/4R	Alexander AYS	B53F	1982	Ex Midland Scottish, 1985
546	XMS424Y	Leyland Leopard PSU3G/4R	Alexander AYS	B53F	1982	Ex Midland Scottish, 1985
555	YSF75S	Leyland Leopard PSU3D/4R	Alexander AYS	B53F	1977	Ex Fife Scottish, 1987
556	YSF79S	Leyland Leopard PSU3D/4R	Alexander AYS	B53F	1977	Ex Fife Scottish, 1987
560	YSF87S	Leyland Leopard PSU3D/4R	Alexander AYS	B53F	1977	Ex Fife Scottish, 1987
561	YSF88S	Leyland Leopard PSU3D/4R	Alexander AYS	B53F	1977	Ex Fife Scottish, 1987
563	ULS323T	Leyland Leopard PSU3E/4R	Alexander AYS	B53F	1979	Ex Kelvin Scottish, 1987
570	EGB70T	Leyland Leopard PSU3C/3R	Alexander AYS	B53F	1979	Ex KCB Network, 1995
573	EGB73T	Leyland Leopard PSU3C/3R	Alexander AYS	B53F	1979	Ex KCB Network, 1995

Opposite, top: **Newly into service Dennis Dart 311, P311HSN shows the lines of the East Lancashire Spryte is one of a pair are to be joined by two similar buses later in the year.** *Tony Wilson*
Opposite, bottom: **RoadCar, also part of the Yorkshire Traction group, secured the entire batch of Reeve Burgess-bodied Renault S75 that ran for London Buses. These have been refurbished and shared between the Yorkshire Traction fleets. Three remain with Strathtay Buses, including 210, G893WML which was photographed at Montrose.** *British Bus Publishing*

In 1988 six Leyland Olympians with Alexander bodywork were transferred from Fife Scottish to Strathtay and these now carry consecutive private index marks in the recently-issued PSU series. The vehicles are all fitted with high-back seating. Representing the batch is 921, PSU372.
Phillip Stephenson

712	ULS673T	Leyland Fleetline FE30AGR	Eastern Coach Works	H43/32F	1979	Ex Midland Scottish, 1985
713	YSR152T	Leyland Fleetline FE30AGR	Eastern Coach Works	H43/32F	1978	Ex Northern Scottish, 1985
714	ASA25T	Leyland Fleetline FE30AGR	Eastern Coach Works	H43/32F	1978	Ex Northern Scottish, 1985
715	WGB711W	Leyland Fleetline FE30AGR	Alexander AD	H44/34F	1980	Ex Midland Scottish, 1985
716	LMS168W	Leyland Fleetline FE30AGR	Alexander AD	H44/34F	1980	Ex Midland Scottish, 1985
717	LJA476P	Daimler Fleetline CRG6LXB	Northern Counties	H43/32F	1976	Ex Greater Manchester PTE, 1987
718	LJA477P	Daimler Fleetline CRG6LXB	Northern Counties	H43/32F	1976	Ex Greater Manchester PTE, 1987
719	LJA478P	Daimler Fleetline CRG6LXB	Northern Counties	H43/23F	1976	Ex Greater Manchester PTE, 1987
721	LJA481P	Daimler Fleetline CRG6LXB	Northern Counties	H43/32F	1976	Ex Greater Manchester PTE, 1987

801-808

		MCW Metrobus DR102/28*	Alexander RL	H45/33F	1982-84	Ex Midland Scottish, 1985
					*806/7 are DR102/33; 808 is DR102/47	

801	ULS627X	803	ULS631X	805	ULS633X	807	BLS433Y	808	B97PKS
802	ULS628X	804	ULS632X	806	BLS424Y				

809	D309DSR	MCW Metrobus DR102/52	Alexander RL	H45/33F	1986	
810	D310DSR	MCW Metrobus DR102/52	Alexander RL	H45/33F	1986	
811	D311DSR	MCW Metrobus DR102/52	Alexander RL	H45/33F	1986	

812-816

		MCW Metrobus DR102/60	Alexander RL	H47/33F	1987	

812	ORU738	813	VLT221	814	YJU694	815	143CLT	816	E36LSL

901	SSA8X	Leyland Olympian ONLXB/1R	Alexander RL	H45/32F	1981	Ex Northern Scottish, 1985
902	SSA9X	Leyland Olympian ONLXB/1R	Alexander RL	H45/32F	1981	Ex Northern Scottish, 1985
903	SSA10X	Leyland Olympian ONLXB/1R	Alexander RL	H45/32F	1981	Ex Northern Scottish, 1985
904	SSA11X	Leyland Olympian ONLXB/1R	Alexander RL	H45/32F	1981	Ex Northern Scottish, 1985

905-910

		Leyland Olympian ONLXB/1R	Eastern Coach Works	H45/32F	1982	Ex Northern Scottish, 1985

905	TSO18X	907	TSO25X	908	TSO26X	909	TSO27X	910	TSO28X
906	TSO22X						

The Scottish Bus Handbook

911-919

Leyland Olympian ONLXB/1RV   Alexander RL   H47/32F   1986-87

| 911 | C111BTS | 916 | C116BTS | 917 | D817EES | 918 | D818EES | 919 | D819EES |

920-925

Leyland Olympian ONLXB/1R   Alexander RL   DPH41/32F   1983   Ex Fife Scottish, 1988

| 920 | PSU371 | 922 | PSU373 | 923 | PSU374 | 924 | PSU376 | 925 | PSU375 |
| 921 | PSU372 | | | | | | | | |

951	M951XES	Leyland Olympian YN2RV18Z4	Northern Counties Palatine	DPH43/29F	1995
952	M952XES	Leyland Olympian YN2RV18Z4	Northern Counties Palatine	DPH43/29F	1995
953	M953XES	Leyland Olympian YN2RV18Z4	Northern Counties Palatine	DPH43/29F	1995
954	M954XES	Leyland Olympian YN2RV18Z4	Northern Counties Palatine	DPH43/29F	1995

Meffan:-

PJI6085	Bristol LHS6L	Plaxton Supreme III	C35F	1976	Ex Hall, Kennoway, 1996
XHR877	Leyland Leopard PSU3D/4R	Alexander AT	C49F	1978	Ex Strathtay, 1994
ULS330T	Leyland Leopard PSU3E/4R	Alexander AYS	B53F	1979	Ex Strathtay, 1993
SOI9994	Leyland Leopard PSU5B/4R	Plaxton P'mnt 3200 (1984)	C57F	1978	Ex Clayton, Leicester, 1995
GDF279V	Leyland Leopard PSU5C/4R	Duple Dominant	DP59F	1979	Ex MacEwan's, Amisfield, 1991
KBZ5748	AEC Reliance 6U3ZR	Plaxton Supreme IV	C57F	1979	Ex Shaw Hadwin, Silverdale, 1995
C778GOX	Freight Rover Sherpa	Dormobile	B20F	1985	Ex Freight Rover, Birmingham, 1988
C649XDF	Mercedes-Benz L608D	Alexander AM	B20F	1986	Ex Acorn Mini Travel, Sealand, 1997
C653XDF	Mercedes-Benz L608D	Alexander AM	B20F	1986	Ex Acorn Mini Travel, Sealand, 1997
D566VBV	Freight Rover Sherpa	Dormobile	B16F	1986	Ex Strathtay, 1994
D569VBV	Freight Rover Sherpa	Dormobile	B16F	1986	Ex RoadCar, 1993
D509NWG	Mercedes-Benz L608D	Alexander AM	B20F	1986	Ex RoadCar, 1995
D220GLJ	Freight Rover Sherpa	Dormobile	B16F	1987	Ex MacEwan's, Amisfield, 1991
D703TLG	Mercedes-Benz 609D	PMT	C25F	1987	
E73ECH	Mercedes-Benz 609D	North West Coach Sales	C24F	1988	Ex Wilson, Dalkeith, 1992
E366YGB	Mercedes-Benz 609D	Scott	C27F	1988	
F771VCW	Mercedes-Benz 609D	Reeve Burgess Beaver	C25F	1988	
F485GGG	Mercedes-Benz 811D	Alexander AM	C33F	1988	Ex McConnochie, Port Glasgow, 1992
F215AKG	Freight Rover Sherpa	Carlyle Citybus 2	B20F	1988	Ex RoadCar, 1994
F276KVW	Mercedes-Benz 609D	Devon Conversions	B20F	1988	Ex Southend HA, 1991
H161YSR	Mercedes-Benz 811D	Scott	C33F	1990	
H223MSX	Mercedes-Benz 814D	PMT Ami	C33F	1990	Ex Wilson, Bonnyrigg, 1996

Previous Registrations:

143CLT	E415GES		PSU376	A989FLS
365DXU	D316SGB, WLT759, D841COS		SOI9994	VAL54S
415VYA	D718FES		VLT45	B133PMS
670CLT	GLS266S		VLT93	A127ESG
821DYE	BSG546W, 17CLT, XDS685W		VLT183	BLS110Y
866PYC	JSA105V		VLT217	E104UNE
ASP97T	CRS75T, YJU694		VLT221	E413GES
E36LSL	E416GES, WLT316		VLT298	BMS512Y
FSU309	A126ESG, VLT42, A651XGG		VOH640	CRS64T
HSK765	C258FGG		WGB711W	LMS156W
HSK766	C259FGG		WLT427	B334LSO
HSK791	C260FGG		WLT610	E664UNE, RHE194, E769AHL
HSK792	C261FGG		WLT743	VSS4X
IIB6015	?		WLT784	C262FGG
KBZ5748	EBM444T, 4150RU, TCW781T		WLT917	B333LSO
ORU738	E412GES		WLT921	A342ASF
PJI6085	RYS943R, YSU953, ROP451R, 884RCV		WLT943	D315SGB
PSU371	A985FLS		XHR577	GLS272S
PSU372	A986FLS		XNR453	CRS65T
PSU373	A987FLS		YJU694	E414GES
PSU374	A988FLS		YSR152T	ASA21T
PSU375	A990FLS		YSV318	CRS67T

Livery: Blue, orange and white; yellow and blue (Scottish Citylink) 401-3/25,451-3; cream and lemon (Meffan) 719; white 136-40.

TRAVEL DUNDEE

Tayside Public Transport Company Ltd, 44-48 East Dock Street, Dundee,
Angus, DD1 3JS

Depots :East Dock Street, Dundee, and Friockheim (G & N Wishart).

Subsidiary of National Express plc

1-20				Ailsa B55-10 MkII		Alexander AV		H44/34F*		1980	* 8/10-2/4/5/7-9 are H44/31F	
1 w	CSL601V	7	CSL607V	10	CSL610V	14w	CSL614V	18	CSL618V
2	CSL602V	8	CSL608V	11	CSL611V	15	CSL615V	19	CSL619V
3	CSL603V	9	CSL609V	12w	CSL612V	17	CSL617V	20	CSL620V

21-35				Volvo-Ailsa B55-10 MkII		Alexander AV		H44/34F*		1980	* 34 is H42/34F	
21w	DSP921V	24	DSP924V	27	DSP927V	30	DSP930V	33	DSP933V
22w	DSP922V	25w	DSP925V	28	DSP928V	31	DSP931V	34	DSP934V
23	DSP923V	26	DSP926V	29	DSP929V	32w	DSP932V	35	DSP935V

36-50				Volvo-Ailsa B55-10 MkIII		Alexander RV		H48/36F		1981	
36	HSR36X	39	HSR39X	42	HSR42X	45	HSR45X	48	HSR48X
37	HSR37X	40	HSR40X	43	HSR43X	46	HSR46X	49	HSR49X
38	HSR38X	41	HSR41X	44	HSR44X	47	HSR47X	50	HSR50X

51-60				Volvo-Ailsa B55-10 MkIII		Northern Counties		H48/36F*		1983	*52 is H51/33F	
51	OSN851Y	53	OSN853Y	55	OSN855Y	57	OSN857Y	59	OSN859Y
52	OSN852Y	54	OSN854Y	56	OSN856Y	58	OSN858Y	60	OSN860Y

Following the purchase of Tayside Buses by National Express the name has changed to Travel Dundee - in line with the Travel West Midlands operation - and the livery changed to the latest style applied in the midlands. Most of the Travel Dundee double-deck fleet are Ailsa B55s.
Representing these is 80, A80SSP, an example with East Lancashire bodywork.
Tony Wilson

Opposite, top: **An early effect of the purchase by National Express was the arrival of new Volvo buses. These are Volvo B10Ls with Wright Liberator bodywork. Pictured shortly after its entry into service is 125, P125KSL, seen on service 18 to Kirkton.**
Mark Bailey

Opposite, bottom: **The final Tayside Buses livery style of blue and cream is seen on 101, G101PES, a Volvo B10M designed to carry the double-deck body, in this case an Alexander RV-type.**
Billy Nicol

61-85

61-85 | | Volvo-Ailsa B55-10 MkIII | | East Lancashire | | H48/36F | | 1983-84 | |

61	OSN861Y	66	OSN866Y	72	OSN872Y	77	A77SSP	82	A82SSP
62	OSN862Y	67	OSN867Y	73	OSN873Y	78	A78SSP	83	A83SSP
63	OSN863Y	68	OSN868Y	74	OSN874Y	79	A79SSP	84	A84SSP
64	OSN864Y	70	OSN870Y	75	OSN875Y	80	A80SSP	85	A85SSP
65	OSN865Y	71	OSN871Y	76	A76SSP	81	A81SSP		

86-90

Volvo Citybus B10M-50   East Lancashire   H51/38F*   1984   *89/90 are DPH45/33F

86	A286TSN	87	A287TSN	88	A288TSN	89	PYJ136	90	OTS271

91-105

Volvo Citybus B10M-50   Alexander RV   H47/37F   1989

91	G91PES	94	G94PES	97	G97PES	100	G100PES	103	G103PES
92	G92PES	95	G95PES	98	G98PES	101	G101PES	104	G104PES
93	G93PES	96	G96PES	99	G99PES	102	G102PES	105	G105PES

106	J215OCW	Dennis Lance 11SDA3101	Northern Counties Paladin	B48F	1992	Ex NCounties demonstrator, 1992
107	J120SPF	Dennis Lance 11SDA3101	Plaxton Verde	B47F	1992	Ex Plaxton demonstrator, 1992
108	K408MSL	Dennis Dart 9SDL3011	Plaxton Pointer	B32F	1993	
109	K409MSL	Dennis Dart 9SDL3011	Plaxton Pointer	B32F	1993	
110	K410MSL	Scania N113CRB	East Lancashire	B45F	1993	
111	K411MSL	Scania N113CRB	East Lancashire	B45F	1993	
112	K412MSL	Scania N113CRB	East Lancashire	B45F	1993	
113	K413MSL	Scania N113CRB	East Lancashire	B45F	1993	
114	L3LOW	Scania N113CRL	East Lancashire	B42F	1993	
115	K247HKV	Volvo B10B-58	Northern Counties Paladin	B49F	1993	Ex Volvo demonstrator, 1993
116	M116XSR	Volvo B6-9.9M	Plaxton Pointer	B38F	1995	
117	M117XSR	Volvo B6-9.9M	Plaxton Pointer	B38F	1995	
118	M118XSR	Volvo B6-9.9M	Plaxton Pointer	B38F	1995	
119	M119XSR	Volvo B6-9.9M	Plaxton Pointer	B38F	1995	
120	P120GSR	Dennis Dart SFD412	Plaxton Pointer	B40F	1996	
121	P121GSR	Dennis Dart SLF SFD212	Plaxton Pointer	B37F	1996	

122-141

Volvo B10L   Wright Liberator   B43F   1997

122	P122KSL	126	P126KSL	130	P130KSL	134	P134KSL	138	P138KSL
123	P123KSL	127	P127KSL	131	P131KSL	135	P135KSL	139	P139KSL
124	P124KSL	128	P128KSL	132	P132KSL	136	P136KSL	140	P140KSL
125	P125KSL	129	P129KSL	133	P133KSL	137	P137KSL	141	P141KSL

W141	SSN241R	Ailsa B55-10	Alexander AV	H44/31D	1976	
200	BUS6X	Mercedes-Benz 609D	Scott	C24F	1990	Ex Stark, Bridge of Weir, 1995
201	D701EES	Renault-Dodge S56	Alexander AM	B23F	1987	
202	D702EES	Renault-Dodge S56	Alexander AM	B23F	1987	
204w	D704EES	Renault-Dodge S56	Alexander AM	DP23F	1987	
205	GBZ7212	Mercedes-Benz 811D	Wright Jenkins	B29F	1991	Ex Stark, Bridge of Weir, 1995
206	P206GSR	Optare MetroRider MR17	Optare	B29F	1996	
207	P207GSR	Optare MetroRider MR17	Optare	B29F	1996	
208	P208GSR	Optare MetroRider MR17	Optare	B29F	1996	
223	NSV622	Volvo B58-56	Plaxton Supreme IV Express	C53F	1982	Ex Greyhound, Dundee, 1990
224	VSR591	Volvo B58-56	Plaxton Supreme IV Express	C49FT	1980	Ex Greyhound, Dundee, 1990
225	NSV621	Volvo B58-56	Plaxton Supreme IV Express	C49FT	1980	Ex Greyhound, Dundee, 1990
226	PSR781	Volvo B58-56	Plaxton Supreme IV Express	C49FT	1980	Ex Greyhound, Dundee, 1990
227	TAY71X	Volvo B10M-56	Plaxton Paramount 3200 E	C49F	1983	Ex Greyhound, Dundee, 1990
235	LXJ462	Leyland Tiger TRCTL11/1RH	Reeve Burgess Riviera	C35F	1984	
236	LIW9278	Volvo B10M-61	Ikarus Blue Danube	C49FT	1988	Ex Greyhound, Dundee, 1990
237	LIW9279	Volvo B10M-61	Ikarus Blue Danube	C49FT	1988	Ex Greyhound, Dundee, 1990
W238	CTS917	Volvo B10M-61	Irizar Pyrennean	C49FT	1984	Ex Greyhound, Dundee, 1990
W239	AJX158	Volvo B10M-61	Irizar Pyrennean	C49FT	1984	Ex Greyhound, Dundee, 1990
240	LXI2961	Volvo B10M-61	Irizar Pyrennean	C49FT	1985	Ex Greyhound, Dundee, 1990
241	LXI2630	Volvo B10M-61	Irizar Pyrennean	C49FT	1985	Ex Greyhound, Dundee, 1990
242	6689DP	Volvo B10M-61	Irizar Pyrennean	C49FT	1986	Ex Tramontana, Carfin, 1987
243	666TPJ	Volvo B10M-61	Irizar Pyrennean	C49FT	1987	
244	PSU339	Dennis Javelin 12SDA1911	Duple 320	C55FL	1988	
W245	PSU340	Dennis Javelin 12SDA1911	Duple 320	C53FT	1988	
245?	P10TAY	Volvo B10M-62	Plaxton Première 350	C49FT	1996	
246	USU661	Dennis Javelin 12SDA1911	Duple 320	C53FT	1988	
247	USU662	Dennis Javelin 12SDA1911	Duple 320	C53FT	1988	
249	A9TPT	Volvo B10M-60	Plaxton Paramount 3500 III	C49FT	1991	Ex Park's, Hamilton, 1993
250	ETS117	Volvo B10M-56	Plaxton Supreme V Express	C53F	1982	Ex Greyhound, Dundee, 1990
251	NSV616	Volvo B10M-56	Plaxton Paramount 3200 Ex	C45FT	1983	Ex Greyhound, Dundee, 1990

The Scottish Bus Handbook

As with many cities, Dundee has taken the opportunity to show off its building and features of interest with open-top tours. An older Ailsa WTS272T has been converted for the work. Renumbered 300, is is seen in the city lettered for the City Tour. *CJC*

252	M100TPT	Volvo B10M-62	Plaxton Premiére 350	C49FT	1994	
253	M200TPT	Volvo B10M-62	Plaxton Premiére 350	C49FT	1994	
268w	WTS268T	Ailsa B55-10	Alexander AV	H44/31D	1979	
273w	WTS273T	Volvo-Ailsa B55-10 MkII	Alexander AV	H44/31D	1979	
276w	WTS276T	Volvo-Ailsa B55-10 MkII	Alexander AV	H44/31F	1979	
300	WTS272T	Ailsa B55-10 MkII	Alexander AV	O44/31D	1979	
W300	F365TSX	Mercedes-Benz 811D	Alexander AM	C33F	1988	Ex Stonehouse Mini Coaches, 1990
W301	F196XFS	Mercedes-Benz 811D	Alexander AM	C33F	1989	Ex Weston, Newbridge, 1989
W302	H290WSE	Mercedes-Benz 814D	Reeve Burgess	C33F	1990	Ex Wishart, Friockheim, 1993
W303	J223HDS	Mercedes-Benz 410D	Made to Measure	C16F	1992	Ex Wishart, Friockheim, 1993
W304	H955LOC	Mercedes-Benz 408D	Jordan, Stourport	C16F	1990	Ex Wishart, Friockheim, 1993
W305	G85SVM	Ford Transit 190	Made to Measure	C16F	1990	

Previous Registrations:

2741AP	KES302X	NSV621	DSR477V
666TPJ	D312ETS	NSV622	KSP698X
6689DP	D491NSU	OTS271	A290TSN
A9TPT	H856AHS	PSR781	DSR478V
AJX158	A947VGG	PSU339	E307KES
CTS917	A946VGG	PSU340	E308KES
ETS117	LSP502X	PYJ136	A289TSN
LIW9278	E736KSP	TAY71X	OES342Y, 220BSR
LIW9279	E737KSP	USU661	F313NSP
LXI2630	B918CSU	USU662	F314NSP
LXI2961	B917CSU	VSR591	DSR476V
LXJ462	B835VSR	BUS6X	H780YYS
NSV616	OES343Y	GBZ7212	From new

Livery: White, red and blue; white (Wishart); white and blue (Tayside Greyhound Coaches)

WEST COAST MOTORS

Craig of Campbeltown Ltd, Benmhor, Campbeltown, Argyll & Bute, PA28 6DN

VSB164M	Bedford YRT	Plaxton Derwent	B60F	1974	
KGG184N	Bedford YRQ	Plaxton Elite III	C45F	1975	Ex Earnside, Glenfarg, 1976
RSB7S	Bedford YLQ	Plaxton Supreme III Express	C45F	1977	
WSB187V	Bedford YMT	Duple Dominant	B63F	1979	
FSL615W	Bedford YLQ	Plaxton Supreme IV	C45F	1980	Ex Henderson, Coaltown, 1985
B192XJD	Volvo B10M-56	Plaxton Paramount 3200	C49F	1985	Ex Tellings-Golden Miller, 1989
E114OBF	Volvo B10M-61	Plaxton Paramount 3200 III	C F	1988	Ex Bakers, Biddulph, 1996
E870BGG	Volvo B10M-56	Duple 300	B54F	1988	Ex Hutchison, Overtown, 1996
E871BGG	Volvo B10M-56	Duple 300	B54F	1988	Ex Hutchison, Overtown, 1996
F131YSB	Ford Transit VE6	Deansgate	M14	1988	
F598YSB	Mercedes-Benz 407D	Scott	M15	1988	Ex MacFarlane, Oban, 1994
F532ASB	Volvo B10M-61	Plaxton Paramount 3200 III	C53F	1989	
F727ASB	Volvo B10M-61	Plaxton Paramount 3200 III	C53F	1989	
H165EJU	Toyota Coaster HDB30R	Caetano Optimo II	C21F	1990	Ex Green, Kirkintilloch, 1992
J807HSB	MAN 11.190	Optare Vecta	B41F	1992	
K400WCM	DAF SB3000DKVF601	Van Hool Alizée	C53F	1993	
K500WCM	Ford Transit VE6	Deansgate	M14	1993	
L937WFW	Leyland DAF 400	Leyland DAF	M14	1994	
L100WCM	Optare MetroRider MR15	Optare	B23F	1993	
L400WCM	DAF SB3000DKVF601	Van Hool Alizée	C55F	1993	
L200WCM	Optare MetroRider MR15	Optare	B29F	1994	
L300WCM	Volvo B10M-60	Jonckheere Deauville P599	C53FT	1994	
L500WCM	Dennis Javelin 12SAD2131	Plaxton Premiére 320	C53F	1994	
L700WCM	DAF SB3000WS601	Van Hool Alizée	C53F	1994	
M519RSB	Ford Transit VE6	Ford	M14	1994	
M100WCM	Dennis Javelin 12SAD2131	Plaxton Premiére 320	C53F	1995	
M200WCM	DAF SB3000WS601	Van Hool Alizée	C53F	1995	
M300WCM	DAF SB3000WS601	Van Hool Alizée	C53F	1995	
M400WCM	DAF SB3000WS601	Van Hool Alizée	C53F	1995	
M609RCP	DAF SB3000WS601	Van Hool Alizée	C51FT	1995	Ex Cronin, Cork, 1997
M826RCP	DAF SB3000WS601	Van Hool Alizée	C51FT	1995	Ex Speedlink, 1997
M500WCM	Optare MetroRider MR.	Optare	B23F	1995	
M700WCM	DAF SB3000WS601	Van Hool Alizée	C51FT	1995	Ex Armchair, Brentford, 1995
M800WCM	DAF SB3000WS601	Van Hool Alizée	C51FT	1995	Ex Armchair, Brentford, 1996
N100WCM	Optare MetroRider MR.	Optare	B23F	1995	
N200WCM	Optare MetroRider MR.	Optare	B23F	1995	
N300WCM	Volvo B9M	Van Hool Alizée	C45F	1996	
N400WCM	Mercedes-Benz 814D	Plaxton Beaver	C33F	1996	
P100WCM	DAF SB3000WS601	Van Hool Alizée	C51FT	1997	
P200WCM	DAF SB3000WS601	Van Hool Alizée	C51FT	1997	

Previous Registrations:
K500WCM	K547OGA	M700WCM	M837RCP	M800WCM	M838RCP

Livery: Red and cream; yellow and blue (Scottish Citylink) L300, L400, M100, M700, M800, M609, P100.

Opposite: **West Coast Motors have gained praise for their smart livery and modern vehicles complete with WCM index marks. The upper picture, taken in the Campletown depot, shows N200WCM, now one of five Optare MetroRiders taken into the fleet. The lower picture shows of the of the shorter Volvo model B9M, H251XDS. Fitted with a Van Hool Alizée body the 10-metre vehicle accomodates forty-two passengers. It is seen working Scottish Citylink service 918 and several of the fleet are liveried for this work.** *Mark Bailey/Billy Nicol*

WESTERN BUSES

Western Buses Ltd, Sandgate, Ayr, KA7 1DD

Depots :Harbour Road, Ardrossan; Waggon Road, Ayr; Ayr Road, Cumnock; Eastfield Road, Dumfries; Argyll Road, Dunoon; Vicarton Street, Girvan; Mackinlay Place, Kilmarnock; Brodick; Isle of Arran; Pointhouse, Rothesay; Lewis Street, Stranraer; Rail Station, Whithorn.

001-035

Mercedes-Benz 709D   Alexander Sprint   B25F   1995-96

001	N601VSS	007	N607VSS	021	N621VSS	026	N626VSS	031	N631VSS
002	N602VSS	008	N608VSS	022	N622VSS	027	N627VSS	032	N632VSS
003	N603VSS	009	N609VSS	023	N623VSS	028	N628VSS	033	N633VSS
004	N604VSS	010	N610VSS	024	N624VSS	029	N629VSS	034	N634VSS
005	N605VSS	011	N611VSS	025	N625VSS	030	N630VSS	035	N635VSS
006	N606VSS	012	N612VSS						

101	XSJ656T	Leyland Fleetline FE30AGR	Northern Counties	O44/31F	1978	
102	HDS566H	Daimler Fleetline CRG6LX	Alexander D	O44/31F	1970	Ex Clydeside Scottish, 1989
103	GHV948N	Daimler Fleetline CRG6	Park Royal	O44/27F	1974	Ex Selkent, 1995
104	GHV102N	Daimler Fleetline CRG6	Park Royal	O44/27F	1975	Ex Selkent, 1995
105	UWV607S	Bristol VRT/SL3/6LXB	Eastern Coach Works	CO43/31F	1977	Ex Bluebird Buses, 1996
106u	OSJ636R	Leyland Leopard PSU3C/3R	Alexander AY	B53F	1977	Ex Bluebird, 1996

116-121

Dennis Dorchester SDA811   Alexander TC   C53F*   1987   118-20 are C51F

116	WLT526	118	WLT415	119	D131UGB	120	WLT447	121	WLT501
117	FSU737							

Western Buses continue to expand their Stagecoach Express services in line with demand. Transferred from Cambus in 1996, three vehicles from the Premier Travel operation now sport the Express livery as shown by 131, YSV735, pictured in Dumfries. *Mark Bailey*

122-128

122-128		Volvo B10M-62		Plaxton Premiére Interurban	DP51F	1994	Ex Stagecoach South, 1996				
122	M160CCD	124	M162CCD	126	M164CCD	127	M165CCD	128	M166CCD		
123	M161CCD	125	M163CCD								

129	WLT416	Volvo B10M-60	Plaxton Paramount 3500 III	C51F	1989	Ex Cambus (Premier), 1996
130	YSV730	Volvo B10M-60	Plaxton Paramount 3500 III	C53F	1990	Ex Cambus (Premier), 1996
131	YSV735	Volvo B10M-60	Plaxton Paramount 3500 III	C53F	1991	Ex Cambus (Premier), 1996
132	J917LEM	Volvo B10M-61	Plaxton Paramount 3500 III	C46FT	1991	Ex Bluebird Buses, 1997
133	J919LEM	Volvo B10M-61	Plaxton Paramount 3500 III	C46FT	1991	Ex Bluebird Buses, 1997
135	VLT104	Volvo B10M-60	Plaxton Expressliner	C53F	1990	Ex Bluebird Buses, 1995
136	WLT794	Volvo B10M-60	Plaxton Expressliner	C53F	1990	Ex Bluebird Buses, 1995
137	WLT809	Volvo B10M-60	Plaxton Expressliner	C53F	1990	Ex Dorset Travel, 1995
138	WLT720	Volvo B10M-60	Plaxton Expressliner	C53F	1990	Ex Dorset Travel, 1995
139	WLT727	Volvo B10M-60	Plaxton Expressliner	C53F	1990	Ex Ribble, 1995
140	WLT830	Volvo B10M-60	Plaxton Expressliner	C53F	1990	Ex Ribble, 1995
141	IIL3507	Volvo B10M-60	Plaxton Paramount 3500 III	C51F	1989	Ex Ribble, 1995

142-160

142-160		Volvo B10M-62		Plaxton Premiére Interurban	DP51F	1996					
142	N142XSA	146	N146XSA	150	P150ASA	154	P154ASA	158	P158ASA		
143	N143XSA	147	N247XSA	151	P151ASA	155	P255ASA	159	P159ASA		
144	N144XSA	148	P148ASA	152	P152ASA	156	P156ASA	160	P160ASA		
145	N145XSA	149	P149ASA	153	P153ASA	157	P157ASA				

163	NIB5232	Leyland Tiger TRCTL11/3RH	Plaxton Paramount 3200 II	C51F	1985	Ex Bluebird Buses, 1996
164	NIB5233	Leyland Tiger TRCTL11/3RH	Plaxton Paramount 3200 II	C51F	1985	Ex Bluebird Buses, 1996
165	BYJ919Y	Leyland Tiger TRCTL11/3R	Plaxton Paramount 3200	C50F	1983	Ex Stagecoach South, 1996
166	UWP105	Leyland Tiger TRCTL11/3R	Plaxton Paramount 3200	C50F	1983	Ex Stagecoach South, 1996
168	MSU466	Leyland Tiger TRCTL11/3RH	Duple 340	C55F	1987	Ex Stagecoach South, 1996
169	XDU599	Leyland Tiger TRCTL11/3RZ	Plaxton Paramount 3500 II	C51F	1986	Ex Stagecoach South, 1996
170	VLT54	DAF SB2305DHTD585	Plaxton Paramount 3200 III	C57F	1989	Ex Arran Coaches, 1994

Previously in the Stagecoach South fleet, Western's 126, M164CCD, carries the Plaxton Interurban body, a version of the Première 320 built to meet Stagecoach's requirements. The vehicle was photographed in Irvine while working service X34. *Murdoch Currie*

171	TSU638	Leyland Tiger TRCTL11/3R	Plaxton Paramount 3200 E	C53F	1983	Ex East Midland, 1995
172	13CLT	Leyland Tiger TRCTL11/3RZ	Duple 340	C51F	1987	Ex Kelvin Central, 1990
173	WLT546	Leyland Tiger TRCTL11/3RZ	Duple 340	C51F	1987	Ex Kelvin Central, 1990
178	CSO386Y	Leyland Tiger TRCTL11/2R	Duple Dominant II Express	C47F	1983	Ex Bluebird Buses, 1995
179	UM7681	Leyland Tiger TRCTL11/3RZ	Plaxton Paramount 3200	C57F	1984	Ex East Midland, 1995
180	439UG	Leyland Tiger TRCTL11/3R	Plaxton Paramount 3200	C53F	1985	Ex East Midland, 1995
181	5796MX	Leyland Tiger TRCTL11/3RH	Plaxton Paramount 3500	C51F	1985	Ex East Midland, 1995
182	295UB	Leyland Tiger TRCTL11/3RH	Plaxton Paramount 3500	C53F	1985	Ex East Midland, 1995
183	283URB	Volvo B10M-60	Plaxton Paramount 3500 III	C53F	1987	Ex East Midland, 1995
184	K574DFS	Volvo B10M-60	Plaxton Premiére 320	C51F	1993	Ex Fife Scottish, 1995
186	896HOD	Volvo B10M-61	Plaxton Paramount 3500 II	C51F	1985	Ex Stagecoach South, 1995
187	495FFJ	Volvo B10M-61	Plaxton Paramount 3500 II	C52F	1985	Ex Stagecoach South, 1995
188	L582JSA	Volvo B10M-60	Plaxton Premiére Interurban	DP51F	1993	Ex Bluebird, 1995
189	L583JSA	Volvo B10M-60	Plaxton Premiére Interurban	DP51F	1993	Ex Bluebird, 1995
190	L584JSA	Volvo B10M-60	Plaxton Premiére Interurban	DP51F	1993	Ex Bluebird, 1995

191-197

Volvo B10M-61   Plaxton Paramount 3500   C49F*   1985   *196/7 are C51F

191	VCS391	194	VLT37	195	WLT978	196	WLT465	197	WLT697

198	P198OSE	Volvo B10MA-55	Plaxton Première Interurban	ADP71F	1996	
199	P199OSE	Volvo B10MA-55	Plaxton Première Interurban	ADP71F	1996	
200	D230UHC	Mercedes-Benz L608D	Alexander AM	B20F	1986	Ex Stagecoach South, 1995
203	D41UAO	Mercedes-Benz L608D	Reeve Burgess	B20F	1987	Ex Cumberland, 1995

205-217

Mercedes-Benz L608D   Alexander AM   B21F   1986   Ex Kelvin Scottish, 1987

205	C105KDS	209	D109NUS	211	D111NUS	215	D115NUS	217	D117NUS
206	C106KDS	210	D110NUS	214	D114NUS	216	D116NUS		

219	L882LFS	Mercedes-Benz 709D	Alexander Sprint	B25F	1994	
220	L883LFS	Mercedes-Benz 709D	Alexander Sprint	B25F	1994	
221	G574FSD	Mercedes-Benz 709D	Reeve Burgess Beaver	B25F	1990	Ex Arran Coaches, 1994
222	D122NUS	Mercedes-Benz L608D	Alexander AM	B21F	1986	Ex Kelvin Scottish, 1987
223	D123NUS	Mercedes-Benz L608D	Alexander AM	B21F	1986	Ex Kelvin Scottish, 1987
224u	D124NUS	Mercedes-Benz L608D	Alexander AM	B21F	1986	Ex Kelvin Scottish, 1987
225	L262VSU	Mercedes-Benz 709D	Dormobile Routemaker	B29F	1994	Ex William Hamilton, Maybole, 1995
227	G461SGB	Mercedes-Benz 609D	North West Coach Sales	C24F	1990	Ex Clyde Coast, 1995
228u	D128NUS	Mercedes-Benz L608D	Alexander AM	B21F	1986	Ex Kelvin Scottish, 1987
229	D129NUS	Mercedes-Benz L608D	Alexander AM	B21F	1986	Ex Kelvin Scottish, 1987
232	E638YUS	Mercedes-Benz 609D	Reeve Burgess	C19F	1988	Ex Arran Coaches, 1994
234	C591SHC	Mercedes-Benz L608D	PMT Hanbridge	B20F	1986	Ex Cheltenham & Gloucester, 1995
235	D322MNC	Mercedes-Benz 609D	Made-to-Measure	DP25F	1986	Ex Bluebird Buses, 1997
237	E645KYW	MCW MetroRider MF158/1	MCW	B30F	1988	Ex East London, 1995
239	F114YVP	MCW MetroRider MF158/16	MCW	B28F	1988	Ex East London, 1995
240	F118YVP	MCW MetroRider MF158/16	MCW	B28F	1988	Ex East London, 1995
243	F121YVP	MCW MetroRider MF158/16	MCW	B28F	1988	Ex East London, 1995
244	F128YVP	MCW MetroRider MF158/16	MCW	B28F	1988	Ex East London, 1995
245	G251TSL	Mercedes-Benz 709D	Alexander Sprint	B25F	1990	Ex Bluebird Buses, 1996
246	G252TSL	Mercedes-Benz 709D	Alexander Sprint	B25F	1990	Ex Bluebird Buses, 1996
247	G253TSL	Mercedes-Benz 709D	Alexander Sprint	B25F	1990	Ex Bluebird Buses, 1996

Opposite, top: **In January 1995 Stagecoach acquired A1 Service. This was a complex sale in that Ayrshire Bus Owners was the last Scottish co-operative bus company and was owned by nine separate members. Stagecoach took 75 vehicles with the purchase, not all constituent members sold all their vehicles, and Stagecoach declined to purchase some of the more elderly vehicles. A batch of Volvo Olympians were taken into stock to operate the former A1 service routes and many of these now carry the A1 Services name in Stagecoach font on the blue and cream livery as a reminder of Western's ownership of this service.**
Opposite, bottom: **Western Buses operate two of Stagecoach's Volvo B10MA bendi-buses, both from the Plaxton-bodied order. The second of the pair, 199, P199OSE, was photographed in Glasgow while working service X76 to Kilmarnock.** *Mark Bailey*

The Scottish Bus Handbook

Five MCW MetroRiders from Stagecoach East London and seven originating with Fife Scottish are now operated by Western Buses. Pictured with lettering for the A1 service operation is 240, F118YVP. It is seen passing through Irvine. *Billy Nicol*

248-265 Mercedes-Benz 709D Alexander Sprint B25F 1995

248	M648FYS	252	M652FYS	256	M656FYS	260	M660FYS	263	M663FYS
249	M649FYS	253	M653FYS	257	M657FYS	261	M661FYS	264	M664FYS
250	M650FYS	254	M654FYS	258	M658FYS	262	M662FYS	265	M665FYS
251	M651FYS	255	M655FYS	259	M659FYS				

266	L916UGA	Mercedes-Benz 709D	Dormobile Routemaker	B29F	1993	Ex Clyde Coast, 1995
267	M667FYS	Mercedes-Benz 709D	Alexander Sprint	B25F	1995	
268	M668FYS	Mercedes-Benz 709D	Alexander Sprint	B25F	1995	
269	K208OHS	Mercedes-Benz 709D	Dormobile Routemaker	B29F	1993	Ex Clyde Coast, 1995
270	G72APO	Mercedes-Benz 709D	Alexander AM	DP25F	1990	Ex Stagecoach South, 1997
271	G976ARV	Mercedes-Benz 709D	Alexander AM	B23F	1990	Ex Stagecoach South, 1997
272	K209OHS	Mercedes-Benz 709D	Dormobile Routemaker	B29F	1993	Ex Clyde Coast, 1995
273	D94EKV	Peugeot-Talbot Freeway	Talbot	DP12FL	1987	Ex Sochulbus, Ashford, 1992
274	F334JHS	Peugeot-Talbot Freeway	Talbot	DP12FL	1989	
275	F335JHS	Peugeot-Talbot Freeway	Talbot	DP12FL	1989	
277	G825VGA	Peugeot-Talbot Freeway	Talbot	DP12FL	1990	
279	L577NSB	Mercedes-Benz 709D	Dormobile Routemaker	B21FL	1993	Ex Arran Coaches, 1994
280	L578NSB	Mercedes-Benz 709D	Dormobile Routemaker	B21FL	1993	Ex Arran Coaches, 1994
281	G254TSL	Mercedes-Benz 709D	Alexander Sprint	B25F	1990	Ex Bluebird Buses, 1996
282	G255TSL	Mercedes-Benz 709D	Alexander Sprint	B25F	1990	Ex Bluebird Buses, 1996
283w	F53RFS	MCW MetroRider MF150/98	MCW	B25F	1988	Ex Cheltenham & Gloucester, 1996
284	F51RFS	MCW MetroRider MF150/98	MCW	B25F	1988	Ex Bluebird, 1995
285	F52RFS	MCW MetroRider MF150/98	MCW	B25F	1988	Ex Bluebird, 1995
286w	F63RFS	MCW MetroRider MF150/100	MCW	B25F	1988	Ex Bluebird, 1995
287	F64RFS	MCW MetroRider MF150/99	MCW	B25F	1988	Ex Bluebird, 1995
288	F65RFS	MCW MetroRider MF150/101	MCW	B25F	1988	Ex Bluebird, 1995
289	F54RFS	MCW MetroRider MF150/98	MCW	B25F	1988	Ex Cheltenham & Gloucester, 1996
294	E643DCK	Renault-Dodge S46	Dormobile	B25F	1987	Ex Fife Scottish, 1994
296	E646DCK	Renault-Dodge S46	Dormobile	B25F	1987	Ex Fife Scottish, 1994
297	F197ASD	Mercedes-Benz 609D	Reeve Burgess Beaver	B23F	1988	Ex Clyde Coast, Ardrossan, 1996

The standard single-deck bus for the Stagecoach group is the Volvo B10M with Alexander's PS-type bodywork, though Northern Counties bodies are also supplied. The 1997 intake calls for 160 of the former and 100 of the latter with deliveries about to commence. One of the 1995 intake for the Western Buses fleet is 507, M871ASW, pictured in Union Street, Glasgow on the service to Ayr. *Billy Nicol*

301-310 — Dennis Dart 9.8SDL3017 — Alexander Dash — B40F — 1992

301	J301BRM	303	J303BRM	305	J305BRM	307	J307BRM	309	J309BRM
302	J302BRM	304	J304BRM	306	J306BRM	308	J308BRM	310	J310BRM

312-341 — Volvo B6-9.9M — Alexander Dash — DP40F — 1994

312	M772BCS	321	M721BCS	326	M726BCS	334	M734BSJ	338	M738BSJ
313	M773BCS	322	M722BCS	327	M727BCS	335	M735BSJ	339	M739BSJ
318	M718BCS	323	M723BCS	332	M732BSJ	336	M736BSJ	340	M740BSJ
319	M719BCS	324	M724BCS	333	M733BSJ	337	M737BSJ	341	M741BSJ
320	M720BCS	325	M725BCS						

351-358 — Volvo B6-9.9M — Alexander Dash — B40F — 1994

351	M674SSX	353	M676SSX	355	M678SSX	357	M680SSX	358	M681SSX
352	M675SSX	354	M677SSX	356	M679SSX				

390-398 — Dennis Dart SFD412 — Alexander Dash — B40F* — 1996-97 *395-8 are DP40F

390	P390LPS	392	P392LPS	394	P394LPS	396	P396BRS	398	P398BRS
391	P391LPS	393	P393LPS	395	P395BRS	397	P397BRS		

399	L208PSB	Dennis Dart 9SDL3031	Marshall C36	B39F	1994	Ex Arran Coaches, 1994

427	ESU435	Volvo B10M-61	East Lancashire (1994)	DP51F	1982	
431	VLT154	Volvo B10M-61	East Lancashire (1994)	DP51F	1981	

501	M151FGB	Volvo B10B	Wright Endurance	B51F	1994	Ex A1 Service, 1995

505-512 — Volvo B10M-55 — Alexander PS — DP48F — 1995

505	M488ASW	507	M871ASW	509	M469ASW	511	M483ASW	512	M468ASW
506	M869ASW	508	M485ASW	510	M481ASW				

565-594

| | | | | | | Volvo B10M-55 | Alexander PS | DP48F | 1995 |

565	M480ASW	571	M471ASW	577	M477ASW	583	M466ASW	589	M789PRS
566	M486ASW	572	M472ASW	578	M478ASW	584	M784PRS	590	M790PRS
567	M487ASW	573	M473ASW	579	M479ASW	585	M785PRS	591	M791PRS
568	M489ASW	574	M474ASW	580	M870ASW	586	M786PRS	592	M792PRS
569	M482ASW	575	M475ASW	581	M484ASW	587	M787PRS	593	M793PRS
570	M470ASW	576	M476ASW	582	M872ASW	588	M788PRS	594	M467ASW

597	WLT774	Volvo B10M-56	Duple 300	B53F	1988	Ex A1 Service, 1995
598	WLT538	Volvo B10M-56	Duple 300	B53F	1988	Ex A1 Service, 1995
599	WLT439	Volvo B10M-55	Plaxton Derwent	B55F	1990	Ex A1 Service, 1995
616	N616USS	Volvo B10M-62	Plaxton Expressliner 2	C44FT	1995	
617	N617USS	Volvo B10M-62	Plaxton Expressliner 2	C44FT	1995	
620	TMS404X	Leyland Leopard PSU3G/4R	Alexander AYS	B53F	1982	Ex Fife, 1996
621	TMS405X	Leyland Leopard PSU3G/4R	Alexander AYS	DP49F	1982	Ex Fife, 1996
622	TMS407X	Leyland Leopard PSU3G/4R	Alexander AYS	DP51F	1982	Ex Fife, 1996
623	XMS423Y	Leyland Leopard PSU3G/4R	Alexander AYS	B53F	1982	Ex Fife, 1996
624	WFS136W	Leyland Leopard PSU3F/4R	Alexander AYS	B53F	1980	Ex Bluebird Buses, 1995
625	YSF98S	Leyland Leopard PSU3D/4R	Alexander AYS	B55F	1977	Ex Bluebird Buses, 1995
626	YSF100S	Leyland Leopard PSU3E/4R	Alexander AYS	B53F	1977	Ex Bluebird Buses, 1995
627	NPA229W	Leyland Leopard PSU3E/4R	Plaxton Supreme IV Express	C49F	1981	Ex Bluebird Buses, 1995
629	GMS285S	Leyland Leopard PSU3E/4R	Alexander AYS	B53F	1978	Ex Kelvin Scottish, 1987
630	GMS292S	Leyland Leopard PSU3E/4R	Alexander AYS	B55F	1978	Ex Kelvin Scottish, 1987
631	WFS147W	Leyland Leopard PSU3F/4R	Alexander AYS	B53F	1980	Ex Fife Scottish, 1997
632	CSF163W	Leyland Leopard PSU3F/4R	Alexander AYS	DP49F	1981	Ex Fife Scottish, 1997

633-680

| | | | | | | Leyland Leopard PSU3E/4R* | Alexander AY | B53F* | 1977-80 *637 is DP49F |

*667/70/1/6/8-80 are PSU3D/4R; 633 ex Clydeside Scottish, 1989

633	GCS33V	647	GCS47V	657	GCS57V	665	GCS65V	676	TSJ76S
637	GCS37V	648	GCS48V	658	GCS58V	667	TSJ67S	678	TSJ78S
638	GCS38V	649	GCS49V	660	GCS60V	669	GCS69V	679	TSJ79S
641	GCS41V	651	GCS51V	661	GCS61V	670	TSJ70S	680	TSJ80S
645	GCS45V	653	GCS53V	662	GCS62V	671	TSJ71S		

681	TMS406X	Leyland Leopard PSU3G/4R	Alexander AYS	DP49F	1982	Ex Fife Scottish, 1996
682	GSO82V	Leyland Leopard PSU3E/4R	Alexander AYS	DP49F	1980	Ex Fife Scottish, 1996
683	GSO83V	Leyland Leopard PSU3E/4R	Alexander AYS	DP49F	1980	Ex Fife Scottish, 1996
684	GSO84V	Leyland Leopard PSU3E/4R	Alexander AYS	DP49F	1980	Ex Fife Scottish, 1996
685	TSJ85S	Leyland Leopard PSU3D/4R	Alexander AY	B53F	1978	
686	XMS422Y	Leyland Leopard PSU3G/4R	Alexander AYS	B53F	1982	Ex Fife Scottish, 1996
687	WFS138W	Leyland Leopard PSU3F/4R	Alexander AYS	B53F	1980	Ex Fife Scottish, 1996
688	WFS142W	Leyland Leopard PSU3F/4R	Alexander AYS	B53F	1980	Ex Fife Scottish, 1996
689	GSO77V	Leyland Leopard PSU3E/4R	Alexander AYS	B55F	1980	Ex Highland Country, 1996

691-699

| | | | | | | Leyland Leopard PSU3E/4R* | Alexander AY | B53F | 1977-80 695-7 ex Clydeside Scottish, 1989 |

*691-3 are PSU3D/4R; 692/6 are B55F

691	TSJ31S	693	TSJ33S	696	BSJ896T	698	BSJ930T	699	BSJ931T
692	TSJ32S	695	BSJ895T	697	BSJ917T				

701	UIB3541	Leyland National 11351A/1R		B48F	1979	Ex Kelvin Central, 1989

702-706

| | | | | | | Leyland National 11351A/3R | | B48F | 1978-79 Ex British Airways, Heathrow, 1993 |

702	UIB3542	703	UIB3543	704	OIW7024	705	OIW7025	706	UIB3076

710	KMA399T	Leyland National 11351A/1R(Gardner)		B51F	1979	Ex A1 Service, 1995
721	703DYE	Bedford YMT	Duple Dominant II Express	C49F	1981	Ex Arran Coaches, 1994
729	FSU739	Bedford YNV	Plaxton Paramount 3200 III	C57F	1987	Ex Arran Coaches, 1994

The Scottish Bus Handbook

The number of Leyland Nationals remaining with Western Buses has diminished to a handful of mark 1s, mostly former British Airways examples with three doors when new, and some mark 2s. Representing the latter type is 780, YFS308W photographed in Kilmarnock and fitted with the sign displayed when operating school duties. *Murdoch Currie*

771-791

									Leyland National 2 NL116L11/1R			B52F*	1980-81 Ex Kelvin Scottish, 1988
													*774/5/85/9-91 are B48F

771	WAS771V	775	MDS865V	781	MSO18W	786	SNS826W	790	YFS310W
773	RFS583V	779	RFS579V	783	NLS983W	788	WAS768V	791	YFS309W
774	YFS304W	780	YFS308W	785	NLS985W	789	NLS989W		

792	KRS540V	Leyland National 2 NL106L11/1R		B41F	1980	Ex Bluebird, 1993
793	KRS542V	Leyland National 2 NL106L11/1R		B41F	1980	Ex Bluebird, 1993
795	MSO10W	Leyland National 2 NL106L11/1R		B41F	1980	Ex Bluebird, 1993
796	NLP388V	Leyland National 2 NL116L11/3R		B48F	1980	Ex British Airways, Heathrow, 1993
797	JTF971W	Leyland National 2 NL116AL11/1R		B48F	1981	Ex Mitchell, Plean, 1994
801	UNA863S	Leyland Atlantean AN68A/1R	Park Royal	H43/32F	1978	Ex GM Buses, 1991
802	WVM884S	Leyland Atlantean AN68A/1R	Park Royal	H43/32F	1978	Ex GM Buses, 1991
804	ANA211T	Leyland Atlantean AN68A/1R	Northern Counties	H43/32F	1978	Ex GM Buses, 1991
805	BNC936T	Leyland Atlantean AN68A/1R	Park Royal	H43/32F	1979	Ex GM Buses, 1991
806	RJA702R	Leyland Atlantean AN68A/1R	Northern Counties	H43/32F	1977	Ex GM Buses, 1991
807	UNA772S	Leyland Atlantean AN68A/1R	Northern Counties	H43/32F	1977	Ex GM Buses, 1991
809	VBA161S	Leyland Atlantean AN68A/1R	Northern Counties	H43/32F	1978	Ex GM Buses, 1992
810	UNA824S	Leyland Atlantean AN68A/1R	Park Royal	H43/32F	1977	Ex GM Buses, 1992
811	UNA840S	Leyland Atlantean AN68A/1R	Park Royal	H43/32F	1977	Ex GM Buses, 1992
812	WVM888S	Leyland Atlantean AN68A/1R	Park Royal	H43/32F	1978	Ex GM Buses, 1992
817	HGD213T	Leyland Atlantean AN68A/1R	Alexander AL	H45/33F	1979	Ex A1 Service, 1995
819	KSD62W	Leyland Atlantean AN68B/1R	Alexander AL	H45/33F	1980	Ex A1 Service, 1995
840	ULS660T	Leyland Fleetline FE30AGR	Eastern Coach Works	H43/32F	1979	Ex Kelvin Central, 1989
843	ASA23T	Leyland Fleetline FE30AGR	Eastern Coach Works	H43/32F	1978	Ex Northern Scottish, 1987
847	ASA27T	Leyland Fleetline FE30AGR	Eastern Coach Works	H43/32F	1978	Ex Northern Scottish, 1987

851-889

	Leyland Fleetline FE30AGR			Northern Counties		H44/31F	1978-79		
						859-6/9/80/5/9 ex Clydeside Scottish, 1988-89			

851	XSJ651T	858	XSJ658T	865	XSJ665T	870	BCS870T	880	ECS880V
853w	XSJ653T	859	XSJ659T	866	XSJ666T	871w	BCS871T	882	ECS882V
854	XSJ654T	860w	XSJ660T	867	XSJ667T	877	ECS877V	888	BCS865T
855	XSJ655T	861	XSJ661T	868	XSJ668T	878	ECS878V	889	BCS869T
857w	XSJ657T	862	XSJ662T	869	XSJ669T	879	ECS879V		

892	A308RSU	Volvo Citybus B10M-50	East Lancashire	H47/36F	1983	Ex A1 Service, 1995
893	B24CGA	Volvo Citybus B10M-50	Alexander RV	H47/37F	1985	Ex A1 Service, 1995
894	E864RCS	Volvo Citybus B10M-50	Alexander RV	DPH41/25F	1987	
895	E865RCS	Volvo Citybus B10M-50	Alexander RV	DPH45/35F	1987	
896	E866RCS	Volvo Citybus B10M-50	Alexander RV	DPH45/35F	1987	
897	E867RCS	Volvo Citybus B10M-50	Alexander RV	DPH43/33F	1987	

901-906

	Leyland Olympian ONLXB/1R	Roe		H47/29F	1982-83 Ex A1 Service, 1995	

901	HSB698Y	903	CUB73Y	904	EWY74Y	905	EWY75Y	906	EWY76Y
902	CUB72Y						

907	C800HCS	Leyland Olympian ONLXB/1R	Eastern Coach Works	H45/32F	1986	Ex A1 Service, 1995
908	F41XCS	Leyland Olympian ONCL10/1RZ	Leyland	H47/31F	1989	Ex A1 Service, 1995
909	F524WSJ	Leyland Olympian ONCL10/1RZ	Leyland	H47/31F	1989	Ex A1 Service, 1995
910	F149XCS	Leyland Olympian ONCL10/1RZ	Leyland	H47/31F	1989	Ex A1 Service, 1995
911	PJI4983	Leyland Olympian ONTL11/2RSp	Eastern Coach Works	CH45/24F	1985	Ex Cleveland Transit, 1995

912-932

	Volvo Olympian YN2RC16V3	Alexander RL		H47/32F	1995

912	M490ASW	917	N851VHH	921	N855VHH	925	N859VHH	929	N863VHH
913	M491ASW	918	N852VHH	922	N856VHH	926	N860VHH	930	N864VHH
914	M492ASW	919	N853VHH	923	N857VHH	927	N861VHH	931	N865VHH
915	N849VHH	920	N854VHH	924	N858VHH	928	N862VHH	932	N866VHH
916	N850VHH								

933-938

	Leyland Titan TNLXB2RRSp	Park Royal		H44/26D*	1978-80 Ex East London, 1995
					*Lower deck seating varies; 934-6 ex Selkent, 1995

933	EYE236V	935	CUL179V	937	WYV5T	939	WYV29T	941	EYE246V
934	CUL189V	936	CUL209V	938	WYV27T	940	CUL197V	942	EYE248V

943-949

	Leyland Titan TNLXB2RRSp	Leyland		H44/26D*	1981-83 Ex East London, 1995
					*Lower deck seating varies

943	GYE252W	945	GYE273W	947	OHV684Y	948	A833SUL	949	A876SUL
944	GYE254W	946	GYE281W						

950-960

	Leyland Titan TNLXB2RRSp	Leyland		H44/26D*	1983 Ex Selkent, 1996
					*Lower deck seating varies

950	A824SUL	953	OHV714Y	955	OHV762Y	957	OHV800Y	959	NUW618Y
951	OHV700Y	954	OHV728Y	956	OHV780Y	958	OHV809Y	960	NUW674Y
952	OHV710Y								

964	WYV49T	Leyland Titan TNLXB2RRSp	Park Royal	H44/22D	1979	Ex Selkent, 1995
965	WYV56T	Leyland Titan TNLXB2RRSp	Park Royal	H44/26D	1979	Ex Selkent, 1995
966	CUL208V	Leyland Titan TNLXB2RRSp	Leyland	H44/26D	1980	Ex Selkent, 1995
967	KYV410X	Leyland Titan TNLXB2RRSp	Leyland	H44/24D	1982	Ex Selkent, 1995

Special event vehicles - traditional liveries

1081	YSD350L	Leyland Leopard PSU3/3R	Alexander AY	B41F	1972	
1074	YYS174	Bedford C5Z1	Duple Vista	C21FM	1960	Ex David MacBrayne, 1970
1082	RCS382	Leyland Titan PD3A/3	Alexander	L35/32RD	1961	
1059	UCS659	Albion Lowlander LR3	Alexander	H40/31F	1963	

Previous Registrations:

13CLT	D317SBG	UIB3542	EGT451T
283URB	E561UHS	UIB3543	WGY589S
295UB	B421CMC	UM7681	A317ONE
439UG	B422CMC	UWP105	XUS535Y
495FFJ	B193CGA	VCS391	B191CGA
5796MX	B106REL	VLT37	B194CGA
703DYE	MCS138W	VLT54	G262EHD
896HOD	B192CGA	VLT73	-
BYJ919Y	XUF534Y, 404DCD	VLT104	G386PNV
CSO386Y	ASA10Y, TSV780	VLT154	NCS121W, WLT415, WGB646W
D131UGB	D219NCS, VLT73	WLT415	D218NCS
ESU435	GGE127X, FSU737, TOS550X	WLT416	F252OFP, XDU599, C84PRP
F149XCS	F523WSJ	WLT439	G569ESD
FSU737	D217NCS	WLT447	D220NCS
FSU739	E849AAO	WLT465	B196CGA
H751LSD	H661UWR, 803DYE	WLT501	D221NCS
HDS566H	SMS402H, 703DYE	WLT526	D216NCS
HSB698Y	CUB50Y	WLT538	E159XHS
IIL3507	F410DUG	WLT546	D318SGB
KRS540V	GSO6V	WLT697	B197CGA
KRS542V	GSO8V	WLT720	G345FFX
M151FGB	M1ABO	WLT727	H149CVU
MSU446	D526ESG	WLT774	E158XHS
NIB5232	B47DWE	WLT794	G387PNV
NIB5233	B48DWE	WLT809	G344FFX
OIW7024	GLP433T	WLT830	H150CVU
OIW7025	GLP427T	WLT978	B195CGA
PJI4983	B577LPE	XDU599	C84PRP
TSU638	FKK838Y	YSV730	H403DEG
UIB3076	EGT458T	YSV735	H406GAV
UIB3541	EGB89T		

Not all the Volvo Olympians carry the blue and cream livery. Pictured in corporate colours. Pictured at Irvine cross is 914, N849VHH. *Billy Nicol*

WHITELAW'S

G Whitelaw, Lochpark Industrial Estate, Stonehouse, South Lanarkshire, ML9 3LR

OLS539P	Leyland Leopard PSU3C/3R	Alexander AYS	B53F	1975	Ex MacDonald, Vatisker, 1991
SSU397R	Leyland Leopard PSU3D/4R	Alexander AYS	B53F	1976	Ex Midland Scottish, 1991
XMS245R	Leyland Leopard PSU3C/3R	Alexander AY	B53F	1977	Ex Midland Scottish, 1991
XMS254R	Leyland Leopard PSU3C/3R	Alexander AY	B53F	1977	Ex Midland Scottish, 1991
YSF102S	Leyland Leopard PSU3E/4R	Alexander AYS	B53F	1977	Ex Fife Scottish, 1993
GMS287S	Leyland Leopard PSU3E/4R	Alexander AYS	B53F	1978	Ex Midland Bluebird, 1993
GSG126T	Leyland Leopard PSU3E/4R	Duple Dominant I	C49F	1978	Ex Fife Scottish, 1993
MRJ280W	Leyland Leopard PSU5D/4R	Plaxton Supreme IV	C50F	1981	Ex Ribble, 1991
TPC109X	Leyland Tiger TRCTL11/2R	Eastern Coach Works B51	DP49F	1982	Ex Redby Travel, Sunderland, 1993
WPH112Y	Leyland Tiger TRCTL11/2R	Eastern Coach Works B51	C49F	1982	Ex Redby Travel, Sunderland, 1994
WPH128Y	Leyland Tiger TRCTL11/2R	Eastern Coach Works B51	C53F	1982	Ex Redby Travel, Sunderland, 1993
WPH140Y	Leyland Tiger TRCTL11/2R	Eastern Coach Works B51	C53F	1982	Ex Redby Travel, Sunderland, 1993
D375RHS	Volvo B10M-61	Duple Dominant	B55F	1987	Ex Allander Travel, Millngavie, 1996
D377RHS	Volvo B10M-61	Duple Dominant	B55F	1987	Ex Allander Travel, Millngavie, 1996
D710KG	Freight Rover Sherpa	Carlyle	B20F	1987	Ex Midland Fox, 1996
K740LHP	Volvo B10B-58	Northern Counties Paladin	B51F	1993	Ex Volvo demonstrator, 1993
L51UNS	Volvo B10B-58	Northern Counties Paladin	B51F	1993	
L52UNS	Volvo B10B-58	Northern Counties Paladin	B51F	1993	
L53UNS	Volvo B10B-58	Northern Counties Paladin	B51F	1993	
L54UNS	Volvo B10B-58	Northern Counties Paladin	B51F	1993	
L56UNS	Volvo B10B-58	Northern Counties Paladin	B51F	1993	
L57UNS	Volvo B10B-58	Alexander Strider	B51F	1994	
L58UNS	Volvo B10B-58	Alexander Strider	B51F	1994	
L59UNS	Volvo B10B-58	Alexander Strider	B51F	1994	
9201WW	Volvo B10M-60	Van Hool Alizée	C53F	1994	Ex Park's, Hamilton, 1994
M6BUS	Volvo B10M-62	Van Hool Alizée	C53F	1994	
M7BUS	Volvo B10M-62	Van Hool Alizée	C53F	1994	
7994WW	Volvo B10M-62	Van Hool Alizée	C55F	1995	
M875NWK	Volvo B10B-58	Plaxton Verde	B51F	1995	Ex Volvo demonstrator, 1995
9396WW	Volvo B10M-62	Van Hool Alizée	C53F	1996	
191WHW	Volvo B10M-62	Van Hool Alizée	C53F	1996	

Previous Registrations:

191WHW	From new	7994WW	From new	9201WW	LSK444, L256AHS
7062WW	-	9396WW	From new	F960ASD	

Livery: Red, grey and blue

Opposite, top:
Whitelaw's operate from a base in Stonehouse and are frequently to be seen in Motherwell bus station. At this interchange we see MRJ280W, a Leyland Leopard with Plaxton Supreme bodywork about to return to Stonehouse on service 54. *Phillip Stephenson*

Opposite, bottom:
In 1993/94 a batch of Volvo B10Bs were taken into stock. The body order was divided between Alexander and Northern Counties. Shown here is Strider L59UNS.
Phillip Stephenson

Photographed in Motherwell, Whitelaw's L51UNS is a Volvo B10B with Northern Counties Paladin bodywork. *Malc McDonald*

WHYTES COACHES

W N & WJ Whyte & IAW Urquhart, Scotstown Road, Newmachar, Aberdeenshire, AB2 0PP

USV365	Volvo B10M-61	Caetano Algarve	C53F	1986	Ex A1 (Meney), Ayr, 1991
HSK177	Mercedes-Benz 811D	Reeve Burgess Beaver	C33F	1988	Ex Stringer, Pontefract, 1993
HSK176	Bova FHD12.290	Bova Futura	C53F	1991	
L314KSS	Mercedes-Benz 814D	Plaxton Beaver	C33F	1993	
L958NRS	Van Hool T815	Van Hool Alicron	C49F	1994	
L959NRS	Van Hool T815	Van Hool Alicron	C49F	1994	
M105PRS	MAN 11.190	Caetano Algarve II	C33F	1994	
M106PRS	DAF SB3000WS601	Caetano Algarve II	C53F	1994	
N142VSA	Renault Master T35D	Cymric	M16	1995	
N978NMW	Mercedes-Benz 814D	Plaxton Beaver	C33F	1995	Ex Andy James, Tetbury, 1996
N82LSE	Volvo B10M-62	Caetano Algarve II	C49FT	1996	
N83LSE	Volvo B10M-62	Caetano Algarve II	C49FT	1996	
N84LSE	Volvo B10M-62	Caetano Algarve II	C49FT	1996	
N85LSE	Volvo B10M-62	Caetano Algarve II	C49FT	1996	
P682DRS	Volvo B10M-62	Caetano Algarve II	C49FT	1997	
P683DRS	Volvo B10M-62	Caetano Algarve II	C49FT	1997	
P684DRS	Volvo B10M-62	Caetano Algarve II	C49FT	1997	
P685DRS	Volvo B10M-62	Caetano Algarve II	C49FT	1997	

Previous Registrations:

HSK176	J412XSO, 5423WW	N978NMW	N30ARJ
HSK177	F300RMH	USV365	C706KDS

Livery: Red and gold

Mercedes-Benz 811D GBZ7214 is one a pair of Wright NimBus-bodiedexamples added to the fleet from Stark in 1995. The pair received registrations from their body supplier, a practice more often connected with the latter years of London Buses. The vehicle is seen on service in Greenock.
Malc McDonald

WILSON'S COACHES

R H Wilson & Son, 7 Dartmouth Avenue, Gourock, Renfrewshire, PA19 1JD

MFR42P	Leyland Leopard PSU4C/2R	Alexander AY	DP41F	1976	Ex Lancaster, 1993
C320OFL	Ford Transit 190	Dormobile	B16F	1986	Ex Viscount, 1990
C447SJU	Ford Transit 190	Robin Hood	B16F	1985	Ex Midland Fox, 1994
C470TAY	Ford Transit 190	Robin Hood	B16F	1985	Ex Midland Fox, 1994
C473TAY	Ford Transit 190	Robin Hood	B16F	1985	Ex Midland Fox, 1994
D742PTU	Freight Rover Sherpa	Dormobile	B16F	1986	Ex Boyd, Loans, 1992
D50TKA	Freight Rover Sherpa	Dormobile	B16F	1987	Ex Joszczak, Gourock, 1992
D227GLJ	Freight Rover Sherpa	Dormobile	B16F	1987	Ex Petrie, Lennoxtown, 1992
D505MJA	Iveco Daily 49.10	Robin Hood City Nippy	B21F	1987	Ex Caldwell, Greenock, 1994
D541MJA	Iveco Daily 49.10	Robin Hood City Nippy	B19F	1987	Ex Caldwell, Greenock, 1992
D412FRV	Iveco Daily 49.10	Robin Hood City Nippy	B19F	1987	Ex Ribble, 1994
E283OMG	Mercedes-Benz 609D	Reeve Burgess	C25F	1988	Ex Ash, High Wycombe, 1996
G111OGA	Mercedes-Benz 609D	North West Coach Sales	DP24F	1989	
G198GNY	Mercedes-Benz 811D	Optare StarRider	B33F	1989	Ex Henderson, Hamilton, 1994
G918CLV	Mercedes-Benz 609D	North West Coach Sales	DP24F	1990	Ex Caldwell, Greenock, 1990
GBZ7213	Mercedes-Benz 811D	Wright NimBus	B29F	1991	Ex Stark, Bridge of Wear, 1995
GBZ7214	Mercedes-Benz 811D	Wright NimBus	B29F	1991	Ex Stark, Bridge of Wear, 1995
K391NGG	Mercedes-Benz 709D	Dormobile Routemaker	B29F	1992	Ex Davidson, Whitburn, 1995
L932UGA	Mercedes-Benz 811D	Dormobile Routemaker	B33F	1993	
L966VGE	Mercedes-Benz 709D	Dormobile Routemaker	B29F	1993	
M327TSF	Mercedes-Benz 709D	Alexander AM	B29F	1994	

Previous Registrations:
GBZ7213   From new   GBZ7214   From new

Livery: White and blue

Wilson's Coaches is a minibus operation based on Gourock with most of the later buses being based on Mercedes-Benz chassis.   One of the type not to have the standard Mercedes cowl is Mercedes-Benz 811D G198GNY which carries Optare StarRider bodywork. *Phillip Stephenson*

WILSON'S / NATIONWIDE

Wilson's Coaches Ltd, Medwyn Garage, Peebles Road, Carnwath, North Lanarkshire, ML10 8HU

Depots : Mair Street, Carnwath and Ayr Road, Shawsburn, Larkhall

	GSL896N	Daimler Fleetline CRG6LXB	Alexander AL	H49/34D	1975	Ex Prospect, Lye, 1995
	NGE172P	AEC Reliance 2U3RA	Plaxton Supreme III(1976)	C46F	1964	Ex Nationwide, Carnwath, 1990
	MDF115P	Leyland Leopard PSU3C/4R	Duple Dominant	C53F	1976	Ex Nightingale, Budleigh Salterton, 1986
	PJO448P	Bristol VRT/SL3/6LX	Eastern Coach Works	H43/33F	1976	Ex Moffat & Williamson, Gauldry, 1995
	OJD44R	Bristol LH6L	Eastern Coach Works	B39F	1976	Ex Nationwide, Carnwath, 1990
	MVK542R	Leyland Atlantean AN68A/2R	Alexander AL	H48/33F	1977	Ex Busways, 1996
N	DLS260S	Leyland Leopard PSU3E/4R	Duple Dominant Express	C53F	1977	Ex Scougall, Dunbar, 1991
N	XBF59S	Leyland Leopard PSU3E/4R	Duple Dominant I	C49F	1978	Ex Pride-of-the-Road, Royston, 1991
	JFV313S	Leyland Atlantean AN68/2R	East Lancashire	H50/36F	1978	Ex Blue Bus, Horwich, 1996
	SCN258S	Leyland Atlantean AN68A/2R	Alexander AL	H49/37F	1978	Ex Busways, 1996
	SCN266S	Leyland Atlantean AN68A/2R	Alexander AL	H49/37F	1978	Ex Busways, 1996
	SCN273S	Leyland Atlantean AN68A/2R	Alexander AL	H49/37F	1978	Ex Busways, 1996
	SCN280S	Leyland Atlantean AN68A/2R	Alexander AL	H49/37F	1978	Ex Busways, 1996
	SCN285S	Leyland Atlantean AN68A/2R	Alexander AL	H49/37F	1978	Ex Busways, 1996
	SCN288S	Leyland Atlantean AN68A/2R	Alexander AL	H49/37F	1978	Ex Busways, 1996
	UVK288T	Leyland Atlantean AN68A/2R	Alexander AL	H49/37F	1978	Ex Busways, 1996
	EGB53T	Leyland Leopard PSU3C/3R	Alexander AYS	B53F	1979	
N	DWY665T	Leyland Leopard PSU3E/4R	Plaxton Supreme III Express	C49F	1979	Ex York City & District, 1991
	EWR164T	Bristol VRT/SL3/6LXB	Eastern Coach Works	H43/33F	1979	Ex Stephenson, Rochford, 1993
	MSG914T	Volvo B58-56	Plaxton Supreme IV	C53F	1979	Ex Allan, Gorebridge, 1986
	WDS183V	Volvo B58-61	Plaxton Supreme IV	C53F	1979	Ex Lochview Coaches, Greenock, 1996
	LDS380V	Leyland Leopard PSU3E/4R	Plaxton Supreme IV	C51F	1979	Ex Stewart, Dalmuir, 1986
	DSD964V	Seddon Pennine 7	Alexander AT	C49F	1979	Ex CBC, New Stevenston, 1996
	YHU679V	Volvo B58-61	Duple Dominant II	C57F	1979	Ex French, Coldingham, 1986
	NGD26V	Volvo B58-61	Duple Dominant II	C57F	1980	Ex Southern Coaches, Barrhead, 1985
	NNS234V	Volvo B58-56	Duple Dominant II	C53F	1980	Ex Mace, Glasgow, 1984
	AVK144V	Leyland Atlantean AN68A/2R	Alexander AL	H49/37F	1980	Ex Busways, 1996
	AVK178V	Leyland Atlantean AN68A/2R	Alexander AL	H49/37F	1980	Ex Busways, 1996
N	EYH811V	Leyland Leopard PSU3E/4R	Duple Dominant II Express	DP49F	1980	Ex Andrews, Sheffield, 1991
Nw	LSA22W	Mercedes-Benz L508DG	Mercedes-Benz	M16	1980	Ex Nationwide, Carnwath, 1990
N	SLJ387X	Leyland Leopard PSU5C/4R	Plaxton Supreme IV	DP53F	1981	Ex Midland Coaches, Auchterarder, 1991
N	DBH453X	Leyland Leopard PSU5D/5R	Duple Dominant III	C57F	1982	Ex Safeway, Rainham, 1991
N	YWX537X	Leyland Leopard PSU3E/4R	Duple Dominant IV	C53F	1982	Ex Warrington Coachlines, 1991
N	JSV362	Leyland Tiger TRCTL11/3R	Plaxton Supreme V	C50F	1982	Ex Armchair, Brentford, 1991
N	YPD110Y	Leyland Tiger TRCTL11/2R	Duple Dominant IV Express	C53F	1983	Ex Dorset Travel Services, 1991
	YPD131Y	Leyland Tiger TRCTL11/2R	Duple Dominant IV Express	DP53F	1983	Ex London Country NE, 1991
	YPD134Y	Leyland Tiger TRCTL11/2R	Duple Dominant IV Express	DP53F	1983	Ex London Country NW, 1991
	NDS837Y	Mercedes-Benz L608D	Reeve Burgess	C25F	1983	Ex Nationwide, Carnwath, 1990
N	A620LCP	Ford R1114	Duple Dominant III	C48FT	1983	Ex Nationwide, Carnwath, 1990
N	HIL0C46	Volvo B10M-61	Van Hool Alizée	C53F	1986	Ex Shearings, 1992
	SJI1976	DAF MB200DKFL600	Plaxton Paramount 3500	C51F	1985	Ex Grangeburn, Mothcrwoll, 1997
	C312CES	Leyland Tiger TRCTL11/3RZ	Caetano Algarve	C F	1986	Ex Moffat & Williamson, Gauldry, 1997
	D855LND	Renault-Dodge S56	Northern Counties	B20F	1986	Ex GM Buses, 1992
	NIB6694	DAF SB2300DHS585	Jonckheere Jubilee P50	C51FT	1987	Ex Hallmark, Luton, 1991
N	HIL8645	Volvo B10M-61	Van Hool Alizée	C49FT	1987	Ex Shearings, 1992
	D869MDB	Renault-Dodge S56	Northern Counties	B20F	1987	Ex Midland Choice, Ripley, 1992
	D475PON	MCW MetroRider MF150/14	MCW	B23F	1987	Ex Parfitt's, Rhymney Bridge, 1995
	E124KYW	MCW MetroRider MF150/38	MCW	B23F	1987	Ex Parfitt's, Rhymney Bridge, 1995
	E624BVK	Renault-Dodge S56	Alexander AM	B25F	1987	Ex Busways, 1996
	E627BVK	Renault-Dodge S56	Alexander AM	B25F	1987	Ex Busways, 1996
	E636BVK	Renault-Dodge S56	Alexander AM	B25F	1987	Ex Busways, 1996
	E638BVK	Renault-Dodge S56	Alexander AM	B25F	1987	Ex Busways, 1996
N	NIL1507	Volvo B10M-61	Van Hool Alizée	C55F	1988	Ex Nationwide, Carnwath, 1990
	174NJO	Volvo B9M	Van Hool Alizée	C38F	1988	
N	F656WCK	Mercedes-Benz 609D	Reeve Burgess Beaver	B23F	1988	Ex Whitehead, Darwen, 1993
	F794UVH	Mercedes-Benz 609D	Reeve Burgess Beaver	C25F	1988	Ex Hanson Coach, Halifax, 1995
	STL743	Volvo B10M-61	Van Hool Alizée	C52FT	1988	Ex Clyde Cost, Ardrossan, 1992
	SV2923	Volvo B10M-60	Van Hool Alizée	C53F	1989	
	9712WX	Volvo B10M-60	Van Hool Alizée	C53F	1989	

The Scottish Bus Handbook

Wilson's Coaches of Carnwath also have a base nearer to Glasgow at Larkhall. L972KDT is one of a pair of Volvo B10Ms with Van Hool Alizée delivered during 1994. This vehicle is seen above near the Isle of Skye bridge. *Robert Edworthy*

Many of the minibuses are operated in plain white livery as illustrated by F794UVH a Mercedes-Benz 609D with Reeve Burgess Beaver bodywork. It is seen at Milngavie rail station on tendered service C15 to Kirkintilloch. *Murdoch Currie*

Three of the Leyland Tigers new to London Country reside in the Wilson's fleet though their routes into the fleet have varied. Photographed in Lanark, YPD131Y was previouly with London Country North East and carried Nationwide fleetnames until recently. *Malc McDonald*

	RIB7742	Volvo B10M-60	Van Hool Alizée	C51F	1989	
N	GIL3271	DAF SB3000DKV601	Caetano Algarve	C53F	1989	Ex Nationwide, Carnwath, 1990
	NIL1509	Volvo B10M-60	Van Hool Alizée	C53F	1990	
	G344HSC	Volvo B10M-60	Van Hool Alizée	C53F	1990	
N	J225HDS	Mercedes-Benz 709D	Dormobile Routemaker	B29F	1992	
N	J226HDS	Mercedes-Benz 709D	Dormobile Routemaker	B29F	1992	
N	J227HDS	Mercedes-Benz 811D	Dormobile Routemaker	B33F	1992	
N	J228HDS	Mercedes-Benz 811D	Dormobile Routemaker	B33F	1992	
	J475NJU	Volvo B10M-60	Caetano Algarve II	C49FT	1994	Ex Jeffs, Helmdon, 1997
	K90SOU	Toyota Coaster HDB30R	Caetano Optimo II	C21F	1993	Ex Southern Coaches, Barrhead, 1996
N	NIL1505	Volvo B10M-60	Caetano Algarve II	C49FT	1993	
	K96UFP	Volvo B10M-60	Caetano Algarve II	C49FT	1993	
	L41CAY	Volvo B10M-62	Caetano Algarve II	C53F	1994	
	L42CAY	Volvo B10M-62	Caetano Algarve II	C53F	1994	
	L43CAY	Volvo B10M-62	Caetano Algarve II	C53F	1994	
	L971KDT	Volvo B10M-60	Van Hool Alizée	C55F	1994	
	L972KDT	Volvo B10M-60	Van Hool Alizée	C55F	1994	
	M125UWY	Volvo B10M-62	Plaxton Première 350	C50F	1995	Ex Wallace Arnold, 1997
	M126UWY	Volvo B10M-62	Plaxton Première 350	C50F	1995	Ex Wallace Arnold, 1997

Previous Registrations:

174NJO	F476XMS	JSV362	XPP295X	RIB7742	F812XSG
9712WX	F640XSF	NGE172P	AAG651B	SJI1976	C467SSF, 501KAA
C312CES	C356FVU, 121ASV	NIL1505	K95UFP	STL743	E938SSD
GIL3271	F208PNR	NIL1507	F710SFS	SV2923	F953WSF
HIL8645	D539MVR	NIL1509	G339HSC	WDS138V	LGB853V, 7076LJ, SJI7624
HIL8646	C526DND	NIB6694	E212GNV	YCR874	-

Livery: Red and silver; red, white and orange (Nationwide).

WOODS

P Woods, 20 Calder Place, Hallglen, Falkirk, FK1 2QQ

L85NSF	Mercedes-Benz 709D	Alexander AM	B25F	1994
L86NSF	Mercedes-Benz 709D	Alexander AM	B25F	1994
L87NSF	Mercedes-Benz 709D	Alexander AM	B25F	1994
P145MNB	LDV Convoy	Concept	M16	1997
P146MNB	LDV Convoy	Concept	M16	1997

Livery: White

Index

Reg	Operator	Reg	Operator	Reg	Operator	Reg	Operator
A260YEP	Highland Country	A720YFS	LRT Lothian	AGM688L	Galson Motors	B84WUV	Fife Scottish
A286TSN	Travel Dundee	A721YFS	LRT Lothian	AHN391T	McEwan's	B88PKS	Midland Bluebird
A287TSN	Travel Dundee	A722YFS	LRT Lothian	AJI8353	Marbill	B89PKS	Greater Glasgow
A288TSN	Travel Dundee	A723YFS	LRT Lothian	AJX158	Travel Dundee	B90PKS	Greater Glasgow
A39VDS	Greater Glasgow	A724YFS	LRT Lothian	AKG162A	Bluebird Buses	B91PKS	Greater Glasgow
A306YSJ	AA Buses	A725YFS	LRT Lothian	AKG232A	Bluebird Buses	B92PKS	Greater Glasgow
A308RSU	Western Buses	A726YFS	LRT Lothian	ALD968B	Bluebird Buses	B93PKS	Midland Bluebird
A322BSC	Lowland	A727YFS	LRT Lothian	ALS104Y	Greater Glasgow	B94PKS	Midland Bluebird
A323BSC	Lowland	A728YFS	LRT Lothian	ALS116Y	Lowland	B95PKS	Midland Bluebird
A324BSC	Lowland	A729YFS	LRT Lothian	ALS117Y	Midland Bluebird	B96PKS	Midland Bluebird
A325BSC	Lowland	A730RNS	Greater Glasgow	ALS118Y	Midland Bluebird	B97PKS	Strathtay
A326BSC	Lowland	A730YFS	LRT Lothian	ALS119Y	Lowland	B97WUV	Fife Scottish
A327BSC	Lowland	A731RNS	Greater Glasgow	ALS120Y	Greater Glasgow	B98PKS	Midland Bluebird
A328BSC	Lowland	A731YFS	LRT Lothian	ALS121Y	Greater Glasgow	B99PKS	Midland Bluebird
A329BSC	Lowland	A732PSU	Greater Glasgow	ALS122Y	Midland Bluebird	B100PKS	Midland Bluebird
A343SPS	Shalder	A732RNS	Greater Glasgow	ALS123Y	Midland Bluebird	B101PKS	Midland Bluebird
A371TGB	Greater Glasgow	A732YFS	LRT Lothian	ALS124Y	Midland Bluebird	B102PKS	Midland Bluebird
A372TGB	Greater Glasgow	A733PSU	Greater Glasgow	ALS125Y	Midland Bluebird	B103PKS	Midland Bluebird
A373TGB	Greater Glasgow	A733RNS	Greater Glasgow	ALS126Y	Midland Bluebird	B104PKS	Midland Bluebird
A374TGB	Greater Glasgow	A733YFS	LRT Lothian	ALS127Y	Midland Bluebird	B105PKS	Midland Bluebird
A375TGB	Greater Glasgow	A734PSU	Greater Glasgow	ALS128Y	Midland Bluebird	B106PKS	Midland Bluebird
A386XOS	Stokes	A734RNS	Greater Glasgow	ALS129Y	Midland Bluebird	B108CCS	Fife Scottish
A416SPS	Shalder	A734YFS	LRT Lothian	ALS130Y	Greater Glasgow	B112MSO	Grampian
A441JJC	Bowman	A735PSU	Greater Glasgow	ALS131Y	Greater Glasgow	B113MSO	Grampian
A469GMS	Greater Glasgow	A735RNS	Greater Glasgow	ALS132Y	Midland Bluebird	B114MSO	Grampian
A470GMS	Midland Bluebird	A735YFS	LRT Lothian	ALS133Y	Midland Bluebird	B115MSO	Grampian
A471GMS	Greater Glasgow	A736PSU	Greater Glasgow	ALS134Y	Midland Bluebird	B116MSO	Grampian
A471HNC	Rennie's	A736RNS	Greater Glasgow	ALS135Y	Midland Bluebird	B117MSO	Grampian
A472GMS	Greater Glasgow	A736YFS	LRT Lothian	ALZ2485	Spa Motors	B118MSO	Grampian
A472HNC	Rennie's	A737PSU	Greater Glasgow	ANA211T	Western Buses	B119MSO	Grampian
A473GMS	Greater Glasgow	A737RNS	Greater Glasgow	ANK316X	Midland Bluebird	B120MSO	Grampian
A473HNC	Rennie's	A738RNS	Greater Glasgow	ANV775J	Skye-Ways	B121MSO	Grampian
A474GMS	Greater Glasgow	A739PSU	Greater Glasgow	ARC670T	Docherty of Irvine	B138KSF	LRT Lothian
A475GMS	Greater Glasgow	A739RNS	Greater Glasgow	ASA23T	Western Buses	B139KSF	LRT Lothian
A476GMS	Greater Glasgow	A741PSU	Greater Glasgow	ASA25T	Strathtay	B140KSF	LRT Lothian
A477GMS	Midland Bluebird	A742PSU	Greater Glasgow	ASA27T	Western Buses	B141KSF	LRT Lothian
A478GMS	Greater Glasgow	A743PSU	Greater Glasgow	ASD30T	Steeles	B142KSF	LRT Lothian
A483UYS	Greater Glasgow	A824ASJ	Owens Coaches	ASD31T	J J Mcmenemy	B143KSF	LRT Lothian
A484UYS	Greater Glasgow	A824SUL	Western Buses	ASD32T	Stevenson	B144KSF	LRT Lothian
A562SGA	Greater Glasgow	A825SUL	Fife Scottish	ASJ206T	AA Buses	B145FCS	Keenan of Ayr
A563SGA	Greater Glasgow	A833SUL	Western Buses	ASJ207T	AA Buses	B145KSF	LRT Lothian
A564SGA	Greater Glasgow	A842ASJ	Skye-Ways	ASP97T	Strathtay	B146KSF	LRT Lothian
A566SGA	Greater Glasgow	A848ASJ	Clydeside	ASP209T	Galloways	B147KSF	LRT Lothian
A567SGA	Greater Glasgow	A858SUL	Fife Scottish	AST160W	Greater Glasgow	B148KSF	LRT Lothian
A568SGA	Greater Glasgow	A876SUL	Western Buses	ASU512S	Bruce Coaches	B149GSC	Lowland
A600TNS	Greater Glasgow	A879ASJ	Clydeside	ATA563L	Spa Motors	B149KSF	LRT Lothian
A601TNS	Greater Glasgow	A907LWU	McEwan's	ATV672T	Steeles	B150GSC	Lowland
A602TNS	Greater Glasgow	A940XGG	Bluebird Buses	AUJ735T	Morrison's	B151GSC	Lowland
A603TNS	Greater Glasgow	A941XGG	Bluebird Buses	AUS417S	Golden Eagle	B152GSC	Lowland
A604TNS	Greater Glasgow	A942XGG	Bluebird Buses	AUS418S	Golden Eagle	B153GSC	Lowland
A607THV	Fife Scottish	A967YSX	Fife Scottish	AVK144V	Wilson's, Carnwath	B154GSC	Lowland
A620LCP	Wilson's, Carnwath	A968YSX	Fife Scottish	AVK178V	Wilson's, Carnwath	B155GSC	Lowland
A663WSU	Bluebird Buses	A969YSX	Fife Scottish	AWG623	Midland Bluebird	B156GSC	Lowland
A703YFS	LRT Lothian	A970YSX	Fife Scottish	AYR332T	Docherty of Irvine	B157GSC	Lowland
A704YFS	LRT Lothian	A971YSX	Fife Scottish	B21YYS	Greater Glasgow	B158GSC	Lowland
A705YFS	LRT Lothian	A972YSX	Fife Scottish	B23YYS	Greater Glasgow	B159GSC	Lowland
A706YFS	LRT Lothian	A973YSX	Fife Scottish	B24CGA	Western Buses	B160KSC	Lowland
A707YFS	LRT Lothian	A974YSX	Fife Scottish	B24YYS	Greater Glasgow	B161KSC	Midland Bluebird
A708YFS	LRT Lothian	A981FLS	Greater Glasgow	B25YYS	Greater Glasgow	B162KSC	Midland Bluebird
A709YFS	LRT Lothian	A982FLS	Greater Glasgow	B26YYS	Greater Glasgow	B163KSC	Midland Bluebird
A710YFS	LRT Lothian	A983FLS	Greater Glasgow	B27YYS	Greater Glasgow	B169KSC	Lowland
A711YFS	LRT Lothian	A984FLS	Greater Glasgow	B28YYS	Greater Glasgow	B170KSC	Lowland
A712YFS	LRT Lothian	A985JJU	Bowman	B29YYS	Greater Glasgow	B171KSC	Lowland
A713YFS	LRT Lothian	AAK112T	McGill's	B30YYS	Greater Glasgow	B172KSC	Lowland
A714YFS	LRT Lothian	AAX589A	Bluebird Buses	B31YYS	Greater Glasgow	B173KSC	Lowland
A715YFS	LRT Lothian	AAX600A	Bluebird Buses	B33YYS	Greater Glasgow	B177FFS	Fife Scottish
A716YFS	LRT Lothian	AAX601A	Bluebird Buses	B34YYS	Greater Glasgow	B178FFS	Fife Scottish
A717YFS	LRT Lothian	AAX631A	Bluebird Buses	B43OSB	Bowman	B179FFS	Fife Scottish
A718YFS	LRT Lothian	ABV669A	Fife Scottish	B61GSC	LRT Lothian	B180FFS	Fife Scottish
A719YFS	LRT Lothian	AEF91A	Keenan of Ayr	B62GSC	LRT Lothian	B181FFS	Fife Scottish

The Scottish Bus Handbook

B182FFS	Fife Scottish	B740GSC	LRT Lothian	BLS439Y	Greater Glasgow	C112BTS	Greater Glasgow
B183FFS	Fife Scottish	B741GSC	LRT Lothian	BLS440Y	Greater Glasgow	C112GSJ	AA Buses
B184FFS	Fife Scottish	B742GSC	LRT Lothian	BLS441Y	Greater Glasgow	C113BTS	Greater Glasgow
B185FFS	Fife Scottish	B743GSC	LRT Lothian	BLS442Y	Greater Glasgow	C114BTS	Greater Glasgow
B186FFS	Fife Scottish	B744GSC	LRT Lothian	BLS444Y	Greater Glasgow	C115BTS	Greater Glasgow
B186YUS	Stokes	B745GSC	LRT Lothian	BLS445Y	Greater Glasgow	C116BTS	Strathtay
B192XJD	West Coast Motors	B746GSC	LRT Lothian	BLS446Y	Midland Bluebird	C174VSF	Midland Bluebird
B200DGG	Greater Glasgow	B747GSC	LRT Lothian	BLS672V	Greater Glasgow	C175VSF	Midland Bluebird
B241BYS	Greater Glasgow	B748GSC	LRT Lothian	BNC936T	Western Buses	C176VSF	Midland Bluebird
B242BYS	Greater Glasgow	B749GSC	LRT Lothian	BNC957T	Keenan of Ayr	C177VSF	Midland Bluebird
B243BYS	Greater Glasgow	B750GSC	LRT Lothian	BSJ890T	Clydeside	C178VSF	Midland Bluebird
B244BYS	Greater Glasgow	B751GSC	LRT Lothian	BSJ891T	Clydeside	C179VSF	Midland Bluebird
B245BYS	Greater Glasgow	B752GSC	LRT Lothian	BSJ893T	Clydeside	C180VSF	Midland Bluebird
B246BYS	Greater Glasgow	B753GSC	LRT Lothian	BSJ894T	Clydeside	C181VSF	Midland Bluebird
B247BYS	Greater Glasgow	B754GSC	LRT Lothian	BSJ895T	Western Buses	C182VSF	Midland Bluebird
B248BYS	Greater Glasgow	B755GSC	LRT Lothian	BSJ896T	Western Buses	C183VSF	Midland Bluebird
B249BYS	Greater Glasgow	B756GSC	LRT Lothian	BSJ897T	Clydeside	C185XSK	Highland
B250BYS	Greater Glasgow	B757GSC	LRT Lothian	BSJ898T	Clydeside	C188RVV	Greater Glasgow
B251BYS	Greater Glasgow	B758GSC	LRT Lothian	BSJ899T	Clydeside	C211UPD	Greater Glasgow
B252BYS	Greater Glasgow	B759GSC	LRT Lothian	BSJ900T	Clydeside	C212UPD	Greater Glasgow
B253BYS	Greater Glasgow	B760GSC	LRT Lothian	BSJ901T	Clydeside	C213UPD	Greater Glasgow
B254BYS	Greater Glasgow	B761GSC	LRT Lothian	BSJ902T	Clydeside	C214UPD	Clydeside
B255BYS	Greater Glasgow	B762GSC	LRT Lothian	BSJ903T	Clydeside	C215UPD	Greater Glasgow
B256BYS	Greater Glasgow	B763GSC	LRT Lothian	BSJ904T	Clydeside	C240OFE	Strathtay
B257BYS	Greater Glasgow	B764GSC	LRT Lothian	BSJ905T	Clydeside	C241OFE	Strathtay
B258BYS	Greater Glasgow	B765GSC	LRT Lothian	BSJ906T	Clydeside	C242OFE	Strathtay
B259BYS	Greater Glasgow	B766GSC	LRT Lothian	BSJ907T	Clydeside	C243OFE	Strathtay
B260BYS	Greater Glasgow	B767GSC	LRT Lothian	BSJ908T	Clydeside	C244OFE	Strathtay
B261BYS	Greater Glasgow	B768GSC	LRT Lothian	BSJ912T	Clydeside	C249OFE	Dart
B262BYS	Greater Glasgow	B769GSC	LRT Lothian	BSJ913T	Clydeside	C257SPC	Greater Glasgow
B263BYS	Greater Glasgow	B999YUS	Greater Glasgow	BSJ914T	Clydeside	C263FGG	McGill's
B268KPF	Dochert'y Midland	BAN115H	Skye-Ways	BSJ916T	Clydeside	C264FGG	McGill's
B291YSL	Bluebird Buses	BAO867T	AA Buses	BSJ917T	Western Buses	C279MDS	Argyle Bus Group
B294KPF	Galson Motors	BCS865T	Western Buses	BSJ918T	Clydeside	C308SPL	Argyle Bus Group
B348LSO	Bluebird Buses	BCS869T	Western Buses	BSJ919T	Clydeside	C310SPL	Argyle Bus Group
B349LSO	Bluebird Buses	BCS870T	Western Buses	BSJ920T	Clydeside	C312CES	Wilson's, Carnwath
B350LSO	Bluebird Buses	BCS871T	Western Buses	BSJ921T	Clydeside	C312SPL	Argyle Bus Group
B351LSO	Bluebird Buses	BFS14L	LRT Lothian	BSJ922T	Clydeside	C319CVU	Shalder
B352LSO	Bluebird Buses	BFS34L	LRT Lothian	BSJ923T	Clydeside	C320OFL	R H Wilson's
B353LSO	Bluebird Buses	BFS39L	LRT Lothian	BSJ925T	Clydeside	C339RPE	Moffat & Williamson
B354LSO	Bluebird Buses	BFS40L	LRT Lothian	BSJ926T	Clydeside	C342VVN	Dart
B355LSO	Bluebird Buses	BFS41L	LRT Lothian	BSJ927T	Clydeside	C352SVV	AA Buses
B356LSO	Bluebird Buses	BFS42L	LRT Lothian	BSJ930T	Western Buses	C402VVN	Dart
B357LSO	Bluebird Buses	BFS43L	LRT Lothian	BSJ931T	Western Buses	C421VVN	Dart
B358LSO	Bluebird Buses	BFS44L	LRT Lothian	BSK756	Bluebird Buses	C422VVN	Dart
B359LSO	Bluebird Buses	BFS45L	LRT Lothian	BSK789	Moffat & Williamson	C427VVN	Dart
B360LSO	Bluebird Buses	BFS48L	LRT Lothian	BSK790	Moffat & Williamson	C430VVN	Dart
B404NJF	H-A-D Coaches	BFS49L	LRT Lothian	BSK791	Moffat & Williamson	C434VVN	Dart
B417CVH	Bowman	BFS50L	LRT Lothian	BSS76	Lowland	C447SJU	R H Wilson's
B459WTC	Moffat & Williamson	BGG252S	Lowland	BSV807	Midland Bluebird	C448BKM	Greater Glasgow
B494GBD	Bowman	BGG254S	Lowland	BTE208V	Keenan of Ayr	C449BKM	Clydeside
B509YAT	Shalder	BGG257S	Lowland	BTU557W	Highland Country	C450BKM	Clydeside
B521YTC	Rowe's	BHN601B	Docherty of Irvine	BUH205V	Docherty of Irvine	C451BKM	Clydeside
B579MLS	Greater Glasgow	BHS206X	McGill's	BUS6X	Travel Dundee	C452GKE	Clydeside
B580MLS	Greater Glasgow	BHS207X	McGill's	BVR76T	Highland Country	C452SJU	H-A-D Coaches
B581MLS	Midland Bluebird	BJI6863	Marbill	BXI521	Greater Glasgow	C453GKE	Clydeside
B582MLS	Midland Bluebird	BLS422Y	Greater Glasgow	BYC789B	Highland Country	C454GKE	Clydeside
B583MLS	Midland Bluebird	BLS424Y	Strathtay	BYD93B	Spa Motors	C461JCP	Rennie's
B584MLS	Midland Bluebird	BLS425Y	Greater Glasgow	BYJ919Y	Western Buses	C461SSO	Bluebird Buses
B585MLS	Midland Bluebird	BLS426Y	Greater Glasgow	C63PSG	LRT Lothian	C462SSO	Bluebird Buses
B586MLS	Greater Glasgow	BLS427Y	Greater Glasgow	C64PSG	LRT Lothian	C463SSO	Bluebird Buses
B587MLS	Midland Bluebird	BLS428Y	Greater Glasgow	C80OCW	Stagecoach Glasgow	C466SSO	Bluebird Buses
B588MLS	Midland Bluebird	BLS429Y	Greater Glasgow	C101KDS	Stagecoach Glasgow	C467SSO	Bluebird Buses
B693BPU	Highland Country	BLS430Y	Greater Glasgow	C102KDS	Midland Bluebird	C468SSO	Bluebird Buses
B697BPU	Greater Glasgow	BLS431Y	Greater Glasgow	C103KDS	Grampian	C469SSO	Bluebird Buses
B724AGD	McGill's	BLS433Y	Strathtay	C104KDS	Stagecoach Glasgow	C470SSO	Bluebird Buses
B725AGD	McGill's	BLS435Y	Greater Glasgow	C105KDS	Western Buses	C470TAY	R H Wilson's
B737GSC	LRT Lothian	BLS436Y	Greater Glasgow	C106KDS	Western Buses	C473TAY	R H Wilson's
B738GSC	LRT Lothian	BLS437Y	Midland Bluebird	C111BTS	Strathtay	C518TJF	Scottish Travel
B739GSC	LRT Lothian	BLS438Y	Greater Glasgow	C111JCS	Bluebird Buses	C591SHC	Western Buses

Reg	Operator	Reg	Operator	Reg	Operator	Reg	Operator
C594SHC	Stagecoach Glasgow	C929SLT	Argyle Bus Group	CSL604V	Stevenson	CWG720V	Greater Glasgow
C649XDF	Meffan	C982KHS	Greater Glasgow	CSL605V	Stevenson	CWG771V	Greater Glasgow
C653XDF	Meffan	C983KHS	Greater Glasgow	CSL607V	Travel Dundee	CWG772V	Greater Glasgow
C707JMB	Clydeside	CAS511W	Highland Country	CSL608V	Travel Dundee	D21SAO	Skye-Ways
C708JMB	Clydeside	CAS512W	Highland Country	CSL609V	Travel Dundee	D23WNH	Scottish Travel
C760CWX	Irvines of Law	CAS513W	Highland	CSL610V	Travel Dundee	D31XSS	Shalder
C770SFS	LRT Lothian	CAS514W	Highland	CSL611V	Travel Dundee	D33BVV	Scottish Travel
C771FBH	Shalder	CAS515W	Highland	CSL612V	Travel Dundee	D35DNH	Rennie's
C771SFS	LRT Lothian	CAS516W	Highland	CSL613V	Stevenson	D37UAO	Stagecoach Glasgow
C772SFS	LRT Lothian	CAS517W	Highland Country	CSL614V	Travel Dundee	D38UAO	Stagecoach Glasgow
C773SFS	LRT Lothian	CAS518W	Highland Country	CSL615V	Travel Dundee	D39UAO	Stagecoach Glasgow
C774SFS	LRT Lothian	CAS519W	Oban & District	CSL617V	Travel Dundee	D41UAO	Western Buses
C775SFS	LRT Lothian	CAS520W	Oban & District	CSL618V	Travel Dundee	D42UAO	Stagecoach Glasgow
C776SFS	LRT Lothian	CBZ4622	Allander Travel	CSL619V	Travel Dundee	D43UAO	Stagecoach Glasgow
C777SFS	LRT Lothian	CFM88S	Marbill	CSL620V	Travel Dundee	D46UAO	Stagecoach Glasgow
C778GOX	Meffan	CFS116S	Galloways	CSO386Y	Western Buses	D50TKA	R H Wilson's
C778SFS	LRT Lothian	CFS119S	Highland Country	CSO387Y	Rowe's	D65BSC	LRT Lothian
C779SFS	LRT Lothian	CGG825X	Greater Glasgow	CSO388Y	Rowe's	D66BSC	LRT Lothian
C780SFS	LRT Lothian	CGG829X	Greater Glasgow	CSU219X	Greater Glasgow	D67TLV	Bridge
C781SFS	LRT Lothian	CGG831X	Greater Glasgow	CSU220X	Greater Glasgow	D68TLV	Bridge
C782SFS	LRT Lothian	CGG832X	Greater Glasgow	CSU221X	Greater Glasgow	D710KG	Whitelaw's
C783SFS	LRT Lothian	CGG833X	Greater Glasgow	CSU222X	Greater Glasgow	D81UFV	Stagecoach Glasgow
C784SFS	LRT Lothian	CGG835X	Greater Glasgow	CSU223X	Greater Glasgow	D82CFA	Argyle Bus Group
C785SFS	LRT Lothian	CGG836X	Greater Glasgow	CSU224X	Greater Glasgow	D82UFV	Stagecoach Glasgow
C786SFS	LRT Lothian	CGG837X	Greater Glasgow	CSU225X	Greater Glasgow	D83UFV	Stagecoach Glasgow
C787SFS	LRT Lothian	CGG838X	Greater Glasgow	CSU226X	Greater Glasgow	D86CFA	Argyle Bus Group
C787USG	Fife Scottish	CGG839X	Greater Glasgow	CSU228X	Greater Glasgow	D93VCC	Scottish Travel
C788SFS	LRT Lothian	CJH118V	Rennie's	CSU229X	Greater Glasgow	D94EKV	Western Buses
C788USG	Fife Scottish	CJH122V	Rennie's	CSU230X	Greater Glasgow	D95VCC	Scottish Travel
C789SFS	LRT Lothian	CJH126V	Rennie's	CSU231X	Greater Glasgow	D97VCC	Scottish Travel
C789USG	Fife Scottish	CJU678W	Rennie's	CSU233X	Greater Glasgow	D103CFA	Argyle Bus Group
C790SFS	LRT Lothian	CKS392X	Greater Glasgow	CSU234X	Greater Glasgow	D107NDW	Mackies
C790USG	Fife Scottish	CLC976T	Shalder	CSU235X	Greater Glasgow	D107NUS	Stagecoach Glasgow
C791SFS	LRT Lothian	CMS196	H-A-D Coaches	CSU236X	Greater Glasgow	D108ELS	Midland Bluebird
C791USG	Fife Scottish	CMT871V	Shalder	CSU237X	Greater Glasgow	D108NUS	Stagecoach Glasgow
C792SFS	LRT Lothian	CMT882V	Shalder	CSU238X	Greater Glasgow	D109ELS	Midland Bluebird
C792USG	Fife Scottish	CRG325C	Grampian	CSU239X	Greater Glasgow	D109NUS	Western Buses
C793SFS	LRT Lothian	CRS60T	Bluebird Buses	CSU240X	Greater Glasgow	D110ELS	Midland Bluebird
C793USG	Fife Scottish	CRS61T	Bluebird Buses	CSU241X	Greater Glasgow	D110NUS	Western Buses
C794SFS	LRT Lothian	CRS62T	Bluebird Buses	CSU242X	Greater Glasgow	D111ELS	Midland Bluebird
C794USG	Fife Scottish	CRS63T	Bluebird Buses	CSU243X	Greater Glasgow	D111NUS	Western Buses
C795USG	Fife Scottish	CRS68T	Bluebird Buses	CSU245X	Greater Glasgow	D112NDW	Mackies
C796USG	Fife Scottish	CRS69T	Bluebird Buses	CSU246X	Greater Glasgow	D113NUS	Stagecoach Glasgow
C797USG	Fife Scottish	CRS70T	Bluebird Buses	CSU247X	Greater Glasgow	D114NUS	Western Buses
C798USG	Fife Scottish	CRS71T	Bluebird Buses	CSU920	Bluebird Buses	D115ELS	Midland Bluebird
C799USG	Fife Scottish	CRS73T	Bluebird Buses	CSU921	Bluebird Buses	D115NUS	Western Buses
C800HCS	Western Buses	CRS74T	Bluebird Buses	CSU922	Bluebird Buses	D116ELS	Midland Bluebird
C800USG	Fife Scottish	CSE122T	Shalder	CSU923	Bluebird Buses	D116NUS	Western Buses
C801KHS	Greater Glasgow	CSF155W	Midland Bluebird	CSU932	Greater Glasgow	D116TFT	Paterson's
C801U3G	Fife Scottish	CSF157W	Oban & District	CTS917	Travel Dundee	D117NUS	Western Buses
C802KHS	Greater Glasgow	CSF158W	Fife Scottish	CUB72Y	Western Buses	D118NUS	Stagecoach Glasgow
C802USG	Fife Scottish	CSF159W	Fife Scottish	CUB73Y	Western Buses	D120DWP	Morrison's
C803KHS	Greater Glasgow	CSF160W	Fife Scottish	CUL88V	Clydeside	D120NUS	Grampian
C803USG	Fife Scottish	CSF161W	Fife Scottish	CUL94V	Clydeside	D122FLS	Mackies
C804KHS	Greater Glasgow	CSF162W	Fife Scottish	CUL139V	Clydeside	D122NUS	Western Buses
C804USG	Fife Scottish	CSF163W	Western Buses	CUL143V	Clydeside	D123NUS	Western Buses
C805KHS	Greater Glasgow	CSF164W	Fife Scottish	CUL152V	Clydeside	D124NUS	Western Buses
C805SDY	Grampian	CSF165W	Fife Scottish	CUL176V	Western Buses	D126NUS	Scottish Travel
C805USG	Fife Scottish	CSF166W	Fife Scottish	CUL189V	Western Buses	D128NUS	Western Buses
C806KHS	Greater Glasgow	CSF167W	Fife Scottish	CUL197V	Western Buses	D129NUS	Western Buses
C806USG	Fife Scottish	CSF168W	Fife Scottish	CUL208V	Western Buses	D130NUS	Stagecoach Glasgow
C807KHS	Greater Glasgow	CSF169W	Fife Scottish	CUL209V	Western Buses	D131NUS	Stagecoach Glasgow
C807USG	Fife Scottish	CSG773S	Lowland	CUS296X	Greater Glasgow	D131UGB	Western Buses
C808KHS	Greater Glasgow	CSG774S	Lowland	CUS297X	Greater Glasgow	D134NUS	Slaemuir
C808SDY	Henderson Travel	CSG776S	Lowland	CUS298X	Greater Glasgow	D136NUS	Stagecoach Glasgow
C809KHS	Greater Glasgow	CSG792S	Lowland	CUS299X	Greater Glasgow	D139NUS	Slaemuir
C810KHS	Greater Glasgow	CSG794S	Lowland	CUS300X	Greater Glasgow	D153NON	Highland Country
C812SDY	Midland Bluebird	CSL601V	Travel Dundee	CUS301X	Greater Glasgow	D154NON	Highland
C821SDY	Midland Bluebird	CSL602V	Travel Dundee	CUS302X	Greater Glasgow	D168VRP	Clydeside
C901HWF	Bluebird Buses	CSL603V	Travel Dundee	CWG694V	Moffat & Williamson	D181TSB	Shalder

The Scottish Bus Handbook

Reg	Operator	Reg	Operator	Reg	Operator	Reg	Operator
D184ESC	Midland Bluebird	D403ASF	Lowland	D562RCK	Dart	DSA247T	Midland Bluebird
D185ESC	Midland Bluebird	D403SGS	Orion Autobus	D563RCK	Dart	DSA248T	Midland Bluebird
D186ESC	Midland Bluebird	D412FRV	R H Wilson's	D564RCK	Dart	DSA249T	Lowland
D202SKD	Clydeside	D420ASF	Lowland	D566VBV	Meffan	DSA250T	Lowland
D203SKD	Clydeside	D426JDB	Shalder	D568VBV	Strathtay	DSA251T	Lowland
D204SKD	Clydeside	D428ASF	Oban & District	D569VBV	Meffan	DSA256T	Midland Bluebird
D205SKD	Clydeside	D435RYS	Bluebird Buses	D591MVR	Midland Bluebird	DSA257T	Midland Bluebird
D206SKD	Clydeside	D436RYS	Bluebird Buses	D599MVR	Midland Bluebird	DSB118X	Highland Country
D212SKD	Dart	D460BEO	Skye-Ways	D613MDB	Argyle Bus Group	DSB119X	Highland Country
D214SKD	Dart	D468PON	Clydeside	D614ASG	Fife Scottish	DSD55V	Steeles
D220GLJ	Meffan	D471UGA	Greater Glasgow	D614BCK	McGill's	DSD958V	Lowland
D226UHC	Midland Bluebird	D472UGA	Greater Glasgow	D615ASG	Fife Scottish	DSD964V	Wilson's, Carnwath
D226URG	Dart	D473UGA	Greater Glasgow	D615MVR	Bowman	DSD965V	Lowland
D227GLJ	R H Wilson's	D474UGA	Greater Glasgow	D621MDB	Argyle Bus Group	DSP921V	Travel Dundee
D227UHC	Midland Bluebird	D475PON	Wilson's, Carnwath	D626MDB	Argyle Bus Group	DSP922V	Travel Dundee
D228URG	Dart	D475UGA	Greater Glasgow	D634BBV	Mackies	DSP923V	Travel Dundee
D229UHC	Midland Bluebird	D501RCK	Dart	D660XPS	Shalder	DSP924V	Travel Dundee
D230UHC	Western Buses	D502NWG	Dart	D665NNE	Argyle Bus Group	DSP925V	Travel Dundee
D231URG	Dart	D502RCK	Dart	D674MHS	Greater Glasgow	DSP926V	Travel Dundee
D232UHC	Grampian	D503MJA	Bridge	D675MHS	Greater Glasgow	DSP927V	Travel Dundee
D243NCS	Green Line	D505MJA	R H Wilson's	D677MHS	Greater Glasgow	DSP928V	Travel Dundee
D248NCS	Puma Coaches	D505RCK	Dart	D679MHS	Greater Glasgow	DSP929V	Travel Dundee
D250WTY	Strathtay	D507NWG	Dart	D681MHS	Greater Glasgow	DSP930V	Travel Dundee
D254NCS	Puma Coaches	D508NWG	Dart	D701EES	Travel Dundee	DSP931V	Travel Dundee
D261NCS	Clydeside	D508RCK	Dart	D702EES	Travel Dundee	DSP932V	Travel Dundee
D276FAS	Lowland	D509NWG	Meffan	D703TLG	Meffan	DSP933V	Travel Dundee
D277FAS	Fife Scottish	D510RCK	Avondale	D704EES	Travel Dundee	DSP934V	Travel Dundee
D278FAS	Fife Scottish	D512CSF	Fife Scottish	D713CSC	Fife Scottish	DSP935V	Travel Dundee
D279FAS	Fife Scottish	D512MJA	Bridge	D726YBV	Rennie's	DSV711	Gibson
D283OOK	Bridge	D512RCK	Dart	D742PTU	R H Wilson's	DWF188V	Bluebird Buses
D285XCX	Bowman	D513RCK	Dart	D744BRS	Bluebird Buses	DWF190V	Bluebird Buses
D301SDS	Puma Coaches	D513RTT	McEwan's	D750DSH	Lowland	DWF191V	Bluebird Buses
D304MHS	Green Line	D515RCK	Avondale	D751DSH	Lowland	DWF193V	Bluebird Buses
D309DSR	Strathtay	D516DSX	Fife Scottish	D752DSH	Lowland	DWF198V	Fife Scottish
D310DSR	Strathtay	D516RCK	Dart	D753DSH	Lowland	DWF199V	Fife Scottish
D311DSR	Strathtay	D517DSX	Fife Scottish	D754DSH	Lowland	DWF200V	Fife Scottish
D318SDS	Clydeside	D517MJA	Bridge	D755DSH	Lowland	DWH696W	Highland
D319SDS	Clydeside	D518DSX	Fife Scottish	D817EES	Strathtay	DWY665T	Wilson's, Carnwath
D322MNC	Western Buses	D519DSX	Fife Scottish	D818EES	Strathtay	DYS636T	McGill's
D328DKS	Lowland	D520DSX	Fife Scottish	D819EES	Strathtay	E31BTO	Greater Glasgow
D329DKS	Lowland	D520RCK	Stagecoach Glasgow	D831RYS	Green Line	E36LSL	Strathtay
D330DKS	Lowland	D521DSX	Fife Scottish	D855LND	Wilson's, Carnwath	E39OMS	Slaemuir
D349ESC	Lowland	D521RCK	Avondale	D869MDB	Wilson's, Carnwath	E40OMS	Spa Motors
D350ESC	Lowland	D522DSX	Fife Scottish	D901CSH	Lowland	E52KJU	Argyle Bus Group
D351ESC	Lowland	D523DSX	Fife Scottish	D902CSH	Lowland	E55LBK	Greater Glasgow
D358CBC	Rowe's	D523KSE	Bluebird Buses	D950UDY	Scottish Travel	E60MMT	Midland Bluebird
D369OSU	Greater Glasgow	D524DSX	Fife Scottish	D951VSS	Grampian	E73ECH	Meffan
D370OSU	Greater Glasgow	D524RCK	Dart	D957UDY	Scottish Travel	E76RCS	AA Buses
D371OSU	Greater Glasgow	D525RCK	Stagecoach Glasgow	D971TKC	Moffat & Williamson	E77RCS	AA Buses
D372OSU	Greater Glasgow	D528MJA	Bridge	D982NJS	Shalder	E100LBC	Riddler
D373OSU	Greater Glasgow	D530RCK	Stagecoach Glasgow	DAZ8290	Shuttle Buses	E101JPL	Clydeside
D374OSU	Greater Glasgow	D531RCK	Stagecoach Glasgow	DBH453X	Wilson's, Carnwath	E102JPL	Clydeside
D375OSU	Greater Glasgow	D532MJA	Bridge	DBV31W	Rennie's	E103JPL	Clydeside
D375RHS	Whitelaw's	D532RCK	Grampian	DDZ8844	Bluebird Buses	E106JNH	Grampian
D376OSU	Greater Glasgow	D534RCK	Stagecoach Glasgow	DEX213T	Rennie's	E108JNH	Grampian
D377OSU	Greater Glasgow	D536RCK	Avondale	DGS625	Bluebird Buses	E108JPL	Clydeside
D377RHS	Whitelaw's	D537RCK	Avondale	DJU704	Rowe's	E108LCW	Green Line
D378OSU	Greater Glasgow	D541MJA	R H Wilson's	DLS260S	Wilson's, Carnwath	E110JNH	Grampian
D379OSU	Greater Glasgow	D541RCK	Dart	DLS349V	Oban & District	E112LCW	Green Line
D380OSU	Greater Glasgow	D542RCK	Dart	DLS350V	Oban & District	E114OBF	West Coast Motors
D381OSU	Greater Glasgow	D545RCK	Dart	DLS351V	Midland Bluebird	E122DRS	Grampian
D382OSU	Greater Glasgow	D546RCK	Dart	DLS352V	Midland Bluebird	E122HLK	Strathtay
D383OSU	Greater Glasgow	D548RCK	Dart	DLS357V	Highland	E123DRS	Grampian
D385XRS	Bluebird Buses	D551RCK	Dart	DMS26V	Midland Bluebird	E123RAX	Maynes
D386XRS	Bluebird Buses	D552RCK	Dart	DNK403T	Riddler	E124DRS	Grampian
D387XRS	Bluebird Buses	D553RCK	Dart	DSA238T	Midland Bluebird	E124HLK	Strathtay
D388XRS	Bluebird Buses	D554RCK	Dart	DSA242T	Lowland	E124KYW	Wilson's, Carnwath
D389UGA	Glen Coaches	D555RCK	Dart	DSA243T	Midland Bluebird	E125DRS	Grampian
D389XRS	Bluebird Buses	D556RCK	Henderson Travel	DSA244T	Midland Bluebird	E125KYW	Clydeside
D402ASF	Lowland	D558RCK	Stagecoach Glasgow	DSA245T	Lowland	E126DRS	Grampian

Reg	Operator	Reg	Operator	Reg	Operator	Reg	Operator
E126KYW	Clydeside	E306MSG	LRT Lothian	E366YGB	Meffan	E689WKJ	Shuttle Buses
E127DRS	Grampian	E307MSG	LRT Lothian	E401TBS	Highland Country	E713LYU	Bluebird Buses
E128DRS	Grampian	E307YDS	Greater Glasgow	E404TBS	Highland	E714LYU	Bluebird Buses
E129DRS	Grampian	E308MSG	LRT Lothian	E405TBS	Highland	E756GSH	Lowland
E130DRS	Grampian	E308YDS	Greater Glasgow	E422MAC	Argyle Bus Group	E766MSC	Henderson Travel
E131DRS	Grampian	E309MSG	LRT Lothian	E431JSG	Midland Bluebird	E809JSX	Puma Coaches
E133KYW	Clydeside	E309YDS	Greater Glasgow	E431LDL	Morrison's	E810JSX	Clydeside
E135KYW	Clydeside	E310MSG	LRT Lothian	E431YHL	Moffat & Williamson	E813JSX	Clydeside
E142VGG	Bridge	E310YDS	Greater Glasgow	E432JSG	Midland Bluebird	E814JSX	Docherty of Irvine
E145VGG	Silver Fox	E311MSG	LRT Lothian	E433JSG	Midland Bluebird	E842KAS	Bluebird Buses
E151KYW	Clydeside	E311YDS	Greater Glasgow	E434JSG	Lowland	E864RCS	Western Buses
E152RNY	Green Line	E312MSG	LRT Lothian	E434YSU	Highland Country	E865RCS	Western Buses
E153UKR	Orion Autobus	E312YDS	Greater Glasgow	E435JSG	Lowland	E866RCS	Western Buses
E156UKR	Orion Autobus	E313MSG	LRT Lothian	E436JSG	Midland Bluebird	E867RCS	Western Buses
E156XHS	Henderson Travel	E313YDS	Greater Glasgow	E437JSG	Midland Bluebird	E870BGG	West Coast Motors
E157XHS	Henderson Travel	E314MSG	LRT Lothian	E439JSG	Midland Bluebird	E871BGG	West Coast Motors
E162UKR	Orion Autobus	E314YDS	Greater Glasgow	E441JSG	Midland Bluebird	E909KSG	Fife Scottish
E165TWO	McEwan's	E315MSG	LRT Lothian	E442JSG	Midland Bluebird	E910KSG	Fife Scottish
E168UKR	Orion Autobus	E315YDS	Greater Glasgow	E447JSG	Midland Bluebird	E911AFM	Highland
E179BNS	Greater Glasgow	E316MSG	LRT Lothian	E449JSG	Midland Bluebird	E928XYS	Greater Glasgow
E179UWF	Moffat & Williamson	E316YDS	Greater Glasgow	E450JSG	Midland Bluebird	E929XYS	Greater Glasgow
E180BNS	Greater Glasgow	E317MSG	LRT Lothian	E451JSG	Midland Bluebird	E930XYS	Greater Glasgow
E181BNS	Greater Glasgow	E318MSG	LRT Lothian	E453JSG	Midland Bluebird	E931XYS	Greater Glasgow
E182BNS	Greater Glasgow	E319LHG	Argyle Bus Group	E454JSG	Midland Bluebird	E932XYS	Greater Glasgow
E183BNS	Greater Glasgow	E319MSG	LRT Lothian	E455JSG	Midland Bluebird	E933XYS	Greater Glasgow
E184BNS	Greater Glasgow	E320MSG	LRT Lothian	E456JSG	Midland Bluebird	E934XYS	Greater Glasgow
E185BNS	Greater Glasgow	E321MSG	LRT Lothian	E458JSG	Lowland	E935XYS	Greater Glasgow
E186BNS	Greater Glasgow	E322MSG	LRT Lothian	E459JSG	Midland Bluebird	E937XYS	Greater Glasgow
E187BNS	Greater Glasgow	E323MSG	LRT Lothian	E460JSG	Midland Bluebird	E938XYS	Greater Glasgow
E187HSF	Lowland	E323WYS	Clydeside	E461JSG	Midland Bluebird	E939XYS	Greater Glasgow
E187UKG	McEwan's	E324MSG	LRT Lothian	E462JSG	Midland Bluebird	E940XYS	Greater Glasgow
E188BNS	Greater Glasgow	E324OSC	Slaemuir	E463JSG	Midland Bluebird	E941XYS	Greater Glasgow
E188HSF	Lowland	E324WYS	Clydeside	E466JSG	Midland Bluebird	E942XYS	Greater Glasgow
E188UKG	McEwan's	E325MSG	LRT Lothian	E467JSG	Grampian	E943XYS	Greater Glasgow
E189BNS	Greater Glasgow	E325WYS	Clydeside	E468JSG	Midland Bluebird	E944XYS	Greater Glasgow
E189HSF	Lowland	E326MSG	LRT Lothian	E469JSG	Midland Bluebird	E945XYS	Greater Glasgow
E190BNS	Greater Glasgow	E326WYS	Clydeside	E470JSG	Midland Bluebird	E947BHS	Bluebird Buses
E190HSF	Lowland	E327MSG	LRT Lothian	E477RAV	Scottish Travel	E947XYS	Greater Glasgow
E191BNS	Greater Glasgow	E327WYS	Clydeside	E494HHN	Clydeside	E948XYS	Greater Glasgow
E191UKG	McEwan's	E328MSG	LRT Lothian	E499TSJ	AA Buses	E949XYS	Greater Glasgow
E192BNS	Greater Glasgow	E328WYS	Clydeside	E504YSU	Henderson Travel	E950XYS	Greater Glasgow
E192UKG	McEwan's	E329MSG	LRT Lothian	E506YSU	Slaemuir	E951XYS	Greater Glasgow
E193BNS	Greater Glasgow	E329WYS	Clydeside	E507HHN	Clydeside	E952XYS	Greater Glasgow
E193UKG	McEwan's	E330MSG	LRT Lothian	E508HHN	Clydeside	E953XYS	Greater Glasgow
E194BNS	Greater Glasgow	E330WYS	Clydeside	E508YSU	Henderson Travel	E954XYS	Greater Glasgow
E194HFV	Green Line	E331MSG	LRT Lothian	E511YSU	Avondale	E955XYS	Greater Glasgow
E194UKG	McEwan's	E331WYS	Clydeside	E518JHG	Avondale	E956XYS	Greater Glasgow
E195BNS	Greater Glasgow	E332MSG	LRT Lothian	E565MAC	Argyle Bus Group	E974VWY	Slaemuir
E196BNS	Greater Glasgow	E332WYS	Clydeside	E566MAC	Shalder	E987BDS	Riddler
E197BNS	Greater Glasgow	E333MSG	LRT Lothian	E571UKK	Stonehouse	E995WNS	Greater Glasgow
E199BNS	Greater Glasgow	E334MSG	LRT Lothian	E591UHS	Paterson's	E996WNS	Greater Glasgow
E200BNS	Greater Glasgow	E334WYS	Clydeside	E596JSP	Moffat & Williamson	EAG980D	Paterson's
E201BNS	Greater Glasgow	E335MSG	LRT Lothian	E609YPS	Shalder	EAP983V	Bluebird Buses
E202BNS	Greater Glasgow	E335WYS	Clydeside	E614FRN	Puma Coaches	EAP996V	Bluebird Buses
E203BNS	Greater Glasgow	E336WYS	Clydeside	E621BVK	Dart	EBB588W	Bowman
E204BNS	Greater Glasgow	E337WYS	Clydeside	E622BVK	Dart	ECS56V	Clyde Coast
E205BNS	Greater Glasgow	E338WYS	Clydeside	E624BVK	Wilson's, Carnwath	ECS57V	Marbill
E206BNS	Greater Glasgow	E339WYS	Clydeside	E627BVK	Wilson's, Carnwath	ECS877V	Western Buses
E207BNS	Greater Glasgow	E342WYS	Clydeside	E629BVK	Dart	ECS878V	Western Buses
E208BNS	Greater Glasgow	E343WYS	Clydeside	E630MAC	Shalder	ECS879V	Western Buses
E208JST	Skye-Ways	E344WYS	Clydeside	E635LSF	Henderson Travel	ECS880V	Western Buses
E209BNS	Greater Glasgow	E348WYS	Clydeside	E636BVK	Wilson's, Carnwath	ECS882V	Western Buses
E209JKS	Midland Bluebird	E348WYS	Clydeside	E638BVK	Wilson's, Carnwath	ECS883V	Marbill
E283OMG	R H Wilson's	E349WYS	Clydeside	E638YUS	Western Buses	ECS885V	Marbill
E300MSG	LRT Lothian	E350WYS	Clydeside	E643DCK	Western Buses	EDO837	Docherty of Irvine
E301MSG	LRT Lothian	E351WYS	Clydeside	E644DCK	Shuttle Buses	EDS50A	Bluebird Buses
E302MSG	LRT Lothian	E353WYS	Clydeside	E645KYW	Western Buses	EGA609T	Stokes
E303MSG	LRT Lothian	E354WYS	Clydeside	E646DCK	Western Buses	EGB53T	Wilson's, Carnwath
E304MSG	LRT Lothian	E355WYS	Clydeside	E647DCK	Green Line	EGB62T	Oban & District
E305MSG	LRT Lothian	E364YGB	Bluebird Buses	E648CHS	Hutchison	EGB63T	Galson Motors

Reg	Operator	Reg	Operator	Reg	Operator	Reg	Operator
EGB67T	Galson Motors	F61RFS	Puma Coaches	F344MGB	Greater Glasgow	F771VCW	Meffan
EGB70T	Strathtay	F63RFS	Western Buses	F345MGB	Greater Glasgow	F772JYS	Hutchison
EGB73T	Strathtay	F64RFS	Western Buses	F346MGB	Greater Glasgow	F773JYS	Hutchison
EGB74T	Galson Motors	F65RFS	Western Buses	F346WSC	LRT Lothian	F774JYS	Hutchison
EGB76T	Galson Motors	F66RFS	Puma Coaches	F347MGB	Greater Glasgow	F775JYS	Hutchison
ELG516K	Bruce Coaches	F67RFS	Oban & District	F347WSC	LRT Lothian	F776JYS	Hutchison
EMS362V	Midland Bluebird	F68RFS	Puma Coaches	F348WSC	LRT Lothian	F782UJS	Skye-Ways
EMS363V	Midland Bluebird	F69RFS	Oban & District	F349WSC	LRT Lothian	F790LSU	Greater Glasgow
EMS366V	Midland Bluebird	F77HAU	Bluebird Buses	F350WSC	LRT Lothian	F790PSN	Oban & District
ESE353T	Maynes	F85XCS	AA Buses	F351WSC	LRT Lothian	F790UJS	Spa Motors
ESF571W	Lowland	F88GGC	Shuttle Buses	F352WSC	LRT Lothian	F791LSU	Greater Glasgow
ESJ526V	Paterson's	F89JYS	Greater Glasgow	F353WSC	LRT Lothian	F791UJS	Spa Motors
ESJ527V	Paterson's	F90JYS	Greater Glasgow	F354WSC	LRT Lothian	F792LSU	Greater Glasgow
ESK834	Munro's	F91JYS	Greater Glasgow	F355WSC	LRT Lothian	F793LSU	Greater Glasgow
ESK847	Munro's	F92JYS	Greater Glasgow	F356WSC	LRT Lothian	F794LSU	Greater Glasgow
ESK930	Rapsons	F93JYS	Greater Glasgow	F357WSC	LRT Lothian	F794UVH	Wilson's, Carnwath
ESK932	Rapsons	F94JYS	Greater Glasgow	F358WSC	LRT Lothian	F795LSU	Greater Glasgow
ESK934	Rapsons	F95JYS	Greater Glasgow	F359WSC	LRT Lothian	F828APS	Shalder
ESK955	Grampian	F96JYS	Greater Glasgow	F360WSC	LRT Lothian	F862FWB	Bluebird Buses
ESK956	Grampian	F97JYS	Greater Glasgow	F361WSC	LRT Lothian	F888XOE	Maynes
ESK957	Grampian	F98JYS	Greater Glasgow	F362MUT	Bowman	F906YWY	Bridge
ESK958	Midland Bluebird	F99JYS	Greater Glasgow	F362WSC	LRT Lothian	F920YWY	Bridge
ESK981	Rapsons	F111NPU	Greater Glasgow	F363WSC	LRT Lothian	F938TVC	Shalder
ESK983	Rapsons	F112NPU	Greater Glasgow	F364WSC	LRT Lothian	F951CSK	Highland Country
ESK985	Rapsons	F113NPU	Greater Glasgow	F365TSX	Travel Dundee	F953CUA	Green Line
ESK986	Rapsons	F114NPU	Greater Glasgow	F365WSC	LRT Lothian	FAO429V	Bluebird Buses
ESU4X	Greater Glasgow	F114YVP	Western Buses	F366WSC	LRT Lothian	FAS372X	Highland
ESU5X	Greater Glasgow	F115NPU	Greater Glasgow	F367WSC	LRT Lothian	FAS373X	Highland
ESU6X	Greater Glasgow	F118YVP	Western Buses	F368WSC	LRT Lothian	FAS374X	Highland Country
ESU8X	Greater Glasgow	F121YVP	Western Buses	F369WSC	LRT Lothian	FAS375X	Highland
ESU378X	Greater Glasgow	F125HGD	Scottish Travel	F370WSC	LRT Lothian	FAS376X	Highland Country
ESU435	Western Buses	F128YVP	Western Buses	F371WSC	LRT Lothian	FDC409V	Golden Eagle
ESU815X	Stokes	F131YSB	West Coast Motors	F384FYS	Greater Glasgow	FDC410V	Golden Eagle
ESX257	Lowland	F136KAO	Henderson Travel	F385FYS	Greater Glasgow	FDV810V	Bluebird Buses
ETS117	Travel Dundee	F149XCS	Western Buses	F395DOA	H-A-D Coaches	FDV816V	Bluebird Buses
EUS101X	Greater Glasgow	F164XCS	Bluebird Buses	F424GGB	Bluebird Buses	FDV819V	Bluebird Buses
EUS102X	Greater Glasgow	F169FWY	Bluebird Buses	F425ENB	Rowe's	FDV840V	Bluebird Buses
EUS103X	Greater Glasgow	F177FWY	Bluebird Buses	F439KSH	Munro's	FES831W	Bluebird Buses
EUS104X	Greater Glasgow	F180FWY	Bluebird Buses	F450FDB	Irvines of Law	FFS7X	Lowland
EUS105X	Greater Glasgow	F196XFS	Travel Dundee	F466KDB	H-A-D Coaches	FFS9X	Lowland
EUS106X	Greater Glasgow	F197ASD	Western Buses	F469WFX	Shalder	FFS10X	Lowland
EUS107X	Greater Glasgow	F201RVN	Greater Glasgow	F479FGE	Stokes	FGE423X	Moffat & Williamson
EUS108X	Greater Glasgow	F203RVN	Greater Glasgow	F480FGE	Stokes	FGE426X	Moffat & Williamson
EUS109X	Greater Glasgow	F215AKG	Meffan	F485GGG	Meffan	FGG572T	Riddler
EUS110X	Greater Glasgow	F238EDS	Greater Glasgow	F524WSJ	Western Buses	FGG601X	Greater Glasgow
EUS111X	Greater Glasgow	F253MGB	Stevenson	F532ASB	West Coast Motors	FGG602X	Greater Glasgow
EUS112X	Greater Glasgow	F254OFP	H Crawford	F546TMH	Glen Coaches	FGG603X	Greater Glasgow
EUS113X	Greater Glasgow	F256OFP	Galloways	F550TMH	Glen Coaches	FGG604X	Greater Glasgow
EUS114X	Greater Glasgow	F262WSD	AA Buses	F551TMH	Owens Coaches	FGG605X	Greater Glasgow
EUS115X	Greater Glasgow	F276KVW	Meffan	F553TMH	Glen Coaches	FHS749X	Highland Country
EWE811V	Bluebird Buses	F277WAF	Bluebird Buses	F555TMH	Owens Coaches	FJY912E	Marbill
EWE204V	Fife Scottish	F281GNB	Scottish Travel	F598YSB	West Coast Motors	FNM868Y	Midland Bluebird
EWE205V	Bluebird Buses	F286KGK	Fife Scottish	F608HGO	Midland Bluebird	FNS979S	H-A-D Coaches
EWR164T	Wilson's, Carnwath	F290MGB	Greater Glasgow	F615HGO	Midland Bluebird	FSD687V	AA Buses
EWY74Y	Western Buses	F291PAC	Galson Motors	F633JSO	Grampian	FSF728S	Greater Glasgow
EWY75Y	Western Buses	F294GNB	Spa Motors	F634JSO	Grampian	FSL615W	West Coast Motors
EWY76Y	Western Buses	F301MGB	Greater Glasgow	F656WCK	Wilson's, Carnwath	FSU68T	Greater Glasgow
EYE236V	Western Buses	F302MGB	Greater Glasgow	F678LGG	J J Mcmenemy	FSU69T	Greater Glasgow
EYE246V	Western Buses	F303MGB	Greater Glasgow	F680LGG	Maynes	FSU70T	Greater Glasgow
EYE248V	Western Buses	F310MYJ	Fife Scottish	F687ONR	Paterson's	FSU71T	Greater Glasgow
EYH811V	Wilson's, Carnwath	F311MYJ	Fife Scottish	F706WCS	Greater Glasgow	FSU72T	Greater Glasgow
F34CWY	Bridge	F312MYJ	Fife Scottish	F707WCS	Hutchison	FSU73T	Greater Glasgow
F41XCS	Western Buses	F326WCS	Grampian	F708WCS	Hutchison	FSU74T	Greater Glasgow
F44CTX	Rowe's	F334JHS	Western Buses	F709WCS	Hutchison	FSU75T	Greater Glasgow
F46CWY	Bridge	F335JHS	Western Buses	F716SML	Midland Bluebird	FSU76T	Greater Glasgow
F47LRA	Rowe's	F338VSD	Hutchison	F727ASB	West Coast Motors	FSU77T	Greater Glasgow
F51RFS	Western Buses	F339VSD	Hutchison	F747TRE	McEwan's	FSU78T	Greater Glasgow
F52RFS	Western Buses	F343GUS	Stokes	F748MSC	Strathtay	FSU79T	Greater Glasgow
F53RFS	Western Buses	F343MGB	Greater Glasgow	F760VNH	Clydeside	FSU80T	Greater Glasgow
F54RFS	Western Buses	F344GUS	Stokes	F771JYS	Hutchison	FSU81T	Greater Glasgow

FSU82T	Greater Glasgow	FUJ905V	Shalder	G260TSL	Bluebird Buses	G344CSG	LRT Lothian
FSU83T	Greater Glasgow	FXI8035	Mackies	G260VJD	Stonehouse	G344HSC	Wilson's, Carnwath
FSU84T	Greater Glasgow	G32OHS	Argyle Bus Group	G261TSL	Bluebird Buses	G345CSG	LRT Lothian
FSU85T	Greater Glasgow	G58RGG	Clydeside	G261UAS	Rapsons	G362FOP	AA Buses
FSU86T	Greater Glasgow	G67DFS	LRT Lothian	G262TSL	Bluebird Buses	G384OGD	Greater Glasgow
FSU87T	Greater Glasgow	G68DFS	LRT Lothian	G262UAS	Rapsons	G385OGD	Greater Glasgow
FSU88T	Greater Glasgow	G71PYS	Spa Motors	G270GKG	Maynes	G386OGD	Greater Glasgow
FSU89T	Greater Glasgow	G72APO	Western Buses	G270TSL	Bluebird Buses	G387OGD	Greater Glasgow
FSU90T	Greater Glasgow	G82KUB	Irvines of Law	G271GKG	Orion Autobus	G388OGD	Greater Glasgow
FSU91T	Greater Glasgow	G83KUB	Irvines of Law	G271TSL	Bluebird Buses	G389OGD	Greater Glasgow
FSU92T	Greater Glasgow	G85SVM	Travel Dundee	G272TSL	Bluebird Buses	G390OGD	Greater Glasgow
FSU93T	Greater Glasgow	G86KUB	Bluebird Buses	G273HBO	Orion Autobus	G390OGD	Greater Glasgow
FSU94T	Greater Glasgow	G87KUB	Irvines of Law	G273TSL	Bluebird Buses	G391OGD	Greater Glasgow
FSU95T	Greater Glasgow	G91PES	Travel Dundee	G274TSL	Bluebird Buses	G392OGD	Greater Glasgow
FSU96T	Greater Glasgow	G92PES	Travel Dundee	G275TSL	Bluebird Buses	G393OGD	Greater Glasgow
FSU97T	Greater Glasgow	G93PES	Travel Dundee	G276TSL	Bluebird Buses	G394OGD	Greater Glasgow
FSU98T	Greater Glasgow	G94PES	Travel Dundee	G277TSL	Bluebird Buses	G395OGD	Greater Glasgow
FSU99T	Greater Glasgow	G95PES	Travel Dundee	G278TSL	Bluebird Buses	G396OGD	Greater Glasgow
FSU100T	Greater Glasgow	G96PES	Travel Dundee	G279TSL	Bluebird Buses	G397OGD	Greater Glasgow
FSU101T	Greater Glasgow	G97PES	Travel Dundee	G280OGE	Greater Glasgow	G398OGD	Greater Glasgow
FSU102T	Greater Glasgow	G98PES	Travel Dundee	G280TSL	Fife Scottish	G399OGD	Greater Glasgow
FSU103T	Greater Glasgow	G99PES	Travel Dundee	G281OGE	Greater Glasgow	G400OGD	Greater Glasgow
FSU104T	Greater Glasgow	G100PES	Travel Dundee	G281TSL	Fife Scottish	G401OGD	Greater Glasgow
FSU105T	Greater Glasgow	G101PES	Travel Dundee	G282OGE	Greater Glasgow	G402OGD	Greater Glasgow
FSU106T	Greater Glasgow	G102PES	Travel Dundee	G282TSL	Bluebird Buses	G403OGD	Greater Glasgow
FSU107T	Greater Glasgow	G103PES	Travel Dundee	G283OGE	Greater Glasgow	G404OGD	Greater Glasgow
FSU108T	Greater Glasgow	G104PES	Travel Dundee	G283TSL	Bluebird Buses	G405OGD	Greater Glasgow
FSU109T	Greater Glasgow	G105PES	Travel Dundee	G284OGE	Greater Glasgow	G406OGD	Greater Glasgow
FSU110T	Greater Glasgow	G109CSF	Henderson Travel	G284TSL	Bluebird Buses	G407OGD	Greater Glasgow
FSU111T	Greater Glasgow	G111OGA	R H Wilson's	G285OGE	Greater Glasgow	G408OGD	Greater Glasgow
FSU112T	Greater Glasgow	G133AHP	Argyle Bus Group	G285TSL	Bluebird Buses	G409OGD	Greater Glasgow
FSU113T	Greater Glasgow	G144LRM	Green Line	G286OGE	Greater Glasgow	G410OGD	Greater Glasgow
FSU114T	Greater Glasgow	G145LRM	Green Line	G286TSL	Bluebird Buses	G411OGD	Greater Glasgow
FSU115T	Greater Glasgow	G180ORJ	Green Line	G287OGE	Greater Glasgow	G412OGD	Greater Glasgow
FSU116T	Greater Glasgow	G188GSG	Shuttle Buses	G287TSL	Bluebird Buses	G413OGD	Greater Glasgow
FSU117T	Greater Glasgow	G192NWY	Clydeside	G288OGE	Greater Glasgow	G414OGD	Greater Glasgow
FSU118T	Greater Glasgow	G192SCH	Shalder	G288TSL	Bluebird Buses	G415OGD	Greater Glasgow
FSU119T	Greater Glasgow	G193NWY	Clydeside	G289TSL	Bluebird Buses	G416OGD	Greater Glasgow
FSU120T	Greater Glasgow	G193PAO	Bluebird Buses	G290OGE	Greater Glasgow	G421MWY	Clydeside
FSU121T	Greater Glasgow	G194NWY	Clydeside	G290TSL	Bluebird Buses	G432UHS	Greater Glasgow
FSU122T	Greater Glasgow	G194PAO	Bluebird Buses	G291KWY	Strathtay	G438NGE	Strathtay
FSU123T	Greater Glasgow	G195NWY	Clydeside	G291OGE	Greater Glasgow	G454TST	Skye-Ways
FSU124T	Greater Glasgow	G195PAO	Bluebird Buses	G291TSL	Bluebird Buses	G456MGG	Hutchison
FSU126T	Greater Glasgow	G196NWY	Clydeside	G292KWY	Strathtay	G461SGB	Western Buses
FSU127T	Greater Glasgow	G196PAO	Bluebird Buses	G292OGE	Greater Glasgow	G470UHS	Royal Mail
FSU308	Midland Bluebird	G197NWY	Clydeside	G292TSL	Bluebird Buses	G521RDS	Greater Glasgow
FSU309	Strathtay	G197PAO	Bluebird Buses	G293MWU	Strathtay	G522RDS	Greater Glasgow
FSU315	Midland Bluebird	G198GNY	R H Wilson's	G293OGE	Greater Glasgow	G523RDS	Greater Glasgow
FSU318	Midland Bluebird	G198PAO	Bluebird Buses	G294OGE	Greater Glasgow	G524RDS	Greater Glasgow
FSU319	Oban & District	G199NWY	Clydeside	G295OGE	Greater Glasgow	G525RDS	Greater Glasgow
FSU331	Shalder	G199PAO	Bluebird Buses	G296OGE	Greater Glasgow	G526RDS	Greater Glasgow
FSU333	Grampian	G200PAO	Bluebird Buses	G297OGE	Greater Glasgow	G527RDS	Greater Glasgow
FSU334	Midland Bluebird	G201PAO	Bluebird Buses	G298OGE	Greater Glasgow	G528RDS	Greater Glasgow
FSU335	Grampian	G202PAO	Bluebird Buses	G299OGE	Greater Glasgow	G529RDS	Greater Glasgow
FSU371	Moffat & Williamson	G203PAO	Bluebird Buses	G300OGE	Greater Glasgow	G530RDS	Greater Glasgow
FSU372	Moffat & Williamson	G251TSL	Western Buses	G301OGE	Greater Glasgow	G531RDS	Greater Glasgow
FSU374	Moffat & Williamson	G251VPK	Highland Country	G302OGE	Greater Glasgow	G532RDS	Greater Glasgow
FSU375	Moffat & Williamson	G252TSL	Western Buses	G303OGE	Greater Glasgow	G533RDS	Greater Glasgow
FSU380	Midland Bluebird	G252VPK	Highland Country	G304OGE	Greater Glasgow	G534RDS	Greater Glasgow
FSU381	Midland Bluebird	G253TSL	Western Buses	G315TKO	Moffat & Williamson	G535RDS	Greater Glasgow
FSU382	Midland Bluebird	G253VPK	Highland Country	G336CSG	LRT Lothian	G536RDS	Greater Glasgow
FSU383	Midland Bluebird	G254TSL	Western Buses	G337CSG	LRT Lothian	G537RDS	Greater Glasgow
FSU393	Moffat & Williamson	G254VPK	Highland Country	G337KKW	Fife Scottish	G538RDS	Greater Glasgow
FSU394	Moffat & Williamson	G255TSL	Western Buses	G338CSG	LRT Lothian	G539RDS	Greater Glasgow
FSU395	Moffat & Williamson	G255VPK	Highland Country	G338KKW	Fife Scottish	G540RDS	Greater Glasgow
FSU718	Shalder	G256TSL	Bluebird Buses	G339CSG	LRT Lothian	G541RDS	Greater Glasgow
FSU737	Western Buses	G257TSL	Bluebird Buses	G340CSG	LRT Lothian	G542RDS	Greater Glasgow
FSU739	Western Buses	G257VJD	Stonehouse	G341CSG	LRT Lothian	G543RDS	Greater Glasgow
FSV598	Moffat & Williamson	G258TSL	Bluebird Buses	G342CSG	LRT Lothian	G544RDS	Greater Glasgow
FSV634	Midland Bluebird	G259TSL	Bluebird Buses	G343CSG	LRT Lothian	G545RDS	Greater Glasgow

Reg	Operator	Reg	Operator	Reg	Operator	Reg	Operator
G574FSD	Western Buses	G878SKE	Argyle Bus Group	GGA752T	Greater Glasgow	GSC651X	LRT Lothian
G601OSH	Midland Bluebird	G881PAO	Royal Mail	GGA753T	Greater Glasgow	GSC652X	LRT Lothian
G685PNS	Greater Glasgow	G889FJW	Strathtay	GGA754T	Greater Glasgow	GSC653X	LRT Lothian
G686PNS	Greater Glasgow	G891FJW	Strathtay	GGE171T	McGill's	GSC654X	LRT Lothian
G687PNS	Greater Glasgow	G892FJW	Strathtay	GGM77W	Rennie's	GSC655X	LRT Lothian
G688PNS	Greater Glasgow	G892WML	Strathtay	GGM78W	Rennie's	GSC656X	LRT Lothian
G689PNS	Greater Glasgow	G893FJW	Strathtay	GGM79W	Rennie's	GSC657X	LRT Lothian
G690PNS	Greater Glasgow	G893WML	Strathtay	GGV47N	McEwan's	GSC658X	LRT Lothian
G691PNS	Greater Glasgow	G894FJW	Strathtay	GHV102N	Western Buses	GSC659X	LRT Lothian
G692PNS	Greater Glasgow	G895FJW	Strathtay	GHV948N	Western Buses	GSC660X	LRT Lothian
G693PNS	Greater Glasgow	G896FJW	Strathtay	GIL1685	Bryans of Denny	GSC661X	LRT Lothian
G694PNS	Greater Glasgow	G897FJW	Strathtay	GIL3271	Wilson's, Carnwath	GSC662X	LRT Lothian
G695PNS	Greater Glasgow	G899FJW	Strathtay	GIL3316	Spa Motors	GSC663X	LRT Lothian
G696PNS	Greater Glasgow	G900FJW	Strathtay	GIL8469	Rennie's	GSC664X	LRT Lothian
G697PNS	Greater Glasgow	G900GWN	Galson Motors	GIW111	Allander Travel	GSC665X	LRT Lothian
G698PNS	Greater Glasgow	G901FJW	Strathtay	GJI625	Marbill	GSC667X	LRT Lothian
G699PNS	Greater Glasgow	G902MNS	Argyle Bus Group	GJI926	Marbill	GSC854T	Lowland
G700PNS	Greater Glasgow	G917CLV	Bridge	GKE442Y	Clydeside	GSC861T	Midland Bluebird
G701PNS	Greater Glasgow	G918CLV	R H Wilson's	GMB654T	AA Buses	GSD271V	Paterson's
G701RNE	Argyle Bus Group	G964SFT	Morrison's	GMS281S	Greater Glasgow	GSD779	AA Buses
G702PNS	Greater Glasgow	G967CLV	Bridge	GMS285S	Western Buses	GSL896N	Wilson's, Carnwath
G703PNS	Greater Glasgow	G976ARV	Western Buses	GMS286S	Highland Country	GSO1V	Bluebird Buses
G704PNS	Greater Glasgow	GBS84N	Shalder	GMS287S	Whitelaw's	GSO77V	Western Buses
G715OSH	Lowland	GBZ7212	Travel Dundee	GMS288S	Greater Glasgow	GSO78V	Highland
G731FSC	Moffat & Williamson	GBZ7213	R H Wilson's	GMS290S	Greater Glasgow	GSO79V	Highland Country
G733PGA	Slaemuir	GBZ7214	R H Wilson's	GMS292S	Western Buses	GSO80V	Midland Bluebird
G737PGA	Shuttle Buses	GCS31V	Clydeside	GMS293S	Greater Glasgow	GSO82V	Western Buses
G754RVJ	Strathtay	GCS32V	Clydeside	GMS298S	Greater Glasgow	GSO83V	Western Buses
G761WAS	Skye-Ways	GCS33V	Western Buses	GMS300S	Highland	GSO84V	Western Buses
G800GSX	LRT Lothian	GCS34V	Clydeside	GMS301S	Moffat & Williamson	GSO85V	Strathtay
G801GSX	LRT Lothian	GCS35V	Clydeside	GMS304S	Greater Glasgow	GSO86V	Strathtay
G802GSX	LRT Lothian	GCS36V	Highland	GMS307S	Greater Glasgow	GSO88V	Strathtay
G803GSX	LRT Lothian	GCS37V	Western Buses	GMS308S	Oban & District	GSO89V	Bluebird Buses
G804GSX	LRT Lothian	GCS38V	Western Buses	GOH355N	Gibson	GSO90V	Bluebird Buses
G805GSX	LRT Lothian	GCS41V	Western Buses	GPC777V	H Crawford	GSO91V	Bluebird Buses
G806GSX	LRT Lothian	GCS42V	Clydeside	GPS714P	Shalder	GSO92V	Bluebird Buses
G807GSX	LRT Lothian	GCS43V	Highland	GPS715P	Shalder	GSO93V	Bluebird Buses
G808GSX	LRT Lothian	GCS45V	Western Buses	GPS730P	Shalder	GSO94V	Bluebird Buses
G809GSX	LRT Lothian	GCS47V	Western Buses	GRS114E	McEwan's	GSO95V	Bluebird Buses
G810GSX	LRT Lothian	GCS48V	Western Buses	GRS343E	Bluebird Buses	GSU338	Midland Bluebird
G811GSX	LRT Lothian	GCS49V	Western Buses	GSC621X	LRT Lothian	GSU339	Midland Bluebird
G811WST	Skye-Ways	GCS50V	Clydeside	GSC622X	LRT Lothian	GSU341	Fife Scottish
G812GSX	LRT Lothian	GCS51V	Western Buses	GSC623X	LRT Lothian	GSU342	Fife Scottish
G813GSX	LRT Lothian	GCS52V	Highland Country	GSC624X	LRT Lothian	GSU343	Fife Scottish
G814GSX	LRT Lothian	GCS53V	Western Buses	GSC625X	LRT Lothian	GSU344	Fife Scottish
G815GSX	LRT Lothian	GCS55V	Clydeside	GSC626X	LRT Lothian	GSU375	Morrison's
G816GSX	LRT Lothian	GCS56V	Clydeside	GSC627X	LRT Lothian	GSU378	Dochert'y Midland
G817GSX	LRT Lothian	GCS57V	Western Buses	GSC628X	LRT Lothian	GSU390	Grampian
G818GSX	LRT Lothian	GCS58V	Western Buses	GSC629X	LRT Lothian	GSU831T	Marbill
G819GSX	LRT Lothian	GCS59V	Clydeside	GSC630X	LRT Lothian	GSU832T	Marbill
G820GSX	LRT Lothian	GCS60V	Western Buses	GSC631X	LRT Lothian	GSU848T	Oban & District
G821GSX	LRT Lothian	GCS61V	Western Buses	GSC632X	LRT Lothian	GSU851T	Gibson
G822GSX	LRT Lothian	GCS62V	Western Buses	GSC633X	LRT Lothian	GSU852T	Gibson
G823GSX	LRT Lothian	GCS63V	Highland	GSC634X	LRT Lothian	GSU861T	Gibson
G824GSX	LRT Lothian	GCS64V	Clydeside	GSC635X	LRT Lothian	GSU862T	Gibson
G825GSX	LRT Lothian	GCS65V	Western Buses	GSC636X	LRT Lothian	GSU866T	Gibson
G825VGA	Western Buses	GCS66V	Clydeside	GSC637X	LRT Lothian	GSX869T	Lowland
G826GSX	LRT Lothian	GCS67V	Clydeside	GSC638X	LRT Lothian	GSX896T	Midland Bluebird
G827GSX	LRT Lothian	GCS68V	Clydeside	GSC639X	LRT Lothian	GSX897T	Midland Bluebird
G828GSX	Midland Bluebird	GCS69V	Western Buses	GSC640X	LRT Lothian	GSX899T	Lowland
G829GSX	LRT Lothian	GDF279V	Meffan	GSC641X	LRT Lothian	GTO303V	Clydeside
G830GSX	LRT Lothian	GDZ3363	Rennie's	GSC642X	LRT Lothian	GTX740W	Rennie's
G831GSX	LRT Lothian	GEU368N	Paterson's	GSC643X	LRT Lothian	GUA380N	Moffat & Williamson
G831RDS	Shuttle Buses	GFM882	McEwan's	GSC644X	LRT Lothian	GVD47	McGill's
G832GSX	LRT Lothian	GFS410N	Steeles	GSC645X	LRT Lothian	GYE252W	Western Buses
G833GSX	LRT Lothian	GFS443N	LRT Lothian	GSC646X	LRT Lothian	GYE254W	Western Buses
G834GSX	LRT Lothian	GFS447N	LRT Lothian	GSC647X	LRT Lothian	GYE273W	Western Buses
G835GSX	LRT Lothian	GFS448N	LRT Lothian	GSC648X	LRT Lothian	GYE281W	Western Buses
G870SKE	Argyle Bus Group	GGA750T	Greater Glasgow	GSC649X	LRT Lothian	GYS77X	Strathtay
G872SKE	Argyle Bus Group	GGA751T	Greater Glasgow	GSC650X	LRT Lothian		

Reg	Operator	Reg	Operator	Reg	Operator	Reg	Operator
H26KSD	Stonehouse	H544DVM	Park's	HNE254V	Bluebird Buses	HSO281V	Grampian
H34USO	Grampian	H649USH	Lowland	HPY421V	Golden Eagle	HSO283V	Grampian
H35USO	Grampian	H657CST	Royal Mail	HRC102C	Morrison's	HSO284V	Grampian
H36USO	Grampian	H658CST	Royal Mail	HRS261V	Midland Bluebird	HSO285V	Grampian
H37USO	Grampian	H667AGD	Shuttle Buses	HRS262V	Grampian	HSO286V	Grampian
H38USO	Grampian	H675AGD	Argyle Bus Group	HRS263V	Lowland	HSO287V	Grampian
H39USO	Grampian	H716LOL	Stokes	HRS265V	Midland Bluebird	HSO289V	Grampian
H71NFS	LRT Lothian	H717LOL	Stokes	HRS266V	Grampian	HSO290V	Grampian
H72NFS	LRT Lothian	H718LOL	Stokes	HRS267V	Grampian	HSR36X	Travel Dundee
H114YSU	Bryans of Denny	H719LOL	Stokes	HRS268V	Grampian	HSR37X	Travel Dundee
H124YGG	Shuttle Buses	H721YYS	Silver Fox	HRS269V	Grampian	HSR38X	Travel Dundee
H161YSR	Meffan	H724LOL	Maynes	HRS271V	Grampian	HSR39X	Travel Dundee
H165EJU	West Coast Motors	H733HWK	McGill's	HRS273V	Grampian	HSR40X	Travel Dundee
H177OSG	LRT Lothian	H810HVM	Highland Country	HRS274V	Grampian	HSR41X	Travel Dundee
H178OSG	LRT Lothian	H838SLS	Midland Bluebird	HRS275V	Grampian	HSR42X	Travel Dundee
H179OSG	LRT Lothian	H844UUA	Greater Glasgow	HRS276V	Grampian	HSR43X	Travel Dundee
H180OSG	LRT Lothian	H881EEA	Spa Motors	HRS277V	Grampian	HSR44X	Travel Dundee
H181OSG	LRT Lothian	H882LOX	Fife Scottish	HRS278V	Grampian	HSR45X	Travel Dundee
H182OSG	LRT Lothian	H883LOX	Fife Scottish	HRS279V	Grampian	HSR46X	Travel Dundee
H183CNS	Argyle Bus Group	H884LSD	Marbill	HRS280V	Grampian	HSR47X	Travel Dundee
H183OSG	LRT Lothian	H885LOX	Fife Scottish	HRS288V	Midland Bluebird	HSR48X	Travel Dundee
H184OSG	LRT Lothian	H897JCS	Henderson Travel	HSB698Y	Western Buses	HSR49X	Travel Dundee
H185CNS	Argyle Bus Group	H901GNC	Clydeside	HSB703Y	Stokes	HSR50X	Travel Dundee
H185OSG	LRT Lothian	H902GNC	Clydeside	HSB874Y	Clydeside	HSR136W	Bluebird Buses
H185WVH	Stonehouse	H912FDU	Royal Mail	HSF76X	Lowland	HSU247	Midland Bluebird
H186OSG	LRT Lothian	H912HRO	Greater Glasgow	HSF77X	Lowland	HSU273	Midland Bluebird
H187OSG	LRT Lothian	H913XGA	Avondale	HSF78X	Lowland	HSU273N	Riddler
H188OSG	LRT Lothian	H914XGA	Avondale	HSF80X	Lowland	HSU301	Midland Bluebird
H193CVU	Grampian	H925PMS	Midland Bluebird	HSF81X	Lowland	HSU955	Grampian
H223MSX	Meffan	H926PMS	Midland Bluebird	HSF82X	Lowland	HUP760T	Moffat & Williamson
H258AAS	Skye-Ways	H946DRJ	Greater Glasgow	HSF83X	Lowland	HWG207W	Bluebird Buses
H290WSE	Travel Dundee	H947DRJ	Greater Glasgow	HSF84X	Lowland	HWG208W	Fife Scottish
H290XNS	Southern Cs	H949DRJ	Park's	HSF85X	Lowland	IIB3728	Harte
H398SYG	Greater Glasgow	H952DRJ	Park's	HSF86X	Lowland	IIB5213	Harte
H410DPS	Shalder	H955DRJ	Greater Glasgow	HSF87X	Lowland	IIB6015	Strathtay
H455WGG	AA Buses	H955LOC	Travel Dundee	HSF88X	Lowland	IIB6819	Harte
H466WGG	AA Buses	H956DRJ	Park's	HSF91X	Lowland	IIB7633	Harte
H471OSC	Lowland	H972RSG	Midland Bluebird	HSF92X	Lowland	IIL3477	Riddler
H472OSC	Lowland	H973RSG	Midland Bluebird	HSF93X	Lowland	IIL3478	Riddler
H473OSC	Midland Bluebird	H974RSG	Midland Bluebird	HSF94X	Lowland	IIL3504	Fife Scottish
H474OSC	Midland Bluebird	H975RSG	Midland Bluebird	HSF95X	Lowland	IIL3506	Fife Scottish
H475OSC	Midland Bluebird	H976RSG	Midland Bluebird	HSK176	Whytes	IIL3507	Western Buses
H476OSC	Lowland	H991YUS	Avondale	HSK177	Whytes	J8SMT	Midland Bluebird
H477OSC	Midland Bluebird	HCO514	Hutchison	HSK641	Park's	J11AFC	Grampian
H478OSC	Midland Bluebird	HCS260N	Docherty of Irvine	HSK642	Park's	J11GRT	Grampian
H479OSC	Midland Bluebird	HCS787N	Galloways	HSK643	Park's	J11SKY	Skye-Ways
H480OSC	Midland Bluebird	HCS818N	Henderson Travel	HSK644	Park's	J17BUS	Hutchison
H481OSC	Midland Bluebird	HDS83V	Clydeside	HSK644	Park's	J18BUS	Hutchison
H482OSC	Midland Bluebird	HDS566H	Western Buses	HSK645	Park's	J32NKJ	H-A-D Coaches
H483OSC	Midland Bluebird	HDV639E	Bluebird Buses	HSK646	Park's	J48XSC	Royal Mail
H484OSC	Midland Bluebird	HFM561D	Bluebird Buses	HSK647	Park's	J75FPS	Shalder
H485OSC	Midland Bluebird	HGA834T	Bowman	HSK648	Park's	J100SOU	Southern Cs
H486OSC	Midland Bluebird	HGD213T	Western Buses	HSK649	Park's	J113XSX	Greater Glasgow
H487OSC	Midland Bluebird	HGD214T	Keenan of Ayr	HSK650	Park's	J120SPF	Travel Dundee
H488OSC	Midland Bluebird	HGD870L	Greater Glasgow	HSK651	Park's	J120XHH	Bluebird Buses
H489OSC	Midland Bluebird	HGD894L	Keenan of Ayr	HSK652	Park's	J121XHH	Bluebird Buses
H490OSC	Midland Bluebird	HGE51T	Stokes	HSK653	Park's	J122XHH	Bluebird Buses
H491OSC	Midland Bluebird	HGM335E	Bluebird Buses	HSK654	Park's	J137FYS	Greater Glasgow
H492OSC	Midland Bluebird	HIL3188	Shuttle Buses	HSK655	Park's	J138FYS	Greater Glasgow
H493OSC	Midland Bluebird	HIL6811	Rennie's	HSK656	Park's	J144CYO	Galson Motors
H494OSC	Midland Bluebird	HIL6812	Rennie's	HSK657	Park's	J153USF	Royal Mail
H495OSC	Midland Bluebird	HIL7589	Gibson	HSK658	Park's	J154USF	Royal Mail
H496OSC	Midland Bluebird	HIL7590	Gibson	HSK659	Park's	J165USF	Royal Mail
H497OSC	Midland Bluebird	HIL8022	Gibson	HSK660	Park's	J166VSF	Royal Mail
H498OSC	Midland Bluebird	HIL8028	Gibson	HSK760	Bluebird Buses	J196YSS	Bluebird Buses
H499OSC	Midland Bluebird	HIL8645	Wilson's, Carnwath	HSK765	Strathtay	J197YSS	Bluebird Buses
H501OSC	Midland Bluebird	HIL8646	Wilson's, Carnwath	HSK766	Strathtay	J198YSS	Bluebird Buses
H502OSC	Midland Bluebird	HJI380	Irvines of Law	HSK791	Strathtay	J199YSS	Bluebird Buses
H503KSJ	Docherty of Irvine	HJI565	Marbill	HSK792	Strathtay	J200BCS	Munro's
H509AGC	Fife Scottish	HNE252V	Bluebird Buses	HSO61N	Grampian	J203VSF	Royal Mail
H512YCX	McEwan's						

Reg	Operator	Reg	Operator	Reg	Operator	Reg	Operator
J215OCW	Travel Dundee	J506WSX	Lowland	J841VSF	Royal Mail	JFS982X	Midland Bluebird
J216XKY	Shuttle Buses	J507FPS	Bluebird Buses	J842TSC	LRT Lothian	JFS983X	Lowland
J217XKY	Shuttle Buses	J507WSX	Lowland	J843TSC	LRT Lothian	JFS984X	Lowland
J218HDS	Clydeside	J508FPS	Bluebird Buses	J844TSC	LRT Lothian	JFS985X	Lowland
J221VSF	Royal Mail	J508WSX	Lowland	J845TSC	LRT Lothian	JFS986X	Lowland
J223HDS	Travel Dundee	J509FPS	Bluebird Buses	J846TSC	LRT Lothian	JFV313S	Wilson's, Carnwath
J225HDS	Wilson's, Carnwath	J509WSX	Lowland	J847TSC	LRT Lothian	JGE29T	Greater Glasgow
J226HDS	Wilson's, Carnwath	J510FPS	Bluebird Buses	J848TSC	LRT Lothian	JIL3391	Spa Motors
J227HDS	Wilson's, Carnwath	J510WSX	Midland Bluebird	J849TSC	LRT Lothian	JIL4386	Silver Fox
J228HDS	Wilson's, Carnwath	J511FPS	Bluebird Buses	J850TSC	LRT Lothian	JIL5280	Silver Fox
J235LLK	Strathtay	J511WSX	Midland Bluebird	J851TSC	LRT Lothian	JIL5281	Irvines of Law
J277OSJ	AA Buses	J512FPS	Bluebird Buses	J852TSC	LRT Lothian	JIL5809	Shalder
J282EST	Royal Mail	J512WSX	Midland Bluebird	J853TSC	LRT Lothian	JIL7640	Highland Country
J301ASH	Lowland	J513FPS	Greater Glasgow	J854TSC	LRT Lothian	JIL8553	Golden Eagle
J301BRM	Western Buses	J514FPS	Greater Glasgow	J855TSC	LRT Lothian	JIL8559	Golden Eagle
J301FSR	Park's	J515FPS	Greater Glasgow	J856TSC	LRT Lothian	JIL8560	Golden Eagle
J302ASH	Lowland	J516FPS	Greater Glasgow	J857TSC	LRT Lothian	JIL8561	Golden Eagle
J302BRM	Western Buses	J517FPS	Greater Glasgow	J858TSC	LRT Lothian	JIL8562	Golden Eagle
J303ASH	Lowland	J518FPS	Greater Glasgow	J859TSC	LRT Lothian	JKW319W	Greater Glasgow
J303BRM	Western Buses	J544FSU	Royal Mail	J860TSC	LRT Lothian	JKW329W	Greater Glasgow
J304ASH	Lowland	J545FSU	Royal Mail	J861TSC	LRT Lothian	JMB398T	Rennie's
J304BRM	Western Buses	J549FSU	Royal Mail	J862TSC	LRT Lothian	JMC281N	Morrison's
J305BRM	Western Buses	J550FSU	Royal Mail	J863TSC	LRT Lothian	JND260V	Bluebird Buses
J305EST	Royal Mail	J590ESL	Royal Mail	J864TSC	LRT Lothian	JOV739P	Paterson's
J306BRM	Western Buses	J601ESL	Royal Mail	J865TSC	LRT Lothian	JOV756P	Silver Fox
J306EST	Royal Mail	J607KGB	Shuttle Buses	J866TSC	LRT Lothian	JOV769P	Paterson's
J307BRM	Western Buses	J609KGB	Shuttle Buses	J867TSC	LRT Lothian	JOV783P	Stevenson
J308BRM	Western Buses	J621FAS	Royal Mail	J868TSC	LRT Lothian	JOV784P	Silver Fox
J309BRM	Western Buses	J622FAS	Royal Mail	J869TSC	LRT Lothian	JRB741N	Gibson
J310BRM	Western Buses	J624FAS	Royal Mail	J870TSC	LRT Lothian	JSA101V	Bluebird Buses
J310XLS	Midland Bluebird	J625FAS	Royal Mail	J871TSC	LRT Lothian	JSA102V	Bluebird Buses
J330EST	Royal Mail	J626FAS	Royal Mail	J882UNA	McEwan's	JSA103V	Bluebird Buses
J381HYS	Royal Mail	J627FAS	Royal Mail	J902WFS	Royal Mail	JSA104V	Bluebird Buses
J382HYS	Royal Mail	J633AAO	Royal Mail	J913HGD	Scottish Travel	JSD595W	AA Buses
J383HYS	Royal Mail	J641FAS	Royal Mail	J916HGD	Argyle Bus Group	JSV362	Wilson's, Carnwath
J400BCS	Munro's	J642FAS	Royal Mail	J917LEM	Western Buses	JSV426	Grampian
J400SOU	Riddler	J643FAS	Royal Mail	J919LEM	Western Buses	JSX579T	LRT Lothian
J408HYS	Royal Mail	J656AAO	Royal Mail	J956LKO	H Crawford	JSX583T	LRT Lothian
J436GDS	Royal Mail	J657AAO	Royal Mail	J961VSG	Royal Mail	JSX589T	LRT Lothian
J437MDB	Moffat & Williamson	J657ASO	Royal Mail	J962VSG	Royal Mail	JSX590T	LRT Lothian
J440UFS	Henderson Travel	J658AAO	Royal Mail	J963VSG	Royal Mail	JSX591T	LRT Lothian
J450NTT	Park's	J659AAO	Royal Mail	J968KGB	Stonehouse	JSX594T	LRT Lothian
J455FSR	Bluebird Buses	J660AAO	Royal Mail	J969VSG	Royal Mail	JSX595T	LRT Lothian
J456FSR	Bluebird Buses	J661AAO	Royal Mail	J970VSG	Royal Mail	JSX596T	LRT Lothian
J460YDT	AA Buses	J716USF	Slaemuir	J971VSG	Royal Mail	JSX597T	LRT Lothian
J470FRS	Royal Mail	J756ASO	Royal Mail	J972VSG	Royal Mail	JSX598T	LRT Lothian
J471ASO	Royal Mail	J774WLS	Midland Bluebird	J973VSG	Royal Mail	JTF971W	Western Buses
J472FSR	Royal Mail	J775WLS	Midland Bluebird	J974VSG	Royal Mail	JVK240P	Greater Glasgow
J473FSR	Royal Mail	J776WLS	Midland Bluebird	J975VSG	Royal Mail	K1GRL	Stonehouse
J474FRS	Royal Mail	J778WLS	Midland Bluebird	J979WFS	Royal Mail	K1GRT	Grampian
J475FRS	Royal Mail	J779WLS	Midland Bluebird	JAK209W	Bluebird Buses	K3GRT	Grampian
J475NJU	Wilson's, Carnwath	J799FTS	Riddler	JAK210W	Bluebird Buses	K4GRT	Grampian
J476FRS	Royal Mail	J801WFS	Fife Scottish	JAK212W	Bluebird Buses	K5SKY	Skye-Ways
J478FSR	Royal Mail	J802WFS	Fife Scottish	JAZ9850	Highland Country	K7SKY	Skye-Ways
J479FSR	Royal Mail	J803WFS	Fife Scottish	JAZ9851	Highland Country	K15BUS	Hutchison
J480FSR	Royal Mail	J804WFS	Fife Scottish	JAZ9852	Highland Country	K16BUS	Hutchison
J481FSR	Royal Mail	J805WFS	Fife Scottish	JAZ9853	Highland Country	K67HSA	Grampian
J482FSR	Royal Mail	J807HSB	West Coast Motors	JAZ9854	Highland Country	K90SOU	Wilson's, Carnwath
J483FSR	Royal Mail	J807WFS	Fife Scottish	JAZ9855	Highland Country	K91RGA	McGill's
J498VMS	Mackies	J831VSF	Royal Mail	JAZ9856	Highland Country	K92RGA	McGill's
J500BCS	Munro's	J832VSF	Royal Mail	JAZ9857	Highland Country	K95RGA	Bridge
J501FPS	Bluebird Buses	J833VSF	Royal Mail	JAZ9858	Highland Country	K96RGA	Bridge
J502FPS	Bluebird Buses	J834VSF	Royal Mail	JAZ9859	Highland Country	K96UFP	Wilson's, Carnwath
J503FPS	Bluebird Buses	J836TSC	LRT Lothian	JD3164	Docherty Midland	K101XHG	Bluebird Buses
J503WSX	Lowland	J837TSC	LRT Lothian	JDE189X	McEwan's	K102XHG	Bluebird Buses
J504FPS	Bluebird Buses	J838TSC	LRT Lothian	JFS166X	Lowland	K103XHG	Bluebird Buses
J504WSX	Lowland	J839TSC	LRT Lothian	JFS928T	Lowland	K104XHG	Bluebird Buses
J505FPS	Bluebird Buses	J840TSC	LRT Lothian	JFS929T	Lowland	K105XHG	Bluebird Buses
J505WSX	Lowland	J841TSC	LRT Lothian	JFS980X	Midland Bluebird	K106XHG	Bluebird Buses
J506FPS	Bluebird Buses			JFS981X	Midland Bluebird	K107XHG	Bluebird Buses

Reg	Operator	Reg	Operator	Reg	Operator	Reg	Operator
K108XHG	Bluebird Buses	K413MSL	Travel Dundee	K718ASC	Fife Scottish	KGG118Y	Greater Glasgow
K109XHG	Bluebird Buses	K422BSG	Royal Mail	K719ASC	Fife Scottish	KGG119Y	Greater Glasgow
K110XHG	Bluebird Buses	K423BSG	Royal Mail	K720ASC	Fife Scottish	KGG120Y	Greater Glasgow
K112CSG	LRT Lothian	K424BSG	Royal Mail	K721ASC	Fife Scottish	KGG121Y	Greater Glasgow
K113CSG	LRT Lothian	K426BSG	Royal Mail	K722ASC	Fife Scottish	KGG122Y	Greater Glasgow
K114CSG	LRT Lothian	K444GSM	Bruce Coaches	K723ASC	Fife Scottish	KGG123Y	Greater Glasgow
K115CSG	LRT Lothian	K473EDT	Midland Bluebird	K724ASC	Fife Scottish	KGG124Y	Greater Glasgow
K116CSG	LRT Lothian	K477SSM	McEwan's	K725ASC	Fife Scottish	KGG126Y	Greater Glasgow
K117CSG	LRT Lothian	K478SSM	McEwan's	K731AOG	Argyle Bus Group	KGG127Y	Greater Glasgow
K118CSG	LRT Lothian	K485FFS	Fife Scottish	K732AOG	Argyle Bus Group	KGG128Y	Greater Glasgow
K119CSG	LRT Lothian	K486FFS	Fife Scottish	K740LHP	Whitelaw's	KGG129Y	Greater Glasgow
K120CSG	LRT Lothian	K487FFS	Fife Scottish	K770AFS	Shuttle Buses	KGG130Y	Greater Glasgow
K121CSG	LRT Lothian	K488FFS	Fife Scottish	K776AFS	Rowe's	KGG131Y	Greater Glasgow
K122CSG	LRT Lothian	K489FFS	Fife Scottish	K813EET	Silver Fox	KGG132Y	Greater Glasgow
K123CSG	LRT Lothian	K490FFS	Fife Scottish	K822HUM	Gibson	KGG133Y	Greater Glasgow
K175YVC	Lowland	K491FFS	Fife Scottish	K823HUM	Gibson	KGG134Y	Greater Glasgow
K200SOU	Southern Cs	K492FFS	Fife Scottish	K825HUM	Moffat & Williamson	KGG135Y	Greater Glasgow
K202OHS	Scottish Travel	K493FFS	Fife Scottish	K828HUM	Moffat & Williamson	KGG136Y	Greater Glasgow
K203OHS	Scottish Travel	K494FFS	Fife Scottish	K831HUM	Moffat & Williamson	KGG137Y	Greater Glasgow
K204OHS	Scottish Travel	K500WCM	West Coast Motors	K872CSF	LRT Lothian	KGG138Y	Greater Glasgow
K208OHS	Western Buses	K504NST	Highland Country	K873CSF	LRT Lothian	KGG139Y	Greater Glasgow
K209OHS	Western Buses	K508ESS	Bluebird Buses	K874CSF	LRT Lothian	KGG140Y	Greater Glasgow
K222GSM	Riddler	K509ESS	Bluebird Buses	K875CSF	LRT Lothian	KGG141Y	Greater Glasgow
K241BSG	Royal Mail	K510ESS	Bluebird Buses	K876CSF	LRT Lothian	KGG142Y	Greater Glasgow
K242BSG	Royal Mail	K511ESS	Bluebird Buses	K877CSF	LRT Lothian	KGG143Y	Greater Glasgow
K247HKV	Travel Dundee	K513BSX	Midland Bluebird	K877DSG	McEwan's	KGG145Y	Greater Glasgow
K253BSG	Royal Mail	K514BSX	Lowland	K878CSF	LRT Lothian	KGG146Y	Greater Glasgow
K256BSG	Royal Mail	K515BSX	Midland Bluebird	K879CSF	LRT Lothian	KGG147Y	Greater Glasgow
K257BSG	Royal Mail	K515ESS	Bluebird Buses	K880CSF	LRT Lothian	KGG149Y	Greater Glasgow
K258BSG	Royal Mail	K516BSX	Midland Bluebird	K881CSF	LRT Lothian	KGG150Y	Greater Glasgow
K259BSG	Royal Mail	K517BSX	Midland Bluebird	K882CSF	LRT Lothian	KGG151Y	Greater Glasgow
K261BSG	Royal Mail	K518ESS	Bluebird Buses	K883CSF	LRT Lothian	KGG152Y	Greater Glasgow
K262BSG	Royal Mail	K537RGX	Midland Bluebird	K884CSF	LRT Lothian	KGG153Y	Greater Glasgow
K263BSG	Royal Mail	K561GSA	Bluebird Buses	K885CSF	LRT Lothian	KGG154Y	Greater Glasgow
K265DSG	Royal Mail	K562GSA	Bluebird Buses	K886CSF	LRT Lothian	KGG155Y	Greater Glasgow
K265SSD	Silver Fox	K563GSA	Bluebird Buses	K886UDB	Slaemuir	KGG156Y	Greater Glasgow
K275DSG	Royal Mail	K564GSA	Bluebird Buses	K887CSF	LRT Lothian	KGG157Y	Greater Glasgow
K279BSG	Royal Mail	K565GSA	Bluebird Buses	K889CSF	LRT Lothian	KGG158Y	Greater Glasgow
K300SOU	Southern Cs	K566GSA	Bluebird Buses	K890CSF	LRT Lothian	KGG159Y	Greater Glasgow
K301MSN	Strathtay	K567GSA	Bluebird Buses	K891CSF	LRT Lothian	KGG160Y	Greater Glasgow
K302MSN	Strathtay	K568GSA	Bluebird Buses	K892CSF	LRT Lothian	KGG161Y	Greater Glasgow
K303MSN	Strathtay	K569GSA	Bluebird Buses	K893CSF	LRT Lothian	KGG162Y	Greater Glasgow
K304MSN	Strathtay	K570GSA	Bluebird Buses	K894CSF	LRT Lothian	KGG163Y	Greater Glasgow
K305MSN	Strathtay	K571LTS	Bluebird Buses	K924RGE	Midland Bluebird	KGG164Y	Greater Glasgow
K331BSG	Royal Mail	K572LTS	Bluebird Buses	K931BSG	Royal Mail	KGG165Y	Greater Glasgow
K332MOS	Allander Travel	K573LTS	Bluebird Buses	K945SGG	McGill's	KGG166Y	Greater Glasgow
K350SDS	Greater Glasgow	K574DFS	Western Buses	K946SGG	McGill's	KGG167Y	Greater Glasgow
K390BSG	Royal Mail	K574LTS	Bluebird Buses	K947SGG	McGill's	KGG168Y	Greater Glasgow
K391NGG	R H Wilson's	K575LTS	Bluebird Buses	K950HSA	Grampian	KGG160Y	Greater Glasgow
K392BSG	Royal Mail	K576LTS	Bluebird Buses	KBV139S	H Crawford	KGG170Y	Greater Glasgow
K400WCM	West Coast Motors	K577LTS	Bluebird Buses	KBZ3627	Lowland	KGG171Y	Greater Glasgow
K401HRS	Grampian	K578LTS	Bluebird Buses	KBZ3628	Lowland	KGG184N	West Coast Motors
K401JSR	Strathtay	K600SOU	Southern Cs	KBZ3629	Lowland	KHG193T	Rowe's
K402HRS	Grampian	K601ESH	Fife Scottish	KBZ5748	Meffan	KKG109W	McGill's
K402JSR	Strathtay	K602ESH	Fife Scottish	KCB758	Greater Glasgow	KKV698V	Skye-Ways
K403HRS	Grampian	K603ESH	Fife Scottish	KEX532	Lowland	KKY220W	Fife Scottish
K404HRS	Grampian	K604ESH	Fife Scottish	KGG101Y	Greater Glasgow	KKY222W	Bluebird Buses
K405HRS	Grampian	K605ESH	Fife Scottish	KGG102Y	Greater Glasgow	KMA399T	Western Buses
K406HRS	Grampian	K614OJR	H Crawford	KGG103Y	Greater Glasgow	KPS701T	Shalder
K407HRS	Grampian	K620DMS	Mackies	KGG104Y	Greater Glasgow	KRM430W	Bluebird Buses
K408BSG	Royal Mail	K651DLS	Midland Bluebird	KGG105Y	Greater Glasgow	KRS531V	Bluebird Buses
K408HRS	Grampian	K652DLS	Midland Bluebird	KGG106Y	Greater Glasgow	KRS532V	Bluebird Buses
K408MSL	Travel Dundee	K653DLS	Midland Bluebird	KGG107Y	Greater Glasgow	KRS536V	McGill's
K409BSG	Royal Mail	K654DLS	Midland Bluebird	KGG108Y	Greater Glasgow	KRS540V	Western Buses
K409BSG	Royal Mail	K655DLS	Midland Bluebird	KGG109Y	Greater Glasgow	KRS542V	Western Buses
K409HRS	Grampian	K656DLS	Midland Bluebird	KGG110Y	Greater Glasgow	KRS682V	Bluebird Buses
K409MSL	Travel Dundee	K657DLS	Midland Bluebird	KGG111Y	Greater Glasgow	KSA179P	Rennie's
K410MSL	Travel Dundee	K657NGB	Henderson Travel	KGG112Y	Greater Glasgow	KSD62W	Western Buses
K411MSL	Travel Dundee	K658DLS	Midland Bluebird	KGG115Y	Greater Glasgow	KSD90W	Rowe's
K412MSL	Travel Dundee	K659DLS	Midland Bluebird	KGG116Y	Greater Glasgow	KSD93W	Rowe's

The Scottish Bus Handbook

Western Buses fleet includes a group of vehicles known as Special Event Vehicles and these are mostly vintage examples reflecting the company's past. Purchased from David MacBrayne in 1970, YYS174 is a Bedford C5Z1 and is to be found operating on the attractive Isle of Arran in the traditional MacBrayne livery. *Tony Wilson*

KSD99W	Rennie's	KSU394	Lowland	L53LSG	Clydeside	L109OSX	Midland Bluebird
KSD100W	Rennie's	KSU834	Midland Bluebird	L53UNS	Whitelaw's	L110OSX	Midland Bluebird
KSD103W	Rowe's	KSX102X	LRT Lothian	L54LSG	Clydeside	L139XDS	Avondale
KSD110W	Rowe's	KSX103X	LRT Lothian	L54UNS	Whitelaw's	L140MAK	Midland Bluebird
KSD112W	Rowe's	KSX104X	LRT Lothian	L56UNS	Whitelaw's	L140XDS	Avondale
KSK930	Hutchison	KSX105X	LRT Lothian	L57UNS	Whitelaw's	L142XDS	Oban & District
KSK931	Hutchison	KWA213W	Bluebird Buses	L58UNS	Whitelaw's	L143XDS	H-A-D Coaches
KSK932	Hutchison	KWA215W	Bluebird Buses	L59UNS	Whitelaw's	L144XDS	H-A-D Coaches
KSK933	Hutchison	KWA216W	Bluebird Buses	L60HMS	Midland Bluebird	L145XDS	H-A-D Coaches
KSK934	Hutchison	KWA217W	Fife Scottish	L70LRT	LRT Lothian	L146XDS	H-A-D Coaches
KSK948	Park's	KWA219W	Bluebird Buses	L73NSX	LRT Lothian	L155UNS	Greater Glasgow
KSK949	Park's	KYN285X	Clydeside	L80SOU	Southern Cs	L156UNS	Greater Glasgow
KSK950	Park's	KYV372X	Clydeside	L81CNY	Greater Glasgow	L157UNS	Greater Glasgow
KSK951	Park's	KYV408X	Clydeside	L82CNY	Greater Glasgow	L158UNS	Greater Glasgow
KSK952	Park's	KYV410X	Western Buses	L83XDS	Bruce Coaches	L159UNS	Greater Glasgow
KSK953	Park's	KYV455X	Fife Scottish	L85CNY	Greater Glasgow	L160UNS	Greater Glasgow
KSK954	Park's	L2SKY	Skye-Ways	L85NSF	Woods	L161UNS	Greater Glasgow
KSK976	Park's	L3LOW	Travel Dundee	L86CNY	Greater Glasgow	L162UNS	Greater Glasgow
KSK977	Park's	L6DMC	Docher'y Midland	L86NSF	Woods	L163UNS	Greater Glasgow
KSK978	Park's	L10BUS	Hutchison	L87NSF	Woods	L164UNS	Greater Glasgow
KSK979	Park's	L11BUS	Hutchison	L91NSF	Henderson Travel	L165UNS	Greater Glasgow
KSK980	Park's	L23WGA	Hutchison	L92NSF	Henderson Travel	L166UNS	Greater Glasgow
KSK981	Park's	L25LSG	Henderson Travel	L95GAX	Glen Coaches	L167UNS	Greater Glasgow
KSK982	Park's	L25LSX	Clydeside	L100JLB	Bluebird Buses	L168UNS	Greater Glasgow
KSK983	Park's	L26JSA	Bluebird Buses	L100WCM	West Coast Motors	L169UNS	Greater Glasgow
KSK984	Park's	L27JSA	Bluebird Buses	L101JSA	Bluebird Buses	L170UNS	Greater Glasgow
KSK985	Park's	L28JSA	Bluebird Buses	L101WYS	Greater Glasgow	L171UNS	Greater Glasgow
KSK986	Park's	L41CAY	Wilson's, Carnwath	L102JSA	Bluebird Buses	L172UNS	Greater Glasgow
KSU388	Lowland	L42CAY	Wilson's, Carnwath	L102WYS	Greater Glasgow	L173UNS	Greater Glasgow
KSU389	Lowland	L43CAY	Wilson's, Carnwath	L103WYS	Greater Glasgow	L174UNS	Greater Glasgow
KSU390	Lowland	L51LSG	Clydeside	L104WYS	Greater Glasgow	L175UNS	Greater Glasgow
KSU391	Lowland	L51UNS	Whitelaw's	L105XSU	Greater Glasgow	L176UNS	Greater Glasgow
KSU392	Lowland	L52LSG	Clydeside	L106XSU	Greater Glasgow	L177UNS	Greater Glasgow
KSU393	Lowland	L52UNS	Whitelaw's	L106YGD	Hutchison	L178UNS	Greater Glasgow

Reg	Operator	Reg	Operator	Reg	Operator	Reg	Operator
L179UNS	Greater Glasgow	L308VSU	Greater Glasgow	L563JLS	Midland Bluebird	L850WDS	Marbill
L180UNS	Greater Glasgow	L309PSC	Fife Scottish	L564JLS	Midland Bluebird	L851WDS	Marbill
L181UNS	Greater Glasgow	L309VSU	Greater Glasgow	L565JLS	Midland Bluebird	L852WDS	Marbill
L182UNS	Greater Glasgow	L310PSC	Fife Scottish	L566JLS	Midland Bluebird	L854WDS	H-A-D Coaches
L183UNS	Greater Glasgow	L310VSU	Greater Glasgow	L577NSB	Western Buses	L857WDS	Marbill
L184UNS	Greater Glasgow	L314KSS	Whytes	L578HSG	Fife Scottish	L860LFS	Clydeside
L185UNS	Greater Glasgow	L315JSA	Bluebird Buses	L578NSB	Western Buses	L861LFS	Clydeside
L186UNS	Greater Glasgow	L316JSA	Bluebird Buses	L579HSG	Fife Scottish	L862LFS	Clydeside
L187UNS	Greater Glasgow	L380PAS	Highland Country	L579JSA	Bluebird Buses	L863LFS	Clydeside
L188UNS	Greater Glasgow	L400WCM	West Coast Motors	L580HSG	Fife Scottish	L864LFS	Clydeside
L189UNS	Greater Glasgow	L423MVV	Fife Scottish	L580JSA	Bluebird Buses	L865LFS	Clydeside
L190UNS	Greater Glasgow	L424LLS	Mackies	L581HSG	Fife Scottish	L866LFS	Clydeside
L191UNS	Greater Glasgow	L424MVV	Fife Scottish	L581JSA	Bluebird Buses	L867LFS	Clydeside
L192UNS	Greater Glasgow	L425MVV	Fife Scottish	L582HSG	Fife Scottish	L868LFS	Clydeside
L193UNS	Greater Glasgow	L426MVV	Fife Scottish	L582JSA	Western Buses	L869LFS	Clydeside
L194UNS	Greater Glasgow	L427MVV	Fife Scottish	L583HSG	Fife Scottish	L870LFS	Clydeside
L195UNS	Greater Glasgow	L428MVV	Fife Scottish	L583JSA	Western Buses	L882LFS	Western Buses
L196MHL	Munro's	L447OSC	Rennie's	L584HSG	Fife Scottish	L883LFS	Western Buses
L196UNS	Greater Glasgow	L456JCK	LRT Lothian	L584JSA	Western Buses	L897RUF	H Crawford
L197UNS	Greater Glasgow	L500SOU	Southern Cs	L585HSG	Fife Scottish	L906LFS	H Crawford
L198UNS	Greater Glasgow	L500WCM	West Coast Motors	L585JSA	Bluebird Buses	L907JSF	Royal Mail
L199UNS	Greater Glasgow	L501KSA	Grampian	L586HSG	Fife Scottish	L908JSF	Royal Mail
L200WCM	West Coast Motors	L502KSA	Grampian	L586JSA	Bluebird Buses	L916UGA	Western Buses
L201KFS	Midland Bluebird	L502YGD	Oban & District	L587HSG	Fife Scottish	L917UGA	Shuttle Buses
L201UNS	Greater Glasgow	L503KSA	Grampian	L587JSA	Bluebird Buses	L922UGA	Avondale
L202KFS	Midland Bluebird	L504KSA	Grampian	L588HSG	Fife Scottish	L932UGA	R H Wilson's
L202UNS	Greater Glasgow	L505KSA	Grampian	L588JSA	Bluebird Buses	L937WFW	West Coast Motors
L203KSX	Midland Bluebird	L506KSA	Grampian	L588JSG	Clydeside	L950MSC	LRT Lothian
L204KSX	Midland Bluebird	L507KSA	Grampian	L589HSG	Fife Scottish	L951MSC	LRT Lothian
L205KSX	Midland Bluebird	L508KSA	Grampian	L590HSG	Fife Scottish	L952MSC	LRT Lothian
L206KSX	Midland Bluebird	L509KSA	Grampian	L592RST	Rapsons	L953MSC	LRT Lothian
L207KSX	Midland Bluebird	L510KSA	Grampian	L628AYS	Glen Coaches	L954MSC	LRT Lothian
L208KSX	Midland Bluebird	L511KSA	Grampian	L630AYS	Riddler	L955MSC	LRT Lothian
L208PSB	Western Buses	L512KSA	Grampian	L637DNA	Slaemuir	L956MSC	LRT Lothian
L209KSX	Midland Bluebird	L513KSA	Grampian	L651HKS	Fife Scottish	L957MSC	LRT Lothian
L210KSX	Midland Bluebird	L514KSA	Grampian	L652HKS	Fife Scottish	L958MSC	LRT Lothian
L210RST	Maynes	L518KSX	Lowland	L653HKS	Fife Scottish	L958NRS	Whytes
L211KSX	Midland Bluebird	L519KSX	Lowland	L654HKS	Fife Scottish	L959MSC	LRT Lothian
L212KSX	Midland Bluebird	L520KSX	Lowland	L655HKS	Fife Scottish	L959NRS	Whytes
L213KSX	Midland Bluebird	L521KSX	Lowland	L656HKS	Fife Scottish	L960KMS	Bryans of Denny
L232LSC	Royal Mail	L522KSX	Lowland	L657HKS	Fife Scottish	L960MSC	LRT Lothian
L262VSU	Western Buses	L523KSX	Midland Bluebird	L658HKS	Fife Scottish	L961KMS	Bryans of Denny
L263AAG	Oban & District	L524KSX	Midland Bluebird	L659HKS	Fife Scottish	L961MSC	LRT Lothian
L263VSU	Argyle Bus Group	L525KSX	Midland Bluebird	L670PWT	Hutchison	L962MSC	LRT Lothian
L264AAG	Oban & District	L526KSX	Midland Bluebird	L676VSM	McEwan's	L963MSC	LRT Lothian
L266VUS	H Crawford	L527KSX	Midland Bluebird	L677VSM	McEwan's	L964MSC	LRT Lothian
L267CCK	Fife Scottish	L531XUT	Bruce Coaches	L684UYS	Hutchison	L965MSC	LRT Lothian
L268CCK	Fife Scottish	L538XUT	Grampian	L685UYS	Hutchison	L966MSC	LRT Lothian
L269CCK	Fife Scottish	L550JFS	Bluebird Buses	L700WCM	West Coast Motors	L966VGE	R H Wilson's
L292USU	Stokes	L551HMS	Midland Bluebird	L703AGA	Davidson Buses	L967MSC	LRT Lothian
L293USU	Stokes	L551USU	Greater Glasgow	L704AGA	Rowe's	L968MSC	LRT Lothian
L300WCM	West Coast Motors	L552GMS	Midland Bluebird	L705AGA	McGill's	L969MSC	LRT Lothian
L301JSA	Bluebird Buses	L552HMS	Midland Bluebird	L720JKS	Lowland	L970MSC	LRT Lothian
L301PSC	Fife Scottish	L552USU	Greater Glasgow	L721JKS	Lowland	L970VGE	Argyle Bus Group
L301VSU	Greater Glasgow	L553GMS	Midland Bluebird	L722JKS	Lowland	L971KDT	Wilson's, Carnwath
L302JSA	Bluebird Buses	L553HMS	Midland Bluebird	L723JKS	Lowland	L971MSC	LRT Lothian
L302PSC	Fife Scottish	L553USU	Greater Glasgow	L724JKS	Lowland	L972KDT	Wilson's, Carnwath
L302VSU	Greater Glasgow	L554GMS	Midland Bluebird	L725JKS	Lowland	L972MSC	LRT Lothian
L303JSA	Bluebird Buses	L554HMS	Midland Bluebird	L726JKS	Lowland	L973MSC	LRT Lothian
L303PSC	Fife Scottish	L554USU	Greater Glasgow	L727JKS	Lowland	L974MSC	LRT Lothian
L303VSU	Greater Glasgow	L555GMS	Midland Bluebird	L827YGA	Greater Glasgow	L975MSC	LRT Lothian
L304PSC	Fife Scottish	L555HMS	Midland Bluebird	L828YGA	Greater Glasgow	L976MSC	LRT Lothian
L304VSU	Greater Glasgow	L556GMS	Midland Bluebird	L829YGA	Greater Glasgow	L977MSC	LRT Lothian
L305PSC	Fife Scottish	L556HMS	Midland Bluebird	L830YGA	Greater Glasgow	L978MSC	LRT Lothian
L305VSU	Greater Glasgow	L557GMS	Midland Bluebird	L831YGA	Greater Glasgow	L979MSC	LRT Lothian
L306PSC	Fife Scottish	L557JLS	Midland Bluebird	L832YGA	Greater Glasgow	L980MSC	LRT Lothian
L306VSU	Greater Glasgow	L558JLS	Midland Bluebird	L833YDS	Henderson Travel	L981MSC	LRT Lothian
L307PSC	Fife Scottish	L559JLS	Midland Bluebird	L833YGA	Greater Glasgow	L982MSC	LRT Lothian
L307VSU	Greater Glasgow	L561JLS	Midland Bluebird	L836MWT	Bryans of Denny	L983MSC	LRT Lothian
L308PSC	Fife Scottish	L562JLS	Midland Bluebird	L845RST	Rapsons	L984AJU	Spa Motors

The Scottish Bus Handbook

Reg	Operator	Reg	Operator	Reg	Operator	Reg	Operator
LAT662	Lowland	LSK475	Grampian	LSU396V	Greater Glasgow	M117RMS	Clydeside
LAZ4475	Clydeside	LSK476	Grampian	LSU397V	Greater Glasgow	M117XSR	Travel Dundee
LAZ5847	Clydeside	LSK478	Rennie's	LSU398V	Greater Glasgow	M118RMS	Clydeside
LAZ6739	Clydeside	LSK479	Rennie's	LSU399V	Greater Glasgow	M118XSR	Travel Dundee
LBZ6829	Galson Motors	LSK481	Park's	LSU400V	Greater Glasgow	M119RMS	Clydeside
LCS317W	Paterson's	LSK483	Park's	LSU401V	Greater Glasgow	M119XSR	Travel Dundee
LCS624W	Paterson's	LSK495	Park's	LSU402V	Greater Glasgow	M120RMS	Clydeside
LDS201A	Bluebird Buses	LSK496	Park's	LSU403V	Greater Glasgow	M121RMS	Clydeside
LDS210A	Bluebird Buses	LSK497	Park's	LSU404V	Greater Glasgow	M125UWY	Wilson's, Carnwath
LDS380V	Wilson's, Carnwath	LSK498	Park's	LSU405V	Greater Glasgow	M126UWY	Wilson's, Carnwath
LEO736Y	Fife Scottish	LSK499	Park's	LSU406V	Greater Glasgow	M133FGD	H Crawford
LFJ848W	McEwan's	LSK500	Park's	LSU407V	Greater Glasgow	M134SKY	Skye-Ways
LFJ849W	McEwan's	LSK501	Park's	LSU917	Grampian	M135SKY	Skye-Ways
LFJ850W	McEwan's	LSK502	Park's	LSX16P	Fife Scottish	M151FGB	Western Buses
LGA14P	Paterson's	LSK503	Park's	LSX17P	Fife Scottish	M151PKS	Lowland
LGE724Y	Greater Glasgow	LSK504	Park's	LSX32P	Fife Scottish	M152PKS	Lowland
LHL247P	McEwan's	LSK505	Park's	LUA268V	Rowe's	M160CCD	Western Buses
LHS741V	Marbill	LSK506	Park's	LUA280V	Highland Country	M161CCD	Western Buses
LHS747V	Marbill	LSK507	Park's	LUS431Y	Greater Glasgow	M162CCD	Western Buses
LHS748V	Allander Travel	LSK508	Park's	LUS432Y	Greater Glasgow	M163CCD	Western Buses
LHS751V	Marbill	LSK509	Park's	LUS433Y	Greater Glasgow	M164CCD	Western Buses
LIB5441	Gibson	LSK510	Park's	LUS434Y	Greater Glasgow	M165CCD	Western Buses
LIW1926	H Crawford	LSK511	Park's	LUS435Y	Greater Glasgow	M166CCD	Western Buses
LIW3462	Henderson Travel	LSK512	Park's	LUS436V	Greater Glasgow	M189RLS	Bryans of Denny
LIW9278	Travel Dundee	LSK513	Park's	LUS437Y	Greater Glasgow	M1GRT	Grampian
LIW9279	Travel Dundee	LSK514	Park's	LUS438Y	Greater Glasgow	M200TPT	Travel Dundee
LJA476P	Strathtay	LSK527	Grampian	LUS439Y	Greater Glasgow	M200WCM	West Coast Motors
LJA477P	Strathtay	LSK529	Grampian	LUS440Y	Greater Glasgow	M201VSX	LRT Lothian
LJA478P	Strathtay	LSK530	Grampian	LWB383P	Rowe's	M202VSX	LRT Lothian
LJA481P	Strathtay	LSK546	Grampian	LWV268P	Gibson	M203VSX	LRT Lothian
LJI978	Marbill	LSK547	Bluebird Buses	LWV269P	Galson Motors	M204VSX	LRT Lothian
LKP381P	Marbill	LSK548	Bluebird Buses	LXI2630	Travel Dundee	M205VSX	LRT Lothian
LKP384P	Stevenson	LSK555	Park's	LXI2961	Travel Dundee	M206VSX	LRT Lothian
LMS154W	Clydeside	LSK570	Grampian	LXJ462	Travel Dundee	M207VSX	LRT Lothian
LMS168W	Strathtay	LSK571	Grampian	M6BUS	Whitelaw's	M208VSX	LRT Lothian
LMS372W	Highland Country	LSK572	Grampian	M6SKY	Skye-Ways	M209VSX	LRT Lothian
LMS373W	Highland	LSK573	Grampian	M7BUS	Whitelaw's	M210VSX	LRT Lothian
LMS374W	Midland Bluebird	LSK830	Park's	M8SKY	Skye-Ways	M211VSX	LRT Lothian
LMS375W	Highland Country	LSK831	Park's	M10ULF	Greater Glasgow	M212VSX	LRT Lothian
LMS376W	Midland Bluebird	LSK835	Park's	M21LYV	Royal Mail	M213VSX	LRT Lothian
LMS377W	Midland Bluebird	LSK839	Park's	M62DSJ	McEwan's	M214VSX	LRT Lothian
LMS378W	Midland Bluebird	LSK844	Park's	M65FDS	Clydeside	M215VSX	LRT Lothian
LMS379W	Midland Bluebird	LSO82P	Skye-Ways	M67FDS	Clydeside	M216VSX	LRT Lothian
LMS380W	Oban & District	LSU368V	Greater Glasgow	M68UWB	H Crawford	M217VSX	LRT Lothian
LMS381W	Midland Bluebird	LSU369V	Greater Glasgow	M69UWB	H Crawford	M218VSX	LRT Lothian
LMS382W	Midland Bluebird	LSU370V	Greater Glasgow	M95EGE	Argyle Bus Group	M219VSX	LRT Lothian
LMS383W	Highland	LSU371V	Greater Glasgow	M100AAB	AA Buses	M220VSX	LRT Lothian
LMS384W	Midland Bluebird	LSU372V	Greater Glasgow	M100TPT	Travel Dundee	M221VSX	LRT Lothian
LMS385W	Strathtay	LSU373V	Greater Glasgow	M100WCM	West Coast Motors	M222GSM	Maynes
LMS386W	Midland Bluebird	LSU374V	Greater Glasgow	M102CCD	Fife Scottish	M223VSX	LRT Lothian
LPS210T	Shalder	LSU375V	Greater Glasgow	M102RMS	Clydeside	M224VSX	LRT Lothian
LPS850V	Shalder	LSU376V	Greater Glasgow	M103CCD	Fife Scottish	M225VSX	LRT Lothian
LPS963V	Shalder	LSU377V	Greater Glasgow	M103RMS	Clydeside	M226VSX	LRT Lothian
LPY458W	McEwan's	LSU378V	Greater Glasgow	M104CCD	Fife Scottish	M227VSX	LRT Lothian
LRS292W	Grampian	LSU379V	Greater Glasgow	M104RMS	Clydeside	M228VSX	LRT Lothian
LRS293W	Grampian	LSU380V	Greater Glasgow	M105PRS	Whytes	M229VSX	LRT Lothian
LRS294W	Grampian	LSU381V	Greater Glasgow	M105RMS	Clydeside	M229WSG	Royal Mail
LRS295W	Grampian	LSU382V	Greater Glasgow	M106PKS	Lowland	M230VSX	LRT Lothian
LRS296W	Grampian	LSU383V	Greater Glasgow	M106PRS	Whytes	M231VSX	LRT Lothian
LRS297W	Grampian	LSU385V	Greater Glasgow	M106RMS	Clydeside	M232VSX	LRT Lothian
LRS298W	Grampian	LSU386V	Greater Glasgow	M107RMS	Clydeside	M233VSX	LRT Lothian
LRS299W	Grampian	LSU387V	Greater Glasgow	M108RMS	Clydeside	M234VSX	LRT Lothian
LRS300W	Grampian	LSU388V	Greater Glasgow	M109RMS	Clydeside	M268POS	H Crawford
LSA22W	Wilson's, Carnwath	LSU389V	Greater Glasgow	M110RMS	Clydeside	M269POS	H Crawford
LSC936T	Lowland	LSU390V	Greater Glasgow	M112RMS	Clydeside	M270POS	H Crawford
LSC938T	Lowland	LSU391V	Greater Glasgow	M113RMS	Clydeside	M271POS	H Crawford
LSD732W	AA Buses	LSU392V	Greater Glasgow	M114RMS	Clydeside	M272POS	H Crawford
LSJ871W	AA Buses	LSU393V	Greater Glasgow	M115RMS	Clydeside	M274TSB	H Crawford
LSJ872W	AA Buses	LSU394V	Greater Glasgow	M116RMS	Clydeside	M275FNS	Harte
LSK444	Park's	LSU395V	Greater Glasgow	M116XSR	Travel Dundee	M275TSB	H Crawford

The Scottish Bus Handbook

Reg	Operator	Reg	Operator	Reg	Operator	Reg	Operator
M276FNS	Argyle Bus Group	M516RSS	Grampian	M664FYS	Western Buses	M778TFS	Fife Scottish
M277FNS	Argyle Bus Group	M517RSS	Grampian	M665FYS	Western Buses	M779PRS	Greater Glasgow
M277TSF	Davidson Buses	M518RSS	Grampian	M667FYS	Western Buses	M779TFS	Fife Scottish
M278FNS	Argyle Bus Group	M519RSB	West Coast Motors	M668FYS	Western Buses	M780PRS	Greater Glasgow
M283SMS	Bryans of Denny	M519RSS	Grampian	M670SSX	Fife Scottish	M780TFS	Fife Scottish
M284SMS	Midland Bluebird	M520RSS	Grampian	M671SSX	Fife Scottish	M781PRS	Greater Glasgow
M300WCM	West Coast Motors	M521RSS	Grampian	M672SSX	Fife Scottish	M784PRS	Western Buses
M306XSN	Strathtay	M522RSS	Grampian	M673SSX	Fife Scottish	M785PRS	Western Buses
M307XSN	Strathtay	M523RSS	Grampian	M674SSX	Western Buses	M786PRS	Western Buses
M310KRY	Clyde Coast	M524RSS	Grampian	M675SSX	Western Buses	M787PRS	Western Buses
M314PKS	Fife Scottish	M527RSO	Bluebird Buses	M676SSX	Western Buses	M788PRS	Western Buses
M315PKS	Fife Scottish	M528RSO	Bluebird Buses	M677SSX	Western Buses	M789PRS	Western Buses
M317RSO	Bluebird Buses	M529RSO	Bluebird Buses	M678SSX	Western Buses	M790PRS	Western Buses
M318RSO	Bluebird Buses	M530RSO	Bluebird Buses	M679CSU	Hutchison	M791EUS	Argyle Bus Group
M319RSO	Bluebird Buses	M531RSO	Bluebird Buses	M679SSX	Western Buses	M791PRS	Western Buses
M320RSO	Bluebird Buses	M532RSO	Bluebird Buses	M680SSX	Western Buses	M792EUS	Argyle Bus Group
M321RSO	Bluebird Buses	M533RSO	Bluebird Buses	M681SSX	Western Buses	M792PRS	Western Buses
M327TSF	R H Wilson's	M534RSO	Bluebird Buses	M700SOU	Southern Cs	M793EUS	Argyle Bus Group
M341WSL	Moffat & Williamson	M535RSO	Bluebird Buses	M700WCM	West Coast Motors	M793PRS	Western Buses
M386KVR	AA Buses	M536RSO	Bluebird Buses	M702XSG	Royal Mail	M794EUS	Argyle Bus Group
M387KVR	AA Buses	M537RSO	Bluebird Buses	M709VSC	Royal Mail	M799EUS	Argyle Bus Group
M388KVR	AA Buses	M538RSO	Bluebird Buses	M711RVN	Docherty of Irvine	M800SOU	Southern Cs
M389KVR	AA Buses	M539RSO	Bluebird Buses	M718BCS	Western Buses	M800WCM	West Coast Motors
M394MRW	Greater Glasgow	M540RSO	Bluebird Buses	M719BCS	Western Buses	M804ASM	McEwan's
M395KVR	AA Buses	M541RSO	Bluebird Buses	M720BCS	Western Buses	M818ECS	Allander Travel
M396KVR	AA Buses	M542RSO	Bluebird Buses	M721BCS	Western Buses	M826RCP	West Coast Motors
M397KVR	AA Buses	M543RSO	Bluebird Buses	M722BCS	Western Buses	M834DUS	Greater Glasgow
M399OMS	Lowland	M544RSO	Bluebird Buses	M723BCS	Western Buses	M835DUS	Greater Glasgow
M400WCM	West Coast Motors	M555GSM	Maynes	M724BCS	Western Buses	M836DUS	Greater Glasgow
M415GUS	Davidson Buses	M567RMS	Midland Bluebird	M725BCS	Western Buses	M837DUS	Greater Glasgow
M422GUS	Argyle Bus Group	M568RMS	Midland Bluebird	M726BCS	Western Buses	M838DUS	Greater Glasgow
M423GUS	Argyle Bus Group	M569RMS	Midland Bluebird	M727BCS	Western Buses	M839DUS	Greater Glasgow
M428RRN	Greater Glasgow	M570RMS	Midland Bluebird	M732BSJ	Western Buses	M840DUS	Greater Glasgow
M435ECS	Glen Coaches	M571RMS	Midland Bluebird	M733BSJ	Western Buses	M841DDS	Clydeside
M442ECS	Glen Coaches	M576TSG	Davidson Buses	M734BSJ	Western Buses	M841DUS	Greater Glasgow
M444GSM	Maynes	M578BSM	McEwan's	M735BSJ	Western Buses	M842DDS	Clydeside
M466ASW	Western Buses	M583SSX	Argyle Bus Group	M736BSJ	Western Buses	M842DUS	Greater Glasgow
M467ASW	Western Buses	M589OSO	Bluebird Buses	M737BSJ	Western Buses	M843DDS	Clydeside
M468ASW	Western Buses	M590OSO	Bluebird Buses	M738BSJ	Western Buses	M843DUS	Greater Glasgow
M469ASW	Western Buses	M591OSO	Bluebird Buses	M739BSJ	Western Buses	M844DDS	Clydeside
M470ASW	Western Buses	M592OSO	Bluebird Buses	M740BSJ	Western Buses	M844DUS	Greater Glasgow
M471ASW	Western Buses	M593OSO	Bluebird Buses	M741BSJ	Western Buses	M845DDS	Clydeside
M472ASW	Western Buses	M594OSO	Bluebird Buses	M753TSF	Royal Mail	M845DUS	Greater Glasgow
M473ASW	Western Buses	M594RFS	Henderson Travel	M754TSF	Royal Mail	M846DDS	Clydeside
M474ASW	Western Buses	M595OSO	Bluebird Buses	M760GGE	Marbill	M846DUS	Greater Glasgow
M475ASW	Western Buses	M596OSO	Bluebird Buses	M761GGE	Henderson Travel	M847DDS	Clydeside
M476ASW	Western Buses	M597OSO	Bluebird Buses	M765PRS	Greater Glasgow	M847DUS	Greater Glasgow
M477ASW	Western Buses	M597SSB	Bryans of Denny	M766PRS	Greater Glasgow	M848DUS	Greater Glasgow
M478ASW	Western Buses	M597SSB	Stonehouse	M766WSC	Glen Coaches	M849DUS	Greater Glasgow
M479ASW	Western Buses	M598OSO	Bluebird Buses	M767PRS	Greater Glasgow	M853TSF	Royal Mail
M480ASW	Western Buses	M598RFS	Stonehouse	M768PRS	Greater Glasgow	M867FSU	Hutchison
M481ASW	Western Buses	M599GMR	Galson Motors	M769PRS	Greater Glasgow	M868FSU	Hutchison
M481CSD	Marbill	M623WAS	Highland	M770PRS	Greater Glasgow	M869ASW	Western Buses
M482ASW	Western Buses	M630RCP	AA Buses	M770TFS	Fife Scottish	M870ASW	Western Buses
M483ASW	Western Buses	M648FYS	Western Buses	M771PRS	Greater Glasgow	M870DYS	Greater Glasgow
M484ASW	Western Buses	M649FYS	Western Buses	M771TFS	Fife Scottish	M871ASW	Western Buses
M485ASW	Western Buses	M650FYS	Western Buses	M772BCS	Western Buses	M871DYS	Greater Glasgow
M485VST	Highland	M651FYS	Western Buses	M772PRS	Greater Glasgow	M872ASW	Western Buses
M486ASW	Western Buses	M652FYS	Western Buses	M772TFS	Fife Scottish	M875NWK	Whitelaw's
M487ASW	Western Buses	M653FYS	Western Buses	M773BCS	Western Buses	M877DDS	Davidson Buses
M487WAS	Highland	M654FYS	Western Buses	M773PRS	Greater Glasgow	M877PRS	Greater Glasgow
M488ASW	Western Buses	M655FYS	Western Buses	M773TFS	Fife Scottish	M878DDS	Argyle Bus Group
M489ASW	Western Buses	M656FYS	Western Buses	M774PRS	Greater Glasgow	M880DDS	Argyle Bus Group
M490ASW	Western Buses	M657FYS	Western Buses	M774TFS	Fife Scottish	M883DDS	Argyle Bus Group
M491ASW	Western Buses	M658FYS	Western Buses	M775PRS	Greater Glasgow	M900SOU	Southern Cs
M492ASW	Western Buses	M659FYS	Western Buses	M775TFS	Fife Scottish	M901NKS	Munro's
M498XSP	Moffat & Williamson	M660FYS	Western Buses	M776PRS	Greater Glasgow	M933LPM	Skye-Ways
M500GSM	Maynes	M661FYS	Western Buses	M776TFS	Fife Scottish	M939EYS	Greater Glasgow
M500WCM	West Coast Motors	M662FYS	Western Buses	M777GSM	Maynes	M940EYS	Greater Glasgow
M510JRY	Stonehouse	M663FYS	Western Buses	M778PRS	Greater Glasgow	M941EYS	Greater Glasgow

The Scottish Bus Handbook

M942EYS	Greater Glasgow	MIL9320	Clydeside	N7DOT	AA Buses
M944TSX	Fife Scottish	MIL9752	Highland Country	N10SOU	Southern Cs
M945TSX	Fife Scottish	MIL9753	Highland Country	N26KYS	Argyle Bus Group
M946TSX	Fife Scottish	MIL9754	Highland Country	N27KYS	Argyle Bus Group
M947TSX	Fife Scottish	MIL9755	Highland Country	N30SOU	Southern Cs
M948TSX	Fife Scottish	MIL9756	Highland Country	N34GSX	Slaemuir
M949EGE	AA Buses	MNS6Y	Fife Scottish	N61CSC	Midland Bluebird
M949TSX	Fife Scottish	MNS7Y	Fife Scottish	N62CSC	Midland Bluebird
M950EGE	AA Buses	MNS8Y	Fife Scottish	N63CSC	Midland Bluebird
M950TSX	Fife Scottish	MNS9Y	Fife Scottish	N64CSC	Midland Bluebird
M951TSX	Fife Scottish	MNS10Y	Fife Scottish	N65CSC	Midland Bluebird
M951XES	Strathtay	MOD572P	Moffat & Williamson	N66CSC	Midland Bluebird
M952TSX	Fife Scottish	MPL125W	Keenan of Ayr	N67CSC	Midland Bluebird
M952XES	Strathtay	MPL137W	Keenan of Ayr	N68CSC	Midland Bluebird
M953TSX	Fife Scottish	MPS666V	Shalder	N69CSC	Midland Bluebird
M953XES	Strathtay	MRJ280W	Whitelaw's	N70CSC	Midland Bluebird
M954TSX	Fife Scottish	MSF126P	Galloways	N74BFS	LRT Lothian
M954XES	Strathtay	MSF127P	Galloways	N75CSX	LRT Lothian
M955TSX	Fife Scottish	MSF477P	LRT Lothian	N77JDS	Docherт'y Midland
M956TSX	Fife Scottish	MSG914T	Wilson's, Carnwath	N81PUS	Argyle Bus Group
M975WES	Moffat & Williamson	MSL64X	Rowe's	N82LSE	Whytes
M988CYS	Marbill	MSL275X	Oban & District	N82PUS	Argyle Bus Group
MAP351W	Galson Motors	MSL278X	Oban & District	N83LSE	Whytes
MAU146P	Bluebird Buses	MSL281X	Moffat & Williamson	N84LSE	Whytes
MAZ6509	Spa Motors	MSO10W	Western Buses	N85LSE	Whytes
MBS281W	Rapsons	MSO18W	Western Buses	N89OGG	Greater Glasgow
MBZ7159	Park's	MSU300Y	Stokes	N91OGG	Greater Glasgow
MDF115P	Wilson's, Carnwath	MSU445	Fife Scottish	N92OGG	Greater Glasgow
MDL650R	Lowland	MSU466	Western Buses	N93HSJ	Paterson's
MDS697P	Greater Glasgow	MSU499	Fife Scottish	N93OGG	Greater Glasgow
MDS712P	Greater Glasgow	MTV762P	Moffat & Williamson	N94HSJ	Paterson's
MDS862V	Greater Glasgow	MUS309Y	Greater Glasgow	N94OGG	Greater Glasgow
MDS865V	Western Buses	MUS310Y	Greater Glasgow	N95ALS	Fife Scottish
MEL556P	Irvines of Law	MUS311Y	Greater Glasgow	N95OGG	Greater Glasgow
MES228P	Moffat & Williamson	MUS312Y	Greater Glasgow	N96ALS	Fife Scottish
MFR42P	R H Wilson's	MUS313Y	Greater Glasgow	N96OGG	Greater Glasgow
MFR126P	McEwan's	MVK503R	Greater Glasgow	N97ALS	Fife Scottish
MGG396P	Shalder	MVK508R	Steeles	N97OGG	Greater Glasgow
MGP226L	Highland	MVK520R	Greater Glasgow	N98OGG	Greater Glasgow
MHS4P	Bluebird Buses	MVK542R	Wilson's, Carnwath	N100WCM	West Coast Motors
MHS5P	Bluebird Buses	N1BUS	Stonehouse	N101WSB	Oban & District
MHS39P	Greater Glasgow	N1SKY	Skye-Ways	N103CKU	Greater Glasgow
MIB5088	Galloways	N2SBL	Shuttle Buses	N104CKU	Greater Glasgow
MIB7416	Bluebird Buses	N2SOU	Southern Cs	N107GSJ	Steeles
MIL4693	AA Buses	N4SKY	Skye-Ways	N107VKS	Lowland
MIL5980	Irvines of Law	N5BUS	Stonehouse	N117FSM	McEwan's
MIL6675	Highland Country	N6SOU	Southern Cs	N120OGG	Greater Glasgow

N121OGG	Greater Glasgow
N122OGG	Greater Glasgow
N122RJF	Silver Coach Lines
N123OGG	Greater Glasgow
N123RJF	Silver Coach Lines
N124OGG	Greater Glasgow
N124RJF	Silver Coach Lines
N125OGG	Greater Glasgow
N126OGG	Greater Glasgow
N127OGG	Greater Glasgow
N128OGG	Greater Glasgow
N129OGG	Greater Glasgow
N130OGG	Greater Glasgow
N131OGG	Greater Glasgow
N132OGG	Greater Glasgow
N133OGG	Greater Glasgow
N134HSD	H Crawford
N134OGG	Greater Glasgow
N135OGG	Greater Glasgow
N136OGG	Greater Glasgow
N136YMS	Clydeside
N137OGG	Greater Glasgow
N137YMS	Clydeside
N138OGG	Greater Glasgow
N138YMS	Clydeside
N139YMS	Clydeside
N139YST	Rapsons
N140ESC	Glen Coaches
N141VDU	Greater Glasgow
N142VSA	Whytes
N142XSA	Western Buses
N143XSA	Western Buses
N144XSA	Western Buses
N145XSA	Western Buses
N146XSA	Western Buses
N148DSL	Strathtay
N148XSA	Bluebird Buses
N149DSL	Strathtay
N149XSA	Bluebird Buses
N150DSL	Strathtay
N150XSA	Bluebird Buses
N151DSL	Strathtay
N151XSA	Bluebird Buses
N152XSA	Bluebird Buses
N153XSA	Bluebird Buses
N154XSA	Bluebird Buses
N167DSP	Docherт'y Midland

N474MUS is shown in the McGill's livery of fawn and red while passing through Paisley on its way to Paisley Cross. The Northen Counties Paladin body is often found on the popular Dennis Dart Chassis.
Mark Bailey

N190OGG	Greater Glasgow	N410CSG	Royal Mail	N609VSS	Western Buses	N807PDS	Argyle Bus Group
N199OGG	Greater Glasgow	N411CSG	Royal Mail	N610VSS	Western Buses	N808PDS	Argyle Bus Group
N200WCM	West Coast Motors	N412CSG	Royal Mail	N610WND	AA Buses	N809PDS	Argyle Bus Group
N201NHS	Clydeside	N413CSG	Royal Mail	N611VSS	Western Buses	N812NHS	Allander Travel
N201NHS	Clydeside	N414CSG	Royal Mail	N611WND	AA Buses	N813NHS	Allander Travel
N201NHS	Clydeside	N415CSG	Royal Mail	N612VSS	Western Buses	N814WSB	Docherty of Irvine
N201VSA	Grampian	N418CSF	Royal Mail	N612WND	AA Buses	N849VHH	Western Buses
N202NHS	Clydeside	N436FSC	Royal Mail	N616USS	Western Buses	N850VHH	Western Buses
N202VSA	Grampian	N437FSC	Royal Mail	N617USS	Western Buses	N851ASF	Rowe's
N202WSB	Oban & District	N439FSC	Royal Mail	N618USS	Bluebird Buses	N851VHH	Western Buses
N203NHS	Clydeside	N439GHG	McGill's	N619USS	Bluebird Buses	N852ASF	Rowe's
N203VSA	Grampian	N440GHG	McGill's	N620USS	Bluebird Buses	N852VHH	Western Buses
N204NHS	Clydeside	N447CSG	Royal Mail	N621VSS	Western Buses	N853VHH	Western Buses
N204VSA	Grampian	N451FSC	Royal Mail	N622VSS	Western Buses	N854VHH	Western Buses
N205VSA	Grampian	N452FSC	Royal Mail	N623VSS	Western Buses	N855VHH	Western Buses
N206VSA	Grampian	N453FSC	Royal Mail	N624VSS	Western Buses	N856VHH	Western Buses
N207GCS	Marbill	N455FSC	Royal Mail	N625VSS	Western Buses	N857VHH	Western Buses
N207NHS	Clydeside	N456FSC	Royal Mail	N626VSS	Western Buses	N858VHH	Western Buses
N208GCS	Marbill	N457FSC	Royal Mail	N627VSS	Western Buses	N859VHH	Western Buses
N208NHS	Clydeside	N460KMW	Maynes	N628VSS	Western Buses	N860DSP	Moffat & Williamson
N209FSM	McEwan's	N473MUS	McGill's	N629VSS	Western Buses	N860VHH	Western Buses
N210ESF	Henderson Travel	N474MUS	McGill's	N630VSS	Western Buses	N861DSP	Moffat & Williamson
N210FSM	McEwan's	N500GSM	Maynes	N631VSS	Western Buses	N861VHH	Western Buses
N226GSC	Royal Mail	N525VSA	Grampian	N632VSS	Western Buses	N862VHH	Western Buses
N228MUS	Argyle Bus Group	N526VSA	Grampian	N633VSS	Western Buses	N863VHH	Western Buses
N240WDO	Maynes	N527VSA	Grampian	N634VSS	Western Buses	N864VHH	Western Buses
N247XSA	Western Buses	N528VSA	Grampian	N635VSS	Western Buses	N865VHH	Western Buses
N249PGD	Avondale	N529VSA	Grampian	N636VSS	Bluebird Buses	N866VHH	Western Buses
N250CSG	Rennie's	N530VSA	Grampian	N637VSS	Bluebird Buses	N885FSM	McEwan's
N250PGD	Avondale	N531VSA	Grampian	N638VSS	Bluebird Buses	N888GSM	Maynes
N253PGD	Argyle Bus Group	N532VSA	Grampian	N639VSS	Bluebird Buses	N905AAS	Rapsons
N254PGD	Argyle Bus Group	N533VSA	Grampian	N640VSS	Bluebird Buses	N906AAS	Rapsons
N256PGD	Argyle Bus Group	N534VSA	Grampian	N659ESN	Moffat & Williamson	N929LSU	Greater Glasgow
N257PGD	Argyle Bus Group	N535VSA	Grampian	N680GSC	Rennie's	N930LSU	Greater Glasgow
N258PGD	Argyle Bus Group	N536VSA	Grampian	N681GSC	Rennie's	N931LSU	Greater Glasgow
N276HSD	H Crawford	N537VSA	Grampian	N686WLS	Midland Bluebird	N932LSU	Greater Glasgow
N277HSD	H Crawford	N538VSA	Grampian	N687WLS	Midland Bluebird	N933LSU	Greater Glasgow
N300WCM	West Coast Motors	N539VSA	Grampian	N688WLS	Midland Bluebird	N934LSU	Greater Glasgow
N308DSL	Strathtay	N549NYS	Bruce Coaches	N689WLS	Midland Bluebird	N935ETU	Argyle Bus Group
N309DSL	Strathtay	N550GFS	Maynes	N690WLS	Midland Bluebird	N935LSU	Greater Glasgow
N311BYA	Park's	N550NYS	Bruce Coaches	N703FSM	McEwan's	N936ETU	Argyle Bus Group
N312BYA	Park's	N552FSC	Royal Mail	N704FSM	McEwan's	N936LSU	Greater Glasgow
N313BYA	Park's	N553FSC	Royal Mail	N705FSM	McEwan's	N937LSU	Greater Glasgow
N314BYA	Park's	N554FSC	Royal Mail	N706FSM	McEwan's	N938LSU	Greater Glasgow
N316VMS	Fife Scottish	N558FSC	Royal Mail	N750LUS	Argyle Bus Group	N939LSU	Greater Glasgow
N317VMS	Fife Scottish	N561SJF	Fife Scottish	N752LUS	Argyle Bus Group	N940LSU	Greater Glasgow
N318VMS	Fife Scottish	N562SJF	Fife Scottish	N753LSU	Stokes	N941LSU	Greater Glasgow
N319VMS	Fife Scottish	N572VMS	Midland Bluebird	N753LUS	Argyle Bus Group	N941MGG	Argyle Bus Group
N320VMS	Fife Scottish	N573VMS	Midland Bluebird	N754LUS	Argyle Bus Group	N942LSU	Greater Glasgow
N321VMS	Fife Scottish	N574VMS	Midland Bluebird	N764CAS	Rapsons	N942MGG	Argyle Bus Group
N322VMS	Fife Scottish	N582XSA	Bluebird Buses	N791SJU	Irvines of Law	N943LSU	Greater Glasgow
N323VMS	Fife Scottish	N583WND	Davidson Buses	N792SJU	Irvines of Law	N943MGG	Slaemuir
N324VMS	Fife Scottish	N583XSA	Bluebird Buses	N797FSD	Marbill	N944LSU	Greater Glasgow
N325VMS	Fife Scottish	N584WND	Davidson Buses	N798FSD	Marbill	N944MGG	Rennie's
N326VMS	Fife Scottish	N584XSA	Bluebird Buses	N798PDS	Avondale	N944SOS	Greater Glasgow
N327VMS	Fife Scottish	N585WND	AA Buses	N799FSD	Marbill	N945LSU	Greater Glasgow
N328VMS	Fife Scottish	N586WND	AA Buses	N799PDS	Avondale	N945SOS	Greater Glasgow
N329VMS	Fife Scottish	N590GBW	AA Buses	N801FSD	Marbill	N946LSU	Greater Glasgow
N400SOU	Southern Cs	N591GBW	AA Buses	N801PDS	Argyle Bus Group	N946SOS	Greater Glasgow
N400WCM	West Coast Motors	N592GBW	AA Buses	N802NHS	Park's	N947LSU	Greater Glasgow
N401GSX	LRT Lothian	N594GBW	AA Buses	N802PDS	Argyle Bus Group	N947SOS	Greater Glasgow
N402GSX	LRT Lothian	N601VSS	Western Buses	N803NHS	Park's	N948GSG	Royal Mail
N403GSX	LRT Lothian	N602VSS	Western Buses	N803PDS	Argyle Bus Group	N948LSU	Greater Glasgow
N404GSX	LRT Lothian	N603VSS	Western Buses	N804NHS	Park's	N948SOS	Greater Glasgow
N405GSX	LRT Lothian	N604VSS	Western Buses	N804PDS	Argyle Bus Group	N949LSU	Greater Glasgow
N406GSX	LRT Lothian	N605VSS	Western Buses	N805NHS	Park's	N949SOS	Greater Glasgow
N407CSG	Royal Mail	N606VSS	Western Buses	N805PDS	Argyle Bus Group	N950LSU	Greater Glasgow
N407GSX	LRT Lothian	N607VSS	Western Buses	N806NHS	Park's	N950SOS	Greater Glasgow
N408CSG	Royal Mail	N608OGE	Hutchison	N806PDS	Argyle Bus Group	N951LSU	Greater Glasgow
N409CSG	Royal Mail	N608VSS	Western Buses	N807NHS	Park's	N951SOS	Greater Glasgow

N952LSU	Greater Glasgow	NCS26P	Docherty of Irvine	NRS314W	Grampian	OGG182Y	Greater Glasgow
N952SOS	Greater Glasgow	NDL655R	Lowland	NRS315W	Grampian	OGG183Y	Greater Glasgow
N953LSU	Greater Glasgow	NDL656R	Lowland	NSC822X	Mackies	OGG184Y	Greater Glasgow
N953SOS	Greater Glasgow	NDS837Y	Wilson's, Carnwath	NSG636A	Bluebird Buses	OGG185Y	Greater Glasgow
N954LSU	Greater Glasgow	NEG322	Riddler	NSJ550X	AA Buses	OGG186Y	Greater Glasgow
N954SOS	Greater Glasgow	NFL881	Morrison's	NSK267T	Highland Country	OGG188Y	Greater Glasgow
N955LSU	Greater Glasgow	NFS170Y	Fife Scottish	NSK272T	Highland Country	OGG189Y	Greater Glasgow
N955SOS	Greater Glasgow	NFS171Y	Fife Scottish	NSP332R	Docherty of Irvine	OGG190Y	Greater Glasgow
N956LSU	Greater Glasgow	NFS172Y	Fife Scottish	NSP334R	Fife Scottish	OGG191Y	Greater Glasgow
N956SOS	Greater Glasgow	NFS173Y	Fife Scottish	NSP336R	Fife Scottish	OHV684Y	Western Buses
N957LSU	Greater Glasgow	NFS174Y	Fife Scottish	NSV616	Travel Dundee	OHV700Y	Western Buses
N957SOS	Greater Glasgow	NFS175Y	Fife Scottish	NSV621	Travel Dundee	OHV710Y	Western Buses
N958LSU	Greater Glasgow	NFS176Y	Fife Scottish	NSV622	Travel Dundee	OHV714Y	Western Buses
N958SOS	Greater Glasgow	NFS177Y	Fife Scottish	NSX248T	LRT Lothian	OHV728Y	Western Buses
N959LSU	Greater Glasgow	NFS178Y	Fife Scottish	NSX249T	LRT Lothian	OHV762Y	Western Buses
N959SOS	Greater Glasgow	NFS179Y	Fife Scottish	NSX250T	LRT Lothian	OHV780Y	Western Buses
N960LSU	Greater Glasgow	NFS984T	Lowland	NTF9	Docherty of Irvine	OHV800Y	Western Buses
N960SOS	Greater Glasgow	NGD26V	Wilson's, Carnwath	NUD801W	Lowland	OHV801Y	Fife Scottish
N961LSU	Greater Glasgow	NGE172P	Wilson's, Carnwath	NUF276	Bluebird Buses	OHV809Y	Western Buses
N961SOS	Greater Glasgow	NIB4138	Bluebird Buses	NUW618Y	Western Buses	OHY789R	McEwan's
N962LSU	Greater Glasgow	NIB5232	Western Buses	NUW674Y	Western Buses	OIB3519	Spa Motors
N962SOS	Greater Glasgow	NIB5233	Western Buses	NVY148	Silver Fox	OIW7024	Western Buses
N963LSU	Greater Glasgow	NIB5455	Bluebird Buses	NXX451	Rennie's	OIW7025	Western Buses
N963SOS	Greater Glasgow	NIB6694	Wilson's, Carnwath	OEM782S	Rennie's	OJD11R	Keenan of Ayr
N964LSU	Greater Glasgow	NIL1505	Wilson's, Carnwath	OEM792S	Rennie's	OJD44R	Wilson's, Carnwath
N964SOS	Greater Glasgow	NIL1507	Wilson's, Carnwath	OEM801S	Rennie's	OJE533	Galson Motors
N965LSU	Greater Glasgow	NIL1509	Wilson's, Carnwath	OEM802S	Rennie's	OJI5506	Allander Travel
N965SOS	Greater Glasgow	NIL5363	Dart	OEX798W	Rowe's	OJI8324	Moffat & Williamson
N966LSU	Greater Glasgow	NIL5364	Dart	OFA590	Stonehouse	OKK154	Riddler
N966SOS	Greater Glasgow	NIL5365	Dart	OFA990	Morrison's	OKM317	AA Buses
N967LSU	Greater Glasgow	NIL5366	Dart	OFS668Y	LRT Lothian	OLS539P	Whitelaw's
N967SOS	Greater Glasgow	NIL5367	Dart	OFS669Y	LRT Lothian	OMS910W	Bluebird Buses
N968LSU	Greater Glasgow	NIL5368	Dart	OFS670Y	LRT Lothian	OPC37R	Gibson
N968SOS	Greater Glasgow	NIL5369	Dart	OFS671Y	LRT Lothian	OPS899X	Shalder
N969LSU	Greater Glasgow	NIL5370	Dart	OFS672Y	LRT Lothian	ORS60R	Grampian
N969SOS	Greater Glasgow	NIL5371	Dart	OFS673Y	LRT Lothian	ORS201R	Midland Bluebird
N970LSU	Greater Glasgow	NIL5372	Dart	OFS674Y	LRT Lothian	ORS202R	Midland Bluebird
N970SOS	Greater Glasgow	NIL5373	Dart	OFS675Y	LRT Lothian	ORS203R	Midland Bluebird
N971LSU	Greater Glasgow	NIL5374	Dart	OFS676Y	LRT Lothian	ORS204R	Midland Bluebird
N971MGG	Stokes	NIW2230	AA Buses	OFS677Y	LRT Lothian	ORS205R	Midland Bluebird
N971SOS	Greater Glasgow	NIW8920	Steeles	OFS678Y	LRT Lothian	ORS208R	Midland Bluebird
N972LSU	Greater Glasgow	NJS246	Rapsons	OFS679Y	LRT Lothian	ORS209R	Midland Bluebird
N972SOS	Greater Glasgow	NJT34P	Irvines of Law	OFS680Y	LRT Lothian	ORS211R	Midland Bluebird
N973LSU	Greater Glasgow	NLE515	Shuttle Buses	OFS681Y	LRT Lothian	ORS215R	Midland Bluebird
N973SOS	Greater Glasgow	NLP388V	Western Buses	OFS682Y	LRT Lothian	ORS216R	Midland Bluebird
N974LSU	Greater Glasgow	NLS981W	Midland Bluebird	OFS683Y	LRT Lothian	ORS217R	Midland Bluebird
N975LSU	Greater Glasgow	NLS983W	Western Buses	OFS684Y	LRT Lothian	ORU738	Strathtay
N976LSU	Greater Glasgow	NLS984W	Midland Bluebird	OFS685Y	LRT Lothian	OSC47V	Fife Scottish
N977LSU	Greater Glasgow	NLS985W	Western Buses	OFS686Y	LRT Lothian	OSC48V	Fife Scottish
N978LSU	Greater Glasgow	NLS989W	Western Buses	OFS687Y	LRT Lothian	OSC49V	Fife Scottish
N978NMW	Whytes	NMY643E	Bluebird Buses	OFS688Y	LRT Lothian	OSC50V	Fife Scottish
N979LSU	Greater Glasgow	NNH190Y	Greater Glasgow	OFS689Y	LRT Lothian	OSC51V	Fife Scottish
N980LSU	Greater Glasgow	NNS234V	Wilson's, Carnwath	OFS690Y	LRT Lothian	OSC52V	Fife Scottish
N981LSU	Greater Glasgow	NOC308R	Marbill	OFS691Y	LRT Lothian	OSC53V	Fife Scottish
N982LSU	Greater Glasgow	NOC458R	Marbill	OFS692Y	LRT Lothian	OSC54V	Fife Scottish
N983ESD	Rowe's	NPA229W	Western Buses	OFS693Y	LRT Lothian	OSC55V	Fife Scottish
N983LSU	Greater Glasgow	NPG266W	Silver Fox	OFS694Y	LRT Lothian	OSC56V	Fife Scottish
N984LSU	Greater Glasgow	NRS301W	Grampian	OFS695Y	LRT Lothian	OSC57V	Fife Scottish
N985LSU	Greater Glasgow	NRS302W	Grampian	OFS696Y	LRT Lothian	OSC60V	Fife Scottish
N985ODS	Golden Eagle	NRS303W	Grampian	OFS697Y	LRT Lothian	OSC61V	Fife Scottish
N986LSU	Greater Glasgow	NRS304W	Grampian	OFS698Y	LRT Lothian	OSC62V	Fife Scottish
N987LSU	Greater Glasgow	NRS305W	Grampian	OFS699Y	LRT Lothian	OSC63V	Fife Scottish
N988LSU	Greater Glasgow	NRS306W	Grampian	OFS700Y	LRT Lothian	OSC64V	Fife Scottish
N991KUS	Argyle Bus Group	NRS307W	Grampian	OFS701Y	LRT Lothian	OSC66V	Fife Scottish
N992KUS	Marbill	NRS308W	Grampian	OFS702Y	LRT Lothian	OSC601V	LRT Lothian
N993KUS	Marbill	NRS309W	Grampian	OFS911M	LRT Lothian	OSC602V	LRT Lothian
N999GSM	Maynes	NRS310W	Grampian	OFS912M	LRT Lothian	OSC603V	LRT Lothian
NAH136P	Irvines of Law	NRS311W	Grampian	OGD660V	Greater Glasgow	OSC604V	LRT Lothian
NAL51P	Highland	NRS312W	Grampian	OGG179Y	Greater Glasgow	OSC605V	LRT Lothian
NBZ2604	J J Mcmenemy	NRS313W	Grampian	OGG181Y	Greater Glasgow	OSC606V	LRT Lothian

The Volvo Ailsa was built mainly for the Scottish bus market and, with Alexander bodywork, provides a local product. Volvo, who assemble the B6, B10 and Olympian in Scotland, dominate the British market for buses, especially for the double-decks. Pictured in Dundee, still with Tayside names, is Travel Dundee's 14, CSL614V. *Tony Wilson*

OSC607V	LRT Lothian	OSN855Y	Travel Dundee	OVT798	Midland Bluebird	P124KSL	Travel Dundee
OSC608V	LRT Lothian	OSN856Y	Travel Dundee	OVV850R	Fife Scottish	P125KSL	Travel Dundee
OSC609V	LRT Lothian	OSN857Y	Travel Dundee	OWR552M	Spa Motors	P126KSL	Travel Dundee
OSC610V	LRT Lothian	OSN858Y	Travel Dundee	OYJ64R	Rennie's	P127KSL	Travel Dundee
OSC611V	LRT Lothian	OSN859Y	Travel Dundee	OYS188M	Greater Glasgow	P128KSL	Travel Dundee
OSC612V	LRT Lothian	OSN860Y	Travel Dundee	P2GRT	Grampian	P129KSL	Travel Dundee
OSC613V	LRT Lothian	OSN861Y	Travel Dundee	P2HAD	H-A-D Coaches	P130KSL	Travel Dundee
OSC614V	LRT Lothian	OSN862Y	Travel Dundee	P2UVG	Greater Glasgow	P131KSL	Travel Dundee
OSC615V	LRT Lothian	OSN863Y	Travel Dundee	P2WBC	Bryans of Denny	P132KSL	Travel Dundee
OSC616V	LRT Lothian	OSN864Y	Travel Dundee	P3BUS	Stonehouse	P133KSL	Travel Dundee
OSC617V	LRT Lothian	OSN865Y	Travel Dundee	P3HAD	H-A-D Coaches	P134KSL	Travel Dundee
OSC618V	LRT Lothian	OSN866Y	Travel Dundee	P4GRT	Grampian	P135KSL	Travel Dundee
OSC619V	LRT Lothian	OSN867Y	Travel Dundee	P10TAY	Travel Dundee	P136KSL	Travel Dundee
OSC620V	LRT Lothian	OSN868Y	Travel Dundee	P20GRT	Grampian	P137KSL	Travel Dundcc
OSD720H	Paterson's	OSN870Y	Travel Dundee	P20SOU	Southern Cs	P138KSL	Travel Dundee
OSF925M	LRT Lothian	OSN871Y	Travel Dundee	P25RFS	Greater Glasgow	P139KSL	Travel Dundee
OSF928M	LRT Lothian	OSN872Y	Travel Dundee	P26RFS	Greater Glasgow	P140KSL	Travel Dundee
OSF939M	LRT Lothian	OSN873Y	Travel Dundee	P50SOU	Southern Cs	P141KSL	Travel Dundee
OSF942M	LRT Lothian	OSN874Y	Travel Dundee	P59KSK	Royal Mail	P145MNB	Woods
OSG53V	Lowland	OSN875Y	Travel Dundee	P60SOU	Southern Cs	P146MNB	Woods
OSG65V	Midland Bluebird	OSR203R	Highland Country	P69PSB	Silver Fox	P148ASA	Western Buses
OSG71V	Lowland	OTB55	H-A-D Coaches	P70JDS	Docherty Midland	P149ASA	Western Buses
OSG71V	Midland Bluebird	OTS271	Travel Dundee	P70SOU	Southern Cs	P150ASA	Western Buses
OSJ616R	Marbill	OTU971V	Spa Motors	P76KSC	LRT Lothian	P151ASA	Western Buses
OSJ617R	H-A-D Coaches	OUC57R	Marbill	P77JDS	Docherty Midland	P151KSM	McEwan's
OSJ634R	Bluebird Buses	OUS11Y	Greater Glasgow	P78OSC	LRT Lothian	P151LSC	Dart
OSJ635R	Bluebird Buses	OUS12Y	Greater Glasgow	P100WCM	West Coast Motors	P152ASA	Western Buses
OSJ636R	Western Buses	OUS13Y	Greater Glasgow	P106MFS	Greater Glasgow	P152FBC	Rennie's
OSJ643R	Bluebird Buses	OUS14Y	Greater Glasgow	P107MFS	Greater Glasgow	P152KSM	McEwan's
OSJ644R	Bluebird Buses	OUS15Y	Greater Glasgow	P108MFS	Greater Glasgow	P152LSC	Dart
OSK784	Bluebird Buses	OUS16Y	Greater Glasgow	P109MFS	Greater Glasgow	P153ASA	Western Buses
OSN851Y	Travel Dundee	OUS17Y	Greater Glasgow	P120GSR	Travel Dundee	P153FBC	Rennie's
OSN852Y	Travel Dundee	OUS18Y	Greater Glasgow	P121GSR	Travel Dundee	P153KSM	McEwan's
OSN853Y	Travel Dundee	OUS19Y	Greater Glasgow	P122KSL	Travel Dundee	P154ASA	Western Buses
OSN854Y	Travel Dundee	OUS20Y	Greater Glasgow	P123KSL	Travel Dundee	P154FBC	Rennie's

The Scottish Bus Handbook

Liveried for the Clyde Coaster service is Clydeside's 805, P805RWU seen heading fo Greenock in May 1997. The vehicle is one of the 1996 intake of low-floor Dennis Darts that are fitted with Plaxton Pointer bodywork. *Nick Coleman*

P156ASA	Western Buses	P193UNS	Greater Glasgow	P219SGB	Clydeside	P274PSX	LRT Lothian
P157ASA	Western Buses	P194TGD	Greater Glasgow	P220SGB	Clydeside	P275PSX	LRT Lothian
P158ASA	Western Buses	P195TGD	Greater Glasgow	P221SGB	Clydeside	P276PSX	LRT Lothian
P159ASA	Western Buses	P196TGD	Greater Glasgow	P222GSM	Maynes	P277PSX	LRT Lothian
P160ASA	Western Buses	P197TGD	Greater Glasgow	P223SGB	Clydeside	P278PSX	LRT Lothian
P166LSC	Stonehouse	P198OSE	Western Buses	P224SGB	Clydeside	P278VUS	H Crawford
P171DMS	Midland Bluebird	P198TGD	Greater Glasgow	P225SGB	Clydeside	P279PSX	LRT Lothian
P172DMS	Midland Bluebird	P199OSE	Western Buses	P226SGB	Clydeside	P279VUS	H Crawford
P173DMS	Lowland	P199TGD	Greater Glasgow	P227SGB	Clydeside	P281PSX	LRT Lothian
P174DMS	Lowland	P200WCM	West Coast Motors	P240OSF	Henderson Travel	P282PSX	LRT Lothian
P174TGD	Greater Glasgow	P201NSC	Midland Bluebird	P240VGD	Bruce Coaches	P283PSX	LRT Lothian
P175TGD	Greater Glasgow	P201TGD	Greater Glasgow	P251PSX	LRT Lothian	P284PSX	LRT Lothian
P176TGD	Greater Glasgow	P202NSC	Midland Bluebird	P252PSX	LRT Lothian	P285PSX	LRT Lothian
P177TGD	Greater Glasgow	P202TGD	Greater Glasgow	P253PSX	LRT Lothian	P310HSN	Strathtay
P178TGD	Greater Glasgow	P203CGA	Hutchison	P254PSX	LRT Lothian	P311HSN	Strathtay
P179TGD	Greater Glasgow	P203NSC	Midland Bluebird	P255ASA	Western Buses	P316UHS	Irvines of Law
P180TGD	Greater Glasgow	P203TGD	Greater Glasgow	P255PSX	LRT Lothian	P341ASO	Bluebird Buses
P181TGD	Greater Glasgow	P204NSC	Midland Bluebird	P256PSX	LRT Lothian	P342ASO	Bluebird Buses
P182TGD	Greater Glasgow	P204TGD	Greater Glasgow	P257PSX	LRT Lothian	P343ASO	Bluebird Buses
P183TGD	Greater Glasgow	P205NSC	Midland Bluebird	P258PSX	LRT Lothian	P344ASO	Bluebird Buses
P184TGD	Greater Glasgow	P206GSR	Travel Dundee	P259PSX	LRT Lothian	P345ASO	Bluebird Buses
P185TGD	Greater Glasgow	P206NSC	Midland Bluebird	P260PSX	LRT Lothian	P346ASO	Bluebird Buses
P186TGD	Greater Glasgow	P207GSR	Travel Dundee	P261PSX	LRT Lothian	P347ASO	Bluebird Buses
P187TGD	Greater Glasgow	P207NSC	Midland Bluebird	P262PSX	LRT Lothian	P348ASO	Bluebird Buses
P188TGD	Greater Glasgow	P208GSR	Travel Dundee	P263PSX	LRT Lothian	P349ASO	Bluebird Buses
P188UNS	Greater Glasgow	P208NSC	Midland Bluebird	P264PSX	LRT Lothian	P350ASO	Bluebird Buses
P189TGD	Greater Glasgow	P209NSC	Midland Bluebird	P265PSX	LRT Lothian	P351ASO	Bluebird Buses
P189UNS	Greater Glasgow	P210NSC	Midland Bluebird	P266PSX	LRT Lothian	P352ASO	Bluebird Buses
P190TGD	Greater Glasgow	P211NSC	Midland Bluebird	P267PSX	LRT Lothian	P361DSA	Stagecoach Glasgow
P190UNS	Greater Glasgow	P212NSC	Midland Bluebird	P268PSX	LRT Lothian	P362DSA	Stagecoach Glasgow
P191TGD	Greater Glasgow	P213NSC	Midland Bluebird	P269PSX	LRT Lothian	P363DSA	Stagecoach Glasgow
P191UNS	Greater Glasgow	P214NSC	Lowland	P270PSX	LRT Lothian	P364DSA	Stagecoach Glasgow
P192TGD	Greater Glasgow	P215NSC	Lowland	P271PSX	LRT Lothian	P365DSA	Stagecoach Glasgow
P192UNS	Greater Glasgow	P217SGB	Clydeside	P272PSX	LRT Lothian	P366DSA	Stagecoach Glasgow
P193TGD	Greater Glasgow	P218SGB	Clydeside	P273PSX	LRT Lothian	P367DSA	Stagecoach Glasgow

Reg	Operator	Reg	Operator	Reg	Operator	Reg	Operator
P368DSA	Stagecoach Glasgow	P490TGA	Argyle Bus Group	P548TYS	Greater Glasgow	P613CMS	Fife Scottish
P369DSA	Stagecoach Glasgow	P491BRS	Bluebird Buses	P549BSS	Grampian	P613WSU	Greater Glasgow
P370DSA	Stagecoach Glasgow	P491FAS	Rapsons	P549NSC	Royal Mail	P614WSU	Greater Glasgow
P371DSA	Stagecoach Glasgow	P491TGA	Argyle Bus Group	P549TYS	Greater Glasgow	P615WSU	Greater Glasgow
P372DSA	Stagecoach Glasgow	P492BRS	Bluebird Buses	P550MSF	Spa Motors	P616WSU	Greater Glasgow
P373DSA	Stagecoach Glasgow	P492FAS	Rapsons	P550NSC	Royal Mail	P617WSU	Greater Glasgow
P373XGG	Clyde Coast	P492TGA	Argyle Bus Group	P550XTL	Silver Coach Lines	P618WSU	Greater Glasgow
P374DSA	Stagecoach Glasgow	P493BRS	Bluebird Buses	P551XTL	Silver Coach Lines	P619WSU	Greater Glasgow
P375DSA	Stagecoach Glasgow	P494BRS	Bluebird Buses	P552XTL	Silver Coach Lines	P620WSU	Greater Glasgow
P376DSA	Stagecoach Glasgow	P495BRS	Bluebird Buses	P553KSD	Marbill	P621WSU	Greater Glasgow
P377DSA	Stagecoach Glasgow	P496BRS	Bluebird Buses	P554KSD	Marbill	P622WSU	Greater Glasgow
P378DSA	Stagecoach Glasgow	P497BRS	Bluebird Buses	P555GSM	Maynes	P623WSU	Greater Glasgow
P379DSA	Stagecoach Glasgow	P498BRS	Bluebird Buses	P563MSX	Fife Scottish	P624WSU	Greater Glasgow
P380DSA	Stagecoach Glasgow	P499BRS	Bluebird Buses	P564MSX	Fife Scottish	P625NSE	Bluebird Buses
P381DSA	Stagecoach Glasgow	P500GSM	Maynes	P565MSX	Fife Scottish	P625WSU	Greater Glasgow
P382DSA	Stagecoach Glasgow	P502VUS	Hutchison	P566MSX	Fife Scottish	P626NSE	Bluebird Buses
P383DSA	Stagecoach Glasgow	P502XGA	Allander Travel	P567MSX	Fife Scottish	P626WSU	Greater Glasgow
P384DSA	Stagecoach Glasgow	P503VUS	Hutchison	P568MSX	Fife Scottish	P627WSU	Greater Glasgow
P385DSA	Stagecoach Glasgow	P503XGA	Allander Travel	P569MSX	Fife Scottish	P628WSU	Greater Glasgow
P386DSA	Stagecoach Glasgow	P503XSH	Lowland	P572NSC	Royal Mail	P629WSU	Greater Glasgow
P387ARY	Rennie's	P504VUS	Hutchison	P573NSC	Royal Mail	P630WSU	Greater Glasgow
P388ARY	Rennie's	P504XSH	Lowland	P574NSC	Royal Mail	P631WSU	Greater Glasgow
P389ARY	Rennie's	P505VUS	Hutchison	P575DMS	Midland Bluebird	P632WSU	Greater Glasgow
P390LPS	Western Buses	P505XSH	Lowland	P575NSC	Royal Mail	P633WSU	Greater Glasgow
P390OFS	Glen Coaches	P506VUS	Hutchison	P576DMS	Midland Bluebird	P634WSU	Greater Glasgow
P391LPS	Western Buses	P506XSH	Lowland	P576NSC	Royal Mail	P635WSU	Greater Glasgow
P392LPS	Western Buses	P507VUS	Hutchison	P577DMS	Midland Bluebird	P648FST	Rapsons
P393LPS	Western Buses	P508VUS	Hutchison	P578DMS	Midland Bluebird	P649FST	Rapsons
P394LPS	Western Buses	P519PYS	Greater Glasgow	P579NSC	Royal Mail	P670EWB	Fife Scottish
P395BRS	Western Buses	P520PYS	Greater Glasgow	P580NSC	Royal Mail	P671EWB	Fife Scottish
P396BRS	Western Buses	P521PYS	Greater Glasgow	P581NSC	Royal Mail	P682DRS	Whytes
P397BRS	Western Buses	P522PYS	Greater Glasgow	P582NSC	Royal Mail	P683DRS	Whytes
P398BRS	Western Buses	P523PYS	Greater Glasgow	P583NSC	Royal Mail	P684DRS	Whytes
P408KSX	LRT Lothian	P524PYS	Greater Glasgow	P583RGB	Glen Coaches	P685DRS	Whytes
P409KSX	LRT Lothian	P525PYS	Greater Glasgow	P585WSU	Greater Glasgow	P736FMS	Mackies
P410KSX	LRT Lothian	P526PYS	Greater Glasgow	P586WSU	Greater Glasgow	P737FMS	Mackies
P411KSX	LRT Lothian	P526UGA	Argyle Bus Group	P587WSU	Greater Glasgow	P738FMS	Mackies
P412KSX	LRT Lothian	P527PYS	Greater Glasgow	P588WSU	Greater Glasgow	P739FMS	Mackies
P413KSX	LRT Lothian	P527UGA	Argyle Bus Group	P589WSU	Greater Glasgow	P741HND	AA Buses
P414KSX	LRT Lothian	P528PYS	Greater Glasgow	P590WSU	Greater Glasgow	P748WSU	Greater Glasgow
P414MFS	Henderson Travel	P528UGA	Argyle Bus Group	P591WSU	Greater Glasgow	P749WSU	Greater Glasgow
P415KSX	LRT Lothian	P529PYS	Greater Glasgow	P592WSU	Greater Glasgow	P750WSU	Greater Glasgow
P416KSX	LRT Lothian	P529UGA	Argyle Bus Group	P593WSU	Greater Glasgow	P751WSU	Greater Glasgow
P417KSX	LRT Lothian	P530PYS	Greater Glasgow	P594WSU	Greater Glasgow	P752WSU	Greater Glasgow
P418KSX	LRT Lothian	P531TYS	Greater Glasgow	P595WSU	Greater Glasgow	P753WSU	Greater Glasgow
P419KSX	LRT Lothian	P532TYS	Greater Glasgow	P596WSU	Greater Glasgow	P754WSU	Greater Glasgow
P420KSX	LRT Lothian	P533TYS	Greater Glasgow	P597WSU	Greater Glasgow	P756WSU	Greater Glasgow
P421KSX	LRT Lothian	P534TYS	Greater Glasgow	P598WSU	Greater Glasgow	P757WSU	Greater Glasgow
P422KSX	LRT Lothian	P535TYS	Greater Glasgow	P599WSU	Greater Glasgow	P758WSU	Greater Glasgow
P423KSX	LRT Lothian	P536TYS	Greater Glasgow	P601WSU	Greater Glasgow	P759WSU	Greater Glasgow
P424KSX	LRT Lothian	P537TYS	Greater Glasgow	P602WSU	Greater Glasgow	P760WSU	Greater Glasgow
P425KSX	LRT Lothian	P538TYS	Greater Glasgow	P603WSU	Greater Glasgow	P761WSU	Greater Glasgow
P426KSX	LRT Lothian	P539TYS	Greater Glasgow	P604WSU	Greater Glasgow	P761XHS	Greater Glasgow
P427KSX	LRT Lothian	P540BSS	Grampian	P605WSU	Greater Glasgow	P762WSU	Greater Glasgow
P428KSX	LRT Lothian	P540TYS	Greater Glasgow	P606CMS	Fife Scottish	P762XHS	Greater Glasgow
P429KSX	LRT Lothian	P541BSS	Grampian	P606WND	AA Buses	P763XHS	Greater Glasgow
P430KSX	LRT Lothian	P541TYS	Greater Glasgow	P606WSU	Greater Glasgow	P764XHS	Greater Glasgow
P431KSX	LRT Lothian	P542BSS	Grampian	P607CMS	Fife Scottish	P765XHS	Greater Glasgow
P432KSX	LRT Lothian	P542TYS	Greater Glasgow	P607WSU	Greater Glasgow	P766XHS	Greater Glasgow
P433KSX	LRT Lothian	P543BSS	Grampian	P608CMS	Fife Scottish	P767XHS	Greater Glasgow
P438NSC	Royal Mail	P543TYS	Greater Glasgow	P608WSU	Greater Glasgow	P768XHS	Greater Glasgow
P454MFS	Henderson Travel	P544BSS	Grampian	P609CMS	Fife Scottish	P769XHS	Greater Glasgow
P454SSK	Morrison's	P544TYS	Greater Glasgow	P609WSU	Greater Glasgow	P770XHS	Greater Glasgow
P455MFS	Henderson Travel	P545BSS	Grampian	P610CMS	Fife Scottish	P771BJF	Owens Coaches
P463NSC	Royal Mail	P545TYS	Greater Glasgow	P610WSU	Greater Glasgow	P771XHS	Greater Glasgow
P464NSC	Royal Mail	P546BSS	Grampian	P611CMS	Fife Scottish	P774XHS	Greater Glasgow
P465NSC	Royal Mail	P546TYS	Greater Glasgow	P611WSU	Greater Glasgow	P779BJF	Owens Coaches
P466NSC	Royal Mail	P547BSS	Grampian	P612CMS	Fife Scottish	P798KSF	Glen Coaches
P467JSP	Dochert'y Midland	P547TYS	Greater Glasgow	P612RGB	Stonehouse	P799KSF	Rowe's
P489TGA	Clyde Coast	P548BSS	Grampian	P612WSU	Greater Glasgow	P801RWU	Clydeside

The Scottish Bus Handbook

Reg	Operator	Reg	Operator	Reg	Operator	Reg	Operator
P802RWU	Clydeside	PRA112R	Bluebird Buses	PUX705M	Shalder	RDS602W	Greater Glasgow
P803RWU	Clydeside	PRU917R	Fife Scottish	PVS20W	Shalder	RDS603W	Greater Glasgow
P804RWU	Clydeside	PSC55Y	LRT Lothian	PYB464	Spa Motors	RDS604W	Greater Glasgow
P805RWU	Clydeside	PSC56Y	LRT Lothian	PYJ136	Travel Dundee	RDS605W	Greater Glasgow
P806DBS	Clydeside	PSC57Y	LRT Lothian	RAN644R	Highland Country	RDS606W	Greater Glasgow
P807DBS	Clydeside	PSC58Y	LRT Lothian	RAN645R	Highland Country	RDS607W	Greater Glasgow
P808DBS	Clydeside	PSF311Y	Lowland	RAX804M	Keenan of Ayr	RDS608W	Greater Glasgow
P809DBS	Clydeside	PSF313Y	Lowland	RCH155R	Spa Motors	RDS609W	Greater Glasgow
P810DBS	Clydeside	PSF314Y	Lowland	RCS382	Western Buses	RDS611W	Greater Glasgow
P825PSG	Silver Coach Lines	PSF315Y	Lowland	RCS702R	H-A-D Coaches	RDS613W	Greater Glasgow
P852VUS	Greater Glasgow	PSF316Y	Lowland	RDS540W	Greater Glasgow	RDS614W	Greater Glasgow
P853VUS	Greater Glasgow	PSR781	Travel Dundee	RDS541W	Greater Glasgow	RDS615W	Greater Glasgow
P854VUS	Greater Glasgow	PSU314	Lowland	RDS542W	Greater Glasgow	RDS617W	Greater Glasgow
P855VUS	Greater Glasgow	PSU315	Lowland	RDS543W	Greater Glasgow	RDS618W	Greater Glasgow
P856VUS	Greater Glasgow	PSU316	Lowland	RDS544W	Greater Glasgow	RFS579V	Western Buses
P857VUS	Greater Glasgow	PSU317	Lowland	RDS545W	Greater Glasgow	RFS580V	Lowland
P858VUS	Greater Glasgow	PSU318	Lowland	RDS546W	Greater Glasgow	RFS583V	Western Buses
P859VUS	Greater Glasgow	PSU319	Lowland	RDS547W	Greater Glasgow	RGD383W	Bowman
P860VUS	Greater Glasgow	PSU320	Lowland	RDS548W	Greater Glasgow	RGD968W	Paterson's
P861VUS	Greater Glasgow	PSU321	Lowland	RDS549W	Greater Glasgow	RHK402M	Spa Motors
P877MNE	Stagecoach Glasgow	PSU322	Lowland	RDS550W	Greater Glasgow	RHK403M	Spa Motors
P877YKS	Midland Bluebird	PSU339	Travel Dundee	RDS551W	Greater Glasgow	RIB4309	Bluebird Buses
P878MNE	Stagecoach Glasgow	PSU340	Travel Dundee	RDS552W	Greater Glasgow	RIB7742	Wilson's, Carnwath
P878YKS	Midland Bluebird	PSU371	Strathtay	RDS553W	Greater Glasgow	RIB8035	Morrison's
P879YKS	Midland Bluebird	PSU372	Strathtay	RDS554W	Greater Glasgow	RIB9362	McEwan's
P881MNE	Stagecoach Glasgow	PSU373	Strathtay	RDS555W	Greater Glasgow	RJA702R	Western Buses
P883MNE	Stagecoach Glasgow	PSU374	Strathtay	RDS556W	Greater Glasgow	RJA801R	Marbill
P884MNE	Stagecoach Glasgow	PSU375	Strathtay	RDS557W	Greater Glasgow	RJI1890	Clyde Coast
P885MNE	Stagecoach Glasgow	PSU376	Strathtay	RDS558W	Greater Glasgow	RJI4578	Irvines of Law
P885USU	Irvines of Law	PSU609	Grampian	RDS559W	Greater Glasgow	RJI5351	Dart
P886MNE	Stagecoach Glasgow	PSU610	Silver Coach Lines	RDS560W	Greater Glasgow	RJI6395	Clyde Coast
P889MNE	Stagecoach Glasgow	PSU611	Silver Coach Lines	RDS561W	Greater Glasgow	RJI6494	Clyde Coast
P891MNE	Stagecoach Glasgow	PSU612	Silver Coach Lines	RDS562W	Greater Glasgow	RJI7949	Clyde Coast
P893MNE	Stagecoach Glasgow	PSU613	Silver Coach Lines	RDS563W	Greater Glasgow	RJI7976	Clyde Coast
P894MNE	Stagecoach Glasgow	PSU614	Silver Coach Lines	RDS564W	Greater Glasgow	RJI8711	Clyde Coast
P904DST	Highland Country	PSU615	Silver Coach Lines	RDS565W	Greater Glasgow	RJI8712	Clyde Coast
P905DST	Highland Country	PSU616	Silver Coach Lines	RDS566W	Greater Glasgow	RJI8713	Clyde Coast
P906DST	Highland Country	PSU617	Silver Coach Lines	RDS567W	Greater Glasgow	RJT153R	Fife Scottish
P907DST	Highland Country	PSU618	Silver Coach Lines	RDS568W	Greater Glasgow	RJT155R	Bluebird Buses
P930YSB	Argyle Bus Group	PSU622	Midland Bluebird	RDS569W	Greater Glasgow	RMS398W	Midland Bluebird
P931YSB	Argyle Bus Group	PSU623	Grampian	RDS570W	Greater Glasgow	RMS399W	Midland Bluebird
P932YSB	Argyle Bus Group	PSU624	Grampian	RDS571W	Greater Glasgow	RMS400W	Midland Bluebird
P936YSB	Argyle Bus Group	PSU625	Midland Bluebird	RDS572W	Greater Glasgow	RMS401W	Greater Glasgow
P937YSB	Argyle Bus Group	PSU626	Grampian	RDS573W	Greater Glasgow	RMS402W	Greater Glasgow
P938YSB	Harte	PSU627	Grampian	RDS574W	Greater Glasgow	RNP957P	Shalder
P991TGB	Stonehouse	PSU628	Grampian	RDS575W	Greater Glasgow	RPR716R	Fife Scottish
P995RHS	Hutchison	PSU629	Grampian	RDS576W	Greater Glasgow	RRA221X	Docherty of Irvine
PAG318H	Docherty of Irvine	PSU631	Grampian	RDS577W	Greater Glasgow	RRS46R	Bluebird Buses
PAU200R	Marbill	PSU698	Silver Coach Lines	RDS578W	Greater Glasgow	RRS47R	Bluebird Buses
PES190Y	Bluebird Buses	PSU968	Grampian	RDS579W	Greater Glasgow	RRS48R	Bluebird Buses
PEX386R	Rennie's	PSV223	Hutchison	RDS580W	Greater Glasgow	RRS50R	Bluebird Buses
PFG362	Mackies	PSX180Y	Fife Scottish	RDS581W	Greater Glasgow	RRS53R	Bluebird Buses
PGA826V	Greater Glasgow	PSX181Y	Fife Scottish	RDS582W	Greater Glasgow	RSB7S	West Coast Motors
PGA832V	Greater Glasgow	PSX182Y	Fife Scottish	RDS583W	Greater Glasgow	RSC190Y	Fife Scottish
PGA833V	McEwan's	PSX183Y	Fife Scottish	RDS584W	Greater Glasgow	RSC191Y	Fife Scottish
PGA834V	Greater Glasgow	PSX184Y	Fife Scottish	RDS585W	Greater Glasgow	RSC192Y	Fife Scottish
PGA835V	Greater Glasgow	PSX185Y	Fife Scottish	RDS586W	Greater Glasgow	RSC194Y	Fife Scottish
PHH409R	Rennie's	PSX186Y	Fife Scottish	RDS587W	Greater Glasgow	RSX591V	Lowland
PIB9211	Rennie's	PSX187Y	Fife Scottish	RDS588W	Greater Glasgow	RTH924S	Fife Scottish
PIJ601	Rennie's	PSX188Y	Fife Scottish	RDS589W	Greater Glasgow	RUS326R	Rennie's
PIJ5751	Bowman	PSX189Y	Fife Scottish	RDS591W	Greater Glasgow	RUS327R	Rennie's
PIW2891	Rennie's	PTT71R	McEwan's	RDS592W	Greater Glasgow	RUS330R	Rennie's
PJI1825	Gibson	PUF249M	Maynes	RDS593W	Greater Glasgow	RUS331R	Rennie's
PJI4983	Western Buses	PUS150W	Greater Glasgow	RDS594W	Greater Glasgow	RVB973S	Fife Scottish
PJI6085	Meffan	PUS151W	Greater Glasgow	RDS595W	Greater Glasgow	RVB974S	Fife Scottish
PJJ16S	Fife Scottish	PUS152W	Greater Glasgow	RDS597W	Greater Glasgow	RVB978S	Fife Scottish
PJO448P	Wilson's, Carnwath	PUS153W	Greater Glasgow	RDS598W	Greater Glasgow	RYG386R	Spa Motors
PNW344W	McEwan's	PUS154W	Greater Glasgow	RDS599W	Greater Glasgow	RYK820Y	Fife Scottish
PRA109R	Bluebird Buses	PUS155W	Greater Glasgow	RDS600W	Greater Glasgow	SAO410R	Bluebird Buses
PRA110R	Bluebird Buses	PUS156W	Greater Glasgow	RDS601W	Greater Glasgow	SAO412R	Bluebird Buses

The Scottish Bus Handbook

Reg	Operator	Reg	Operator	Reg	Operator	Reg	Operator
SAS855T	Highland Country	SSX603V	Lowland	TJI1692	Argyle Bus Group	TSJ90S	Henderson Travel
SAS856T	Highland Country	SSX604V	Lowland	TJI3140	Galloways	TSJ593S	Lowland
SAS857T	Highland Country	SSX605V	Lowland	TJI3141	Galloways	TSJ596S	Lowland
SAS858T	Highland	SSX606V	Lowland	TJI3142	Galloways	TSJ599S	Lowland
SAS859T	Highland	SSX607V	Lowland	TJI3143	Galloways	TSJ600S	Lowland
SAS860T	Highland	SSX608V	Midland Bluebird	TJI5390	AA Buses	TSN576M	Rowe's
SBA202R	Keenan of Ayr	SSX609V	Lowland	TJI5391	AA Buses	TSO12X	Bluebird Buses
SCN244S	Fife Scottish	SSX610V	Lowland	TJI5392	AA Buses	TSO13X	Bluebird Buses
SCN258S	Wilson's, Carnwath	SSX612V	Lowland	TJI5393	AA Buses	TSO14X	Bluebird Buses
SCN261S	Fife Scottish	SSX613V	Lowland	TJI5394	AA Buses	TSO15X	Bluebird Buses
SCN266S	Wilson's, Carnwath	SSX618V	Lowland	TJI5399	AA Buses	TSO16X	Bluebird Buses
SCN272S	Greater Glasgow	SSX619V	Lowland	TJI6494	Clyde Coast	TSO17X	Bluebird Buses
SCN273S	Wilson's, Carnwath	SSX620V	Lowland	TJI6494	Clyde Coast	TSO18X	Strathtay
SCN280S	Wilson's, Carnwath	SSX621V	Lowland	TMA254V	Bowman	TSO20X	Bluebird Buses
SCN285S	Wilson's, Carnwath	SSX622V	Lowland	TME134M	Skye-Ways	TSO21X	Bluebird Buses
SCN288S	Wilson's, Carnwath	SSX624V	Midland Bluebird	TMS403X	Midland Bluebird	TSO22X	Strathtay
SCS384M	Docherty of Irvine	SSX625V	Midland Bluebird	TMS404X	Western Buses	TSO23X	Bluebird Buses
SDA617S	Paterson's	SSX627V	Lowland	TMS405X	Western Buses	TSO24X	Bluebird Buses
SDD137R	Gibson	SSX628V	Lowland	TMS406X	Western Buses	TSO25X	Strathtay
SFJ124R	McEwan's	SSX629V	Lowland	TMS407X	Western Buses	TSO26X	Strathtay
SFJ151R	Gibson	SSX630V	Lowland	TMS408X	Midland Bluebird	TSO27X	Strathtay
SFV428P	Paterson's	STG476Y	Keenan of Ayr	TMS409X	Strathtay	TSO28X	Strathtay
SIB8045	Paterson's	STJ31T	Highland Country	TMS410X	Midland Bluebird	TSO29X	Bluebird Buses
SJI1976	Wilson's, Carnwath	STJ34T	Highland Country	TMS411X	Midland Bluebird	TSO30X	Bluebird Buses
SJW515	AA Buses	STL743	Wilson's, Carnwath	TMS412X	Midland Bluebird	TSO31X	Bluebird Buses
SL8207	Mackies	SUS600W	Greater Glasgow	TMU847Y	McEwan's	TSO32X	Bluebird Buses
SL8417	Mackies	SUS601W	Greater Glasgow	TND139X	Highland Country	TSU638	Western Buses
SL8852	Mackies	SUS602W	Greater Glasgow	TOS866X	Argyle Bus Group	TSU642W	Clydeside
SLJ387X	Wilson's, Carnwath	SUS603W	Greater Glasgow	TPC108X	Greater Glasgow	TSU643W	Greater Glasgow
SMS120P	Highland Country	SUS604W	Greater Glasgow	TPC109X	Whitelaw's	TSU644W	Greater Glasgow
SMS123P	Highland Country	SUS605W	Greater Glasgow	TPD106X	Clydeside	TSU645W	Greater Glasgow
SMS124P	Highland Country	SUS606W	Greater Glasgow	TPD116X	Clydeside	TSU646W	Greater Glasgow
SMS125P	Highland Country	SUS607W	Greater Glasgow	TPD130X	Clydeside	TSU647W	Greater Glasgow
SMS128P	Highland Country	SV2923	Wilson's, Carnwath	TPJ67S	McEwan's	TSU648W	Greater Glasgow
SMS130P	Highland Country	SWW299R	Moffat & Williamson	TPU70R	Paterson's	TSU649W	Greater Glasgow
SNS826W	Western Buses	TAG516M	Paterson's	TRS333	Grampian	TSU650W	Greater Glasgow
SOI9994	Meffan	TAP288R	Galson Motors	TRY51S	Galson Motors	TSU651	Grampian
SSA2X	Bluebird Buses	TAY71X	Travel Dundee	TSD285	Docherty of Irvine	TSU651W	Greater Glasgow
SSA3X	Bluebird Buses	TDR725	Dochert'y Midland	TSJ31S	Western Buses	TSU652W	Greater Glasgow
SSA4X	Bluebird Buses	TDS611R	McGill's	TSJ32S	Western Buses	TSU653W	Greater Glasgow
SSA5X	Bluebird Buses	TFN990T	Fife Scottish	TSJ33S	Western Buses	TSU682	Midland Bluebird
SSA6X	Bluebird Buses	TFS106Y	LRT Lothian	TSJ35S	Clydeside	TSV497	Hutchison
SSA7X	Bluebird Buses	TFS107Y	LRT Lothian	TSJ36S	Clydeside	TSV612	Midland Bluebird
SSA8X	Strathtay	TGD221R	Bowman	TSJ37S	Clydeside	TSV677	Bowman
SSA9X	Strathtay	TGE825R	Greater Glasgow	TSJ38S	Clydeside	TSV718	Bluebird Buses
SSA10X	Strathtay	TGE840R	Greater Glasgow	TSJ39S	Clydeside	TSV719	Bluebird Buses
SSA11X	Strathtay	TGG378W	Greater Glasgow	TSJ41S	Clydeside	TSV720	Bluebird Buses
SSC108P	Lowland	TGG381W	Greater Glasgow	TSJ42P	Clydeside	TSV721	Bluebird Buses
SSN239S	Clyde Coast	TGG383W	Greater Glasgow	TSJ43S	Clydeside	TSV722	Bluebird Buses
33N241R	Travel Dundee	TGG384W	Greater Glasgow	TSJ44S	Clydeside	TSV778	Bluebird Buses
SSN247S	Clyde Coast	TGG385W	Greater Glasgow	TSJ47S	Clydeside	TSV779	Bluebird Buses
SSN248S	Clyde Coast	TGG386W	Greater Glasgow	TSJ50S	Clydeside	TSV780	Bluebird Buses
SSN253S	Paterson's	TGG742R	Greater Glasgow	TSJ51S	Clydeside	TSV781	Bluebird Buses
SSN255S	Paterson's	TGG744R	Greater Glasgow	TSJ52S	Clydeside	TTK248	Galson Motors
SSU397R	Whitelaw's	TGG745R	Greater Glasgow	TSJ53S	Clydeside	TVP856S	Highland Country
SSU727	Oban & District	TGG749R	Greater Glasgow	TSJ54S	Clydeside	TVP862S	Highland Country
SSU816	Midland Bluebird	TGG754R	Greater Glasgow	TSJ56S	Clydeside	TVP864S	Highland Country
SSU821	Midland Bluebird	TGG760R	Rennie's	TSJ58S	Clydeside	TVP865S	Highland Country
SSU827	Midland Bluebird	THB420Y	Shalder	TSJ60S	Clydeside	TYS255W	Lowland
SSU829	Midland Bluebird	THB424Y	Shalder	TSJ63S	Clydeside	TYS264W	Lowland
SSU831	Midland Bluebird	THB541Y	Keenan of Ayr	TSJ67S	Western Buses	TYS268W	Irvines of Law
SSU837	Midland Bluebird	THX642S	Shuttle Buses	TSJ70S	Western Buses	TYS270W	Moffat & Williamson
SSU841	Midland Bluebird	TIA6937	Golden Eagle	TSJ71S	Western Buses	UAS63T	Highland Country
SSU851	Oban & District	TIB4022	Paterson's	TSJ76S	Western Buses	UAS64T	Highland
SSU857	Midland Bluebird	TIB8511	Greater Glasgow	TSJ78S	Western Buses	UAS65T	Highland Country
SSU859	Midland Bluebird	TIB8512	Greater Glasgow	TSJ79S	Western Buses	UAS66T	Highland
SSU861	Midland Bluebird	TIB8513	Greater Glasgow	TSJ80S	Western Buses	UAS67T	Highland Country
SSU897	Midland Bluebird	TIW572S	Marbill	TSJ84S	Clydeside	UAS68T	Highland
SSX597V	Lowland	TJI1328	Keenan of Ayr	TSJ85S	Western Buses	UAS69T	Highland Country
SSX602V	Lowland	TJI1687	Rennie's	TSJ87S	Clydeside	UAS70T	Highland Country

The Scottish Bus Handbook

UAS71T	Highland Country	ULS643X	Midland Bluebird	VJI6963	Dart	WGB711W	Strathtay
UBM880	Stonehouse	ULS659T	Highland	VLT37	Western Buses	WHH414S	Rennie's
UCS659	Western Buses	ULS660T	Western Buses	VLT45	Strathtay	WHH415S	Fife Scottish
UCS896S	Clyde Coast	ULS673T	Strathtay	VLT54	Western Buses	WIA20	Docherty of Irvine
UFG50S	Greater Glasgow	ULS713X	Midland Bluebird	VLT77	Fife Scottish	WJM806T	Galloways
UFS875R	Fife Scottish	ULS714X	Midland Bluebird	VLT93	Strathtay	WLT357	Greater Glasgow
UFS876R	Fife Scottish	ULS716X	Midland Bluebird	VLT104	Western Buses	WLT388	Greater Glasgow
UFS877R	Fife Scottish	ULS717X	Midland Bluebird	VLT154	Western Buses	WLT408	Greater Glasgow
UFS878R	Fife Scottish	UM7681	Western Buses	VLT183	Strathtay	WLT415	Western Buses
UFT921T	Bowman	UMB985	Stonehouse	VLT217	Strathtay	WLT416	Western Buses
UGB193W	Greater Glasgow	UNA772S	Western Buses	VLT221	Strathtay	WLT427	Strathtay
UGB196W	Greater Glasgow	UNA824S	Western Buses	VLT272	Bluebird Buses	WLT439	Western Buses
UGB202W	Greater Glasgow	UNA840S	Western Buses	VLT298	Strathtay	WLT447	Western Buses
UGE388W	McGill's	UNA863S	Western Buses	VML5G	Silver Fox	WLT465	Western Buses
UGE389W	McGill's	UNS973W	Golden Eagle	VNB169L	Moffat & Williamson	WLT501	Western Buses
UGG394R	Greater Glasgow	UOT648	Bluebird Buses	VOH640	Strathtay	WLT526	Western Buses
UGG396R	Greater Glasgow	URB160S	Rennie's	VPR487S	Fife Scottish	WLT538	Western Buses
UGG398R	Greater Glasgow	URS316X	Grampian	VRM622S	Gibson	WLT546	Western Buses
UIB3076	Western Buses	URS317X	Grampian	VSB164M	West Coast Motors	WLT610	Strathtay
UIB3541	Western Buses	URS318X	Grampian	VSR591	Travel Dundee	WLT677	Greater Glasgow
UIB3542	Western Buses	URS319X	Grampian	VST915	Docherty of Irvine	WLT678	Greater Glasgow
UIB3543	Western Buses	URS320X	Grampian	VSX490V	Riddler	WLT697	Western Buses
UJI2169	Galloways	URS321X	Grampian	VTV167S	Fife Scottish	WLT720	Western Buses
UJI5786	AA Buses	URS322X	Grampian	VTV171S	Bluebird Buses	WLT724	Midland Bluebird
UJI5787	AA Buses	URS323X	Grampian	VUD29X	McEwan's	WLT727	Western Buses
UJI5789	AA Buses	URS324X	Grampian	VXI8734	Lowland	WLT741	Greater Glasgow
UJI8218	Shuttle Buses	URS325X	Grampian	VXU444	Midland Bluebird	WLT743	Strathtay
UJT366	H-A-D Coaches	URS326X	Grampian	VYJ893	McGill's	WLT760	Greater Glasgow
ULS96X	Greater Glasgow	URS327X	Grampian	WAG370X	Greater Glasgow	WLT770	Greater Glasgow
ULS97X	Greater Glasgow	URS328X	Grampian	WAG373X	Greater Glasgow	WLT774	Western Buses
ULS98X	Greater Glasgow	URS329X	Grampian	WAG374X	Greater Glasgow	WLT784	Strathtay
ULS99X	Greater Glasgow	URS330X	Grampian	WAG376X	Greater Glasgow	WLT794	Western Buses
ULS100X	Midland Bluebird	USE500R	Shalder	WAG377X	Greater Glasgow	WLT809	Western Buses
ULS101X	Midland Bluebird	USJ491Y	AA Buses	WAG378X	Greater Glasgow	WLT830	Western Buses
ULS102X	Midland Bluebird	USK500Y	Rapsons	WAG379X	Greater Glasgow	WLT910	Greater Glasgow
ULS103X	Midland Bluebird	USU661	Travel Dundee	WAG381X	Greater Glasgow	WLT917	Strathtay
ULS104X	Midland Bluebird	USU662	Travel Dundee	WAG513K	Docherty of Irvine	WLT921	Strathtay
ULS105X	Midland Bluebird	USV365	Whytes	WAO643Y	Bluebird Buses	WLT924	Clydeside
ULS106X	Midland Bluebird	USV809	Paterson's	WAS768V	Western Buses	WLT943	Strathtay
ULS107X	Midland Bluebird	USV810	Paterson's	WAS769V	Greater Glasgow	WLT956	Clydeside
ULS108X	Midland Bluebird	USX51V	LRT Lothian	WAS771V	Western Buses	WLT974	Clydeside
ULS109X	Midland Bluebird	USX53V	LRT Lothian	WBN467T	Greater Glasgow	WLT976	Greater Glasgow
ULS110X	Midland Bluebird	USX54V	LRT Lothian	WCK126V	Gibson	WLT978	Western Buses
ULS111X	Midland Bluebird	UVK288T	Wilson's, Carnwath	WCK129V	Gibson	WNH51W	Shuttle Buses
ULS112X	Midland Bluebird	UVK293T	Greater Glasgow	WCW312R	Clydeside	WPH112Y	Whitelaw's
ULS113X	Midland Bluebird	UWP105	Western Buses	WCW314R	Clydeside	WPH116Y	Greater Glasgow
ULS114X	Midland Bluebird	UWV605S	Bluebird Buses	WDS183V	Wilson's, Carnwath	WPH119Y	Galson Motors
ULS115X	Midland Bluebird	UWV607S	Western Buses	WDS210V	Clydeside	WPH128Y	Whitelaw's
ULS317T	Greater Glasgow	UWV608S	Bluebird Buses	WDS212V	Clydeside	WPH140Y	Whitelaw's
ULS323T	Strathtay	UWV609S	Bluebird Buses	WDS216V	Clydeside	WSB187V	West Coast Motors
ULS324T	Irvines of Law	UWV611S	Bluebird Buses	WEX828X	McEwan's	WSH433V	Spa Motors
ULS330T	Meffan	UWV613S	Bluebird Buses	WFS135W	Bluebird Buses	WSU209	Stokes
ULS333T	Highland	UWV617S	Fife Scottish	WFS136W	Western Buses	WSU437S	Greater Glasgow
ULS337T	Highland Country	UWY62L	Spa Motors	WFS137W	Bluebird Buses	WSU438S	Greater Glasgow
ULS338T	Midland Bluebird	VAO488Y	Lowland	WFS138W	Western Buses	WSU440S	Greater Glasgow
ULS619X	Greater Glasgow	VBA161S	Western Buses	WFS139W	Fife Scottish	WSU447	Grampian
ULS620X	Midland Bluebird	VCD296S	Marbill	WFS140W	Fife Scottish	WSU447S	Greater Glasgow
ULS622X	Midland Bluebird	VCS391	Western Buses	WFS141W	Fife Scottish	WSU448S	Marbill
ULS623X	Midland Bluebird	VCU305T	Greater Glasgow	WFS142W	Western Buses	WSU453S	Greater Glasgow
ULS624X	Midland Bluebird	VCU308T	Greater Glasgow	WFS143W	Midland Bluebird	WSU460	Grampian
ULS626X	Greater Glasgow	VCU311T	Greater Glasgow	WFS144W	Midland Bluebird	WSU475	Clydeside
ULS627X	Strathtay	VCU313T	Greater Glasgow	WFS145W	Oban & District	WSU476	Clydeside
ULS628X	Strathtay	VDV123S	Moffat & Williamson	WFS146W	Midland Bluebird	WSU479	Midland Bluebird
ULS629X	Greater Glasgow	VEL374	Spa Motors	WFS147W	Western Buses	WSU487	Midland Bluebird
ULS630X	Midland Bluebird	VFS324V	Lowland	WFS150W	Fife Scottish	WSU489	Midland Bluebird
ULS631X	Strathtay	VFS432V	Lowland	WFS151W	Oban & District	WSU557	Stokes
ULS632X	Strathtay	VHV109G	Skye-Ways	WFS152W	Highland Country	WSU857	Stokes
ULS633X	Strathtay	VJI3001	Shuttle Buses	WFS153W	Highland	WSU858	Stokes
ULS635X	Greater Glasgow	VJI6961	Dart	WFS154W	Midland Bluebird	WSU859	Stokes
ULS640X	Midland Bluebird	VJI6962	Dart	WGB497W	Greater Glasgow	WSU860	Stokes

The Scottish Bus Handbook

WSU864	Stokes	XSG67R	Highland Country	XUS614S	Greater Glasgow	YSF91S	Highland Country
WSU871	Stokes	XSG68R	Highland Country	XUS615S	Greater Glasgow	YSF94S	Highland
WSV135	Midland Bluebird	XSG69R	Highland Country	XUS616S	Greater Glasgow	YSF95S	Highland
WSV136	Lowland	XSG70R	Galloways	XUS617S	Greater Glasgow	YSF96S	Highland Country
WSV137	Lowland	XSH464V	Munro's	XUS618S	Greater Glasgow	YSF98S	Western Buses
WSV138	Lowland	XSJ646T	Marbill	XUS619S	Greater Glasgow	YSF100S	Western Buses
WSV140	Midland Bluebird	XSJ651T	Western Buses	XUS620S	Greater Glasgow	YSF102S	Whitelaw's
WSV540	AA Buses	XSJ653T	Western Buses	XUS621S	Greater Glasgow	YSF103S	Highland
WTS258T	Paterson's	XSJ654T	Western Buses	XWL539	Grampian	YSF104S	Highland Country
WTS268T	Travel Dundee	XSJ655T	Western Buses	XXI7400	Royal Mail	YSG631W	Lowland
WTS269T	Docherty of Irvine	XSJ656T	Western Buses	XYS596S	McGill's	YSG632W	Lowland
WTS270T	Stevenson	XSJ657T	Western Buses	YBK159	Moffat & Williamson	YSG633W	Lowland
WTS271T	Stevenson	XSJ658T	Western Buses	YBK335V	Moffat & Williamson	YSG634W	Lowland
WTS272T	Travel Dundee	XSJ659T	Western Buses	YBK336V	Moffat & Williamson	YSG635W	Lowland
WTS273T	Travel Dundee	XSJ660T	Western Buses	YBK337V	Moffat & Williamson	YSG636W	Lowland
WTS274T	Docherty of Irvine	XSJ661T	Western Buses	YBK338V	Moffat & Williamson	YSG637W	Lowland
WTS276T	Travel Dundee	XSJ662T	Western Buses	YBK339V	Moffat & Williamson	YSG638W	Lowland
WTS277T	Docherty of Irvine	XSJ665T	Western Buses	YBK340V	Moffat & Williamson	YSG639W	Lowland
WTU471W	Rennie's	XSJ666T	Western Buses	YBK341V	Moffat & Williamson	YSG640W	Lowland
WUS567S	Greater Glasgow	XSJ667T	Western Buses	YBK342V	Moffat & Williamson	YSG642W	Lowland
WUS570S	Greater Glasgow	XSJ668T	Western Buses	YBK343V	Moffat & Williamson	YSG643W	Lowland
WVM884S	Western Buses	XSJ669T	Western Buses	YBK344V	Moffat & Williamson	YSG645W	Lowland
WVM888S	Western Buses	XSS331Y	Grampian	YBL526	Mackies	YSG646W	Midland Bluebird
WYV5T	Western Buses	XSS332Y	Grampian	YBW600R	Paterson's	YSG647W	Lowland
WYV27T	Western Buses	XSS333Y	Grampian	YBW606R	Moffat & Williamson	YSG650W	Lowland
WYV29T	Western Buses	XSS334Y	Grampian	YCS88T	Clydeside	YSG654W	Lowland
WYV49T	Western Buses	XSS335Y	Grampian	YCS90T	Clydeside	YSG655W	Lowland
WYV56T	Western Buses	XSS336Y	Grampian	YCS91T	Clydeside	YSG656W	Midland Bluebird
WYV60T	Clydeside	XSS337Y	Grampian	YCS94T	Clydeside	YSG657W	Midland Bluebird
XAK912T	Rennie's	XSS338Y	Grampian	YCS96T	Clydeside	YSG658W	Lowland
XAK915T	Rennie's	XSS339Y	Grampian	YCS97T	Clydeside	YSG659W	Lowland
XAP643S	Fife Scottish	XSS340Y	Grampian	YCS98T	Clydeside	YSG660W	Midland Bluebird
XAT11X	Allander Travel	XSS341Y	Grampian	YFB7V	Morrison's	YSJ14T	AA Buses
XBF59S	Wilson's, Carnwath	XSS342Y	Grampian	YFS304W	Western Buses	YSO33Y	Bluebird Buses
XCC95V	Galson Motors	XSS343Y	Grampian	YFS307W	Greater Glasgow	YSO34Y	Bluebird Buses
XCD108	Rennie's	XSS344Y	Grampian	YFS308W	Western Buses	YSO35Y	Bluebird Buses
XDU599	Western Buses	XSS345Y	Grampian	YFS309W	Western Buses	YSO36Y	Bluebird Buses
XHR877	Meffan	XSS39Y	Strathtay	YFS310W	Western Buses	YSO37Y	Bluebird Buses
XIB9829	Spa Motors	XSS40Y	Strathtay	YFS438	Mackies	YSO38Y	Bluebird Buses
XKW870	Owens Coaches	XSS41Y	Strathtay	YFS92S	Greater Glasgow	YSO39Y	Bluebird Buses
XMS245R	Whitelaw's	XSS42Y	Strathtay	YHS282S	Greater Glasgow	YSO40Y	Bluebird Buses
XMS254R	Whitelaw's	XSS43Y	Strathtay	YHU679V	Wilson's, Carnwath	YSO41Y	Bluebird Buses
XMS420Y	Fife Scottish	XSV229	Hutchison	YIJ3053	Keenan of Ayr	YSO42Y	Bluebird Buses
XMS421Y	Midland Bluebird	XSV270	Mackies	YJF16Y	Midland Bluebird	YSO43Y	Bluebird Buses
XMS422Y	Western Buses	XUF456	Hutchison	YJU694	Strathtay	YSO231T	Grampian
XMS423Y	Western Buses	XUS579S	Greater Glasgow	YMB515W	Rennie's	YSO233T	Midland Bluebird
XMS424Y	Strathtay	XUS583S	Greater Glasgow	YMS705R	Marbill	YSO234T	Midland Bluebird
XMS425Y	Midland Bluebird	XUS586S	Greater Glasgow	YMS712R	Marbill	YSO235T	Midland Bluebird
XNR453	Strathtay	XUS587S	Greater Glasgow	YMS85R	Mackies	YSO236T	Midland Bluebird
XPW879X	McEwan's	XUS590G	Greater Glasgow	YPD110Y	Wilson's, Carnwath	YSO237T	Midland Bluebird
XRC487	Bluebird Buses	XUS592S	Greater Glasgow	YPD131Y	Wilson's, Carnwath	YSR152T	Strathtay
XRM772Y	Bluebird Buses	XUS593S	Greater Glasgow	YPD134Y	Wilson's, Carnwath	YSU865	Clydeside
XRR50S	Clydeside	XUS594S	Greater Glasgow	YPL83T	McEwan's	YSU866	Clydeside
XRY278	Marbill	XUS595S	Greater Glasgow	YSD350L	Western Buses	YSU989	Maynes
XSA5Y	Rennie's	XUS596S	Greater Glasgow	YSF75S	Strathtay	YSU990	Maynes
XSA218S	Midland Bluebird	XUS599S	Greater Glasgow	YSF76S	Highland Country	YSV318	Strathtay
XSA219S	Midland Bluebird	XUS601S	Greater Glasgow	YSF77S	Highland	YSV586	Galson Motors
XSA220S	Midland Bluebird	XUS602S	Greater Glasgow	YSF78S	Highland Country	YSV730	Western Buses
XSA221S	Midland Bluebird	XUS603S	Greater Glasgow	YSF79S	Strathtay	YSV735	Western Buses
XSA223S	Midland Bluebird	XUS605S	Greater Glasgow	YSF83S	Highland Country	YSV904	Riddler
XSA224S	Midland Bluebird	XUS606S	Greater Glasgow	YSF84S	Highland	YTE591V	Highland Country
XSA225S	Midland Bluebird	XUS607S	Greater Glasgow	YSF87S	Strathtay	YWX537X	Wilson's, Carnwath
XSA226S	Midland Bluebird	XUS608S	Greater Glasgow	YSF88S	Strathtay	YYS174	Western Buses
XSA227S	Midland Bluebird	XUS610S	Greater Glasgow	YSF90S	Highland Country		

ISBN 1 897990 20 0
Typeset by Bill Potter
Published by *British Bus Publishing Ltd*
The Vyne, 16 St Margarets Drive, Wellington,
Telford, Shropshire, TF1 3PH

Printed by Graphics & Print Ltd
Unit A13, Stafford Park 15
Telford, Shropshire, TF3 3BB